Fishes of the World

Fishes of the World

JOSEPH S. NELSON

Associate Professor of Zoology
Department of Zoology
The University of Alberta, Edmonton

A WILEY-INTERSCIENCE PUBLICATION

JOHN WILEY & SONS
New York • Chichester • Brisbane • Toronto • Singapore

Library of Congress Cataloging in Publication Data

Nelson, Joseph S
    Fishes of the world.

    "A Wiley-Interscience publication."
    Bibliography: p.
    Includes index.
    1. Fishes—Classification. I. Title.

QL618.N4   597'.001'2   76-14959
ISBN 0-471-01497-4

Printed in the United States of America

10 9 8 7 6 5

Preface

One purpose dominated the writing of this book—to present a modern
introductory systematic treatment of all major fish groups. A knowledge
of the diversity, evolution, and classification of fishes is of interest to all
persons working with these aquatic vertebrates. Our views of fish phylogeny have changed radically in the last few decades and consequently
this classification is different from older classifications such as those
found in Jordan (1923), Regan (1929), Berg (1940, 1955), Bertin and
Arambourg (1958), and Nikolskii (1961). This book is intended to fill
a need that many teachers feel exists for both the lecture and laboratory
portions of a course in ichthyology or biology of fishes. It is hoped that
it will also be helpful to others who wish to review or refer to fish
classification.

The plan of the book is simple. The introduction deals in an elementary way with fish diversity and abundance, following which a brief
review of the classification of lower chordates puts the fishes in perspective. The fishes are presented in linear order in a manner that
would best seem to reflect their postulated evolutionary relationships.
Alternate schemes of classification recognized in recent literature are
often referred to. Evolutionary trends are mentioned for some of the
groups. Categories are given down at least to family level and frequently
lower. A relatively large number of categories are recognized to pro-

vide a better presentation of postulated relationships. The categories of the higher taxa, and their endings in parentheses when consistent, are as follows in order of rank: phylum, subphylum, superclass, grade, subgrade, class, subclass, infraclass, division, superorder, series, order (*iformes*), suborder (*oidei*), infraorder (*oidea*), superfamily (*oidae*), family (*idae*), subfamily (*inae*), tribe (*ini*), genus, and subgenus. The ending I use for the little-used infraorder category is recommended for super-families by the *International Code of Zoological Nomenclature*. Not all categories are employed within a particular taxon. A dagger denotes those of the level of suborder or higher that do not contain living species. Those who find this number a cumbersome proliferation may wish to use only the such familiar ones as class, order, suborder, and family (as given in Appendix I). For each family the most appropriate common name known to me, if any, and a brief mention of its range, has been added. An outline drawing illustrates most of the families, sometimes for lower levels of classification. A short description is given for most categories; some are inconsistently brief, usually as a consequence of the lack of diagnostic features and my lack of information on them. For some families interesting life-history or biological notes are given with the maximum length of the largest species and, when possible, the number of recognized (valid) genera and species. These figures are always for living forms, never fossil. In many cases they may disagree by a considerable amount with other recent works and may quickly become obsolete. The total number of recognized fish species in this book is estimated to be 18,818. For this edition it is assumed that a knowledge of fish anatomy will be obtained elsewhere. The generalized maps in Appendix II which show the distribution of some fish groups are based primarily on the acknowledged sources. In all cases it should be remembered that limits are usually based on scattered populations of one species. The maps are intended to show basic distributions only and are not necessarily accurate in detail.

Readers will find that the following books, among others, supplement this one in various ways. Such books as Alexander (1967), Gosline (1971), Lagler, Bardach, and Miller (1962), Marshall (1965), Nikolskii (1963, 1965), and Norman and Greenwood (1963) include information on functional morphology and general fish biology and ecology. References to the literature on various extant groups can be found in Blackwelder (1972) and Lindberg (1971). The latter valuable work also contains a set of keys to the fish families. The Norman manuscript (1957) provides keys and synonymies to most extant genera recognized up to the early 1940's. Hubbs and Lagler (1964) contains information on making meristic counts and morphometric measurements. Ecological and physiological information can be found in various articles in Hoar and Randall

(1969–1971). Breder and Rosen (1966) describe modes of reproduction in various fish groups. Bennett (1971) and Bardach, Ryther, and Mc-Larney (1972) discuss fish management and aquaculture. Schwartz (1972) offers a world listing of various hybrid crosses and Bailey et al. (1970) lists all species recorded in Canada and the United States. A series of papers, in which synonymies and references for extinct and extant taxa of fishes entitled "A catalog of world fishes" by the late Henry W. Fowler are presented, is being issued by the *Quarterly Journal of the Taiwan Museum* (published by the Taiwan Museum, Taipei), beginning with Volume 17 for 1964. Unfortunately this work is incomplete and out of date. Helpful elementary or popular books which usually emphasize economically important fishes and many good books on aquarium fishes are also available.

The ichthyologist is a student of fish systematics. In addition to constructing phylogenies and classifications and determining evolutionary trends based on comparative information from morphological and other studies, he often attempts to explain diversity and to identify the selective forces at work which adapt the fish to its environment. He attempts to determine why some groups are more successful than others and to learn how morphology determines function and how ways of life can determine morphology. We are trying to explain the biological significance of the differences we observe and not only to deal with them taxonomically.

Laboratories of ichthyology courses are generally designed to demonstrate the diversity of fishes and their probable course of evolution and to provide some training in identification. Sections may be designed to show diverse adaptations to common functions in which fish are used as examples to show various phenomena. Collecting trips, curatorial functions, and special projects (e.g., skeletal preparation, staining, and clearing) may also be involved. The laboratory can be a good place to discuss taxonomic problems as well.

In the laboratory portion of some courses stress is given to the local fish fauna. For this purpose there are many fine regional books. However, it is also highly desirable to have a broad look at fish classification and to place one's local fauna in perspective to all fishes. Students in most tropical and subtropical areas (or living near large museums) will obviously be better off than those in northern inland areas (such as the students in my ichthyology course).

Students concerned with the systematics of fishes, ichthyology in the strict sense, will obtain a good understanding of the principles, theory, and assumptions of systematics and taxonomy in such books as Blackwelder (1967), Boydan (1973), Crowson (1970), Hennig (1966), Jardine and Sibson (1971), Mayr (1963, 1969), Simpson (1961), Sneath and

Sokal (1973), and Sokal and Sneath (1963). These books plus articles in the journal *Systematic Zoology* will reveal the considerable fundamental differences that exist in the principles of classification. All of this should be part of the student's background. An understanding of how knowledge is obtained is far better than just learning the end results. Particular philosophies and approaches in fish systematics may be found in many of the works listed in the bibliography (e.g., Greenwood et al., 1966; Nelson, 1969a, 1972c; Rosen and Patterson, 1969; Smith and Koehn, 1971).

In fish systematics today there is a vast amount of revisionary work being done. A great deal more is needed if we are to achieve our goal of trying to unravel the history of evolution of the heterogeneous assemblage of fishes. Many questions will likely always remain unanswered. It is often impossible to distinguish between primitive (ancestral) characters and derived characters (although attempts should be made to determine if diagnostic characters are primitive or derived). The evidence for evolution is overwhelming; the problems that beset us, however, in reconstructing its pathway are immense. We are like the early geographer who was convinced that the earth was round but knew little of the details. To our regret we will probably never have a complete fossil record or a time machine that will allow us to gather detail in a manner comparable to what the early geographer could do with his ships and instruments. In many groups the fossil record is either not known or too poorly known to be of any help in tracing the evolutionary path of extant species. As noted in an earlier study on sticklebacks (Nelson, 1971:439), "The paucity of . . . fossils, however, makes criteria of constancy and consistency impossible to establish and places an undesirably large burden of evidence on new finds for those workers bent on deriving extant species from whatever extinct species are known." Fossils fill in the gaps in our study of diversity and are invaluable in showing relationships, but they do not necessarily represent forms on the main evolutionary pathway. Ironically it is the gaps in the fossil record that permit us to define discrete groups. As our knowledge grows our ability to erect well-defined groups decreases.

As long as there are active, creative ichthyologists there will be major disagreements in our classification in the foreseeable future (similarly there is disagreement in almost all important fields of biology). Fish classification is in a dynamic state and the student pursuing ichthyology will find that all groups can be reworked. There are many challenges, both in developing the theory of classification and in its actual practice. It has been a difficult task to try to present the most modern, up-to-date classification while at the same time not prematurely accepting some new, unorthodox view of phylogeny before it has been "tested" and has gained some acceptance.

To keep up to date the worker must use such bibliographic aids as *Biological Abstracts* and *Science Citation Index* and monitor the numerous journals that carry ichthyological articles. *Zoological Record* is an excellent guide to systematic literature but, unfortunately, is several years behind. Because classifications eventually become obsolete (as will most biological information) the beginner should regard them as working frameworks that will provide a basis for building as advances are made. If however, any beginner should question the value of learning a classification, it should be remembered that they are useful vehicles on which to base an understanding of biology (learning a classification is probably best done by most by looking at the groups and picturing their relationships). We do not stop using objects or acquiring the present state of knowledge merely because our technical knowledge is going to improve.

The bibliography does not contain all the pertinent literature. It includes some of the more important or useful works that have come to my attention. An attempt has been made to list regional works, systematic revisions, and other important biological studies.

I am grateful to many individuals who have helped in various ways with the book. The majority of the line drawings were executed by Mr. R. Kureluk. Virtually all were based on figures from regional works. Many ichthyologists provided encouragement, advice, or information which helped in writing the manuscript. In particular, I should like to thank Drs. R. M. Bailey, P. L. Forey, C. Gruchy, C. L. Hubbs, C. C. Lindsey, D. E. McAllister, J. R. Nursall, C. R. Robins, W. B. Scott, S. H. Weitzman, and N. J. Wilimovsky for their varied contributions and help. Needless to say, the work has been greatly aided by the numerous excellent revisions that have recently been done. I sincerely look forward to suggestions and new published information from all workers for future editions. Some information, primarily from the literature, was derived from work supported by the National Research Council of Canada, grant number A-5457. The Zoology Department of The University of Alberta was most generous in providing for assistance in typing the manuscript. Finally, my thanks to my wife Claudine and children, Brenda, Janice, Mark, and Karen, for their help with "little" things during its preparation.

Joseph S. Nelson

Edmonton, Alberta, Canada
May 1976

Contents

Fishes of the World

Introduction

Fish exhibit enormous diversity in their morphology, in the habitats they occupy, and in their biology. Unlike the other commonly recognized vertebrate groups, fish are a heterogeneous assemblage. From lamprey and hagfish to lungfish and flatfish, they include a vast array of distantly related vertebrates. Many are even more closely related to mammals than to certain other fish. Despite this diversity and the dilemma that evolution does not always make definitions easy, fish can be simply defined as aquatic poikilotherm vertebrates that have gills throughout life and limbs, if any, in the shape of fins. The body of information known about them is so vast that their study can include all facets of biology. On the other hand, they are attractive to the researcher because of the wealth of information still to be found.

NUMBERS

Fishes constitute almost half the total number of vertebrates. An estimated 18,818 living species compared with 21,100 extant tetrapods (a total of about 39,900 recognized vertebrate species) have been described. Other workers, for various reasons, have arrived at different estimates, most of which range between 17,000 and 30,000, for the numbers of currently recognized fish species. The number arrived at here is slightly larger than the approximate figure of 18,300 given by R. M. Bailey in Bailey and Cavender (1971) but smaller than Cohen's (1970) 20,600 (mean of his extremes). Cohen placed the number of Ostariophysi at 6200, compared with my 5000. Some groups are expanding with newly described species, whereas others are decreasing, for species are being synonymized faster than the new ones are described. However, a net increase is shown every year, and the number of new species of fishes described annually exceeds that of the new tetrapods. Bird and mammal species are not likely to rise much above the present 12,300. Amphibians and reptiles may increase significantly (perhaps at a relatively slow rate because herpetologists are far fewer than other vertebrate systematists). The eventual number of fish species may be 50% greater than presently recognized, with close to 28,000 extant. In contrast to amphibians, reptiles, and mammals, the known diversity of living fishes exceeds that of known fossil taxa. On the other hand, there is a much richer and more informative fossil fish fauna than is known for birds (even relative to their numbers).

Approximate numbers of recognized extant families, genera, and species in the 46 orders of fishes that contain living representatives. The number of freshwater species is an estimate of the species always or almost always confined to fresh water (or inland lakes, regardless of salinity). It basically includes all species in Darlington's (1957) primary division families, most in his secondary division families, and many in his peripheral division families. It excludes commonly diadromous fishes that may have landlocked populations.

Order	Families	Genera	Species	Freshwater species
Petromyzoniformes	1	9	31	24
Myxiniformes	1	5	32	0
Heterodontiformes	1	1	6	0
Hexanchiformes	2	4	6	0
Lamniformes	7	56	199	0
Squaliformes	3	19	76	0
Rajiformes	8	49	315	10
Chimaeriformes	3	6	25	0
Ceratodiformes	1	1	1	1
Lepidosireniformes	2	2	5	5
Coelacanthiformes	1	1	1	0
Polypteriformes	1	2	11	11
Acipenseriformes	2	6	25	15

(*Continued*)

Order	Families	Genera	Species	Freshwater species
Semionotiformes	1	1	7	7
Amiiformes	1	1	1	1
Osteoglossiformes	4	9	15	15
Mormyriformes	2	11	101	101
Clupeiformes	4	72	292	25
Elopiformes	3	5	11	0
Anguilliformes	22	133	603	0
Notacanthiformes	3	6	24	0
Salmoniformes	24	145	508	80
Gonorynchiformes	4	7	16	14
Cypriniformes	26	634	3000	3000
Siluriformes	31	470	2000	1950
Myctophiformes	16	73	390	0
Polymixiiformes	1	1	3	0
Percopsiformes	3	5	8	8
Gadiformes	10	168	684	5
Batrachoidiformes	1	18	55	2
Lophiiformes	15	57	215	0
Indostomiformes	1	1	1	1
Atheriniformes	16	167	827	500
Lampridiformes	10	18	35	0
Beryciformes	15	39	143	0
Zeiformes	6	25	50	0
Syngnathiformes	6	44	200	2
Gasterosteiformes	2	7	10	3
Synbranchiformes	3	7	13	8
Scorpaeniformes	21	260	1000	100
Dactylopteriformes	1	4	4	0
Pegasiformes	1	2	5	0
Perciformes	147	1257	6880	950
Gobiesociformes	3	42	144	2
Pleuronectiformes	6	117	520	3
Tetraodontiformes	8	65	320	8
Totals	450	4032	18,818	6851

MORPHOLOGICAL DIVERSITY

Fishes range in size from a tiny 12 mm adult Philippine goby to the giant 15 m whale shark. They have stringlike to ballshaped bodies. Some species are brilliantly colored; others are drab (e.g., see Burgess and Axelrod, 1972-continuing). Some are sleek and graceful, moving with little resistance through the water (which is 800 times denser than air); others are described by the general public as ugly and grotesque, their livelihood not depending on speed.

Fins may be missing or highly modified into holdfast organs or as a lure for attracting prey. About 50 species of teleosts lack eyes (mostly cyprinids, siluriforms, amblyopsids, ophidiids, and gobiids). Scales may be present or absent in closely related species. Their bodies may be inflatable or encased in inflexible bony armor. Internal anatomical diversity in hard and soft parts is also enormous. Many bizarre specializations exist. Some insight into the morphological diversity will be found in the taxonomic section.

HABITAT DIVERSITY

Fishes live in almost every conceivable type of aquatic habitat. They are found in South America's Lake Titicaca, the world's highest large lake (3812m), where a group of cyprinodontids have undergone much radiation, in Lake Baikal, the world's deepest (at least 1000 m), and 7000 m below the surface of the ocean. Some species live in almost pure fresh water of 0.01‰ (parts per thousand) total dissolved solids (most lakes are between 0.05 and 1‰) or in very salty lakes of 100‰ (ocean water is close to 35‰). They may be confined to total darkness in caves, or as in Tibet, China, and India, to fast torrential streams. In Africa a *Tilapia* occurs in hot soda lakes which have temperatures as high as 44°C, whereas under the Antarctic ice sheet *Trematomus* lives at about −2°C. Many species have acquired air-breathing organs and find a living in stagnant, tropical swamps; others demand well-oxygenated waters to sustain life. An individual species may tolerate a wide range of temperatures, in which case it is said to be eurythermal, or a narrow range (stenothermal). Similarly, it may tolerate a wide range of salinity (euryhaline) or only a narrow range (stenohaline).

DISTRIBUTION AND ZOOGEOGRAPHY

Both freshwater and marine fish are found throughout the world. As a group they have shown a remarkable ability to overcome barriers. Areas recently exposed from the last ice age tend to have a relatively sparse fish fauna. The study of species dispersal following glaciation or the uplift of land from the ocean (e.g., Central America) is an exciting field that involves geology, geography, and systematics (e.g., geographic variation). At a different level in zoogeography many studies have been made of the affinities of families in different areas and their centers of origin and patterns of dispersal. Another interesting field lies in attempting to determine the implications and importance of continental drift, outlined in detail by Dietz and Holden (1970), on past fish dispersal. Myers (1966) believes that the many similarities between the freshwater fish of South America and Africa are best explained by continental drift.

In both fresh and marine waters the largest number of species occurs in the tropics and there is a progressive reduction toward the polar areas (although numbers of individuals in certain northern species are great). The most species of freshwater fishes occur in southeast Asia, but the Amazon, the world's largest river, has almost as many. Most oceanic islands and many large continental islands lack indigenous freshwater species, although Australia and New Zealand have a few (most of which in the former and all in the latter are closely related to marine or diadromous species). Western Europe has a relatively sparse freshwater fauna. In tropical areas Africa exhibits the most diversity of non-ostariophysan freshwater fish; South America exhibits surprisingly little. In temperate areas eastern North America shows the greatest diversity in non-ostariophysan freshwater fishes. In marine waters the Indo-Pacific (Red Sea and Indian Ocean to northern Australia and Polynesia) is the richest, the most species occurring in the New Guinea to Queensland area. The West Indian or Caribbean fauna (southern Florida to northern Brazil) is also a rich one. One large reef (Alligator Reef off Florida) supports a total of 517 species (Starck, 1968). The west African fauna, however, is relatively poor. Arctic and Antarctic faunas are depauperate. In all, then, the greatest numbers of species in the world inhabit the southeastern Asian region.

All individuals of most species of fish live entirely either in fresh or marine waters. A few are diadromous, regularly living part of their lives in fresh water and part in the oceans. Among them most are anadromous, spawning in fresh water but spending much of their time in the sea. A few are catadromous, spawning in the oceans but returning to fresh water. Classification as marine, diadromous, or freshwater is impossible, except perhaps as a generalization, for some species. Just as in an otherwise marine family there may be one species confined to fresh water so in some species there are populations that occur in an environment opposite to that of most of their fellow members. Individuals in some otherwise marine species ascend rivers for short distances in part of their range, and those of some species that are usually freshwater are anadromous in some areas.

Many fresh and marine water species are also common in brackish water estuaries. About 6850 species normally live in the freshwater lakes and rivers that cover only about 1% of the earth's surface and account for a little less than 0.01% of its water (the mean depth of the lakes is only a few meters). About twice that number (11,650) live all their lives in the oceans, which cover about 70% of the earth's surface, account for 97% of its water, and have a mean depth of about 3700 m.

Few or no fish occur indiscriminately throughout fresh or marine waters. Many environmental factors influence just where a certain species will predominate. In freshwater environments species may show a preference for lakes or streams. Between lakes they may show a preference for deep, cold, oligotrophic lakes or for shallower, warmer, and more productive eutrophic lakes. In lake waters they may show a preference (horizontal and vertical) for the open-water limnetic zone, the benthic area, or shallow littoral areas. They may even be restricted to certain types of bottom or thrive best under certain physicochemical conditions. Stream fishes may prefer riffle or quiet areas, and a zonation of species is usually found from the headwaters to the mouth. In the oceans the vast majority of fishes, perhaps 9100 species in all, are coastal or littoral. Most of those living beyond the 200 m deep continental shelf (oceanic species) are deep-sea (mesopelagic, bathypelagic, abyssopelagic, or benthic at various depths) and number about 2300; only a small minority, perhaps 250, regularly live close to the surface in the well-lighted upper 200 m zone (epipelagic). The epipelagic and mesopelagic fishes, which consist of both large predators and small plankton feeders, are varied, whereas most of the bathypelagic and abyssal fishes are relatively small.

Many species have limited ranges [the smallest is perhaps that of *Cyprinodon diabolis,* found only in one spring in Nevada (Brown, 1971)] and many areas have a high degree of endemism. Marine fish have the obvious land (notably the New and Old World land masses) and mid-ocean barriers as well as many ecological and physiological barriers; freshwater species are limited by marine and land barriers. Geological changes and broad ecological tolerances (and perhaps slow evolutionary rates) have allowed some species to develop remarkably large ranges. Approximately 107 marine species are believed to extend around the world in tropical or subtropical waters (Briggs, 1960), among which about 14 are shore species, 90 are oceanic (48 in the upper 200 m and 42 below this depth), and only three are benthic. Many more genera are represented in the Pacific and Atlantic but almost always different species are involved. Representatives of many

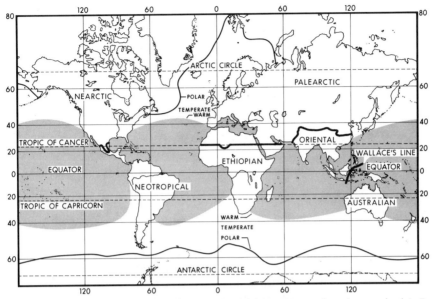

Commonly recognized zoogeographical regions of the continents (based on work of A. R. Wallace) and broad thermal zones of the ocean. The zoogeographical regions are useful summators of numbers and proportion of endemic organisms and help in understanding the evolutionary and geographic history of a group. The Nearctic and Palearctic are frequently combined into one region, the Holarctic. The thermal divisions of the sea denote warm water, temperate water, and polar water regions (based on part of a figure given in Hesse, Allee, and Schmidt, 1951). Zoogeographic regions, which express degrees of endemism, are also recognized in the oceans [e.g., Indo-West Pacific (-Indo-Pacific in text), tropical western Atlantic, tropical eastern Atlantic, North Pacific, North Atlantic, Mediterranean-East Atlantic]. As in continental zoogeographic regions, marine oceans share different similarities with one another; for example, in many families the tropical eastern Pacific shows a greater resemblance to the western Atlantic than to the Indo-West Pacific because of the mid-Pacific barrier and the relatively recent marine connection across the Isthmus of Panama.

marine genera occur in the temperate and polar faunas of both hemispheres. Some are surface-bound, others are deep-water. This complete equatorial discontinuity or bipolarity has been termed antitropicality by Hubbs (1952). The vast majority of genera, however, are tropical; most of the rest occur either in the Northern or the Southern Hemisphere, never both. We know little of the abyssal depths and its species composition. Many abyssal species have been found at widely separated localities, which suggests that some, at least, may be virtually worldwide. No freshwater species is circumtropical, but two species, *Esox lucius* and *Lota lota*, are circumpolar and several others are almost so. Many freshwater fishes have shown a remarkable

ability to disperse across newly exposed land areas following glaciation. No freshwater genus has an antitropical distribution.

The map on p. 7 shows the major zoogeographic regions of the
continents and the broad thermal zones of the ocean. Detailed studies
of distributional patterns and their relation to environmental variables
form an important part of zoogeography.

BIOLOGICAL DIVERSITY

The diversity in fish behavior is as great as in their morphology. Some
species travel in schools, others are highly territorial, some exhibit
parental care for their offspring, and others scatter millions of eggs to
the hazards of predation. Interesting commensal relationships exist
with other fish and other animals. Fish are adapted to a wide variety of
foods. Some are specialized or highly adapted to feed on plants, zoo-
plankton, or coral. Almost all classes of animal can serve as food. A few
species are parasitic on other species or on the female of their own.
Some produce venom, electricity, sound, or light, and a few are known
to be hermaphrodites or to exhibit sex reversal. Fish in all types of
aquatic environment may migrate phenomenal distances, a field rich in
research on homing mechanisms. The larvae and early juveniles of
some oceanic species (e.g., the many flyingfishes and the dolphins)
regularly inhabit shore waters, whereas the larvae of many shore fishes
inhabit oceanic waters. In fresh water *Oncorhynchus keta* and *O.
tshawytscha* migrate 3000 km up the Yukon River to their spawning
grounds without feeding. Many other fish are known to live out their
lives in very restricted areas.

IMPORTANCE TO MAN

Fishes, like many other forms of life, are of immense value to mankind.
They have long been a staple item in the diet of many peoples. Today
they form an important element in the economy of many nations while
giving incalculable recreational and psychological value to the natural-
ist, sportsman, and home aquarist. They are also the subject of international and domestic agreements and disagreements. Adverse effects
(e.g., from poisonous and man-eating species) are of immense concern
in some areas. Many government institutions are devoted to the study
of their biology and propagation. Particular aspects of phenomena of

various species have lent themselves to studies in behavior, ecology, evolution, genetics, and physiology. They are used as general indicators or summators of pollution, partly to the direct benefit of man and partly to protect what man considers a valuable and necessary part of his heritage and life. We consider it desirable to maintain the diversity that the systematist studies.

CLASSIFICATION AND DIVERSITY

As noted in the preface, many different classifications and approaches to classification exist. Comparative information on diversity is essential, however, before any classification of species can be constructed. This is true regardless of which of the following approaches is taken: a phenetic approach by a numerical taxonomist in which numerous characters are given equal weight (except to correct for correlations) (e.g., Sokal and Sneath, 1963; Sneath and Sokal, 1973; Jardine and Sibson, 1971; Smith and Koehn, 1971); a genealogical approach (cladism) with a search for sister groups in which taxa are classified according to their recency of common descent (e.g., Hennig, 1966; Nelson, 1969a, 1972c; Greenwood, Miles, and Patterson, 1973); or a classical evolutionary approach by a phylogenetic systematist (e.g., Simpson, 1961; Mayr, 1969). In the latter some workers may philosophically prefer a vertical classification (e.g., Greenwood et al., 1966) or a horizontal classification (e.g., Gosline, 1971). Problems arise in regard to lumping and splitting, depending, in part, on whether we are impressed with the similarities or the differences with the group, when we attempt to translate our phylogenetic ideas into a classification. There can be subjective and objective elements and a particular category can have a different composition, depending on the worker involved. Mayr (1969) gives an excellent review (from the viewpoint largely favored in this classification) of the various methods and principles of zoological classification. Many differences of opinion exist in regard to the validity of the various approaches (e.g., see the journal *Systematic Zoology*, No. 4, for 1973).

Skeletal studies from extinct and extant material have been used most extensively but considerable use is also being made of soft anatomy, karyotypes, ecology, behavior, and mode of reproduction. Many serological and biochemical differences exist between various populations and species [e.g., de Ligny (1969) and Love (1970)] which can be useful when shown to have a hereditary basis. The diversity of distribution and habitat occupied (e.g., freshwater or marine) can also be considered. However, a detailed knowledge of continental drift and the location of epicontinental seas usually does not help much in inferring relationships of an old group, but when it is combined with a good phylogeny established on other criteria (including fossils of a known age) it can present an exciting story on evolution and may even reinforce our view of the evolution of the group when a plausible story emerges. Great caution must be used, however, in invoking continental drift as a mechanism for dispersal because oceans are not necessarily complete barriers to groups normally living only in fresh water.

In order to understand the strength of the various sections of a classification and of our knowledge of relationships it is useful to identify diagnostic characters as primitive or derived (advanced) (e.g., see Fraser, 1972). Such a categorization or statement of recognition regarding which groups are weakly classified on the basis of shared primitive characters or strongly classified on the basis of numerous shared derived characters is not attempted here.

Phylogenetic relationships are more reliable when they are based on a great diversity of sources of information. Classifications erected on only one source of data are not likely to last long. On the other hand, different lines of evidence sometimes suggest different relationships. The tasks of tracing phylogenies and erecting classifications are further complicated because it appears that the same levels of specialization have been independently attained along different phyletic lines. Of course, it is not always certain whether characters are similar in different taxa because of convergent evolution or because the bearers shared a common ancestry; for example, a consideration of all the comparative information on the diversity within the Pacific salmon *Oncorhynchus* exposes numerous different trends and results in the problem of how to polarize the trends objectively. It is possible that certain characters developed independently in different species in a complicated mosaic manner such that it may be impossible to weight the various characters objectively unless we have an exceptionally complete fossil record. Whether a certain character is derived or primitive, even when a fossil record is present, is an argument that will persist in the literature. We usually cannot be absolutely certain whether a fossil lies on a side stem or in the main evolutionary line. Alternative explanations exist for most phylogenies. Even in the face of overwhelming problems, however, it is best to present classifications as models or hypotheses that can be tested against future evidence and be made as consistent as possible with all available evidence. No classification to date can claim to present the final truth.

CLASSIFICATION OF THE PHYLUM CHORDATA

The phylum Chordata has been used by most workers to encompass members of the subphyla Hemichordata (acorn worms), Urochordata (tunicates or sea-squirts), Cephalochordata (lancelets), and Vertebrata. The first three are commonly called the protochordates. Pogonophora may be considered as a "lower chordate," as suggested by Halstead (1969), and included in the chordates, thereby making five subphyla with living representatives. Jefferies' (1968) subphylum Calcichordata, known only from fossils, is included here in the Chordata. The six groups are thought to have shared a general common ancestry from, or at least with, the echinoderms. As is true for most groups, a great deal of disagreement exists on the classification and interrelations of

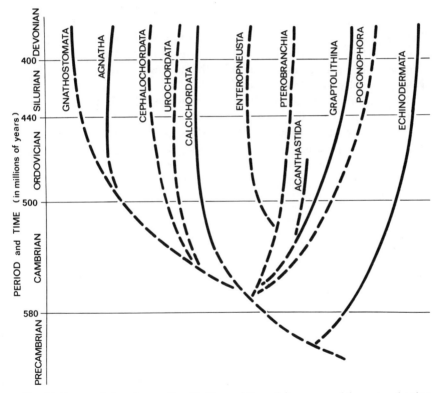

One highly speculative view on the affinities and time of divergence of the major chordate groups and their allies. Much uncertainty exists and numerous other relationships for the groups have been proposed and will undoubtedly continue to be proposed. The solid line for each group denotes the extent in time of known fossils.

these groups. Many modern workers include only the Urochordata, Cephalochordata, and Vertebrata in the Chordata (e.g., Barrington, 1965) because the other three groups have only a remote affinity, at best, with the latter three.

Despite agreement by most recent workers that chordates have had an echinoderm ancestry (Bone, 1960; Denison, 1971a; Dillion, 1965; Romer, 1970; Tarlo, 1960), some authors continue to raise old ideas that they believe contradict our classical echinoderm-chordate scheme. Sillman (1960) argues for a nautiloid cephalopod origin of the primitive vertebrate ostracoderms, whereas Jensen (1963), also on anatomical evidence, argues that the hoplonemerteans gave rise to the vertebrates through the myxinoids, with the echinoderms and "lower" chordates being much later degenerate offshoots. As at any level in taxonomic categories, evidence may often be interpreted in many ways when critically examined. It is well that there are people willing and daring enough to take these "far-out" views. As Kerkut (1960) makes clear, we often tend to be naive in our outlook; however, the echinoderm-chordate theory seems by far the best founded view. Chordates, echinoderms, and perhaps chaetognaths (arrow worms) may be placed in the superphylum Deuterostomia.

The general classification of the lower nonfishlike chordates, in what might be termed the liberal viewpoint of most workers, is given below. The ancestors of vertebrates, thus fishes, are almost certainly to be found in one of these groups. The phylogenetic diagram on p. 11 expresses one view of the interrelations of these groups.

Phylum Chordata

† SUBPHYLUM CALCICHORDATA (Class Stylophora, Class Caroidea)

Calcichordates are interpreted to be a primitive chordate with strong echinoderm affinities [placed by many in the phylum Echinodermata (Denison, 1971a)] and believed to be ancestral to all other chordate groups (Jefferies, 1968; Jefferies and Prokop, 1972). Eaton (1970) agrees with Jefferies that they are closer to chordates than to echinoderms and further believes that ostracoderms probably arose from certain mitrates in perhaps the early Ordovician. This subphylum contains two orders, Cornuta and Mitrata, and is known from Cambrian to Devonian times.

SUBPHYLUM HEMICHORDATA

Hemichordates possess pharyngeal gill openings (absent in *Rhabdopleura*) but lack an endostyle (homologous with the thyroid gland) and notochord. When the embryology is known, they are clearly deuterostomes (the anus develops from the blastopore and the mouth represents a new opening; the coelom is enterocoelic). Some workers prefer to recognize hemichordates as a separate phylum because of the dif-

13

ferences with other chordates but they are retained here simply to express the view (hypothesis) that they have closer affinities with the chordates than with any other group. Their classification is provisional.

The biology of living forms is reviewed by Barrington (1965).

Five classes, two of which are known only as fossils, and about 85 living species.

† Class GRAPTOLITHINA (Graptolites)

Cambrian to Mississippian forms, which, according to Kozlowski (1966) and Bulman (1970), are related to the pterobranchs. Graptolites were colonial, marine organisms which secreted a sclerotized exoskeleton with characteristic growth bands. There were both sessile and pelagic forms. Bulman (1970) recognizes six orders: the sessile Upper Cambrian-Mississippian Dendroidea; the sessile Upper Cambrian-Silurian Tuboidea; the encrusting Ordovician Camaroidea; the encrusting Ordovician Crustoidea; the sessile or encrusting Ordovician Stolonoidea; and the planktonic Ordovician-Lower Devonian Graptoloidea.

† Class ACANTHASTIDA

Colonial, sessile Lower Ordovician forms up to 5 mm in diameter; their upper surface is convex and bears long spines; thought to be related to the graptolites (Kozlowski, 1966; Bulman, 1970:138). This group, based on the only known genus *Acanthastus,* was described by R. Kozlowski in 1949.

Class PLANCTOSPHAEROIDEA

Based on two specimens taken in the Bay of Biscay and described in 1936 (Bulman, 1970:17). *Planctosphaera* may be the larvae of an unknown type of hemichordate.

Class ENTEROPNEUSTA (Acorn Worms)

Wormshaped marine animals with a proboscis, collar, and trunk and live mostly in burrows in shallow waters. They possess gill slits and a dorsal nerve cord (with a primitive nerve net lying within the epidermis) and have a microscopic ciliated tornaria larvae which has many echinoderm characteristics. Acorn worms lack an external skeleton (coenoecium) and there are no certain fossils. Maximum length about 2.5 m, attained in *Balanoglossus gigas;* most less than 30 cm.

About 12 genera (e.g., *Balanoglossus, Ptychodera,* and *Saccoglossus*) with about 65 species.

Class PTEROBRANCHIA

Small (body up to 7 mm) colonial or pseudocolonial sedentary marine animals with a ciliated lophophore; an external cuticular skeleton is present. Known as fossils from the Lower Ordovician, Upper Cretaceous, and Eocene (Bulman, 1970). Eaton (1970) believes that some early members may have been the ancestral forms to echinoderms and chordates (through the mitrates). The class contains two orders with about 20 living species.

Order CEPHALODISCA.   Zooids free; no true colonies; living forms with four to nine pairs of arms with tentacles. Contains the fossil *Eocephalodiscus* and *Pterobranchites* and the living *Atubaria* (one species from near Japan) and *Cephalodiscus* (four subgenera; most species in the Antarctic).

Order RHABDOPLEURIDA.   Zooids attached; true colonies; living forms with two tentacular arms. Contains the fossil *Rhabdopleurites* and *Rhabdopleuroides* and the living *Rhabdopleura* (eastern Atlantic, South Pacific, and Antarctic).

SUBPHYLUM POGONOPHORA (Beard Worms)

Beard worms are highly aberrant, elongate, tube-living animals. The gut is absent in the larval and adult stages; blastopore absent in embryo; circulatory system closed and with haemoglobin; tentacles present; body divided into three regions, with a corresponding tripartite coelom (formation thought to be enterocoelous); segmented posterior end; sexes separate. For more on this group see Ivanov (1955, 1963) and Southward (1971).

Pogonophorans are marine, worldwide, and usually confined to cold, deep waters in soft sediments. Most species occur in the abyssal zone in Far Eastern seas. They were discovered in 1900 and thought to be polychaete annelids. The first published description (1914) contained the name first used by K. E. Johansson in 1937 (as Pogonofora). Some possible pogonophoran fossils have been described, the oldest being the Lower Cambrian *Hyolithellus*, which appears to be similar to living pogonophorans.

Pogonophorans have usually been regarded as deuterostomes which shared a common ancestry with hemichordates (especially the enteropneustans). Recently, however, it has been suggested that they are more closely related to the Annelida than to the Deuterostomia and therefore belong to the Protostomia. Some have suggested that polychaetes, pogonophorans, lophophorates, and pterobranch hemichordates shared a common ancestry. Southward (1971) favors an annelid affinity but prefers to recognize them as a separate phylum. Harland et al. (1967) consider them both under the Chordata (p. 607) and Mollusca (p. 621). The group is retained here in Chordata until further work clarifies the existing differences of opinion. Maximum length normally about 30 cm; diameter only about 2 mm.

Two orders, Thecanephria and Athecanephria, with about 14 genera (e.g., *Birsteinia, Lamellisabella,* and *Siboglinum*) and about 100 species.

SUBPHYLUM UROCHORDATA (Tunicata: the Tunicates)

Their tadpole larvae possess gill slits, dorsal hollow nerve cord, notochord, and a muscular, unsegmented tail; the adults are sessile filter feeders usually lacking the above features. An endostyle, homologous with the thyroid, is present. The following classification is based largely on Berrill (1950). There is no fossil record. About 1600 species are known.

Class ASCIDIACEA

Larvae free-swimming, tadpolelike (short-lived and nonfeeding); adults sessile benthic, solitary or colonial, and without a tail.

Ascidians are marine and worldwide, extending from the intertidal to well into the abyssal-benthic region, occurring on almost any substrate; for example, *Ascidia, Boltenia, Botryllus, Ciona, Corella, Molgula, Pyura,* and *Styela.*

Class THALIACEA (Salps)

Larvae and adults transparent, pelagic (adults may be solitary or colonial). They tend to be planktonic but are generally capable of weak movements. Remarkable life cycles are characteristic of this group, with sexual and asexual reproductive stages occurring. The most complex cycle occurs in *Doliolum*.

Order PYROSOMIDA. Marine seas except the Arctic. Tubular colonies with a common atrial chamber. They can emit a strong phosphorescent light. The colonies usually vary in length from about 3 cm to 1 m. One genus, *Pyrosoma*.

Order DOLIOLIDA (Cyclomyaria). Marine; primarily tropical to temperate. Generally barrel-shaped with eight or nine muscle bands around the body; for example, *Doliolum*.

Order SALPIDA (Hemimyaria). Marine, all seas. Cylindrical or prismshaped; for example, *Iasis, Thalia,* and *Salpa*.

Class APPENDICULARIA (Larvacea)

Pelagic; Arctic to Antarctic. Larval characteristic (such as the tail) are retained in the adult; for example, *Appendicularia* and *Oikopleura*.

SUBPHYLUM CEPHALOCHORDATA (Acrania, in part)

The notochord extends to the anterior end of the body, in front of the brain. Cranium is absent; no vertebrae; no cartilage or bone; heart consisting of a contractile vessel; no red corpuscles; brain consisting of only two pairs of cerebral lobes; two pairs of cerebral nerves; nonuniting dorsal and ventral nerve roots; liver diverticulum; segmented musculature; epidermis with a single layer of cells; protonephridia with solenocytes for excretion; endostyle present (with iodine-fixing cells; it becomes the thyroid of vertebrates).

About 23 species; no fossil record.

At most, members of the subphyla Cephalochordata and Vertebrata (Agnatha and Pisces only) are normally considered as fish or fishlike and treated in "fish" books. Some workers restrict the term fish, in the narrowest sense, to the Osteichthyes. It is the ichthyologist who generally studies the lancelets and "fish."

Cephalochordates and vertebrates share the following attributes: notochord present (at least in embryo), a dorsal tubular central nervous system, paired lateral gill slits (at least in embryo), postanal tail, hepatic portal system, and endostyle (homologous with the thyroid).

Order AMPHIOXIFORMES (Lancelets). The lancelets are small (up to 9 cm long), slender, fishlike animals, probably close to the ancestral vertebrate lineage.

Lancelets spend most of their time buried in sand in shallow waters. They feed by straining minute organisms from the water that is constantly drawn in through the mouth.

Many workers recognize only one family, Branchiostomidae, and two genera, *Branchiostoma* and *Asymmetron*. Larvae previously classified in *Amphioxides* are now thought to belong to other known genera.

Family BRANCHIOSTOMIDAE.   Marine, primarily tropical; Atlantic, Indian, and Pacific.

Two genera, *Amphioxus* and *Branchiostoma*, with about 14 species.

Family EPIGONICHTHYIDAE.   Marine; Atlantic, Indian, and Pacific.

Two genera, *Asymmetron* and *Epigonichthys*, and about nine species.

†CONODONTOPHORIDA (Subphylum? Conodontochordata). Position uncertain

This is a poorly known group that occurs worldwide and ranges from Cambrian to Triassic times; it is receiving a great deal of attention by paleontologists. Most workers agree that conodonts were planktonic or free swimming and marine; however, a great many ideas exist on their affinities. Some workers believe them to be either fish remains or to belong to a group closely related to primitive vertebrates; others believe that they represent the jaw apparatus of an annelidlike group. The average size of these calcium phosphate structures ranges from 0.1 to 2 mm and are thus the right size for fish teeth or annelid jaws. Evidence is put forth by some workers that they were planktonic wormlike animals with a lophophore around the mouth, possibly bearing some remote affinity with brachiopods. On the other hand, chordatelike organisms about 70 mm long with a dorsal nerve cord have been found with conodonts, but it is not entirely certain whether the organism was a conodont carrier or a conodont eater. A small minority of conodonts are known to form apparatuses in which the individual elements may have different shapes.

Two orders (or classes) can be recognized: Westergaardodinida (with one family) and Conodontophorida (with 20 families).

More information on this group can be found in Halstead (1969:12), Lindström (1964), Lindström and Zeigler (1972), and Rhodes (1972). The last two are symposia and contain numerous references.

SUBPHYLUM VERTEBRATA (Craniata)

The notochord never extends in front of brain; cranium present; vertebrae usually present; cartilage or bone or both are present; heart chambered; red blood corpuscles usually present; brain well developed; 10 to 12 pairs of cranial nerves; dorsal and ventral nerve roots usually uniting; nephridia absent; epidermis with several cell layers; endostyle only in larval lampreys (ammocoetes) and transformed into thyroid tissue in all others.

It is possible that the two basic branches, the agnathans and gnathostomes, evolved independently from a common acraniate ancestor in the Cambrian or earlier (Jarvik, 1968b:502). This seems more plausible than the attempts to derive gnathostomes from the pteraspid line of the agnathans.

SUPERCLASS AGNATHA (Cyclostomata, Marsipobranchii)

Members of this superclass have no jaws (a biting apparatus, not derived from gill arches, is present in some fossil forms); no pelvic fins; two (vertical) semicircular canals (only one canal, but two ampullae, reported for Myxiniformes); vertebral centra never present (only the notochord); gills covered with endoderm and directed internally; gill arch skeleton fused with neurocranium, external to gill lamellae; gills opening to surface through pores rather than through slits; bony exoskeleton in most.

Agnathans first appear in the fossil record in the Middle Ordovician and have their greatest radiation in the Silurian and Lower Devonian.

In older works two artificial assemblages are usually recognized, the extinct agnathans are lumped together as the ostracoderms and living species as the cyclostomes.

About 14 genera with 63 extant species.

Class CEPHALASPIDOMORPHI

Superorder CEPHALASPIDOMORPHA (Monorhina)

Bone, when present, with true bone cells (except in anaspids); pectoral fins sometimes present; single median nostril (nasohypophysial) opening between eyes with pineal eye behind.

† Order CEPHALASPIDIFORMES (Class Cephalaspides, Berg, 1940, and Order Osteostraci, Romer, 1966). Ten pairs of external ventral gill openings; eyes are dorsal; tail heterocercal, with a pair of horizontal caudal flaps in ventral position (Heintz, 1967); cephalic shield with "electric organs"; body with dorsoventrally elongated scales; head depressed anteriorly, triangular posteriorly; body slightly compressed; mouth ventral. Maximum length about 60 cm; most are much smaller.

Seven families; for example, Cephalaspidae, Hemicyclaspidae, and Tremataspidae. Upper Silurian to Upper Devonian, predominantly freshwater.

Order PETROMYZONIFORMES (Hyperoartii) (Class Petromyzones, Berg, 1940, and Suborder Petromyzontoidei, Romer, 1966). Seven pairs of external lateral gill openings; eyes are lateral (except in *Mordacia*); tail isocercal in adults, hypocercal in ammocoete larvae; body naked, eel-like; no bone; no paired fins.

One family, Recent and fossil.

Although the petromyzonids and myxinids are sometimes classified together, to the exclusion of fossil agnathans (e.g., Romer, 1966), it is well established that they are phylogenetically far apart (Stensio, 1968). Both the cephalaspids (Stensio, 1968) and anaspids (Halstead, 1969) have been postulated as having the closest affinity with the petromyzonids.

Family PETROMYZONIDAE (Petromyzontidae)—Lampreys. Anadromous and freshwater; cool zones of the world (see map on p. 323).

One or two dorsal fins are present; eyes well developed in adult; barbels absent; teeth on oral disc and tongue (except in fossil form); dorsal and ventral nerve roots separated; nasohypophyseal sac with external opening only; spiral valve and cilia in intestinal tract; small cerebellum; sexes separate; eggs small, not yolky, occurring in the thousands; larval stage (ammocoete) undergoes radical metamorphosis in fresh water. Ripe female lampreys can have an anal finlike fold but Vladykov (1973) notes the presence of a true anal fin in one female *Petromyzon*.

Lampreys are either parasitic or nonparasitic and both life-history types may exist in individuals of the same species or characterize individuals of closely related species. It is believed that most nonparasitic species have been independently derived from a parasitic species. The parasitic phase, after metamorphosis from the ammocoete larvae but before reproducing, goes through a period of feeding on blood from other fish (very rarely on other animals) by rasping through their skin. The nonparasitic phase reproduces, without feeding, after metamorphosis. It is always confined to fresh water, whereas the parasitic form may be freshwater or anadromous. No parasitic freshwater lampreys are known from the Southern Hemisphere. Maximum length of larvae about 10 cm and parasitic adult about 0.9 m.

Four subfamilies [given family status in Hubbs and Potter (1971)], one known only from fossils, and nine genera with 31 extant species. About 24 species are almost always confined to fresh water. The first subfamily listed is restricted to the Northern Hemisphere, generally north of 30°N, whereas the next two are restricted to the Southern Hemisphere south of 34°S. The following classification is based largely on Hubbs and Potter (1971).

SUBFAMILY PETROMYZONINAE. Supraoral plate (immediately anterior to the front edge of the esophageal opening) single and never with more than three cusps; transverse lingual lamina (extending across the tongue) straight or incurved; largest cusp, if developed, median; slight lateral bulge in midgut.

Ichthyomyzon: freshwater; eastern North America; parasitic and nonparasitic; seven species.

Petromyzon marinus: anadromous (landlocked in Great Lakes region); Atlantic drainages of Canada, United States, Iceland, and Europe (including the Mediterranean); parasitic.

Caspiomyzon wagneri: Caspian Sea basin; probably parasitic.

Eudontomyzon: freshwater; Black Sea drainage (primarily Danube basin), China, and Korea; parasitic and nonparasitic; four species.

Tetrapleurodon: freshwater; Rio Lerma system of Mexico; parasitic and nonparasitic; two species.

Okkelbergia aepyptera: freshwater; southeastern United States; nonparasitic.

Lampetra: anadromous and freshwater; Eurasia and North America; parasitic and nonparasitic; 11 species.

Three subgenera as follows:

Entosphenus: coastal regions of North Pacific in North America and Asia; two species.

Lethenteron: circumarctic drainage basins, coastal regions of western Alaska, and eastern North America; four species.

Lampetra: coastal regions of Europe (to Italy) and western North America; five species.

SUBFAMILY GEOTRIINAE.   Supraoral plate single with four prongs; transverse lingual lamina strongly trident, bident at maturity; two well-developed diverticulae in midgut; caudal and second dorsal fins well separated in the immature (continuous or contiguous in other lampreys).

Geotria (=*Exomegas*) *australis:* anadromous; southern Australia, Tasmania, New Zealand, Chile, Argentina, and the Falkland and South Georgia islands; parasitic.

SUBFAMILY MORDACIINAE.   Supraoral plate paired, each plate with three teeth; transverse lingual lamina incurved, largest cusp at each lateral edge; one well-developed diverticula in midgut; eyes dorsolateral in immature and dorsal in mature (lateral in other lampreys).

Mordacia: anadromous and freshwater; southeastern Australia, Tasmania, and Chile; parasitic and nonparasitic; three species.

SUBFAMILY MAYOMYZONINAE.   Teeth absent (except on tongue). Its only species, *Mayomyzon pieckoensis,* is known from the Pennsylvanian (Bardack and Zangerl, 1968, 1971).

† **Order ANASPIDIFORMES (Subclass Birkeniae, Berg, 1940, and Order Anaspida, Romer, 1966).**   Up to 15 pairs of external lateral gill openings; eyes lateral; tail hypocercal; body usually with dorsoventrally elongated scales (virtually naked in *Jamoytius*); body fusiform and some-

what compressed; mouth terminal; bone cells absent. Maximum length about 15 cm.

Five families; for example, Birkeniidae, Endeiolepidae, and Jamoytiidae. Upper Silurian to Upper Devonian, predominantly freshwater.

Class PTERASPIDOMORPHI

Superorder PTERASPIDOMORPHA (Diplorhina)

Bone, when present, lacks true bone cells; there are no pectoral fins. The acellular nature of the bone may be a primitive rather than a secondary condition, unlike acellular bone in higher fishes which is derived from cellular bone.

Order MYXINIFORMES (Hyperotreti) (Class Myxini, Berg, 1940, and Suborder Myxinoidei, Romer, 1966).   One to 16 pairs of external gill openings; body naked, eellike; no bone; no paired fins.

One family, Recent.

Moy-Thomas and Miles (1971) agree that the cephalaspidiforms, petromyzoniforms, and anaspidiforms are more closely related to one another than to the myxiniforms but believe that the myxiniforms are more closely related to them than to other agnathans. They recognize this in their classification by placing the myxiniforms in the Cephalaspidomorphi but in a taxonomic unit of their own (the Hyperotreti) as opposed to the cephalaspidiforms, petromyzoniforms, and anaspidiforms (the Hyperoartii).

Family MYXINIDAE—Hagfishes.   Marine; temperate zones of the world.

The dorsal fin is absent (the caudal fin extends onto part of dorsal surface); eyes are degenerate; barbels present around biting mouth; teeth only on tongue (plus one on "palate"); dorsal and ventral nerve roots united; nasohypophyseal sac not blind, opening into pharynx; no spiral valve or cilia in intestinal tract; numerous mucous pores along body (shown in sketch); no cerebellum; ovaries and testes in same individual but only one gonad functional (not hermaphrodite); eggs large, yolky, up to 30 per individual; no metamorphosis.

Hagfish are scavenger feeders (mostly eating the insides of dying or dead invertebrates and fish). They are the only vertebrate in which the bodily fluids are isosmotic with seawater. Maximum length up to about 0.8 m.

Five genera with about 32 species.

The following classification is based largely on Adam and Strahan (1963) and C. L. Hubbs (personal communication, 1972).

SUBFAMILY MYXININAE. Efferent branchial ducts open by a common external aperture on each side. The pharyngocutaneous duct which exits the pharynx behind the gills is present only on the left side and probably functions to permit the pharynx to be flushed, thus clearing particles too large for the afferent branchial ducts.

Myxine: anal fin ending posterior to branchial aperture; five or six pairs of gill pouches. Atlantic and Pacific; about nine species.

Notomyxine tridentiger: the pharyngocutaneous duct opens separately to the exterior, leaving two apertures on the left side instead on one as in all other Myxininae (in which it opens into the left common branchial aperture). Buenos Aires to Tierra del Fuego.

Neomyxine biplinicata: a pair of short ventrolateral finfolds behind the branchial region (finfolds are absent in other hagfishes). Cook Strait, New Zealand.

Nemamyxine: anal fin extending anterior to branchial apertures. New Zealand and Patagonia; two species.

SUBFAMILY EPTATRETINAE. Efferent branchial ducts open separately to the exterior with 5 to 16 external gill openings.

Eptatretus (=*Bdellostoma, Paramyxine,* and *Polistotrema*).

Atlantic and Pacific; about 19 species.

† **Order PTERASPIDIFORMES (Class Pteraspides, Berg, 1940, and Heterostraci, Romer, 1966).** Single external lateral gill opening; eyes lateral; tail hypocercal (this, however, is questioned by Denison, 1971b); anal fin absent; probably two olfactory capsules with only an internal opening into mouth area. Maximum length 1.5 m, usually much smaller.

Eleven families; for example, Cyathaspidae, Drepanaspidae, and Pteraspidae (e.g., *Pteraspis*).

Lower Silurian to Upper Devonian. Some isolated plates of Middle Ordovician, which may be pteraspid, are known.

†Order THELODONTIFORMES (Subclass? Coelolepides, Berg, 1940, and Order? Coelolepida, Romer, 1966). Similar to Pteraspidiformes but with anal fin present; entire body covered with placoidlike denticles; head depressed. Maximum length about 40 cm.

Two families, Thelodontidae (e.g., *Thelodus* and *Turinia*) and Phlebolepidae (e.g., *Lanarkia* and *Phlebolepis*). Upper Silurian to Lower Devonian.

Palaeospondylus: position uncertain; Middle Devonian of Scotland. Paired fins are evident in this fish which has a maximum length of 5 cm. Its affinities are completely unknown. Various workers have postulated it to be the larval form of some preceding group (e.g., myxiniforms) or of one of several gnathostome groups. There is some evidence that true jaws existed, but it is retained in Agnatha following Moy-Thomas and Miles (1971).

SUPERCLASS GNATHOSTOMATA

Members of this superclass have jaws that are derived from modified gill arches; paired limbs usually present; three semicircular canals; vertebral centra usually present; gills covered with ectoderm and directed externally; gill arches not fused with neurocranium—internal to gill lamellae; gills opening to surface in Pisces through slits [opercular opening (when present) may be porelike]; bony exoskeleton rarely developed.

The first jawed vertebrates, the acanthodians, appear in the Upper Silurian.

Two grades: Pisces (with four classes, as follows) and Tetrapoda (with four classes—Amphibia, Reptilia, Aves, and Mammalia). Mayr (1969) estimates that the number of living tetrapod species is 21,100, about half the number he gives for vertebrates (41,700).

Nelson (1969a) presents a radically different classification of the gnathostomes based on the sister-group model of W. Hennig. In this system a genealogical approach is used in which sister groups are coordinate taxa of the same absolute estimated age. Different rates of evolution, size of gaps in separating groups, diversity of the taxa, etc., are ignored. The classification attempts to give a strict interpretation of the concepts of phylogeny. Some results are a marked lowering of the relative ranks of mammals and birds, the combination of birds and crocodiles into a common taxon, and the inclusion of all tetrapods in the class Teleostomi. In Nelson's classification (1969a), the superclass Gnathostomata contains the classes Elasmobranchiomorphi and Teleostomi. The latter contains the subclasses Actinopterygii (with infraclasses Chondrostei and Neopterygii) and Sarcopterygii (with infraclasses Brachiopterygii, Coelacanthini, Dipnoi, and Choanata).

GRADE PISCES

The jawed aquatic vertebrates in this grade have gills throughout life and paired limbs, if any, in shape of fins, that are not polydactylous.

The most primitive known gnathostomes are postulated by Jarvik (1968b:505) to be the crossopterygians (acanthodians, however, appear first in the fossil record). The interrelations of the various major groups are unknown. All appear distinct when first present in the fossil record.

Grade Pisces contains two subgrades and four classes with a total of about 18,755 extant species. Two major phyletic lines are recognized: the Elasmobranchiomorphi and the Teleostomi.

SUBGRADE ELASMOBRANCHIOMORPHI

This is a poorly defined group used to indicate that placoderms probably bear a closer relation to the chondrichthyans than to the osteichthyans.

† Class PLACODERMI

Body covered with bony plates (containing bone cells); head shield usually movably articulated with the trunk shield; tail usually heterocercal; internal skeleton ossified.

Most Lower and Middle Devonian placoderms were freshwater; the Upper Devonian were mainly marine. Most were bottom-living fish with depressed bodies. A rapid replacement of placoderms by the chondrichthyans occurred at the end of the Devonian.

The arrangement of orders follows Moy-Thomas and Miles (1971).

† **Order ARTHRODIRIFORMES (Class Coccostei, Berg, 1940, and Order Arthrodira, Romer, 1966).** Full complement of dermal bones on head and usually the trunk; craniothoracic joint with fossa on head, condyle on trunk. Arthrodires were primarily large predators. Maximum length about 9 m.

Lower Devonian to Upper Devonian.

Suborder Arctolepoidei (Dolichothoracoidei). Trunk shield long; eyes small; pectoral spines immovable.

Four families.

Suborder Brachythoracoidei. Trunk shield short; eyes large; no immovable pectoral spines. Some were completely nektonic rather than benthic.

Fourteen families; for example, Coccosteidae, Dinichthyidae, and Titanichthyidae.

† **Order PTYCTODONTIFORMES.** Dermal armor on head and trunk greatly reduced; large sexually dimorphic pelvic fins with claspers in males (fertilization was probably internal); many resemblances with living holocephalans. Maximum length about 20 cm.

One family, Ptyctodontidae (e.g., *Ctenurella* and *Rhamphodopsis*). Devonian.

† **Order PHYLLOLEPIFORMES.** Armor on trunk greatly reduced; body much depressed; concentric and transverse ridges on head and trunk shields.

One family, Phyllolepidae. Upper Devonian.

† **Order PETALICHTHYIFORMES.** Trunk shield has long lateral spinal plates; eyes dorsal. Maximum length seldom more than 0.5 m.

Includes the orders Macropetalichthyiformes and Stensioelliformes (Stegoselachii), Berg (1940).

Three families; for example, Macropetalichthyidae (e.g., *Lunaspis*). Devonian to Mississippian.

† Order RHENANIFORMES. Mosaic of small bones on head shield between the large plates; mouth subterminal. Maximum length seldom more than 0.3 m.

Two Devonian families: Palaeacanthaspidae—long dorsal spine; Gemuendinidae—small dorsal spine; body strongly depressed with large pectoral fins and raylike body.

† Order ANTIARCHIFORMES (Class Pterichthys of Berg, 1940, and Order Antiarchi of Romer, 1966). Head shield smaller than trunk shield; trunk shield has a movable spinelike pectoral fin; no anal fin; eyes dorsal and closely placed; pineal organ between eyes; mouth subterminal; craniothoracic joint with condyles on head, fossae on body. Maximum length about 30 cm.

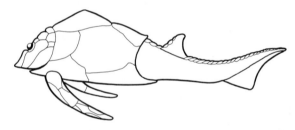

Three families, Asterolepidae (e.g., *Asterolepis* and *Bothriolepis*), Remigolepidae, and Wudinolepidae. Devonian, freshwater.

Class CHONDRICHTHYES—Cartilaginous Fishes

The cartilaginous skeleton is often calcified but never ossified, and the skull lacks sutures in living forms. Teeth usually not fused to jaws and replaced serially; horny, soft fin rays unsegmented and epidermal in origin (ceratotrichia); nasal openings on each side usually single (imperfectly divided by a flap into incurrent and excurrent openings) and more or less ventral; biting edge of upper jaw formed by palatoquadrate; swim bladder and lung absent; intestinal spiral valve present; internal fertilization in modern forms—males with pelvic claspers which are inserted in the female cloaca and oviduct(s); embryo encapsulated in a leatherlike case (gestation periods of two years are known, the longest of any vertebrate); high blood concentration of urea and trimethylamine oxide (converted from toxic ammonia) allows water to be drawn freely into the body.

Two main lines of evolution can be recognized—the elasmobranchs and holocephalans (ranked as subclasses). It is probable that these two lineages had separate origins within the placoderms with elasmobranchs being derived from the petalichthyiforms (via the cladoselachimorphs) and holocephalans being derived from the ptyctodontiforms (via the iniopterygiforms).

Extant taxa constitute 6 orders, 24 families, 135 genera, and about 627 species.

Subclass ELASMOBRANCHII

Five to seven separate gill openings on each side; dorsal fin(s) and spines, if present, are rigid; males without clasper organ on head; dermal placoid scales often present; palatoquadrate (upper jaw) not fused to cranium (suspension amphistylic or hyostylic); teeth numerous; some ribs usually present; spiracle opening (remains of hyoidean gill slit) usually present. Middle Devonian to Recent.

Elasmobranchs are typically predaceous fishes that rely more on smell (the olfactory capsules are relatively large) than sight (the eyes are relatively small) for obtaining their food.

Compagno (1973) has proposed a new (and provisional) classification of living elasmobranchs that differs in many ways with the one given here. Although it presents modern views on elasmobranch phylogeny, it is a split classification in which 49 families compare with the 21 I recognize. Compagno recognizes four superorders (with 49 families): Squalomorphii, with the orders Hexanchiformes, Squaliformes (Echinorhinidae and Squalidae), and Pristiophoriformes; Batoidea, with the orders Rajiformes (Rhinidae, Rhynchobatidae, Rhinobatidae, Platyrhinidae, Arhynchobatidae, Rajidae, Pseudorajidae, and Anacanthobatidae), Pristiformes, Torpediniformes (Torpedinidae, Hypnidae, Narcinidae, and Narkidae), Myliobatiformes (Dasyatidae, Potamotrygonidae, Urolophidae, Gymnuridae, Myliobatidae, Rhinopteridae, and Mobulidae); Squatinomorphii (with only *Squatina*); and Galeomorphii, with the orders Heterodontiformes, Orectolobiformes, Lamniformes, and Carcharhiniformes.

Compagno also prefers to place living elasmobranchs (he estimates 700 to 800 or more species) and the fossil hybodonts and ctenacanths in the cohort Euselachii, in opposition to the extinct cladoselachians, cladodonts, xenacanths, and edestoids.

About 128 genera with 602 living species.

† Superorder CLADOSELACHIMORPHA

Cladodont-type tooth (tall central cusp and one or more pairs of lateral cusps on a broad base); claspers usually absent (*Diademodus,* which may be related to *Cladoselache,* had claspers); amphistylic jaw suspension; no anal fin; paired fins in shape of triangular flaps; radials of fins unsegmented and extending almost to the edge of the fin.

† **Order CLADOSELACHIFORMES.**   Two dorsal fins, each with a spine.
One family.

Family CLADOSELACHIDAE.   Upper Devonian to Mississippian.

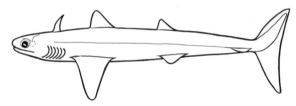

Maximum length about 2 m.
Includes the well-known *Cladoselache. Diademodus* may belong here, although it had claspers and probably lacked dorsal fin spines.

† **Order CLADODONTIFORMES.**   One dorsal fin, without a spine.
One family.

Family CLADODONTIDAE.   Middle Devonian to Mississippian (? Permian).

Includes *Cladodus* (a genus to which a number of primitive but unrelated species have been assigned), *Denaea,* and *Symmorium.*

† Superorder XENACANTHIMORPHA (Subclass Xenacanthi, Berg, 1940, and Order Pleuracanthodii, Romer, 1966)

† Order XENACANTHIFORMES. Pleuracanth-type tooth (three cusps of variable size, usually two prominent lateral cusps and a smaller median one). Claspers in male; amphistylic jaw suspension; elongate dorsal fin base; diphycercal tail; two anal fins; cephalic spine; radials of pectorals jointed and ending well before fin margin.
   One family.

Family XENACANTHIDAE. Freshwater; Late Devonian to Triassic.

For example, *Xenacanthus.*

Superorder SELACHIMORPHA (Pleurotremata)—Sharks

Gill openings mainly lateral. Anterior edge of pectoral fin not attached to side of head; anal fin present or absent; pectoral girdle halves not joined dorsally (fused ventrally).
   The well-known terms for vertebral types (astrospondylic, tectospondylic, and cyclospondylic) lump unrelated groups and Applegate (1967) has proposed a new system.
   Thirteen families contain about 80 genera and 287 living species.

† Order CTENACANTHIFORMES. Two dorsal fins, each with a spine. Anal fin near caudal fin; cladodont-type tooth; amphistylic jaw suspension.
   One family.

Family CTENACANTHIDAE. Upper Devonian and Mississippian.

Maximum length about 2.5 m.
   Bandringa, Ctenacanthus, Goodrichthys, and *Tristychius* are included.

†Order HYBODONTIFORMES. Hybodontids have the features given above for the closely related ctenacanthids. They differ, among other features, in their internal fin structure. Males have hooked spines above the eye which may have functioned as cephalic claspers during copulation.

It is generally believed that modern sharks are derived from hybodontidlike fishes. The amphistylic jaw suspension is transformed to a hyostylic one in the majority of living sharks (correlated with their protrusible jaws).

Four families (e.g., Coronodontidae and Hybodontidae). Pennsylvanian to Cretaceous (the dominant selachians of the Triassic and Jurassic).

Order HETERODONTIFORMES.   Two dorsal fins, each with a spine. Anal fin present; five gill slits; eyes without nictitating fold; spiracle present; nostrils connected with mouth by deep groove.

Family HETERODONTIDAE—Bullhead, Horn, or Port Jackson Sharks.   Marine; tropical Indian and Pacific (South Africa to Japan and Australia and New Zealand; eastern Pacific from California to Galapagos Islands and Peru).

One genus, *Heterodontus,* with six species.

Order HEXANCHIFORMES (Notidanoidei).   One dorsal fin, without spine; anal fin present; six or seven gill slits; eyes without nictitating fold; spiracle present.

Family CHLAMYDOSELACHIDAE—Frill Shark.   Marine; Japan, California, and Europe.

Six gill openings, margin of first gill continuous across throat; mouth terminal.

One species, *Chlamydoselachus anguineus.*

Family HEXANCHIDAE—Cow Sharks.   Marine; Atlantic, Indian, and Pacific.

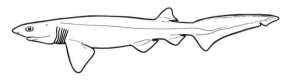

Six or seven gill openings, margin of first gill not continuous across throat; mouth ventral. Three genera and five species: *Hexanchus griseus* and *H. vitulus* with six gill openings and *Heptranchias* and *Notorynchus* with seven gill openings; three species.

Order LAMNIFORMES (Galeoidea).   Two dorsal fins (one dorsal fin in the scyliorhinid *Pentanchus*), without spines; anal fin present; five gill slits; gill rakers absent except as noted; spiracle present except as noted.
About 56 genera and 199 species.

Suborder Lamnoidei (Isurida).   Eyes without nictitating membrane.

Family RHINCODONTIDAE—Whale Shark.   Marine; pelagic tropical.

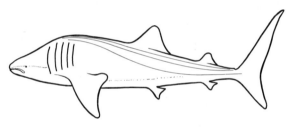

Mouth terminal; gill openings exceptionally large; fifth gill opening behind origin of pectoral, over fin base; gill rakers elongate, plankton feeders; teeth reduced.
World's largest fish with lengths up to 15.2 m (perhaps up to about 18 m).
One species, *Rhincodon typus*, first described under the generic name *Rhiniodon* in 1828 (Penrith, 1972) but the well-known name *Rhincodon* is best retained.

Family ORECTOLOBIDAE—Carpet or Nurse Sharks.   Marine; all oceans.

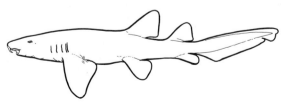

Mouth ventral; fourth and fifth gill openings behind origin of pectoral, over fin base; nostril connected to mouth by a deep groove, with a well-developed barbel; first dorsal fin posteriorly placed. Young born alive in some; in others the females lay eggs.

Maximum length about 4.2 m, attained in several species (e.g., *Ginglymostoma cirratum*).

About 11 genera (e.g., *Ginglymostoma*, *Orectolobus*, and *Stegostoma*) and about 25 species.

Family ODONTASPIDIDAE (Carchariidae)—Sand Tigers.   Marine; Atlantic, Indian, and Pacific.

Mouth ventral; fifth gill opening well in front of pectoral fin.

Subfamily Odontaspidinae (sand sharks).   Jaws not greatly protrusible.

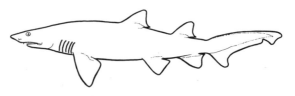

One genus, *Odontaspis* (= *Carcharias*, and *Pseudocarcharias* which probably deserves generic rank), with six species.

Subfamily Scapanorhynchinae (goblin sharks).   Jaws greatly protrusible; rostral projection.

One species, *Scapanorhynchus* (= *Mitsukurina*) *owstoni*. The living species, known only from a few specimens, is usually placed in *Mitsukurina* with the earlier discovered fossil form placed in *Scapanorhynchus*.

Family LAMNIDAE.   Marine; all oceans.

The following subfamilies are given family status by some workers.

The Alopiinae bears some relationship to Odontaspidae, whereas the Cetorhinae has a close affinity to the Lamninae.

Subfamily Alopiinae (thresher sharks).   Upper lobe of caudal fin greatly elongate, caudal fin almost one-half of total length; third to fifth gill openings over origin of pectoral fin.

One genus, *Alopias,* with five species.

SUBFAMILY CETORHININAE (BASKING SHARKS). Gill openings exceptionally large; gill rakers elongate, plankton feeders, teeth reduced; tail nearly symmetrical with keel on caudal peduncle; fifth gill opening in front of pectoral fin.

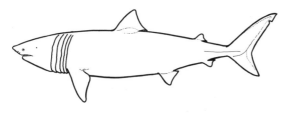

World's second largest fish, attains lengths up to 13.6 m.
One genus, *Cetorhinus,* with two species.

SUBFAMILY LAMNINAE (ISURIDAE) (MACKEREL SHARKS). Caudal peduncle with a distinct keel; teeth large; fifth gill opening in front of pectoral fin; spiracle sometimes absent.

Some are maneaters (e.g., the dreaded white shark, *Carcharodon carcharias*) in lengths about 7 m.
Three genera, *Carcharodon, Isurus,* and *Lamna,* and about seven species.

Suborder Scyliorhinoidei. Nictitating fold or membrane usually present.

Family SCYLIORHINIDAE—Cat Sharks. Marine; temperate, and tropical.

Nictitating membrane absent but longitudinal fold along lower eyelid usually present; fifth gill opening over origin of pectoral fin.

SUBFAMILY PSEUDOTRIAKINAE. First dorsal fin base longer than tail length and well anterior to origin of pelvics.

One genus, *Pseudotriakis,* with two species.

SUBFAMILY SCYLIORHININAE. The first dorsal fin base is shorter than tail length and at least one-half its base posterior to the origin of pelvics.

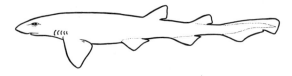

TRIBE SCYLIORHININI. Eleven genera (e.g., *Apristurus, Atelomycterus, Cephaloscyllium, Conoporoderma, Galeus, Holohalaelurus, Pentanchus* (which has one dorsal fin), *Schroederichthys,* and *Scyliorhinus*), with about 54 species.

TRIBE PROSCYLLINI. Two monotypic genera, *Eridacnis* and *Proscyllium.*

Family CARCHARHINIDAE. Marine; all oceans.

Fifth gill opening over or behind origin of pectoral fin.

SUBFAMILY TRIAKINAE (SMOOTH DOGFISHES). Teeth usually low with three or more cusps.

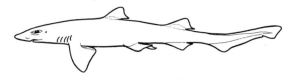

Eleven genera with about 35 species.

TRIBE LEPTOCHARIINI.   One species, *Leptocharias smithii*.

TRIBE TRIAKINI.   About six genera (e.g., *Galeorhinus, Iago, Mustelus, Triakis,* and *Scylliogaleus*).

TRIBE HEMIGALEINI.   Four genera, *Dirrhizodon, Chaenogaleus, Hemigaleus,* and *Paragaleus*.

SUBFAMILY CARCHARHININAE (REQUIEM SHARKS).   Teeth usually bladelike with one cusp.

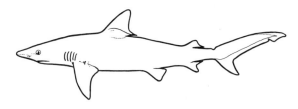

Carcharhinus leucas, the bull shark, of the Atlantic and Pacific oceans, is found in some lakes and streams in Mexico, Central America, and northern South America; it also occurs inland up the Amazon River as far as Peru (Thorson, 1972).

Eleven genera with about 50 species.

TRIBE GALEOCERDINI.   One genus, *Galeocerdo* (tiger sharks), with perhaps two species.

TRIBE SCOLIODONTINI.   One genus, *Scoliodon,* with several species.

TRIBE CARCHARHININI.   Nine genera, *Carcharhinus, Hypoprion, Isogomphodon, Lamiopsis, Loxodon, Negaprion, Prionace, Rhizoprionodon,* and *Triaenodon,* with about 45 species.

Family SPHYRNIDAE—Hammerhead Sharks.   Marine (occasionally brackish); all oceans (primarily in warm coastal waters).

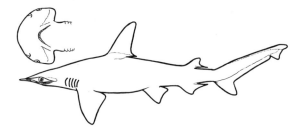

Lateral expansion of the head (with the eyes and nasal openings farther apart than in other sharks which may confer an advantage in homing in on food); spiracle absent. A great deal of variation between species in the development of the lateral lobes is illustrated in Gilbert (1967). *Sphyrna* (*Eusphyra*) *blochii*, sometimes placed in its own genus, *Eusphyra,* has an extremely wide and hammerlike head (with narrow extensions), whereas in *S. tiburo* it is evenly rounded and spadelike.

These sharks are closely related to the Carcharhininae but differ in many cranial characters associated with the sphyrnid cephalic hydrofoil or "hammer." Large individuals are highly dangerous and there are many records of fatal attacks on humans. Maximum length 4.5 m, attained in *Sphyrna tudes.*

One genus, *Sphyrna,* with nine species (Gilbert, 1967).

Order SQUALIFORMES (Tectospondyli). Two dorsal fins, with or without spines; anal fin absent; five or six gill slits.

About 19 genera and 76 species.

Suborder Squaloidei. Body sharklike; eyes lateral.

Family SQUALIDAE—Dogfish Sharks. Marine; Atlantic, Indian, and Pacific.

Compagno (1973) favors placing *Echinorhinus* in its own family apart from other squalids. Although there may have been considerable parallelism in the loss of the fin spines in the other members of this family, the relationships of the genera are too poorly known to erect any but a provisional classification.

Several members of this family, such as *Isistius, Euprotomicrus, Centroscyllium,* and *Etmopterus,* are luminescent.

Maximum length 6.3 m, attained by *Somniosus microcephalus.* The world's smallest sharks, two species of *Squaliolus,* belong to this family. *Euprotomicrus bispinatus,* the next smallest, has a maximum known length of 26.5 cm and weight of 67.6 grams (Hubbs et al., 1967). *Etmopterus hillianus* reaches about 35 cm.

SUBFAMILY DALATIINAE (SLEEPER SHARKS). Second dorsal and usually the first without spines.

At least seven genera (e.g., *Centroscymnus, Dalatias, Euprotomicrus, Isistius, Scymnodon, Somniosus,* and *Squaliolus*) and about 15 species.

SUBFAMILY ECHINORHININAE (BRAMBLE SHARKS).   No dorsal fin spines; spinelike tubercles over body.

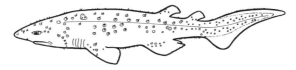

Two species, *Echinorhinus brucus* from most oceans and the rare *E. cooki* from the Pacific (Garrick, 1960).

SUBFAMILY SQUALINAE (DOGFISH SHARKS).   Each dorsal fin preceded by a spine (may be short).

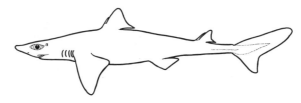

Eight genera with about 44 species.

TRIBE ETMOPTERINI.   Three genera, *Aculeola, Centroscyllium,* and *Etmopterus.*

TRIBE SQUALINI.   Three genera, *Centrophorus, Cirrhigaleus,* and *Squalus.*

TRIBE DEANIINI.   One genus, *Deania,* with about five species.

TRIBE OXYNOTINI.   One genus, *Oxynotus,* with three species.

Family PRISTIOPHORIDAE—Saw Sharks.   Marine; South Africa and Indo-Pacific (Australia to Japan).

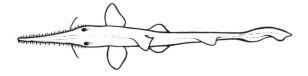

Snout produced in a long flat blade with teeth on each side (teeth unequal in size, usually alternating large and small, and weakly embedded); one pair of long barbels; no dorsal fin spines (sometimes present as internal rudiments).

Pristiophorids have many raylike characters and probably have a relatively close affinity to the Batoidimorpha, as do the squatinids.

Two genera, *Pristiophorus* (five gill openings) and *Pliotrema* (six gill openings), with four species.

Suborder Squatinoidei. Body raylike; eyes dorsal.

Family SQUATINIDAE—Angel Sharks. Marine; Atlantic and Pacific.

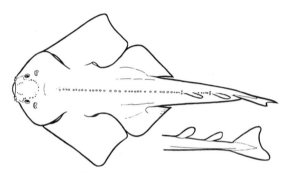

Two spineless dorsal fins; no anal fin; five gill openings; spiracle large; mouth almost terminal; nostrils terminal with barbels on anterior margin.

One genus, *Squatina*, with 11 species.

Superorder BATOIDIMORPHA (Hypotremata)—Rays

Gill openings ventral; anterior edge of the greatly enlarged pectoral fin attached to side of head anterior to the five gill openings; anal fin absent; eyes and spiracles on dorsal surface; pectoral girdle halves joined dorsally; nictitating membrane absent; body generally strongly depressed; ceratotrichia reduced; jaws protrusible; teeth pavementlike; in most, water for breathing taken in chiefly through the spiracle rather than the mouth (except for those living off the bottom); habitat generally benthic; most give birth to live young (Rajidae, however, have eggs encased in a horny capsule); no electric organs in head region except in Torpedinidae. Upper Jurassic to Recent.

Order RAJIFORMES. If the relationships suggested by Compagno (1973) were to be recognized in the following classification, the following suborders and superfamilies could be erected: Pristioidei with Pristidae, Rajoidei with the superfamilies Rhinobatoidae and Rajoidae, Torpedinoidei with Torpedinidae, and Myliobatoidei with the superfamilies Dasyatoidae and Myliobatoidae.

Eight families with about 49 genera and 315 species.

Family PRISTIDAE—Sawfishes. Marine; Atlantic, Indian, and Pacific; freshwater in some areas.

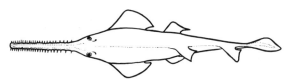

Snout produced in a long flat blade with teeth on each side (teeth of equal size and embedded in deep sockets); barbels absent; body somewhat sharklike, although the head is depressed; two distinct dorsal fins and a caudal fin.

One genus, *Pristis* (with two subgenera, *Anoxypristis*, for *P. cuspidatus*, and *Pristis*), with six species.

Family RHINOBATIDAE—Guitarfishes. Marine; Atlantic, Indian, and Pacific.

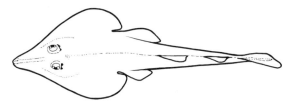

Body intermediate between sharklike and skatelike; tail stout, not definitely marked off from body; two distinct dorsal fins and a caudal fin; denticles over body form a row on midline of back; tail without spine.

About 45 species.

SUBFAMILY RHINOBATINAE. Caudal fin not bilobed; origin of first dorsal behind pelvics.

TRIBE RHINOBATINI. Four genera, *Aptychotrema, Rhinobatos, Trygonorrhina*, and *Zapteryx*.

TRIBE PLATYRHININI. Three genera, *Platyrhina, Platyrhinoidis*, and *Zanobatus*.

SUBFAMILY RHYNCHOBATINAE. Caudal fin bilobed; origin of first dorsal over or in front of pelvics.

TRIBE RHYNCHOBATINI. One genus, *Rhynchobatus,* probably with two species.

TRIBE RHININI. One Indo-Pacific species, *Rhina ancylostoma.*

Family TORPEDINIDAE—Electric Rays. Marine; Atlantic, Indian, and Pacific.

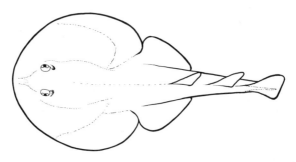

Powerful electric organs, derived from branchial muscles, in head region; skin soft and loose; eyes small to obsolete; caudal fin well developed; dorsal fins 0-2 (on which basis some workers have recognized three families or subfamilies).

Four species are blind; the two species of *Typhlonarke* endemic to New Zealand and *Benthobatis moresbyi* off southern India have concealed eyes, whereas *Narke impennis* of the Bay of Bengal has minute sunken eyes (Garrick, 1951).

Nine genera with at least 35 species.

SUBFAMILY TORPEDININAE. Disc truncate or emarginate anteriorly; jaws extremely slender; no labial cartilages; rostrum absent or reduced.

TRIBE TORPEDININI. Tail and dorsal and caudal fins well developed. One genus, *Torpedo,* with several species.

TRIBE HYPNINI. Tail and dorsal and caudal fins very small. One Australian species, *Hypnos subnigrum.*

SUBFAMILY NARCININAE. Disc rounded anteriorly; jaws stout; strong labial cartilages; rostrum present.

TRIBE NARCININI.   Deep groove around mouth and lips; jaws long and strongly protractile; rostrum broad; usually two dorsal fins.

Four genera, *Benthobatis*, *Diplobatis*, *Discopyge*, and *Narcine*.

TRIBE NARKINI.   Shallow groove around mouth; jaws short and weakly protractile; rostrum narrow; usually a single dorsal fin.

At least three genera, *Heteronarce* (has two dorsal fins), *Narke* (= *Temera*, which lacks a dorsal fin and is usually given generic rank), and *Typhlonarke*.

Family RAJIDAE—Skates.   Marine, all oceans.

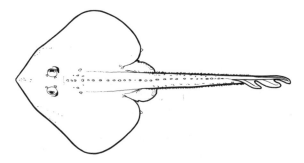

Caudal fin reduced or absent; tail extremely slender; weak electric organs derived from caudal muscles; dorsal fins 0-2; most with prickles on skin, often with a row along midline of back. Eggs encased in horny capsule with four long tips.

The following first two and last two subfamilies are recognized as families by Bigelow and Schroeder (1962); Hulley (1972) placed *Gurgesiella* in its own family.

SUBFAMILY ANACANTHOBATINAE.   No dorsal fin; caudal fin well-developed or not; upper surface smooth; pelvic fins divided into two distinct lobes, the anterior lobe limblike; tip of snout with a filament (expanded terminally in *Springeria*).

Two genera, *Anacanthobatis* and *Springeria*, with five species, known from South Africa, Natal, and tropical western Atlantic.

SUBFAMILY ARHYNCHOBATINAE.   One dorsal fin; caudal fin complete.

One species, *Arhynchobatis asperrimus*, endemic to New Zealand and known only from a few specimens, all of which are females (Garrick, 1954, 1957).

SUBFAMILY GURGESIELLINAE.   No dorsal fin; pelvic fin outer angles pointed; rostral filament short.

Two species, *Gurgesiella atlantica* and *G. furvescens,* known from the tropical western Atlantic and off Chile.

SUBFAMILY PSEUDORAJINAE.   No dorsal fin; caudal fin well-developed; upper surface with prickles; pelvic fins not divided into lobes; outer angles broadly rounded; snout terminating in a short, fleshy appendage (rostral filament).

One species, *Pseudoraja fisheri,* known from the gulfs of Mexico and Honduras.

SUBFAMILY RAJINAE.   Two dorsal fins; caudal fin usually poorly developed.

Six genera [e.g., *Breviraja, Cruriraja, Raja* (the most specious elasmobranch genus), and *Sympterygia*] with at least 110 species.

Family DASYATIDAE (Trygonidae).   Marine; Atlantic, Indian, and Pacific (a few species occasionally occur in brackish and fresh water).

Outer anterior margin of pectorals continuous along side of head, no separate cephalic or subrostral fins; no distinct dorsal fin (completely absent in most species); most species with one or more long poisonous spines on tail (pain said to be excruciating to humans).

SUBFAMILY DASYATINAE (STINGRAYS OR WHIPRAYS).   Disc less than 1.3 times as broad as long; no caudal fin; tail long (distance from cloaca to tip much longer than breadth of disc).

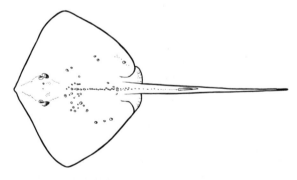

Five genera (e.g., *Dasyatis* and *Himantura*) with about 35 species.

SUBFAMILY GYMNURINAE (BUTTERFLY RAYS). Disc extremely broad (more than 1.5 times as broad as long); no caudal fin; tail short (distance from cloaca to tip much shorter than breadth of disc).

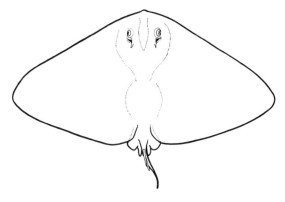

Two genera, *Aetoplatea* and *Gymnura,* with about 10 species.

SUBFAMILY UROLOPHINAE (ROUND RAYS). Disc less than 1.3 times as broad as long; well-developed caudal fin; tail moderately long.

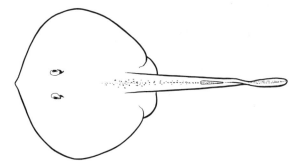

Three genera, *Trygonoptera, Urolophus,* and *Urotrygon,* with about 20 species.

Family POTAMOTRYGONIDAE—River Stingrays. Freshwater; South America (Atlantic drainage), and possibly Africa (Benoue River of the Niger System) and the Mekong River in northern Laos.

Similar to the Dasyatinae; the major difference is the long, median, anteriorly directed process from the pelvis which is absent in the Dasyatidae (but present in the Myliobatidae and Mobulidae). T. B. Thorson and his colleagues have found these rays to have low urea concentrations in the blood, unlike other members of the class Chondrichthyes.

Castex (1967), in a study of the venomous rays, listed 19 South American species (the only *Disceus* and 18 *Potamotrygon*), a recently discovered *Potamotrygon* in Nigeria, and the two or more unnamed species from Laos. He mentions the need to determine the validity of the named species (various intermediate forms between "species" are known) and the relation between the South American, African, and Asiatic species.

Two genera, *Disceus* and *Potamotrygon,* with at least 10 species.

Family MYLIOBATIDAE—Eagle Rays.   Marine; Atlantic, Indian, and Pacific.

Head elevated and distinct from disc; eyes and spiracles lateral on head; gill openings about length of eye; tail much longer than disc; venomous spine(s) present in some; small dorsal fin; no caudal fin; pectoral fins reduced or absent opposite the eyes, but with an anterior subdivision that unites below the tip of the snout forming a subrostral lobe. Some are famous for their ability to leap high into the air from the water.

Subfamily Myliobatinae (eagle rays).   Anterior face of cranium nearly straight; subrostral fin not incised.

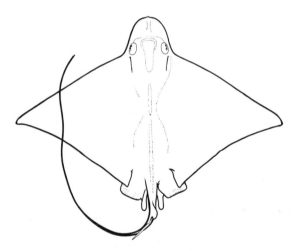

Four genera, *Aetobatus, Aetomylaeus, Myliobatis,* and *Pteromylaeus,* with about 15 species.

SUBFAMILY RHINOPTERINAE (COW-NOSED RAYS). Anterior face of cranium concave; subrostral fin incised (bilobed).
One genus, *Rhinoptera*, with 10 species.

Family MOBULIDAE—Manta Rays and Devil Rays. Marine; Atlantic, Indian, and Pacific.

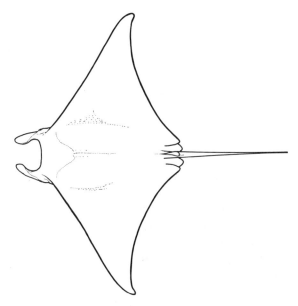

Head distinct from disc; eyes and spiracles lateral on head; gill openings much longer than eye; tail much longer than disc; spine(s) present in some; small dorsal fin; no caudal fin. Members of this family are the only living vertebrates with three functional paired limbs (the cephalic pair assist in feeding; they are essentially the anterior subdivision of the pectorals).

Some mantas grow to a width of about 6.1 m and a weight of more than 1360 kg; largest members of the superorder (and like the whale shark and basking shark, strain their food out of the water).

Two genera, *Manta* with mouth terminal and *Mobula* with mouth ventral, and 10 species.

†Order HELICOPRIONIFORMES (Helicoprionida). Position uncertain. Probably elasmobranchs, affinities unknown; possess tooth whorls superficially similar to those of the edestids.
One family Helicoprionidae (e.g., *Campyloprion* and *Helicoprion*). Pennsylvanian to Permian.

†**Order BRADYODONTIFORMES (Bradyodonti).** Position uncertain. Elasmobranchs of uncertain relationships. All have pavementlike crushing dentition and holostylic jaw suspension. Some are known only from their teeth.

Five families [Petalodontidae, Psammodontidae, Copodontidae, Chondrenchelyidae, and Edestidae (e.g., *Erikodus, Fadenia, Ornithoprion,* and *Sarcoprion*)]. Late Devonian to Permian. Moy-Thomas and Miles (1971) gave ordinal status to these five families and included them in the Holocephali.

Romer (1966) placed the edestids in the hybodontoids. Bendix-Almgreen (1968) noted that the bradyodonts may be a heterogeneous assemblage and not necessarily ancestral to the chimaerids. Patterson (1968a) placed the better known bradyodonts in the Holocephali. The scheme followed here for the bradyodonts and holocephalans takes some features from Romer (1966) and Patterson (1968a).

Subclass HOLOCEPHALI

Gill cover over the four gill openings, leaving one opening on each side; palatoquadrate fused to cranium (holostylic); no spiracle opening; teeth as a few grinding plates (except in the iniopterygians); no cloaca, separate anal and urogenital openings; skin in adult naked; no stomach; no ribs; males with clasping organ on head (in addition to the pelvic claspers). This group may be allied to the ptyctodontid placoderms. The anatomy of the group is discussed in detail by Patterson (1965) and Stahl (1967). Upper Devonian to Recent.

†**Order INIOPTERYGIFORMES.** Large pectoral fins appearing to originate from the nape of the neck; dentition sharklike.

The recently discovered iniopterygians appear to be morphological intermediates (but not strict phylogenetic intermediates) between chimaeroids and elasmobranchs (Zangerl and Case, 1973; Zangerl, 1973). They possibly shared a common ancestry with the Chimaeriformes, both being derived from an early elasmobranch ancestor.

About five genera (e.g., *Iniopteryx*) have been described. Pennsylvanian, North America.

Order CHIMAERIFORMES

†*Suborder Helodontoidei.* One family, Helodontidae (e.g., *Helodus* and *Psephodus*). Upper Devonian to Lower Permian.

Romer (1966) placed the helodonts with the bradyodonts but Patterson (1968a) placed them in the Chimaeriformes and included two other well-known bradyodonts (Chondrenchelyidae and Edestidae) in the Holocephali as separate orders.

†Suborder Cochliodontoidei.   Known only from the mandible and dentition.

One family, Cochliodontidae (e.g., *Cochliodus, Deltodus,* and *Sandalodus*). Upper Devonian to Permian.

This group is placed in the bradyodonts in most older works.

†Suborder Menaspoidei.   One family, Menaspidae (e.g., *Menaspis* and *Deltoptychius*). Mississippian to Upper Permian.

†Suborder Myriacanthoidei.   Three families. Jurassic.

†Suborder Squalorajoidei.   One family, Squalorajidae. Jurassic.

Suborder Chimaeroidei.   Two dorsal fins, the first erectile, with short base, and preceded by an erectile spine, the second nonerectile, low, and with long base; mouth inferior. In living forms, at least, fertilization is internal; the deposited egg is encased in a brown horny capsule. Water for breathing is chiefly taken in through the nostrils.

Chimaeroids have probably descended from the squalorajoids and myriacanthoids which in turn can be traced back to the menaspoids (Patterson, 1965).

Six extant genera with about 25 species. Many authors place all species into one family, Chimaeridae, rather than in three as is done here. Jurassic to Recent.

Family CALLORHYNCHIDAE—Plownose Chimaeras.   Marine; Southern Hemisphere (off southern South America, New Zealand, southern Australia, southern Africa etc.).

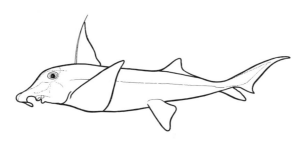

Snout with elongate, flexible, hooklike process; tail heterocercal.
  One genus, *Callorhynchus*, with as many as four species.

Family CHIMAERIDAE—Shortnose Chimaeras or Ratfishes. Marine; Atlantic
and Pacific.

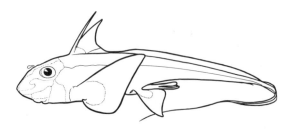

Snout short and rounded; tail diphycercal. Egg capsule tadpole-shaped
with rearward filament. A poison gland is associated with the dorsal
spine and the venom is painful to man.
  Two genera, *Chimaera* (with anal fin separate from caudal fin) and *Hy-drolagus* (with anal fin joined to caudal fin) and about 15 species. *Chimaera* has six species and occurs in the northern Atlantic, Japan and
northern China, and South Africa, whereas *Hydrolagus* has about nine
species and occurs primarily in the northern Atlantic, off South Africa,
and in many areas in the Pacific (e.g., California to Alaska, Japan, New
Zealand, and Australia).

Family RHINOCHIMAERIDAE—Longnose Chimaeras. Marine; Atlantic and
Pacific.

Snout long and pointed, not hooklike; tail diphycercal; anal fin separated
from caudal in *Neoharriotta* and joined with it in the other genera.
  Three genera: *Harriotta* of the western and eastern Atlantic, Japan,
New Zealand, and lower California, with possibly two species; *Neoharriotta* of the southern Caribbean Sea and West Africa with two species;
and *Rhinochimaera* of Japan, northeastern Atlantic (off Ireland), and
western North Atlantic (seven specimens taken in 1952 and 1953 off
southwestern Nova Scotia and Massachusetts) with two species (Bigelow
and Schroeder, 1953; Bullis and Carpenter, 1966; Leim and Scott, 1966;
Garrick, 1971). Of the six species four are in the Atlantic and two in the
Pacific.

SUBGRADE TELEOSTOMI

This is a poorly defined group. Its only merit is to indicate that acanthodians probably bear a closer relation to the osteichthyans than to the chondrichthyans.

†Class ACANTHODII

True bone present; jaws formed by palatoquadrate and Meckel's cartilage, both ossified; mandibular arch (palatoquadrate), probably closely associated with hyoid arch, with the spiracular gill cleft (homologous with spiracle of other fish and eustachian tube of tetrapods) virtually closed; dermal operculum (associated with hyoid arch); five gill arches; notochord generally persistent; ganoid scales present; stout spines present before the dorsal, anal, and paired fins (up to six paired spines present between the pectorals and pelvics in some); caudal fin heterocercal. Upper Silurian to Lower Permian.

The acanthodians, with their large eyes and small nasal capsules, were probably mid- and surface-water feeders. The Silurian were marine but the Devonian were mainly freshwater. They are the earliest known true jawed fishes. Maximum length 2 m, usually less than 20 cm.

A variety of views have been expressed about acanthodian relationships. Watson (1937), in his review of the group, felt that they were the most primitive known gnathostomes. He placed them in the Aphetohyoidea, along with several other groups, which had equal rank as the Pisces. In many classifications of the 1930s to 1950s they were placed in the class Placodermi. Berg (1940) recognized acanthodians in their own class and placed them immediately before his class Elasmobranchii. Romer (1966) provisionally considered them as the most primitive subclass of the Osteichthyes because of certain resemblances to the actinopterygians but Nelson (1968a) felt that their closest relationship was with the elasmobranchiomorphs. Jarvik (1968b:517) favored placing them between the Chondrichthyes and Osteichthyes. The view of Moy-Thomas and Miles (1971) and Miles (1973) that they are more closely related to the latter is accepted here as the most probable hypothesis.

The classification of this group follows Miles (1973), who suggests that the acanthodiforms and ischnacanthiforms are more closely related to each other than either group is to the climatiiforms.

†Order ACANTHODIFORMES. Three families, Acanthodidae (e.g., *Acanthodes,* which is one of the last known survivors of the class), Cheiracanthidae (e.g., *Cheiracanthus*), and Mesacanthidae (e.g., *Mesacanthus*). Lower Devonian to Lower Permian (Antarctica, Asia, Australia, Europe, and North America).

†**Order ISCHNACANTHIFORMES.**   One family, Ischnacanthidae (e.g., *Ischnacanthus, Onchus, Protodus,* and *Uraniacanthus*). Upper Silurian to Devonian and possibly to Pennsylvanian [Europe (including Svalbard) and North America].

†**Order CLIMATIIFORMES.**   Dermal plates in shoulder girdle (other acanthodians possess only endoskeletal elements). Upper Silurian to Lower Permian.

Suborder Climatioidei.   Procoracoid absent; prepectoral spines present. Upper Silurian to Permian [Asia, Australia, Europe (including Svalbard), North Africa, and North America].

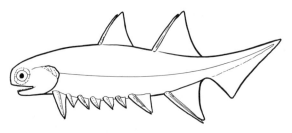

Three families: Climatiidae [e.g., *Brachyacanthus, Climatius* (usually reached only 7.5 cm, shown in figure), *Erriwacanthus, Nostolepis, Parexus* (had exceptionally long dorsal spines), *Ptomacanthus, Sabrinacanthus,* and *Vernicomacanthus*]; Euthacanthidae (*Euthacanthus*); and Gyracanthidae (*Gyracanthus, Gyracanthides,* and *Oracanthus*).

Suborder Diplacanthoidei.   Procoracoid present; prepectoral spines absent; jaws short and toothless.
   One family, Diplacanthidae (*Diplacanthus* and *Rhadinacanthus*). Lower Devonian to Pennsylvanian (Europe and North America).

Class OSTEICHTHYES—Bony Fishes

Skeleton, in part at least, with true bone (endochondral or membrane bone); skull with sutures; teeth usually fused to the bones; soft fin rays usually segmented and dermal in origin (lepidotrichia); nasal openings on each side usually double and more or less dorsal; biting edge of upper jaw usually formed by dermal bones, the premaxillae and maxillae; swim bladder or functional lung usually present; intestinal spiral valve in only a few lower groups; internal fertilization relatively rare—pelvic copulatory device in only one group (phallostethoids); embryos not encapsulated in a case—effective elimination of ammonia allowed; low blood concentration of urea and trimethylamine oxide (except in dipnoans and *Latimeria*)—osmotic balance maintained only by an energy demanding transfer process.

This class is divided into four subclasses. The first two (dipnoans and crossopterygians) are sometimes combined into the subclass Sarcopterygii, the lobe-finned fishes (e.g., Romer, 1966), but they are quite distinct and no intermediate forms have yet been found. Nelson (1969a) presents a very different classification of the major chordate groups based on the sister-group concept of W. Hennig. He employs the subclass Sarcopterygii to include his infraclasses Brachiopterygii, Coelacanthini, Dipnoi, and Choanata (rhipidistians and the tetrapods). Jarvik (1968b: 516) believes that the crossopterygians (and presumably their tetrapod derivatives), brachiopterygians, and actinopterygians form a natural group as opposed to the acanthodians, elasmobranchiomorphs (placoderms, elasmobranchs, and holocephalans), and dipnoans. This view, although possibly correct, is not expressed in the present classification, and the dipnoans, crossopterygians, and actinopterygians are placed in the Class Osteichthyes as favored by Schaeffer (1968: 221) and Moy-Thomas and Miles (1971).

The crossopterygians, dipnoans, and actinopterygians are all definitely represented in the Lower Devonian.

This class contains 424 families, about 3883 genera, and 18,128 species.

Primitive (and advanced) states in the three major subclasses of Osteichthyes:

	Dipneusti	Crossopterygii	Actinopterygii
Tail	heterocercal (diphycercal)	heterocercal (diphycercal)	heterocercal (homocercal)
Dorsal fins	double (single)	double (double)	single (single or double)
Scales	cosmoid (cycloid)	cosmoid (cycloid)	ganoid (cycloid or ctenoid)
Presence of pineal foramen	common (rare)	common (lost)	rare (lost)

Subclass DIPNEUSTI—Lungfishes (see map on p. 324) (Class Dipnoi, Berg, 1940, and Order Dipnoi, Romer, 1966)

Palatoquadrate fused to the lower neurocranium (not fused in the other three subclasses).

The dipnoans have many similarities with amphibians thought to be the result of convergence, not phylogenetic relationship, as proposed by many early workers. It is not agreed on by all workers that dipnoans are closer to the osteichthyans than to the chondrichthyans. Jarvik (1968a) felt that they had some elasmobranch affinities [but without any close relationship to acanthodians (1968a:242)], whereas Bertmar (1968) felt that dipnoans and actinopterygians are relatively close (more so than to crossopterygians). Bertmar (1968), in his embryological study, presented convincing evidence that the dipnoan internal excurrent nostril is a ventrally migrated external excurrent nostril. Thus they are not choanate fishes as are some crossopterygians.

†Superorder DIPTERIMORPHA (Superorder Dipteri, Berg, 1940)

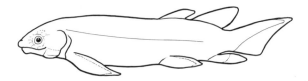

Branchiostegal rays 0–3, gular plates present; caudal fin heterocercal or diphycercal.

Devonian to Triassic.

Moy-Thomas and Miles (1971) recognize six distinct assemblages as orders; namely, Dipteriformes, Holodipteriformes, Rhynchodipteriformes, Phaneropleuriformes, Uronemiformes, and Ctenodontiformes (endings modified).

Superorder CERATODIMORPHA (Superorder Ceratodi, Berg, 1940)

Branchiostegals and gulars absent; caudal fin diphycercal, confluent with dorsal and anal fins; premaxillae and maxillae absent; functional lungs.

Extensive fossil record since the Lower Triassic in addition to the following three extant genera and six species.

Order CERATODIFORMES. Body compressed; pectoral and pelvic fins flipperlike; scales large; air bladder unpaired; larvae without external gills; adults do not estivate.

Family CERATODIDAE—Australian Lungfish. Freshwater; Queensland, Australia.

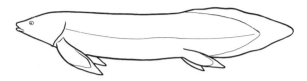

One species, *Neoceratodus forsteri*.

Order LEPIDOSIRENIFORMES. Body cylindrical; pectoral and pelvic fins filamentous, without rays; scales small; air bladder paired; larvae with external gills; adults estivate in dry season.

Family LEPIDOSIRENIDAE—South American Lungfish. Freshwater; Brazil and Paraguay.

Five gill arches and four gill clefts; body very elongate.
    One species, *Lepidosiren paradoxa*.

Family PROTOPTERIDAE—African Lungfishes. Freshwater; Africa.

Six gill arches and five gill clefts; body moderately elongate.
    One genus, *Protopterus*, with four species.

Subclass CROSSOPTERYGII—Fringe-Finned or Tassel-Finned Fishes

Two dorsal fins; paired fins lobate; "cosmoid" scales; hyomandibular involved in suspensorium.
    Andrews (1973) puts forth a provisional classification that suggests different relationships to that proposed here. He places the osteolepiforms, rhizodontiforms, and struniiforms together in one superorder and the porolepiforms and coelacanthiforms in another. The work of

Bjerring (1973), however, suggests that the relationships of the coela-canthiforms are problematical and they are retained here in their own superorder.

†Superorder OSTEOLEPIMORPHA—Rhipidistians
(Superorder Osteolepides, Berg, 1940, and
Suborder Rhipidistia, Romer, 1966)

Caudal fin heterocercal or diphycercal, but not with three lobes; internal nostrils (choanae); branchiostegals 4–13; lepidotrichia (fin rays) branched; many more lepidotrichia in caudal fin than radials. Middle Devonian to Lower Permian. This group gave rise to the tetrapods.

Because rhipidistians are so close to amphibians, some authors combine them with the tetrapods in the group Choanata (e.g., Nelson, 1969a). Maximum length 4 m.

†Order POROLEPIFORMES (Holoptychiiformes). Body plump; pectorals inserted relatively high on body; thick rhombic cosmoid scales to thin cycloid scales; no pineal foramen.

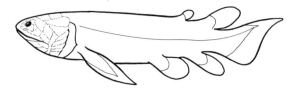

Jarvik (1968b) reviews the evidence that suggests that the urodeles were derived from porolepids, whereas the other tetrapods were derived from the osteolepids.

Two families, Porolepidae and Holoptychiidae. Devonian.

†Order OSTEOLEPIFORMES. Body slender; pectorals usually inserted low on body; thick rhombic scales; pineal foramen present.

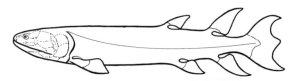

Four families, Osteolepidae, Tristichopteridae, Eusthenopteridae (*Eusthenopteron* is one of the best known of all fossil fishes—see Andrews and Westoll, 1970, and Moy-Thomas and Miles, 1971), and Rhizodopsidae. Middle Devonian to Lower Permian.

†**Order RHIZODONTIFORMES.**   One family Rhizodontidae, containing *Rhizodus, Sauripterus,* and *Strepsodus.* This group is too poorly known for its relationships to be considered.

†**Order STRUNIIFORMES (Onychodontiformes).**   Position uncertain. A poorly known Middle to Upper Devonian group known from two genera (*Onychodus* and *Strunius*) which appears to resemble most closely the rhipidistians (Jarvik, 1968b).

Superorder COELACANTHIMORPHA (Actinistia)

Order COELACANTHIFORMES (Superorder Coelacanthi, Berg, 1940, and Suborder Coelacanthini, Romer, 1966).   Caudal fin diphycercal, consisting of three lobes; external nostrils, no choana; branchiostegals absent; lepidotrichia never branched; lepidotrichia in tail equal to number of radials or somewhat more numerous; anterior dorsal fin in front of center of body. Maximum length about 1.5 m (1.8 m in *Latimeria*).

Several families known only from fossils, Devonian to Cretaceous. One family with a living representative.

Family LATIMERIIDAE—Gombessa.   Marine; South Africa and Comores Archipelago.

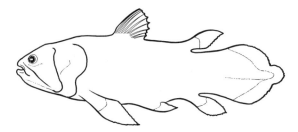

First specimen trawled off East London, South Africa, in 1938. Since 1952 numerous other specimens have been taken, all in the Comores Archipelago, northwest of Madagascar. Length up to 1.8 m.

One species, *Latimeria chalumnae* (J. L. B. Smith, 1940; McAllister, 1971; Thomson, 1973).

Subclass BRACHIOPTERYGII (Cladista)

Rhombic ganoid scales; spiracle present; dorsal fin consisting of 5–18 finlets, each with a single spine to which is attached one or more soft rays; pectoral fin rays supported by numerous ossified radials which attach to a cartilaginous plate and two rods, thence to the scapula and coracoid; no interopercle; a pair of gular plates, no branchiostegals; maxillae firmly united to skull; intestine with spiral valve; lungs partially used in respiration.

Brachiopterygians may be related to Cretaceous palaeoniscids; however, Nelson (1969a) places them in the subclass Sarcopterygii, a group coordinate with the Actinopterygii.

Order POLYPTERIFORMES

Family POLYPTERIDAE—Bichirs.   Freshwater; Africa (see map on p. 324).

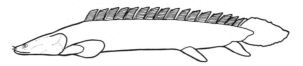

Extensive fossil record in addition to the 11 extant species placed in two genera.

Calamoichthys (=*Erpetoichthys*) *calabaricus* (reedfish), body eellike; pelvics absent.

Polypterus (bichirs), body elongate; pelvics present; 10 species.

Subclass ACTINOPTERYGII—Ray-Finned Fishes

Scales ganoid, cycloid, or ctenoid (absent in many groups); spiracle usually absent; finlets, if present, with rays attached to body, not to a fin spine; pectoral radials (actinosts) attached to the scapulo-coracoid complex; interopercle and branchiostegal rays usually present; gular plate usually absent; internal nostrils absent; nostrils relatively high up on head.

Infraclass CHONDROSTEI

Interoperculum absent; spiracle usually present. Extant taxa in two families, six genera, and 25 species.

The classification of this group is probably more insecure than that for

most other groups. Chondrosteans include all the early lines of actinopterygian evolution. It is a group of great structural diversity.

Classification of the fossil forms is based largely on Moy-Thomas and
Miles (1971) and Romer (1966). The latter author presented most of the
following orders as suborders under the order Palaeonisciformes.

†Order PALAEONISCIFORMES. In many primitive palaeoniscids the
cheekbones form a solid unit (the maxillae, preopercles, and suborbitals
are firmly united), the hyomandibular is oblique, the eyes are large and
far forward, and the tail is strongly heterocercal. More advanced forms
had a hyomandibular in the vertical plane and a breakup of the cheekbones. This permitted more flexibility in the oral-branchial chamber.
The dorsal lobe of the tail became reduced to an abbreviated heterocercal tail. Numerous other evolutionary trends can be noted in pro-
ceeding from the chondrostean level of organization to the holostean
level.

Suborder Palaeoniscoidei. This is a heterogenous group of primitive
chondrosteans. Some classifications recognize as many as 42 families. It
includes the Devonian Cheirolepididae with one genus, *Cheirolepis,* and
the Lower Permian Aeduellidae.

Lower Devonian to Lower Cretaceous.

Suborder Platysomoidei. Body deep and compressed (zeidlike).

Three families, Bobastraniidae, Chirodontidae, and Platysomidae.
Marine and freshwater.

Mississippian to Lower Triassic.

†Order HAPLOLEPIDIFORMES. Body fusiform; fin rays few in
number and not branched.

Three Pennsylvanian genera recognized. Included in the Palaeoniscoidei in Romer (1966).

†Order TARRASIIFORMES. Dorsal and anal fins continuous with the
diphycercal caudal fin; pelvic fins absent; scales absent from most of
body; body elongate; pectoral fins with a rounded fleshy lobe.

Only one or two Mississippian genera recognized.

†Order PHANERORHYNCHIFORMES. Body superficially like that of a sturgeon.

One Pennsylvanian genus, *Phanerorhynchus.* Questionably placed in the Acipenseriformes in Romer (1966).

†Order DORYPTERIFORMES. Body deep and mostly scaleless; pelvic fin in front of pectorals (jugular); caudal peduncle very narrow.

One Upper Permian genus, *Dorypterus.* Placed in the Platysomoidei in Romer (1966).

†Order PTYCHOLEPIFORMES. Triassic and Jurassic.

†Order PHOLIDOPLEURIFORMES. Triassic.

†Order LUGANOIIFORMES. Triassic.

†Order REDFIELDIIFORMES. Triassic.

†Order PERLEIDIFORMES. Triassic and Lower Jurassic.

Order ACIPENSERIFORMES. Caudal fin heterocercal; one branchiostegal ray; gulars absent; skeleton largely cartilagenous; fin rays more numerous than their basals; intestine with spiral valve.

Includes several extinct families from Pennsylvanian to Cretaceous times. Two families with living representatives.

Family ACIPENSERIDAE—Sturgeons. Anadromous and freshwater; Northern Hemisphere (see map on p. 325).

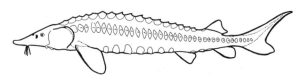

Five rows of bony scutes on body; four barbels in front of mouth; mouth inferior and protrusible; gill rakers fewer than 50; teeth absent in adults; swim bladder large. Maximum length 4.2 m (*Huso huso*).

Four genera with 23 species.

SUBFAMILY ACIPENSERINAE. Spiracle present; snout and caudal peduncle subconical.

Acipenser: range of family. Gill membranes joined to isthmus, mouth transverse. Sixteen species.

Huso: Adriatic Sea to Amur River. Gill membranes joined to one another, mouth crescentic. Two species.

SUBFAMILY SCAPHIRHYNCHINAE. Spiracle absent; snout depressed.

Pseudoscaphirhynchus (= *Kessleria*): Aral Sea basin.
Caudal peduncle short, slightly depressed, and not completely armored. Three species.

Scaphirhynchus: Mississippi basin. Caudal peduncle long, depressed, and completely armored. Two species.

Family POLYODONTIDAE—Paddlefishes. Freshwater; China and United States (see map on p. 325).

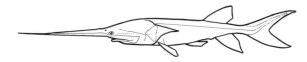

Snout paddlelike; body naked except for a few scales on caudal peduncle; minute barbels on snout; gill rakers long and in the hundreds in the plankton-feeding *Polyodon;* teeth minute; spiracle present; gill cover greatly produced posteriorly.

Two living species, *Polyodon spathula* with a nonprotrusible mouth from the United States (Mississippi drainage) and *Psephurus gladius* with a protrusible mouth from China (Yangtze River).

Infraclass HOLOSTEI

The taxon Holostei, like Chondrostei, includes many distinct evolutionary lines and is not a monophyletic group. Gardiner (1967) believes that the Semionotiformes were derived from the chondrostean Aeduellidae and all other holosteans and the halecostomes from the Parasemionotiformes (Parasemionotidae). The latter group is recognized by most workers, such as Gardiner (1967), Romer (1966), and Schaeffer (1973), as chondrostean, but it is recognized here and by McAllister (1968) and Patterson (1973) as holostean. Nelson (1969a) and Patterson (1973) group the holosteans and teleosts together as the Neopterygii (as also done by some earlier authors).

Patterson (1973) postulates relationships quite different from those presented here. He retains the term holostean informally (as a grade of evolutionary advance). His system, which breaks up the holosteans, is essentially as follows:

Subclass Actinopterygii.

Infraclass Chondrostei.

Infraclass Neopterygii.

Division, *incertae sedis*—Pycnodontidae, Gyrodontidae, Coccodontidae, and Luganoiidae.

Division Ginglymodi—only Lepisosteidae.

Division Halecostomi.

Subdivision, *incertae sedis*—Oligopleuridae and Semionotidae.

Subdivision Halecomorphi: Amiidae (Amiinae and Sinamiinae), Caturidae, and Parasemionotidae.

Subdivision Teleostei.

Cohort, *incertae sedis:* Pholidophoridae, Ichthyokentemidae, Pleuropholidae, Catervariolidae, Aspidorhynchidae, and Pachycormidae; all higher forms would be placed in other cohorts.

In the present classification the extant taxa of holosteans constitute two families, two genera, and eight species.

Order SEMIONOTIFORMES

†*Suborder Semionotoidei.*   One family.

Family SEMIONOTIDAE (Lepidotidae)
Mouth small.

Patterson (1973) feels that this group bears more affinity to the halecostomes than to *Lepisosteus* and places it as a basal grade in his Halecostomi. The family may be polyphyletic.

SUBFAMILY SEMIONOTINAE.   Upper Permian to Cretaceous. Body fusiform; dorsal and anal fins usually short; gular absent.

About 16 genera (e.g., *Acentrophorus, Lepidotes,* and *Semionotus; Dandya* and *Heterostrophus* probably also belong to this subfamily rather than to the Dapediinae). Among all holosteans only *Acentrophorus* is known from the Palaeozoic (Permian).

SUBFAMILY DAPEDIINAE. Upper Triassic to Lower Jurassic; in marine and freshwater deposits; North America, Europe, and India.

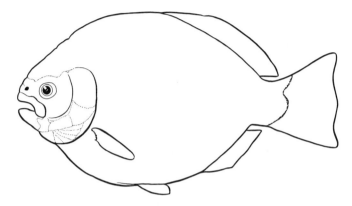

Body deep; dorsal and anal fins long; gular present.

Four genera, *Hemicalypterus, Tetragonolepis, Dapedium,* and *Paradapedium* (Jain, 1973).

Suborder Lepisostoidei (Ginglymodi). One family with extinct genera and one extant genus.

Upper Cretaceous to Recent.

Family LEPISOSTEIDAE—Gars. Freshwater (occasionally brackish, very rarely in marine water); eastern North America, Central America (south to Costa Rica), and Cuba (see map on p. 326).

Body and jaws elongate; mouth with needlelike teeth; abbreviated heterocercal tail; heavy ganoid scales, about 50–65 along lateral line; dorsal fin far back, with few rays; three branchiostegal rays; no gular or interopercle; vomer paired; swim bladder vascularized (thus permitting aerial respiration); vertebrae opisthocoelous [anterior end convex, posterior end concave (as in some reptiles and unlike all other fish)].

The heavily armored predaceous gars usually occur in shallow, weedy areas. Maximum length about 3.0 m, attained in *Lepisosteus spatula.*

The northernmost limit is reached by *Lepisosteus osseus* in southern Quebec, whereas the southernmost limit is reached by *L. tropicus* in Costa Rica. This is also the only species that ranges to Pacific slope drainages (from southern Mexico to Honduras).

One genus, *Lepisosteus,* with seven species. Fossils of *Lepisosteus* are known from North America, Europe, and India, with relatives in Africa.

†Order PYCNODONTIFORMES. Several families (e.g., Pycnodontidae).

Upper Triassic to Eocene.

Order AMIIFORMES

†*Suborder Parasemionotoidei.* Four families, Paracentrophoridae, Parasemionotidae, Catervariolidae, and Promecosominidae. This line gave rise to the Amioidei and Halecostomi.

Triassic and Jurassic.

Suborder Amioidei. Three extinct families [Caturidae (Eugnathidae and Furidae), Macrosemiidae, and Pachycormidae] and the following extant family (which also has many fossils).

Triassic to Recent.

Family AMIIDAE—Bowfin. Freshwater; eastern North America (see map on p. 326).

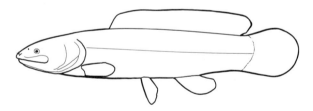

Caudal fin abbreviate heterocercal; dorsal fin base long, with about 48 rays; large median gular plate and 10–13 branchiostegal rays; swim bladder can function as a lung; no pyloric caeca. Maximum length about 90 cm.

One species, *Amia calva.* Fossils of *Amia* are known from North America, Europe, and Asia.

†Infraclass HALECOSTOMI

Recognition of this group follows Arambourg and Bertin (1958) and others. It represents a transition grade between the holosteans and teleosts and has a mosaic of characters between these two groups. It is probably derived from the Parasemionotiformes. Unlike the lower actinopterygians, the tail is externally symmetrical in all members.

†Order ASPIDORHYNCHIFORMES. One family.

Family ASPIDORHYNCHIDAE. Jurassic and Cretaceous.

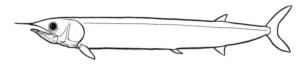

Body elongate with a long, slender snout; dorsal and anal fins opposite one another and placed posteriorly. Appearance superficially like needlefishes. All were probably marine, with lengths up to 1 m.

Two genera, *Aspidorhynchus* and *Belonostomus*.

†Order PHOLIDOPHORIFORMES. This group probably gave rise to the leptolepiforms in the Triassic and, independently, the elopomorph and osteoglossomorph teleostean lines in the Triassic or Jurassic. All major teleostean lines radiate in the Cretaceous.

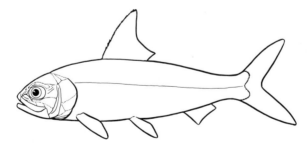

Schaeffer (1972) gives references to studies on various families of the order and describes a Lower Jurassic species (of about 179–161 million years age) from the Antarctica of the presumed freshwater family Archaeomaenidae, previously known only from Australia.

Seven families (Archaeomaenidae, Galkiniidae, Ichthyokentemidae, Ligulellidae, Majokiidae, Pholidophoridae, and Pleuropholidae).

Marine and freshwater.

Middle Triassic to Cretaceous.

Infraclass TELEOSTEI

Teleosts undoubtedly are derivatives of the pholidophorids, and probably rose during Triassic times. The boundary between the two groups is an arbitrary one (defined on the basis of caudal skeleton structure; Patterson, 1967a, 1968b); perhaps the teleost stage was reached through several lines from the pholidophorids. Several lineages with living forms are found in Cretaceous beds.

Teleosts are by far the most abundant (in species) and diversified group of all the vertebrates. About 18,007 extant species placed in 31 orders, 415 families, and 3869 genera represent about 96% of all extant fishes.

Many different classification schemes have been employed to show the presumed relationships within the teleosts. Here I follow the basic scheme of Greenwood et al. (1966) (with many changes resulting from recent works). Three main lineages stressing "vertical" relationships, called divisions, are recognized, each of which possesses primitive or lower teleost forms (names of divisions taken from Greenwood et al., 1967). Gosline (1971) who adheres to a different philosophy of classification divides the teleosts into three stages or grades of evolution ("horizontal" classification). Gosline's lower teleostean group includes members of the divisions Archaeophylaces and Taeniopaedia and basically up to the superorder Paracanthopterygii in the Euteleostei. His intermediate teleostean group, which possesses some advanced characters but has not attained the perciform level, extends inclusively from the Paracanthopterygii to the order Gasterosteiformes. The last group, the higher teleosteans, is basically from the Synbranchiformes onward. These teleosteans are characterized by almost never having more than five soft rays in the pelvic fin.

Greenwood et al. (1966) placed the Archaeophylaces (their Division II) between the Taeniopaedia (their Division I) and the Euteleostei (their Division III). Their placement at the start of the Teleostei follows Nelson (1969a) and Gosline (1971).

†**Order LEPTOLEPIFORMES.** Position uncertain.

† Family **LEPTOLEPIDAE (Leptolepididae).** Probably marine; Triassic to Cretaceous.

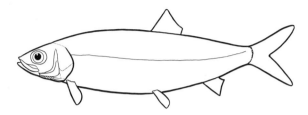

Romer (1966) and many other workers placed this group as the first category in the Teleostei, as I have here. They are thought to be derived from the Pholidophoridae, the forerunners of the Teleostei, and may have given rise to some teleosts (Clupeomorpha?). *Clupavus* (Upper Jurassic to Cretaceous) is thought by Patterson (1967a) to be a leptolepid derivative, but views that it was on a clupeomorph lineage seem very unlikely.

The type genus, *Leptolepis,* underwent a rapid rate of evolution in the Jurassic-Lower Cretaceous. Wenz (1967) gives a good description of *L. coryphaenoides,* a type species that shows considerable variation in certain head parts.

Leptolepids are obviously a transitional form between the halecostomes and teleosteans but are Teleostei as defined by structure of the caudal skeleton (Patterson, 1967a). Until more is known about the affinities of this group they are best not placed in any of the divisions. Indeed, they may not be on the lineage of any of the three divisions recognized here.

Division ARCHAEOPHYLACES (Division II of Greenwood et al., 1966)

The following classification basically follows Greenwood et al. (1966) to family level. Gosline (1971) included all of the following in three suborders and placed them at the start of teleostean classification. The most marked divergence from Greenwood's et al. (1966) classification is the wide separation of Hiodontidae and Notopteridae by Jordan (1923) and McAllister (1968). Both workers considered the hiodontids to be closer allies of the clupeids than of the notopterids. Regan (1929), Berg (1940), Greenwood et al. (1966), and Gosline (1971), however, place hiodontids and notopterids together in the same suborder. Nevertheless, the two families are recognized as being quite distinct.

Berg (1940) and Greenwood et al. (1966) classify notopterids and osteoglossoids in the same order but place mormyrids and gymnarchids in
their own order. Nelson (1968b), on the basis of a study of gill arches,
suggested that the Osteoglossiformes be divided into two divisions, the
notopteroids in one and the osteoglossoids plus mormyroids in the
other. The whole superorder displays a mosaic of ancient teleostean
characters and, as with most groups, the actual lineages are poorly un-
derstood. Phyletic diagrams are given by Nelson (1969b). Characteristics
of the group are given by Nelson (1972a).

One superorder and two orders.

Superorder OSTEOGLOSSOMORPHA

Parasphenoid and tongue bones usually with well-developed teeth; no
supramaxillae; caudal fin with 16 or fewer branched rays; caudal fin
skeleton, except in *Hiodon*, with large first ural centrum and no uro-
dermals; nasal capsule rigid, no antorbital-supraorbital system for
pumping water over olfactory epithelium; epipleural intermuscular
bones absent; intestine passes posteriorly to left of esophagus and stomach (in most other gnathostomes it passes to right); one or two pyloric
caeca.

P. H. Greenwood (in Greenwood, Miles, and Patterson, 1973) has presented new evidence and interpreted it by using cladistic principles to ar-
rive at a scheme different from that which I recognize. First, he prefers
placing the Osteoglossomorpha and Clupeomorpha on the same phyletic line [considering them to be sister groups in Hennig's (1966) ter-
minology]; *Hiodon* and the Clupeomorpha have a similar otophysic (ear-
swim bladder) connection. Second, he recognizes two suborders within
the Osteoglossomorpha: the Notopteroidei with two superfamilies, Hio-
dontoidea (Hiodontidae and Lycopteridae) and Notopteroidea (Notopteridae, Mormyridae, and Gymnarchidae), and the Osteoglossoidei (his
plesiomorph or ancestral group) with Osteoglossidae and Pantodontidae. Among other things, this classification emphasizes several shared
presumed specializations between Notopteridae and Mormyridae and
gives relatively little weight to the mormyrid and gymnarchid brain and
electric organs.

Six families, 20 genera, and about 116 species.

Order OSTEOGLOSSIFORMES. Maxillae-toothed.

†*Suborder Tselfatoidei.* Body deep; mouth bordered by premaxillae
and maxillae; dorsal fin extending along most of back; pectoral fins in-

serted high on body; pelvics absent or present and with six or seven rays; caudal fin deeply forked, with 18 principal rays; palate toothed; most fin rays unsegmented.

Includes several Cretaceous genera, such as *Tselfatia, Protobrama,* and *Plethodus.*

McAllister (1968) felt that the majority of characters would place them near the Elopoidei, Albuloidei, and Clupeoidei. However, Patterson's (1967b) placement in the Osteoglossomorpha is provisionally accepted here. Patterson (1967b) also speculates that the Ichthyodectidae [which includes the giant *Xiphactinus* (=*Portheus*)] might also be placed in this suborder.

The Upper Jurassic *Allothrissops* (and perhaps *Thrissops*) also appears to bear some affinity to the osteoglossomorphs (perhaps giving rise to the ichthyodectids). It also resembles the leptolepids.

Suborder Notopteroidei.   Anterior prongs of the swim bladder pass forward to the ear lateral to the skull (intracranially in *Xenomystus* and *Papyrocranus*).

Eight species.

Superfamily Hiodontoidae

†**Family LYCOPTERIDAE.**   Upper Jurassic to Lower Cretaceous; freshwater; eastern Asia.

This family has usually been associated with the Cyprinidae, of Berg's (1940) basal Clupeiformes, and the Leptolepidae. Its placement here in a superfamily with Hiodontidae follows Greenwood (1970).

Includes the well-known genus *Lycoptera* and several poorly known genera.

Family HIODONTIDAE—Mooneyes.   Freshwater; North America (see map on p. 327).

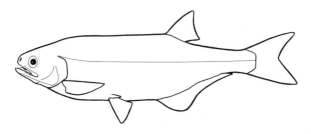

Anal fin moderately long (23–33 rays) and not confluent with the well-developed forked caudal fin; pelvic fins distinct, with seven rays; 7–10 branchiostegal rays; subopercular present; lateral-line scales about 54–61. Length up to 50 cm.

Two species: *Hiodon tergisus* (mooneye) with 11 or 12 principal dorsal fin rays and no keel in front of pelvics; and *Hiodon alosoides* (goldeye) with 9 or 10 principal dorsal fin rays and a keel in front of pelvics.

The only fossil, *Eohiodon*, is from the Eocene of British Columbia, North America (Cavender, 1966).

Superfamily Notopteroidae

Family NOTOPTERIDAE—Featherbacks or Knifefishes. Freshwater (sometimes brackish); Africa to Southeast Asia (see map on p. 327).

Anal fin long (85–141 rays or 100 or more rays in anal and caudal combined) and confluent with a reduced caudal fin; pelvic fins small (3–6 rays) to absent; subopercular absent; lateral-line scales 120–180; ventral scutes 25–45. Length up to 80 cm.

Three genera: *Notopterus* (about four species) occurs in India and Southeast Asia and has a small dorsal fin with 8–10 rays and eight or nine branchiostegal rays; *Papyrocranus afer* occurs in tropical Africa and has six or seven rays in the dorsal fin and 6–9 branchiostegal rays. *Xenomystus nigri* is confined to tropical Africa; it lacks a dorsal fin and has three branchiostegal rays. *Papyrocranus* and *Xenomystus* probably belong on the same phyletic line (and may be placed in the subfamily Xenomystinae, as opposed to the Notopterinae).

Suborder Osteoglossoidei. No intracranial penetration of swim bladder; six pelvic rays; lateral line scales 21–55.

Seven species.

Family OSTEOGLOSSIDAE—Osteoglossids or Bonytongues. Freshwater; circumtropical (see map on p. 328).

Pelvic fins distinctly behind base of pectoral fins; some possess a supra-branchial organ and can utilize atmospheric air; 60–100 vertebrae.

The fossil record includes *Phareodus* from the Eocene of North America.

SUBFAMILY ARAPAIMINAE.   No mandibular barbels; 10 or 11 branchio-stegal rays.

One species, *Arapaima gigas* in South America, grows to 4.5 m and is among the largest freshwater fish.

SUBFAMILY HETEROTINAE.   No mandibular barbels; seven to nine bran-chiostegal rays; parasphenoid teeth absent and tongue teeth reduced.

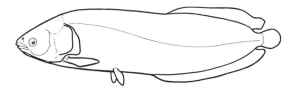

One species, *Heterotis* (=*Clupisudis*) *niloticus* in western Africa.

SUBFAMILY OSTEOGLOSSINAE.   Mandibular barbels present; 10—17 branchiostegal rays.

Osteoglossum bicirrosum (arawana) and *O. ferreirai* occur in South America and have 42–57 dorsal rays; *Scleropages leichardti* and *S. formosus* occur in northern Australia and Southeast Asia and have about 20 dorsal rays.

Family PANTODONTIDAE—Butterflyfish.   Freshwater; tropical western Africa.

Pelvic fins located under the pectoral fins; swim bladder can act as an
air-breathing organ; eight branchiostegal rays; greatly enlarged pectoral
fins; 30 vertebrae. Length up to 10 cm.

One species, *Pantodon buchholzi*.

Order MORMYRIFORMES. Maxillae toothless; enormous cerebellum;
eyes usually small; electric organs derived from caudal muscles; intracranial penetration of swim bladder.

Some mormyrids and the one gymnarchid are known to transmit
weak electric currents and to be capable of detecting extremely weak
charges. They are primarily nocturnal fishes and may use these currents
to locate objects (see Lissman, 1963). Mormyrids, at least, appear to
have considerable learning ability. Their brain size (largely cerebellum),
relative to body weight, is comparable to that of humans.

Family MORMYRIDAE—Elephantfishes. Freshwater; tropical Africa and Nile
(see map on p. 328).

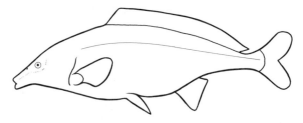

Anal, caudal, and pelvic fins present; caudal peduncle narrow; caudal
fin deeply forked; teeth present on parasphenoid and tongue; 6–8 branchiostegal rays; dorsal fin rays 12–91; anal rays 20–70; dorsal and anal
fins usually opposite and placed back on body; vertebrae 37–64.

The mouth is extremely variable in mormyrids. In some there is a very elongate proboscislike snout with a terminal mouth (e.g., *Gnathonemus curvirostris*); in a few there is an elongate lower jaw (e.g., *Gnathonemus petersii*), whereas in others there is a rounded snout with an undershot mouth (e.g., *Marcusenius*). The fish shown on p. 72 has a moderately developed proboscislike snout. Some bottom-feeding mormyrids have a chin barbel which is absent in the midwater species. Taverne (1968) gives a detailed osteological description of several species. Length reported up to 1.5 m; the maximum length in most species is 9–50 cm.

About 10 genera (e.g., *Gnathonemus*, *Marcusenius*, *Mormyrops*, and *Mormyrus*) and about 100 species.

Family GYMNARCHIDAE. Freshwater; tropical Africa and Nile.

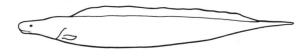

Anal, caudal, and pelvic fins absent; teeth absent from parasphenoid and tongue; four branchiostegal rays; elongate body; long dorsal fin (183–230 rays) which can be used for locomotion (they can move forward or backward equally well by passing reversible wavelike movements along the fin while keeping the body rigid); vertebrae 114–120. Length reported up to 1.5 m but usually less than 0.9 m.

One species, *Gymnarchus niloticus*.

Division TAENIOPAEDIA (Division I of Greenwood et al., 1966)

The elopiforms and clupeiforms were placed in the same order by Berg (1940), along with several other groups; the anguilliforms were placed some distance away. Greenwood et al. (1966) combined the elopiforms and anguilliforms into the same superorder and placed the clupeiforms in a separate superorder. The two superorders were placed in the same division, as also favored by Nelson (1972b) but not by all recent workers. This combination of the superorders Clupeomorpha and Elopomorpha (which may have had separate origins from the pholidophoriforms) should be considered very provisional. Indeed, Greenwood (1968) speculated on a possible osteoglossomorph-clupeomorph relation, whereas Nelson (1973a,b) preferred to recognize four main lineages (with cohort status of his division Teleostei)—Osteoglossomorpha, Taeniopaedia, Clupeomorpha, and Euteleostei—and suggested a relationship between the latter two. The relation of the superorders recognized here is poorly known and they are essentially "loose ends."

In placing elopiforms and anguilliforms in the same superorder, as done by Greenwood et al. (1966) and accepted here, emphasis is given to the occurrence of a leptocephalous larval stage, with many features in common, in the two orders. Gosline (1971), however, emphasized adult characters and combined the elopiforms, gonorynchiforms, and clupeiforms into one order (Clupeiformes). He placed the anguilliforms after the cypriniforms, as did Berg (1940). This difference in classification is partly explained by the fact that Greenwood et al. (1966) and Gosline (1971) follow different principles in their classifications. Greenwood et al. (1966) emphasize lineage concepts. The product tends to be a vertical classification and sometimes results in placing generalized ancestral forms with the specialized descendents. Gosline (1971) combines various primitive groups, each of which may have been the start of a separate lineage. It tends to be a horizontal classification.

Two superorders and four orders.

Superorder CLUPEOMORPHA

No leptocephalous larvae; body compressed in most; all but Engraulidae with swim bladder opening into stomach; swim bladder diverticula connected with ear in a manner unlike that occurring in any other group (ending in two large vesicles within bullae of the prootic and pterotic bones); *recessus lateralis* chamber in neurocranium in most, into which several lateral-line canals of the head open into, not known from any other group; extant forms with a diagnostic caudal fin skeleton (e.g., first hypural completely separate from first ural centrum; first ural centrum reduced in size and fused to the second hypural); temporal foramen present (bordered by the frontals and parietals); branchiostegal rays usually fewer than 15; parasphenoid teeth absent; abdomen often with keeled scutes along the ventral midline; lateral-line pores absent from trunk (except in *Denticeps*); lateral-line canals extending over the gill cover; jaws not protrusile. Most are plankton feeders, with numerous long gill rakers which serve as efficient straining devices.

Four families, 72 genera, and about 292 species.

Order CLUPEIFORMES

Suborder Denticipitoidei

Family DENTICIPITIDAE—Denticle Herring.   Freshwater; southwest Nigeria, Africa.

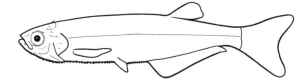

Denticles (odontodes) on all roofing bones of skull; no supramaxilla; 16 principal caudal fin rays; five branchiostegal rays, median pair with denticles on anterior edge; ventral half of head with "furred" appearance from small denticles; lateral line complete.

Family erected in 1959 (Clausen, 1959). A fossil denticipitid (*Palaeodenticeps*) is known from the Oligocene or Miocene from Tanzania, East Africa (Greenwood, 1968).

One species, *Denticeps clupeoides*.

Suborder Clupeoidei. Whitehead (1963a) reviews the groups and gives their characteristics.

Two fossil genera with ventral and dorsal scutes (double-armored) and about 31–36 vertebrae, *Diplomystus* and *Knightia*, should probably be given familial rank (Greenwood, 1968:265). Schaeffer (1947:24) comments on such a move but retains them in the Clupeidae in a group with three Recent clupeid genera, *Potamalosa* and *Hyperlophus* of Australia and *Ethmidium* of Peru and Chile, which also have dorsal scutes (extending from the occiput to the dorsal fin). Dorsal scutes occur as well in *Clupanodon thrissa* of Vietnam, China, and Korea (Nelson and Rothman, 1973), and in present classification of Recent forms the double-armored condition occurs in three different lineages (Pellonulinae, Alosinae, and Dorosomatinae). Nelson (1970a) suggests that the double-armored fossil genera (to which can be added *Gasteroclupea*) may show some relationship with the Pristigasterinae [given superfamily status in Nelson (1970a)]. The double-armored forms are thus not more closely related among themselves but are related to species that lack the dorsal scutes.

The heterogeneous assemblage *Diplomystus* (which lacks a *recessus lateralis*) is geographically widespread and extends from the Cretaceous to the Eocene, whereas *Knightia* is known only from the Eocene in South America. If Greenwood's (1968) recommendation of a separate family for these two fossil genera were accepted, a name other than Diplomystidae (which is preoccupied by a catfish) would have to be chosen.

Family CLUPEIDAE—Herrings (Shads, Sardines, and Menhadens). Primarily marine, some freshwater and anadromous; worldwide (mostly tropical).

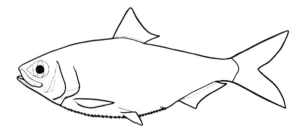

Lateral line existing on a few scales behind the head in some species, absent in others; head scaleless; dorsal and pelvic fins rarely absent (both absent in *Raconda*); mouth inferior, superior, or terminal; teeth small or absent; abdominal scutes usually present [the Dussumieriinae (round herrings) usually lack abdominal scutes, except for a single pelvic scute]; usually 5–10 branchiostegal rays (6–20 in Dussumieriinae) [see Svetovidov (1952), Berry (1964), and Nelson (1967, 1970a) for an account of the family]. Maximum length 75 cm.

A valuable commercial fishery exists for clupeids in many parts of the world. Most species form schools and swim near the surface, usually in coastal waters, feeding on plankton. Fifty genera with about 180 species.

Seven subfamilies [some given family status, e.g., Greenwood (1968) recognizes Dussumieriidae, Congothrissidae, and Pristigasteridae] with living representatives may be recognized tentatively; the following genera are examples:

Dussumieriinae [Whitehead (1963b) recognized seven genera and 10 species of round herrings]: *Dussumieria, Etrumeus, Gilchristella, Jenkinsia,* and *Spratelloides.*

Clupeinae: *Clupea, Harengula, Opisthonema, Sardina,* and *Sardinella.*

Pellonulinae: *Hyperlophus, Pellonula,* and *Potamalosa.*

Alosinae: *Alosa* (=*Pomolobus*), *Brevoortia,* and *Ethmidium.*

Dorosomatinae [Nelson and Rothman (1973) recognized five genera and 17 species of gizzard shads; 12 species are Indo-Pacific; the five *Dorosoma* are North American]: *Anodontostoma, Gonialosa, Nematalosa, Clupanodon* (=*Konosirus*), and *Dorosoma* (=*Signalosa*).

Pristigasterinae (Berry, 1964, recognized eight genera): *Ilisha, Pellona, Pristigaster, Opisthopterus,* and *Raconda.*

Congothrissinae [one genus in Africa, given family status by Poll (1964)]: *Congothrissa.*

Family ENGRAULIDAE (Stolephoridae)—Anchovies. Marine, occasionally fresh-water; Atlantic, Indian, and Pacific.

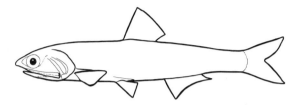

Tip of snout overhanging mouth; upper jaw extending well beyond eye; gill rakers 50 or more on lower limb of first arch in most; teeth small; 7–19 branchiostegal rays; body translucent with a silvery stripe down the side; the vast majority of Old World anchovies possess abdominal scutes; all New World anchovies lack abdominal scutes (except for a single pelvic scute which lacks a keel); luminescent organs have been reported in one species of *Coilia* (Berry, 1964:722).

Twenty genera (e.g., *Anchoa, Anchovia, Anchoviella, Coilia, Engraulis,* and *Stolephorus*) with about 110 species. Nelson (1970a) recognizes two subfamilies, Coilinae and Engraulinae (with the tribes Stolephorini and Engraulini).

Family CHIROCENTRIDAE—Wolf Herring. Marine; Indian (west to South Africa and the Red Sea) and western Pacific (Japan to New South Wales).

Body elongate and compressed; fanglike teeth in the jaws (highly preda-cious fish); spiral valve in intestine; 17–22 gill rakers; no pyloric caeca; scales small; dorsal fin with 16–18 rays; anal fin with 32–35 rays; pelvic fins small, with six or seven rays; pectoral fin with 13–15 rays; 6–8 bran-chiostegal rays; vertebrae 70–74.

Wolf herrings are voracious carnivores, unlike all other clupeoids. Maximum length 3.6 m.

Bardack (1965) gives a detailed description of *Chirocentrus.* He also provides good descriptions of several fossil forms considered by him to be chirocentrids [e.g., *Allothrissops, Ichthyodectes, Gillicus, Thrissops,* and *Xi-phactinus* (= *Portheus*) (which attained lengths of more than 4 m)], but as suggested by Greenwood et al. (1966) they show more affinities with the

Osteoglossomorpha [which, in turn, may be distantly related to the Clupeomorpha as suggested by Greenwood (1968)].

One species, *Chirocentrus dorab* (another species, *C. nudus,* is recognized by some authors).

Superorder ELOPOMORPHA

Leptocephalous larva (ribbonlike, totally unlike the adult); swim bladder not connected with ear (in *Megalops*, however, it does lie against the skull); no *recessus lateralis;* hypurals, when present, on three or more centra; branchiostegal rays usually more than 15; parasphenoid toothed (except in some Notacanthiformes). During metamorphosis from the leptocephalous to the juvenile body form the fish shrinks greatly in length.

In the phylogeny of the Elopomorpha given in Forey (1973a:358) the arrangement of groups proceeds from ancestral to descendent as follows: Megalopidae, Elopidae, Albulidae, Pterothrissidae, Anguilliformes, and Notacanthiformes. Forey postulates that the notacanthiforms evolved from the albuloids (pterothrissids) and that albuloids and megalopids were probably derived from elopids, but the megalopid lineage being older than the albuloid lineage. Greenwood's et al. (1966) classification, which recognizes the three orders accepted here, is not in contradiction with this suggested phylogeny. The evidence, however, can be translated into classification in a way that is different but still not incompatible with a classification suggested by G. J. Nelson, who (Nelson, 1973a,b) expresses the view that albuloids and anguilloids are more closely related to each other than either is to the elopoids (the opposite to what is implied in this classification). This is expressed in his classification by including within his cohort Taeniopaedia two superorders, the Elopomorpha (Elopidae and Megalopidae) and the Anguillomorpha, with the orders Albuliformes (Aulbulidae and Notacanthiformes of this work) and Anguilliformes. Basically, the intermediate evolutionary stage (albuloids) is grouped with the derived forms (notacanthiforms and anguilliforms) rather than with the ancestral forms (elopoids).

Twenty-eight families, 144 genera, and about 638 species.

Order ELOPIFORMES.   Pelvic fins abdominal; body slender, usually compressed; gill openings wide; caudal fin deeply forked; scales cycloid; mesocoracoid and postcleithra present. Leptocephali with a well-developed, forked, caudal fin and a posterior dorsal fin (pelvic fins in older larvae).

Elopomorphs, which are pholidophorid derivatives, cannot be convincingly related to any other lower teleost. Resemblances to other groups consist primarily of primitive characters. Within the superorder, elopids and megalopids have been separate since the Upper Jurassic, whereas the albulids probably are a Lower Cretaceous derivative of the basal elopids with some Cretaceous *Osmeroides* being somewhat intermediate between the two (Forey, 1973a,b). The evidence that the megalopid lineage is possibly older than the albulid lineage could be justification for combining elopids and albulids in classification, as distinct from megalopids. It seems best here, however, to recognize the greater divergence of the albulids and place the elopids and megalopids relatively close, but placement of them in the same family (as in Bailey et al., 1970 and Gosline, 1971) seems inappropriate.

Five genera with about 11 species. Forey (1973b) provides a detailed account of the fossil and extant forms.

Suborder Elopoidei. Gular plate well developed (median); branchiostegal rays 23–35; mouth bordered by premaxillae and toothed maxillae; upper jaw extending past eye; tip of snout not overhanging mouth (mouth terminal or superior); caudal fin with seven hypurals; no sensory canal extending onto the small premaxillae.

Nybelin (1971) recorded many similarities in caudal anatomy between *Elops* and *Coregonus* and postulated a relationship between them. Forey (1973a) suggested that the Elopidae and Salmonidae may have shared a common ancestor, possibly within the Upper Jurassic *Anaethalion* complex (a species assemblage in which some species resemble salmonids, whereas others resemble elopids).

Family ELOPIDAE—Tenpounders. Mainly marine (rarely brackish and freshwater); tropical and subtropical oceans.

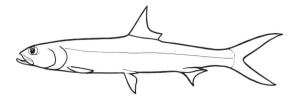

Body rounded (little compressed); mouth terminal; pseudobranchiae large; branchiostegal rays 27–35; dorsal fin rays usually 20–25, the last ray not elongate; anal fin rays usually 13–18; pelvic rays usually 12–16; no conus arteriosus; lateral line tubes unbranched; lateral line scales usually 95–120; insertion of pelvic fin beneath or posterior to origin of dorsal fin; vertebrae 63–79.

One genus, *Elops*, with about five species. Whitehead (1962) presents a key to the six species he recognizes. J. L. B. Smith has speculated that only one valid species exists. Forey (1973b) recognizes the following fossil genera: *Davichthys* and *Anaethalion*. The latter is a generic complex in which some species show a close affinity to other elopoids. The oldest known elopiform is *A. vidali*, found in the Upper Jurassic.

Family MEGALOPIDAE—Tarpons.   Mainly marine (enters fresh waters); tropical and subtropical oceans.

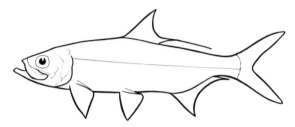

Body compressed; mouth terminal or superior; pseudobranchiae absent; branchiostegal rays 23–27; dorsal fin rays 13–21, the last ray elongate; anal fin rays usually 22–29; pelvic rays 10 or 11; conus arteriosus present; lateral line tubes branched (radiating over surface of lateral line scales); only elopiforms with the swim bladder lying against the skull (there is no intimate association between the swim bladder and the perilymphatic cavity as in clupeoids and notopteroids). Maximum length about 2.2 m, attained in *Tarpon atlanticus*.

Two species, *Megalops cyprinoides* of the Indo-Pacific (Africa to Society Islands) and *Tarpon atlanticus* (=*Megalops atlantica* of most recent authors) of the western Atlantic (Nova Scotia to Brazil and offshore) and off tropical West Africa. The two species can be distinguished as follows:

M. cyprinoides: insertion of pelvic fin beneath origin of dorsal fin; dorsal fin rays 17–21; lateral line scales 37–42; vertebrae 67 or 68;

T. atlanticus: insertion of pelvic fin in advance of origin of dorsal fin; dorsal fin rays 13–16; lateral line scales 41–48; vertebrae 53–57.

Forey (1973b) recognizes the following fossil genera: *Protarpon*, *Promegalops*, *Elopoides*, *Sedenhorstia*, and possibly *Pachythrissops*.

Suborder Albuloidei. Gular plate reduced to a thin median splint or absent; branchiostegal rays 6–16; pelvic rays 10–14; mouth bordered primarily by the premaxillae (maxillae toothed only in Pterothrissinae); upper jaw not extending as far as front of eye; tip of snout overhanging mouth (mouth inferior); caudal fin with six hypurals; infraorbital lateral line canal extending onto premaxillae (rare among living teleosteans).

This was probably the ancestral group (possibly from a stock near *Pterothrissus*) for the anguilliforms and notacanthiforms (Gosline, 1971; Forey, 1973a,b).

Forey (1973b) erected the family Osmeroididae for the extinct *Osmeroides* and *Dinelops* and placed it in this suborder. *Albula* and *Pterothrissus* probably evolved from an osmeroidid, which may in turn have been derived from an elopid.

Family ALBULIDAE—Bonefishes. Marine; tropical seas.

Maximum length about 105 cm, attained in *Albula vulpes*.

Subfamily Albulinae. Most tropical seas (rarely brackish and freshwater).

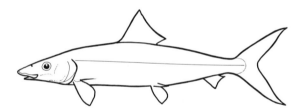

Dorsal fin base short, 16–21 rays (last ray of dorsal fin prolonged into a filament in *Albula nemoptera*); branchiostegal rays 10–16; gill rakers 15–17; lateral line scales 66–84; vertebrae 69–80; small median gular plate; maxillae toothless.

Two species, *Albula vulpes* (most tropical seas) and *A. nemoptera* (=*Dixonina nemoptera*) (Panama to Venezuela in Atlantic and Mexico to Panama in Pacific) (Rivas and Warlen, 1967).

Several fossil *Albula* exist and Forey (1973b) describes *Lebonichthys*.

Subfamily Pterothrissinae. Eastern Atlantic (Gulf of Guinea) and Japan.

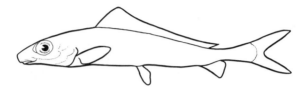

Dorsal fin base long, about 55–65 rays; branchiostegal rays six; lateral line scales 85–112; vertebrae about 107; gular plate absent; maxilla each with six or seven small teeth.

One genus, *Pterothrissus*, with two species: *P. belloci* (from tropical west Africa) and *P. gissu* from Japan.

Forey (1973b) recognizes the fossil genus *Istieus* and possibly *Hajulia*.

Order ANGUILLIFORMES.   Pelvic fins absent (present only in the fossil eel genera *Anguillavus*, which had eight-rayed pelvic fins, and *Enchelurus*); pectoral fins and skeleton entirely absent in some; body elongate (eellike); anal fin usually elongate; gill openings narrow; the two premaxillae, the vomer (usually), and the ethmoid united into a single bone; maxillae toothed, bordering gape; no posttemporal; mesocoracoid and postcleithra absent. Leptocephali with rounded or pointed posteriors and with a many-rayed dorsal fin which is continuous with the caudal but so inconspicuous that it is easily missed.

Eels are primarily specialized for wedging through small openings. Some, in addition, are adapted to burrowing in soft bottoms or to a bathypelagic existence.

One hundred and thirty-three genera, with about 603 species.

Suborder Anguilloidei (Apodes).   Scales, if present, cycloid; symplectic usually absent (hyomandibular united with quadrate); swim bladder present and with a duct; oviducts absent; gills displaced posteriorly; 6–22 branchiostegal rays.

Considerable morphological diversity exists among the pelagic leptocephali larvae, more so than among the adults. Selective pressures on larval characters have generally been different than on adult characters; the larvae and adults give the appearance of having evolved independently. Problems still exist in determining which leptocephali are the young of which adult and the larval forms of some families have not yet been recognized. Most leptocephali are less than 20 cm long before metamorphosis (when there is a loss of certain characters and a contraction in length) but a few are known to exceed 50 cm. Castle (1969) gives a valuable index to the literature of eel larvae.

The following classification is based largely on Nelson (1966), Robins and Robins (1970, 1971), C. R. Robins (pers. comm., 1972), and Smith and Castle (1972). The family Aoteidae, based on *Aotea acus* from Cook Strait, New Zealand, and placed in the Synbranchiformes by its describer, Phillipps (1926), was recognized as an anguilliform family by Berg (1940), Greenwood et al. (1966), and Gosline (1971). Castle (1967:2) in a footnote states that it was based on a damaged *Muraenichthys*. Aoteidae is therefore a junior synonym of Ophichthidae.

Nineteen families, 129 genera, and about 594 species.

Superfamily Anguilloidae

Family ANGUILLIDAE—Freshwater Eels. Usually catadromous; tropical and temperate seas except eastern Pacific and south Atlantic (see map on p. 329).

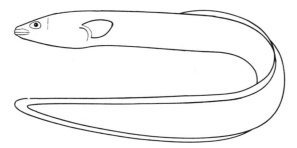

Minute scales present.

The North American and European freshwater eels originate in the Sargasso Sea area. It has been suggested that they do not represent two distinct species but that European eels are strays from the North American *Anguilla rostrata* which develop in cooler regions [see Vladykov (1964) and Smith (1968) for a review of this problem]. This hypothesis, however, is doubtful. Despite much effort many mysteries remain concerning the life history of *A. rostrata;* for example, adults have very rarely been taken in the open ocean (and never off the continental shelf) after they leave the estuaries on their spawning migration.

One genus, *Anguilla*, with about 15 species (Ege, 1939, recognized 16).

Family HETERENCHELYIDAE. Marine, Atlantic.

Two genera, *Pythonichthys* and *Panturichthys*, with seven species.

Family MORINGUIDAE—Worm or Spaghetti Eels. Marine; Indo-Pacific and western Atlantic.

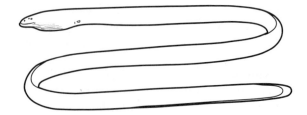

Body extremely elongate, threadlike; no scales; gill openings low on body; dorsal and anal fins reduced to low folds, posteriorly, and confluent with caudal fin; pectorals feeble or absent; eyes small and covered with skin. Marked sexual differences exist, although it is not always certain which males and females are conspecific.

Two genera, *Moringua* (=*Stilbiscus*) and *Neoconger,* with about 10 species.

Superfamily Nemichthyoidae

Family NEMICHTHYIDAE—Snipe Eels.   Deep-sea; Atlantic, Indian, and Pacific.

Extremely long, needlelike, upper and lower jaws.

Six genera (e.g., *Avocettinops, Avocettina, Labichthys, Nematoprora,* and *Nemichthys*), with about 10 species.

Family CYEMIDAE.   Marine; Atlantic, Indian, and Pacific.

Branchiostegal rays and opercular bones absent; gill arches greatly reduced.

One species, *Cyema atrum.*

Superfamily Muraenoidae

Family XENOCONGRIDAE (Echelidae in part)—False Morays.   Marine; Atlantic, Indian, and Pacific.

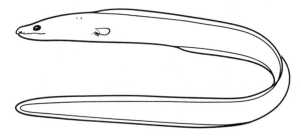

Gill openings restricted to small roundish lateral openings; lateral line pores on head but not on body; one or two branchial pores; no scales; pectoral fins absent in some; all but *Kaupichthys nuchalis* with posterior nostril opening into the lip.

Seven genera, *Chilorhinus, Chlopsis, Catesbya, Kaupichthys, Powellichthys, Robinsia,* and *Xenoconger,* with 15 species, some known only from single specimens. Böhlke (1956) gives a key to most of the species (but recognizes only four genera).

Family MYROCONGRIDAE. Marine; Atlantic.

One species, *Myroconger compressus,* known from only one specimen described by A. Gunther in 1870 and redescribed by Robins and Robins (1966).

Family MURAENIDAE (Heteromyridae)—Moray Eels. Marine; tropical and temperate seas.

Gill openings restricted to small roundish lateral openings; lateral line pores on head but not on body; two branchial pores; fourth branchial arch strengthened and supporting pharyngeal jaws; no scales; pectorals absent; posterior nostril high on head (usually above front portion of eye).

Highly dangerous fishes if provoked because of their bite. Morays tend to be nocturnal and most species occur in shallow water in reefs or rocky areas. Some are highly colorful.

Some morays are involved in ciguatera fish poisoning. This disease occurs largely between 35° N and 34° S and results from eating any one of a large variety of fish species which are ciguatoxic (Halstead, 1967–1970). It is suspected that plant-feeding fishes acquire the toxicity first by feeding on a certain benthic alga; they then pass it on to carnivorous fishes which are the most likely to be poisonous (e.g., *Sphyraena, Caranx, Mycteroperca,* and *Lutjanus*). Maximum length 3.0 m.

Twelve genera with about 100 species.

SUBFAMILY UROPTERYGIINAE. Ossified hypobranchials in first and second arches; vertical fins reduced; rays confined to posterior part of tail.

Three genera, *Uropterygius, Anarchias,* and *Channomuraena.*

SUBFAMILY MURAENINAE. No ossified hypobranchials; vertical fins not reduced; rays confined to posterior part of tail.

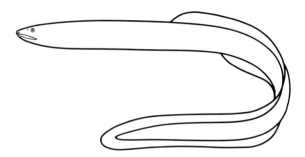

About nine genera, *Echidna, Enchelycore, Enchelynassa, Evenchelys, Gymnomuraena, Gymnothorax, Muraena, Rabula,* and *Stophidon.*

Superfamily Synaphobranchoidae.   Frontals fused; trunk relatively short.
Classification of this group is based primarily on the works of Robins and Robins (1970) and C. H. Robins (1971).

Family SYNAPHOBRANCHIDAE—Cutthroat Eels.   Marine; all seas.

Body scaled; branchial apertures confluent or only slightly separated.

Subfamily Ilyophinae.   One species, *Ilyophis brunneus.*

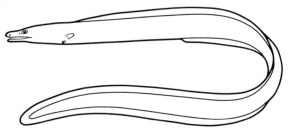

Subfamily Synaphobranchinae.   Three genera, *Diastobranchus, Histiobranchus,* and *Synaphobranchus,* with about 10 species.

Family SIMENCHELYIDAE—Snubnose Parasitic Eel.   Deep-sea; Atlantic and Pacific.

Snout blunt and rounded with terminal slitlike mouth; body slimy; scales embedded in skin; dorsal, anal, and caudal fins confluent; pectoral fins moderate in size. Maximum length about 60 cm.

This eel occurs most commonly between 500 and 1400 m. It is known from the western North Atlantic, the Azores off Africa, Japanese waters, and Cook Strait, New Zealand (Castle, 1961; Leim and Scott, 1966). Although this eel is reported to be parasitic on other fishes (especially halibut), little is known of its feeding habits and food and adults probably also feed on invertebrates and dead fish (Solomon-Raju and Rosenblatt, 1971).

One species, *Simenchelys parasiticus* (which is probably closely related to *Ilyophis*).

Family DYSOMMIDAE—Mustard or Arrowtooth Eels. Marine; Indo-Pacific and Atlantic.

Body scaleless; dorsal, anal, and caudal fins confluent; pectoral fins present (absent in the two species of *Dysommopsis* and *Nettodarus*); vertebrae 122–203.

SUBFAMILY DYSOMMINAE. Four genera, *Atractodenchelys, Dysomma, Dysommina,* and *Dysommopsis,* with at least 10 species.

Works before Robins and Robins (1970) considered *Dysommina rugosa* to be the sole member of a different family, the Dysomminidae (first erected by Böhlke and Hubbs, 1951).

SUBFAMILY NETTODARINAE (TODARIDAE). One species, *Nettodarus brevirostris,* in the Mediterranean Sea.

Superfamily Congroidae

Family MACROCEPHENCHELYIDAE. Marine; Macassar Strait (between Borneo and Celebes).

Body elongate; pectoral fins well developed; mouth subterminal.

One species, *Macrocephenchelys brachialis,* known only from two specimens collected in 1909 (Fowler, 1933:275; Robins and Robins, 1971).

Family COLOCONGRIDAE. Marine; Atlantic, Indian, and Pacific.

One genus, *Coloconger,* with two species.

Family CONGRIDAE—Conger Eels. *Marine; Atlantic and Pacific.*

About 38 genera and 100 species.

SUBFAMILY CONGRINAE.   Pectoral fins well developed.

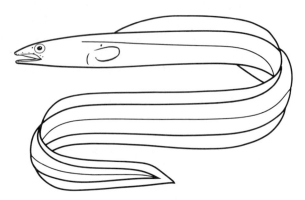

About 30 genera (e.g., *Conger, Oxyconger, and Gnathophis*).

SUBFAMILY BATHYMYRINAE.   *Ariosoma* and *Bathymyrus,* for example.

SUBFAMILY HETEROCONGRINAE (GARDEN EELS).   Pectoral fins minute or absent. Four genera, *Gorgasia, Heteroconger, Nystactichthys,* and *Taenioconger,* with eight species.

Family MURAENESOCIDAE—Pike Eels or Pike Congers.   Marine, Atlantic and Indo-Pacific.

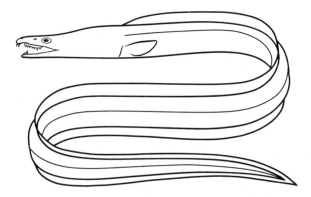

Pectorals well developed; eyes large and covered with skin.
     Three genera, *Muraenesox, Cynoponticus* (=*Phyllogramma*), and *Sauromuraenesox,* with about seven species.

Family NETTASTOMIDAE (Nettastomatidae)—Duckbill or Witch Eels. Marine; Atlantic, Indian, and Pacific.

Six genera, *Nettastoma, Facciolella, Metapomycter, Gavialiceps, Saurenchelys,* and *Venefica,* with about 16 species. The genus *Hoplunnis,* with about four species, probably also belongs here and not in Muraenesocidae where it has usually been placed.

Family SERRIVOMERIDAE. Marine; Atlantic, Indian, and Pacific.

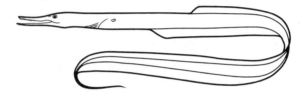

Jaws very elongate.

Four genera, *Platuronides, Serrivomer, Spinivomer,* and *Stemonidium,* with 10 species.

Superfamily Ophichthyoidae

Family OPHICHTHIDAE (Echelidae in part)—Snake Eels. Marine; all seas.

Posterior nostril within or piercing the upper lip; tongue not free; branchiostegal rays numerous and overlapping along the midventral line (forming a basketlike structure termed a jugostegalia in the ventral wall of the throat); neural spines poorly developed or absent; hyomandibulae usually vertical or backwardly inclined (inclined obliquely forward in *Benthenchelys*); pectoral fins present or absent.

Rosenblatt and McCosker (1970) give a key to the 44 genera they recognize. Castle (1972) feels that *Benthenchelys* is a structural intermediate with the Heterocongrinae (family Congridae—particularly with the relatively primitive *Gorgasia*) which also shows some affinity with *Derichthys*.

SUBFAMILY OPHICHTHINAE (SNAKE EELS). Caudal fin absent (strong, spikelike tail); no scales; body usually spotted or striped.

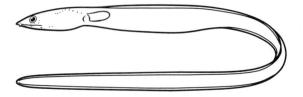

About 21 genera (Rosenblatt and McCosker, 1970, recognize about 35; e.g., *Caecilia, Caecula, Callechelys, Myrichthys, Ophichthus, Sphagebranchus,* and *Verma*) with about 230 species.

SUBFAMILY ECHELINAE (WORM EELS). Caudal fin present; body plain colored.

Ten genera: *Ahlia, Benthenchelys, Echelus, Leptenchelys, Muraenichthys, Myrophis, Neenchelys, Pseudomyrophis, Schismorhynchus,* and *Schultzidia,* with about 40 species. The largest genus, *Muraenichthys,* contains about 19 species in the Indian and Pacific oceans.

Family DERICHTHYIDAE—Longneck Eels. Deep-sea; Atlantic and Pacific.

Series of parallel striations on the head forming part of a sensory system.

SUBFAMILY DERICHTHYINAE. One species, *Derichthys serpentinus* (Castle, 1970).

SUBFAMILY NESSORHAMPHINAE. One species, *Nessorhamphus ingolfianus,* is usually placed in its own family, the Nessorhamphidae. Robins and Robins (1971:148) suggest that it is allied with *Derichthys* and place both species in the same family. Subfamily status is accorded each species in recognition of their many differences.

Suborder Saccopharyngoidei (Lyomeri). Highly aberrant fishes, lacking symplectic bone, opercular bones, branchiostegal rays, scales, pelvic fins, ribs, pyloric caeca, and swim bladder; caudal fin absent or rudimentary; gill openings ventral; dorsal and anal fins long; jaws, hyomandibular, and quadrate greatly elongate; highly distensible pharynx (accommodating extremely large prey); eyes small and placed far forward.

The saccopharyngoids and anguilloids share a relatively close relationship (Böhlke, 1966, and others) but some earlier authors (e.g., V. V.

Tchernavin) have questioned whether they are true bony fishes at all. Orton (1963) describes the saccopharyngoid leptocephalous larvae.

About nine species, all bathypelagic. These are perhaps the most anatomically modified of all vertebrate species.

Family SACCOPHARYNGIDAE—Swallowers. Marine; Atlantic, Indian, and Pacific.

Gill openings closer to end of snout than to anus; mouth large; jaws with curved teeth; pectoral fins well developed.

One genus, *Saccopharynx*, with four species known from a total of 16 specimens.

Family EURYPHARYNGIDAE—Gulpers. Marine; Atlantic, Indian, and Pacific.

Gill openings small, closer to anus than to end of snout; only teleosts with five gill arches and six visceral clefts; mouth enormous; jaws with minute teeth; pectoral fins minute.

At least one species, *Eurypharynx pelecanoides;* perhaps two.

Family MONOGNATHIDAE. Marine, Atlantic and Pacific.

Upper jaw absent (i.e., no maxillae or premaxillae); pectoral fins absent; dorsal and anal fins without skeletal supports.

Two genera, *Monognathus* and *Phasmatostoma*, with three species.

Order NOTACANTHIFORMES (Lyopomi and Heteromi). Body eel-like; posteriorly directed spine on dorsal edge of rear of maxillae; premaxillae and maxillae bordering upper jaw; gill membranes separate; pectoral fins relatively high on body; pelvic fins abdominal, with 7–11 rays (the two fins are usually connected by a membrane); anal fin base long and merged with what remains of the caudal fin; caudal fin skeleton reduced or absent; tail easily regenerated when lost (analogous to loss of tail in lizards?); branchiostegal rays 5–23; swim bladder present. Some have photophores (Marshall, 1962).

Mead (1965), Harrisson (1966), Smith (1970), and Castle (1973) describe the leptocephalouslike larva. Older notacanthiform larvae have pelvic fins and a short-based dorsal fin (both are inconspicuous, however). The larvae, which can be exceptionally large, reach a length of at least 45 cm and possibly as much as 180 cm before metamorphosing into the smaller juvenile (Smith, 1970).

Members of this deep-sea order have been taken between 125 and 4900 m but most seem to occur at depths of 450–2500 m.

Marshall (1962) pointed out the similarities between the Notacanthiformes (Heteromi) and Anguilliformes, but they have perhaps evolved independently from an albuloid stock (Gosline, 1971). Berg (1940) divided the Notacanthiformes into two separate orders (as had also been done earlier by T. Gill), the Halosauriformes (Lyopomi) and Notacanthiformes (Heteromi). McDowell (1973) gives a detailed review of the members of the order.

Six genera with about 24 species (McDowell, 1973).

Suborder Halosauroidei

Family HALOSAURIDAE—Halosaurs. Deep-sea; worldwide.

Maxillae and premaxillae toothed; branchiostegal membranes completely separate, rays 9–23; dorsal fin entirely anterior to anus, with 9–13 soft rays, no spines; lateral line cavernous and extending full length of body, lateroventrally; scales relatively large, fewer than 30 longitudinal rows on each side.

Three genera with 14 species. *Halosaurus,* with eight species, occurs in many areas of the Atlantic, Indian, and Pacific, usually confined to continental margins. *Halosauropsis macrochir* is in the Atlantic and western Indian. *Aldrovandia,* with five species, is in the Atlantic, Indian, and western and central Pacific. In addition, some fossils such as the Upper Cretaceous *Echidnocephalus,* are known.

Suborder Notacanthoidei. Branchiostegal membranes at least partly joined; at least part of the dorsal fin posterior to the anus; lateral line not cavernous and well up on the side; scales relatively small, more than 50 longitudinal rows occur on each side; some have the unique feature of having as many as three spinelike rays in each pelvic fin.

Family LIPOGENYIDAE. Deep-sea; western North Atlantic.

Mouth small, toothless, and suctorial; lower jaw short, lying within the suckerlike opening; branchiostegal rays 5–7; gill rakers absent; pectoral girdle somewhat degenerate, cleithrum and supracleithrum absent; dorsal fin base short, with 9–12 rays (the first few spinelike); anal fin base long, with the first 32–44 rays spinelike, total rays about 116–136; pyloric caeca 5–7; vertebrae about 228–234.

McDowell (1973) and Templeman (1973) each describe nine specimens collected since the holotype (collected in 1887), but all are different specimens.

One species, *Lipogenys gilli.*

Family NOTACANTHIDAE—Spiny Eels. Deep-sea; worldwide.

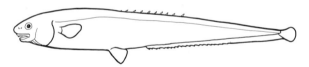

Mouth normal in size, maxillae toothless but premaxillae and dentary are toothed; branchiostegal rays 6–13; well-developed gill rakers; cleithrum and supracleithrum well ossified; dorsal fin with 6–40 isolated spines and no conspicuous soft rays.

Two genera with nine species. *Polyacanthonotus* (*=Macdonaldia*), with three species, has 26–40 dorsal spines and is known from the southern Bering Sea, North Pacific, New Zealand, Caribbean, Mediterranean, and North Atlantic. *Notacanthus,* with six species, has 6–15 dorsal spines and is probably worldwide.

Division EUTELEOSTEI (Division III of Greenwood et al., 1966)

Twenty-five orders, 377 families, 3633 genera, and 17,031 species. The five largest families, Cyprinidae, Gobiidae, Characidae, Cichlidae, and Labridae, contain about 24% of the species of the Division.

Superorder PROTACANTHOPTERYGII

The one order contained herein is considered to be the basal (ancestral) stock of euteleostean evolution.

Order SALMONIFORMES.   Maxillae included in gape of mouth except in Aplochitonidae.

The following classification, to family, is based largely on the modifications of Greenwood et al. (1966) made by McDowall (1969), Rosen and Patterson (1969), and Weitzman (1967b). The view expressed by Nelson (1970b) that salmonoids, argentinoids, galaxioids, and osmeroids are more related to one another than either is to the esocoids [as also expressed in Berg's (1940) classification] is accepted here.

Currently recognized with five extant suborders, 24 families, 145 genera, and 508 species.

Suborder Esocoidei (Haplomi).   No adipose fin; maxillae toothless but in gape of mouth; dorsal and anal fins located posteriorly; no pyloric caeca; no mesocoracoid. Four genera and 10 species.

Family ESOCIDAE—Pikes.   Freshwater; Northern Hemisphere (see map on p. 329).

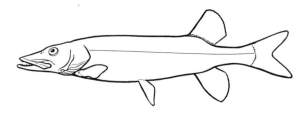

Snout produced; caudal fin forked, with 40–50 rays (17 branched); lateral line complete; infraorbital canal with eight or more pores; 10–20 branchiostegal rays; nasals present; vertebrae 43–67. Maximum length 1.4 m.

One genus, *Esox,* with three species confined to eastern North America, one in Siberia, and the circumpolar *Esox lucius.*

Fossils are known as early as the Oligocene in Europe.

Family UMBRIDAE—Mudminnows.   Freshwater; parts of Northern Hemisphere (see map on p. 330).

Snout not produced; caudal fin rounded, with 20–30 rays (8–16 branched); lateral line faint or absent; infraorbital canal with three or fewer pores; 5–8 branchiostegal rays; nasals absent; vertebrae 32–42. Maximum length 20 cm.

One genus of this family, *Dallia,* has been placed in its own order (Jordan and Evermann, 1896) or family (e.g., McPhail and Lindsey, 1970). Most recent authors place *Dallia, Novumbra,* and *Umbra* in the same family but there is much disagreement on the interrelations. Beamish et al. (1971) feel that this lumping may be ill-advised because of the highly variable chromosome number in the group, which ranges from 22 in *Umbra* to 78 in *Dallia* (all *Esox* have 50). Little is known, however, about the evolutionary stability, and thus the systematic value, of karyotypes. Cavender (1969) claimed that *Dallia* is closer to *Novumbra* than to any other living esocoid but felt it best not to recognize subfamilies. Nelson (1972b) regarded *Dallia* and *Umbra* as relatively close (and placed them in the subfamily Umbrinae, whereas *Novumbra* was put in its own subfamily). In view of disagreements on the interrelations no attempt has been made here to recognize subfamilies.

Three genera with five species. Fossils include *Proumbra* of Oligocene in western Siberia, *Palaeoesox* of Eocene in Germany, and *Novumbra* of Oligocene in North America.

Dallia

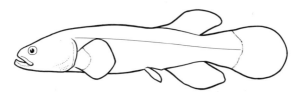

Pectoral rays 32–36; pelvic rays usually two or three (rarely 0 or 1); dorsal rays 10–14; anal rays 12–16; lateral scales 76–100; vertebrae 40–42; Baudelot's ligament ossified (only esocid with it ossified).

One species, *Dallia pectoralis* (Alaska blackfish), freshwater, northeast Siberia and Alaska.

Novumbra

Pectoral rays 18–23; pelvic rays six or seven; dorsal rays 12–15; anal rays 11–13; lateral scales 52–58; vertebrae 37–40.

One species, *Novumbra hubbsi,* confined to the Chehalis River in western Washington.

Umbra

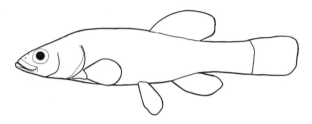

Pectoral rays 11–16; pelvic rays 5–7; dorsal rays 13–17; anal rays 7–10; lateral scales 30–36; vertebrae 32–37.

Three species, two in central and eastern United States and one in southeastern Europe.

The following four suborders are known from the Upper Cretaceous and are described in detail by Goody (1969). They probably represent small radiations from the basal stock, Salmonoidei, from which the Esocoidei is possibly an earlier offshoot. Among the fossil salmoniforms the Ichthyotringoidei, the most primitive, show some affinity with the Elopiformes. Both groups may have had a close relationship in the pholidophorids. Rosen (1973) favors a completely different relationship for these groups, removes them from the Salmoniformes, and places them in the Neoteleostei in his new order Aulopiformes.

†*Suborder Ichthyotringoidei.* Head elongated anteriorly into a prominent rostrum; body short; pectoral skeleton with two postcleithra.
Two families, Ichthyotringidae and Apateopholidae.

†*Suborder Cimolichthyoidei.* Body elongate; interoperculum absent.
Three families, Cimolichthyidae, Dercetidae, and Prionolepididae.

†*Suborder Enchodontoidei.* Body compressed; interoperculum absent.
Two families, Enchodontidae and Eurypholidae.

†*Suborder Halecoidei.* Dorsal fin confined to anterior half of body.
One family.

Suborder Salmonoidei. Seven families, 33 genera, and about 151 species.

Superfamily Salmonoidae. Adipose fin present; mesocoracoid present; pyloric caeca present.

Family SALMONIDAE—Salmonids. Freshwater and anadromous; Northern Hemisphere.

Gill membranes extending far forward, free from isthmus; pelvic axillary process present; last three vertebrae turned up; 11–210 pyloric caeca; 7–20 branchiostegal rays. Maximum length up to 1.5 m. This family has tremendous value in sport and commercial fisheries.

Nine genera with about 68 species.

As suggested in Behnke (1972), the biological diversity in this family is much greater than recognized in our current taxonomy with its nomenclatorial limits. Many biological species exist that are not named. Several "species," such as *Coregonus lavaretus, Coregonus artedii,* and *Salvelinus alpinus,* are each best described as a species complex. Perhaps our realization that salmonid classification, like gasterosteid classification, cannot adequately express evolutionary reality is due to the numerous detailed studies of the family (because of its economic importance), and the problems in trying to express their diversity in binomial taxonomy may not be so unique.

Classification of this group is based largely on Behnke (1968, 1970, 1972), Lindsey and Woods (1970), Norden (1961), and Vladykov (1963).

SUBFAMILY COREGONINAE. Fewer than 15 dorsal fin rays; scales large, fewer than 110 along lateral line; no teeth on maxillae; orbitosphenoid present; suprapreopercular absent.

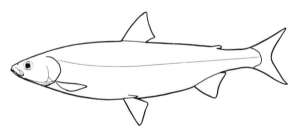

Stenodus leucichthys (inconnu); large mouth with many small teeth on jaws, vomer, and palatine; two flaps between nostrils. Anadromous; arctic Asia and North America.

Prosopium (whitefishes); small mouth with weak or no teeth; single flap between nostrils; basibranchial plate present; young with parr marks.

Freshwater; northern Northern Hemisphere; six species. One species occurs in northern North America and Siberia; three are endemic to Bear Lake, Utah-Idaho, one of which is ciscolike.

Coregonus (whitefishes and ciscoes); small mouth with weak or no teeth; two flaps between nostrils; no basibranchial plate; young without parr marks. Freshwater (occasionally anadromous along Arctic coastline), northern Northern Hemisphere; 25 species (17 ciscoes and eight lake whitefishes).

The two subgenera may not be strictly monophyletic. In North America there is good separation between the two groups in gill raker number; the lake whitefishes almost always have 35 or fewer gill rakers, the ciscoes 36 or more. In Eurasia, however, one lake whitefish (*C. muksun*) usually has 51–56 gill rakers, whereas one cisco (*C. tugun*) has 25–39.

Subgenus *Leucichthys* (ciscoes). Mouth superior or terminal; maxillae normally extending beyond front margin of eye. Usually plankton feeders.

Circumpolar but most species in eastern North America in Great Lakes.

Subgenus *Coregonus* (lake whitefishes). Mouth subterminal; maxillae usually not extending beyond front margin of eye. Bottom and plankton feeders.

Circumpolar but most species in northwestern Eurasia.

The dominant ones are *C. lavaretus* complex in Eurasia and *C. clupeaformis* complex in North America.

SUBFAMILY THYMALLINAE. More than 17 dorsal fin rays; teeth on maxillae; orbitosphenoid absent; suprapreopercular absent.

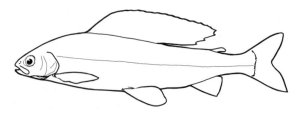

One genus, *Thymallus* (graylings), freshwater; Northern Hemisphere; four species (one in Europe, two in Mongolia, and probably one widespread across northern Asia and North America).

SUBFAMILY SALMONINAE.   Fewer than 16 dorsal fin rays; scales small, more than 110 along lateral line; teeth on maxillae; orbitosphenoid present; suprapreopercular present.

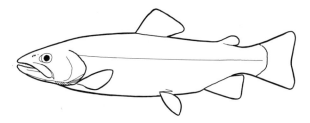

Certain species, such as *Salvelinus fontinalis, Salmo trutta,* and *S. gairdneri* have been introduced virtually throughout the world.

Rounsefell (1962) gives meristic and other data on North American species.

Brachymystax lenok (lenok): freshwater; northern Asia to Korea.

Hucho (huchen or taimen): freshwater and anadromous; northern Asia to Korea, Danube basin of Europe; at least three species (possibly five).

Salvelinus: Subgenus *Salvelinus* (charrs). Freshwater and anadromous; Northern Hemisphere. About six species (e.g., Arctic charr and Dolly Varden).

Subgenus *Baione.* Freshwater and anadromous; eastern North America. One species, *S. fontinalis,* the brook trout.

Subgenus *Cristivomer.* Freshwater; North America. One species, *S. namaycush,* the lake trout.

Salmo (trouts): Subgenus *Salmo.* Freshwater and anadromous; North Atlantic basin (northeastern North America and Europe) and European Arctic. Fall spawning. About five species (e.g., Atlantic salmon and brown trout, both with anadromous and freshwater populations).

Subgenus *Parasalmo.* Freshwater and anadromous; North Pacific basin (eastern slopes of parts of Rocky Mountains in North America) and south to Mexico and Arizona. Spring spawning. About five species (e.g., rainbow and cutthroat trout).

Subgenus *Salmothymus.* Freshwater; southern Yugoslavia. Three species.

Oncorhynchus (Pacific salmon): usually anadromous, occasionally freshwater; North Pacific coastal areas from Japan to California and adjacent parts of Arctic Ocean (see map on p. 330). Fall spawning. About seven species (five of which occur in North America).

Pacific salmon are a rich source of material for studies in raciation (e.g., Simon and Larkin, 1972). They have a strong homing ability, usually returning to their natal streams for spawning. Many studies have been conducted on the mechanisms of various aspects of their migration (e.g., Brannon, 1972, and references therein). *O. gorbuscha* (pink salmon) have a rigid two-year life span, with the even- and odd-year stocks existing alone or together (allochronously in the same stream, with, of course, no gene flow between them). Other species have variable lifespans: *O. nerka* (sockeye) lives as long as eight years in its northern range (Alaska). In one species, *O. nerka,* the anadromous form (sockeye) has throughout most of its range given rise to freshwater populations (kokanee) which occur in sympatry or allopatry (usually in "landlocked" lakes) with the parental anadromous form. *O. gorbuscha* and *O. keta* (chum salmon) usually spawn in the lower reaches of rivers and are the most "marinelike" of all Pacific salmon. All die after spawning.

Bulletins of the International North Pacific Fisheries Commission (Vancouver, Canada), contain many excellent articles on the biology of Pacific salmon. Bulletin 16 for 1965 contains articles on the life history of *O. kisutch* (coho), *O. tschawytscha* (chinook), and *O. masou* (masu); Bulletin 18 for 1966 contains articles on the life history of *O. nerka, O. gorbuscha,* and *O. keta.* Several articles on the biology of *Oncorhynchus* (and other salmonids) are given in Northcote (1969) and osteological information is provided by Hikita (1962), Norden (1961), and Vladykov (1962).

Superfamily Galaxioidae.   Usually no pyloric caeca; no mesocoracoid; no supramaxillae; 18 or fewer principal caudal fin rays; no upturned vertebrae. These cold-water fishes form the dominant element in the freshwater fish fauna of the Southern Hemisphere. Eleven genera and about 58 species.

McDowall (1969) concluded that *Prototroctes* is closely related to *Retropinna,* whereas *Aplochiton* and *Lovettia* are more similar to *Galaxias,* and preferred giving family status to the Prototroctinae and Aplochitoninae. Nelson (1972b) postulated a similar relationship among these genera but placed all the following families in the family Galaxiidae with *Prototroctes, Retropinna,* and *Stokellia* in the same subfamily (Retropinninae) and all other genera in the subfamily Galaxiinae.

The relationship of *Lepidogalaxias salamandroides*, found in one small creek in the southwest of Western Australia, is obscure and is not assigned to any family here. Nelson (1972b:36) noted some similarity with *Dallia* in the pitlines. Rosen (1973:434) evidently assigned it to its own family, Lepidogalaxiidae.

Family RETROPINNIDAE—New Zealand Smelts. Fresh and brackishwater (some partially marine); New Zealand, southeastern Australia, Tasmania, and Chatham Islands.

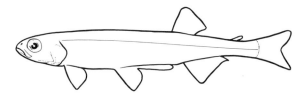

Adipose fin present; head compressed; dorsal fin posterior to pelvics, opposite the anal fin; cycloid scales; caudal fin forked; branchiostegal rays five or six; maxillae with teeth; only left ovary present. Some species appear to be anadromous.

Two genera, *Retropinna* and *Stokellia*, with six species. *Retropinna* has five species in Australia, Tasmania, New Zealand, and Chatham Islands; *Stokellia anisodon* occurs in New Zealand (McDowall, 1969).

Family APLOCHITONIDAE (Haplochitonidae)—Southern Smelts. Fresh and brackishwater; southern South America, Falkland Islands, southeastern Australia, Tasmania, and New Zealand.

Adipose fin present; dorsal fin anteriorly placed; body naked or with scales; forked caudal fin; branchiostegal rays 3–6; maxillae toothless and small, essentially excluded from gape of mouth by premaxillae. Maximum length 30 cm.

SUBFAMILY PROTOTROCTINAE. Scales present; vomerine, palatine, and basibranchial teeth present. Shows much affinity with the retropinnids.

One genus, *Prototroctes*, with two species, one in Australia and one (now extinct) in New Zealand.

SUBFAMILY APLOCHITONINAE. Scales absent; vomerine, palatine, and basibranchial teeth absent; vertebrae 52–72. *Aplochiton* has pyloric caeca but lacks the postcleithrum. Shows some affinity with the galaxiids.

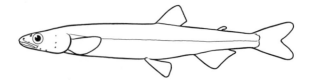

McDowall (1971a) reviews the life history and distribution of the species and describes their morphology. Certain life history stages may be marine.

Two genera, *Aplochiton* and *Lovettia*, with perhaps four species. *Aplochiton* (with two or three species) occurs in Chile, Argentina, Tierra del Fuego, and the Falkland Islands; *Lovettia sealii* is confined to Tasmania. The genera are very different in their morphology and it is not entirely certain that they share a common ancestry.

Family GALAXIIDAE—Galaxiids.   Freshwater and diadromous; Australia, New Zealand, New Caledonia, southernmost Africa, and southern South America.

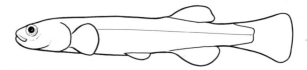

No adipose fin; dorsal fin posteriorly placed, near tail; no scales; rounded caudal fin (except in *Brachygalaxias*); no palatine or maxillae teeth; branchiostegal rays 5–9; pelvic fins absent in most *Neochanna;* pyloric caeca 0–6 (usually two); both ovaries present; vertebrae 37–66.

Most galaxiids are confined to fresh water, although some species are partially anadromous, having larvae that descend streams after hatching and spend some time in the ocean. The 16 cm *Galaxias maculatus* is peculiar among galaxiids in that ripe adults migrate down streams and spawn in esturine grasses in the upper tidal flats at spring tides. The eggs usually hatch after two weeks in future high tides when they are reimmersed in water and the larvae are washed out to sea. The species is marginally catadromous (with a lunar rhythm), although landlocked populations are known. In New Zealand young galaxiids of several species constitute the whitebait commercial and recreational fishery.

Maximum length, 58 cm, attained in *Galaxias argenteus* of New Zealand; most species are less than 20 cm.

Six genera, *Brachygalaxias, Galaxias, Neochanna, Nesogalaxias, Paragalaxias,* and *Saxilaga*, with about 46 species. Species abundance is greatest in Australia, especially in Tasmania and southeastern Australia. There are up to 25 species in Australia (20 *Galaxias*, two *Paragalaxias*, two *Saxi-*

laga, and one *Brachygalaxias;* Lake, 1971), 14 species in New Zealand (11 *Galaxias* and three *Neochanna;* McDowall, 1970), and four species in South America (three *Galaxias* and one *Brachygalaxias;* McDowall, 1971b). Only *Galaxias zebratus* occurs in South Africa and the only species in *Nesogalaxias* is in New Caledonia. The two species placed in *Brachygalaxias* should probably not be considered congeneric; the South American species has priority and the Australian probably shows more affinity with *Galaxias.* The most widespread species, *G. maculatus,* occurs in Australia, Tasmania, Lord Howe Island, New Zealand, Chatham Islands, and southern South America (Chile, Patagonia, Tierra del Fuego, and Falkland Islands) (McDowall, 1972). McDowall (1970, 1971b, 1973a) gives detailed descriptions of many of the species.

Superfamily Osmeroidae. Adipose fin present. Thirteen genera and 25 species.

Family OSMERIDAE—Smelts. Marine, anadromous, and coastal freshwater; Northern Hemisphere in Atlantic and Pacific (see map on p. 331).

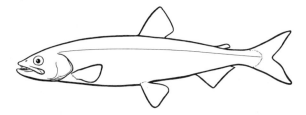

Pelvic axillary process absent; eight pelvic rays and 19 principal caudal rays (17 branched); branchiostegal rays 6–10; teeth on premaxillae, maxillae, dentary, and inner mouth bones; mesocoracoid present; orbitosphenoid absent; pyloric caeca 0–11; last vertebra turned up. Color silvery. Maximum length about 40 cm; most species less than 20 cm.

McAllister (1963) gives a revision of the family.

SUBFAMILY HYPOMESINAE. Two genera, *Hypomesus* and *Mallotus* with four species.

SUBFAMILY OSMERINAE. Four genera, *Allosmerus, Osmerus, Spirinchus, and Thaleichthys,* with six (possibly seven) species.

Family PLECOGLOSSIDAE—Ayu Fish. Anadromous; Japan, Korea, and China.

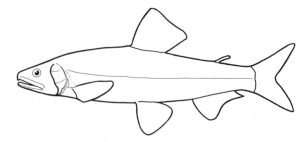

No pelvic axillary process; last vertebrae not turned up; more than 300 pyloric caeca; dorsal rays 10–12; anal rays 9–17; five or six branchiostegal rays.

One species, *Plecoglossus altivelis*.

Family SALANGIDAE—Icefishes.   Anadromous and freshwater; Japan, Korea, China, and Vietnam.

Body transparent and generally scaleless; head depressed; no swim bladder; no pyloric caeca; branchiostegal rays three or four; maxillae with teeth. Neotenic fishes.

Six genera (e.g., *Reganisalanx, Salangichthys,* and *Salanx*) and about 14 species.

Suborder Argentinoidei.   Complex posterior branchial structure ("epibranchial" organ), termed the crumenal organ.

Classification of this group is based partly on Marshall (1966a), Gosline (1969), and Greenwood and Rosen (1971).

Five families, 51 genera, and 109 species.

Superfamily Argentinoidae.   Adipose fin usually present; caudal fin forked; dorsal fin near body center; maxillae and premaxillae (when present) toothless; branchiostegal rays 2–7; lateral line scales 40–70; swim bladder, when present, physoclistic; mesocoracoid present or absent. Many are bathypelagic. Color silvery.

Twelve genera and about 58 species.

Family ARGENTINIDAE—Argentines or Herring Smelts.   Marine; Atlantic, Indian, and Pacific.

SUBFAMILY ARGENTININAE.   Eyes not tubular; adipose fin over anal fin base; dorsal fin origin in front of pelvics; pectoral fin base on ventrolateral surface; mouth small.

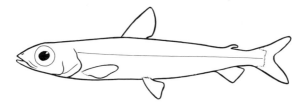

Two genera, *Argentina* and *Glossanodon,* and at least 10 species.

SUBFAMILY XENOPHTHALMICHTHYINAE.   Eyes tubular (protruding anteriorly); no adipose fin; dorsal fin origin behind pelvic fin insertion; pectoral fin base well up on side; mouth small.

One genus, *Xenophthalmichthys,* with two species.

Family BATHYLAGIDAE—Deep-sea Smelts.   Marine; Atlantic, Indian, and Pacific.

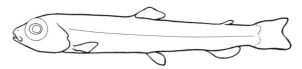

SUBFAMILY BATHYLAGINAE.   Adipose fin present or absent; pectoral fin base near ventral surface; swim bladder absent; no orbitosphenoid.
   One genus, *Bathylagus,* with about 27 species.

SUBFAMILY MICROSTOMATINAE.   Lateral line and lateral line scales extending onto tail; pectoral fin base on side; mesocoracoid absent; orbitosphenoid present.

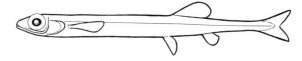

Two genera with about eight species.

Microstoma: no adipose fin; dorsal fin behind pelvics.

Nansenia: adipose fin present; dorsal fin in front of pelvics.

Family OPISTHOPROCTIDAE—Barreleyes or Spookfishes.   Marine; Atlantic, Indian, and Pacific.

Eyes usually tubular; pectoral fin base on side; pelvic fin base on side in some; adipose fin in some; photophores in some; most lack swim bladder.

Six genera (e.g., *Dolichopteryx, Macropinna, Opisthoproctus,* and *Winteria*) with about 11 species.

Superfamily Alepocephaloidae.   Maxillae included in gape; dorsal fin inserted well back on body; no adipose fin; no swim bladder; dark colored fishes.

About 39 genera with 51 species.

Family ALEPOCEPHALIDAE—Slickheads.   Deep-sea; all oceans.

Pelvic fins absent in some; teeth usually small; gill rakers long and numerous; 4–13 branchiostegal rays.

Subfamily Alepocephalinae.   No shoulder sac apparatus with papillae; 5–8 branchiostegal rays.

About 24 genera (e.g., *Alepocephalus, Ericara, Narcetes,* and *Photostylus*), with perhaps 30 species.

SUBFAMILY BATHYPRIONINAE. Body pikelike in shape; relatively large, widely spaced maxillary teeth; 10 pectoral rays; 12 branchiostegal rays.
One species, *Bathyprion danae*.

SUBFAMILY BATHYLACONINAE. Premaxillae minute, maxillae extending well behind eyes; branchiostegal rays form part of the opercular system; cycloid scales.

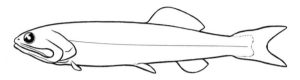

One species, *Bathylaco nigricans*, known only from a few specimens from the Atlantic and Pacific.

SUBFAMILY LEPTOCHILICHTHYINAE. Expanded and toothless maxillae; 13 branchiostegal rays.
One genus, *Leptochilichthys*, with perhaps two species.

Family SEARSIIDAE. Marine; all oceans.

Shoulder sac apparatus produces luminous mucus with conspicuous opening through tubular papilla; 14–28 pectoral rays; 4–8 branchiostegal rays.
Twelve genera (e.g., *Holtbyrnia, Mentodus, Mirorictus, Normichthys, Platytroctes, Sagamichthys,* and *Searsia*) with 17 species.

The following two suborders are provisionally retained in the salmoniforms (after Greenwood et al., 1966). The stomiatoids differ from other salmoniforms in several important details and this suborder, and the giganturoids, which have had an unstable systematic history, should perhaps be removed from the salmoniforms. Indeed, Rosen (1973) has advanced a new classification of euteleosteans in which he places the giganturids in the suborder Alepisauroidei (superfamily Synodontoidea), and that group, plus the aulopoids and stomiatoids, is placed in the Neoteleostei, an advanced group that also contains the Myctophiformes and all higher fishes. He considers the myctophiforms to be closer to the paracanthopterygians and acanthopterygians than to his aulopiforms (Aulopoidei and Alepisauroidei). Rosen also suggests that the enchodontoids and three other related fossil suborders of Goody (1969) are allied to the alepisauroids (and are therefore also neoteleosts). The order Salmoniformes would thus be a much smaller group than that presented here. In addition to the above, Rosen places the Protacanthopterygii and Neoteleostei together in a higher category whose status is equal to the Ostariophysi.

Suborder Stomiatoidei.   Luminescent organs (photophores) present; chin barbel present in some; premaxillae and maxillae in gape of mouth—both have teeth; mouth extending past eye in most; scales, if present, cycloid and easily lost; pectoral, dorsal, or adipose fins absent in some; ventral adipose fin present in some; pelvic fin rays 4–9; branchiostegal rays 5–24.

Classification of this suborder is based on Weitzman (1967a) and Gosline (1971). The ancestral stomiatoid was perhaps allied to the salmonoids and may not have been far from the myctophiform ancestor. Color in most is dark brown or black; some are silvery. Mostly tropical; many are deep-sea.

Eight families, 54 genera, and about 232 species.

Superfamily Gonostomatoidae (Heterophotodermi)

Family GONOSTOMATIDAE—Bristlemouths or Lightfishes.   Marine; Atlantic, Indian, and Pacific.

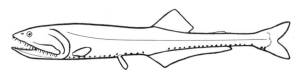

Body elongated, never extremely compressed; pectoral fins low on body; scales absent in some; anal fin rays 12–68; dorsal fin rays 6–20; dorsal adipose fin present or absent; some species of *Ichthyococcus* have a ventral adipose fin in front of the anus; mouth horizontal to moderately oblique.

Twenty-one genera [e.g., *Cyclothone* (perhaps with the greatest abundance of individuals of any fish genus in the world), *Diplophos*, *Gonostoma*, *Maurolicus*, *Pollichthys*, *Polymetme*, and *Vinciguerria*] and about 60 species.

Family STERNOPTYCHIDAE—Marine Hatchetfishes. Marine; Atlantic, Indian, and Pacific.

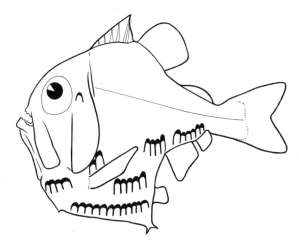

Body deep and extremely compressed; pectoral fins low on body; blade in front of the dorsal fin composed of specialized dorsal pterygiophores; anal fin sometimes divided, rays 11–19; dorsal fin rays 8–17; mouth nearly vertical; eyes sometimes telescopic.

Three genera, *Argyropelecus* (seven species, broadly worldwide, high-sea pelagic, usually 100–600 m), *Sternoptyx* (three species, broadly worldwide, high-sea pelagic, 500–1500 m), and *Polyipnus* [17 species, usually coastal (50–400 m); most species in the western Pacific], with 27 species (Baird, 1971).

Superfamily Stomiatoidae (Lepidophotodermi)

Family CHAULIODONTIDAE—Viperfishes. Marine; Atlantic, Indian, and Pacific.

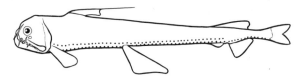

Dorsal fin well in advance of pelvics, shortly behind head; first dorsal fin ray greatly elongated; fanglike teeth on premaxillae and lower jaw; short chin barbel present in some; adipose fins present behind dorsal fin and in front of anal fin; dorsal fin rays 5–7; anal fin rays 10–13.

One genus, *Chauliodus*, with six species.

Family STOMIATIDAE—Scaly Dragonfishes. Marine; Atlantic, Indian, and Pacific.

Body elongate; dorsal fin origin far behind pelvics, above anal fin; long barbel on chin; no adipose fin.

Two genera, *Stomias* with eight species and *Macrostomias longibarbatus*.

Superfamily Astronesthoidae (Gymnophotodermi)

Family ASTRONESTHIDAE—Snaggletooths. Marine; Atlantic, Indian, and Pacific.

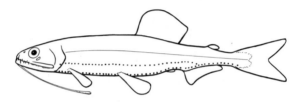

Dorsal fin origin over or behind pelvic fin insertion but well ahead of anal origin; dorsal adipose fin present except in *Rhadinesthes decimus;* ventral adipose fin present in many, in front of anal fin; no scales; barbel on chin; dorsal fin rays 9–21; anal fin rays 12–28.

Six genera (e.g., *Astronesthes, Borostomias,* and *Neonesthes*) with 27 species.

Family MELANOSTOMIATIDAE—Scaleless Black Dragonfishes. Marine; Atlantic, Indian, and Pacific.

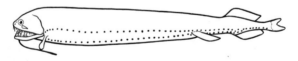

Dorsal fin origin far behind pelvic fin, over anal fin; dorsal adipose fin absent except in *Chirostomias;* no scales; most with barbel on chin; pectoral fins absent in some.

Sixteen genera (e.g., *Bathophilus, Chirostomias, Eustomias, Leptostomias, Melanostomias,* and *Tactostoma*) with at least 90 species.

Family MALACOSTEIDAE—Loosejaws. Marine; Atlantic, Indian, and Pacific.

Jaws elongated, longer than skull; dorsal fin origin far behind pelvic fin, over anal fin; adipose fin and scales absent; chin barbel in most; pectoral fins absent in some; dorsal fin rays 14–28; anal fin rays 17–32.

Four genera, *Aristostomias*, *Malacosteus*, *Photostomias*, and *Ultimostomias*, with 10 species.

Family IDIACANTHIDAE—Black Dragonfishes.   Marine; Atlantic, Indian, and Pacific.

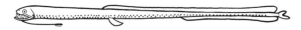

Body eellike; dorsal fin extremely elongate, more than one-half the body length and with 54–74 rays; anal fin rays 29–49; each dorsal and anal fin ray flanked by a spur; no scales; pectoral fins absent in adult; chin barbel only in females.

One genus, *Idiacanthus*, with about three species.

Suborder Giganturoidei.   Provisionally placed in the salmoniforms.

Family GIGANTURIDAE—Giganturids.   Marine; Atlantic, Indian, and Pacific.

Eyes large, tubular, and directed forward; mouth large, extending well behind eyes; sharp depressible teeth in mouth; pectoral fins high on body, above gill opening; body scaleless; no pelvic or adipose fins; caudal fin forked with some rays in lower lobe greatly elongated; no premaxilla, orbitosphenoid, parietal, symplectic, branchiostegal rays, gill rakers, posttemporal, supratemporal, or cleithrum; no swim bladder. Color silvery. The loss of many characters that generally appear late in fish morphogenesis suggests a neotenous condition for these fish.

Two genera, *Bathyleptus* and *Gigantura*, with five species.

Family ROSAURIDAE

May be based on the young of a giganturid; however, an adipose fin is present.

One species, *Rosaura,* based on a single specimen 8.4 mm long (Tucker, 1954).

Superorder OSTARIOPHYSI

The higher classification of this superorder follows Rosen and Greenwood (1970). *Ellopostoma megalomycter,* a freshwater fish from Borneo with certain resemblances to Cobitidae and Kneriidae, cannot be assigned any firm systematic position (Roberts, 1972).

Two series and three orders.

Series ANOTOPHYSI

Order GONORYNCHIFORMES.   Suprabranchial (= epibranchial) organ; mouth small; toothless jaws (but see Phractolaemidae); first three vertebrae specialized and associated with one or more cephalic ribs; 5–7 hypural plates.

Several features suggest some affinity between this order and the clupeoids. Most workers, in a variety of ways, have placed the following families in the order Clupeiformes (or its equivalent).

Four families, seven genera, and about 16 species.

Suborder Chanoidei.   Branchiostegal rays three or four; swim bladder present.

Family CHANIDAE—Milkfish.   Marine and brackish (occasionally freshwater); Indian and tropical Pacific.

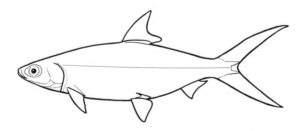

Mouth terminal, toothless; nonprotractile upper jaw; pelvic fin with 11 or 12 rays; cycloid scales; body compressed; dorsal fin rays 13–17; anal fin rays 9–11.

Chanos is of considerable commercial importance as a food-fish in Southeast Asia. In the Philippines and Indonesia, especially, there is an extensive fishpond culture for them. Young are caught close inshore and reared in coastal ponds. Adults feed primarily on plant material. Maximum length 1.7 m.

One species, *Chanos chanos.*

Family KNERIIDAE (includes Cromeriidae).   Freshwater; tropical Africa and Nile.

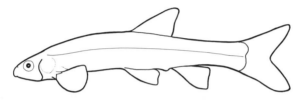

Mouth inferior or subterminal; protractile upper jaw; pelvic rays 6–9. *Kneria* has cycloid scales, whereas *Cromeria nilotica* has a naked body.

Three genera, *Cromeria, Kneria,* and *Parakneria* with about 12 species. *Grasseichthys gabonensis* probably belongs here.

Family PHRACTOLAEMIDAE.   Freshwater; tropical Africa.

Mouth superior; protractile upper jaw; pelvic rays six; cycloid scales; body elongate; jaws with only two teeth (at symphysis of lower jaw).

One species, *Phractolaemus ansorgei.*

Suborder Gonorynchoidei.   Branchiostegal rays four or five; no swim bladder.

Family GONORYNCHIDAE (Gonorhynchidae).   Marine; Indo-Pacific.

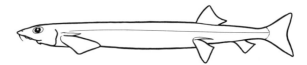

Mouth inferior; protractile upper jaw; barbel at tip of snout; ctenoid scales on body and head; body anguilliform. Maximum length 60 cm.
One species, *Gonorynchus gonorynchus.*

Series OTOPHYSI (Ostariophysi of Greenwood et al., 1966, and Cypriniformes of Berg, 1940)

Distinctive modification of anterior four or more vertebrae (Weberian apparatus); movable bony parts connect the swim bladder to the inner ear for sound transmission. In addition to the diagnostic Weberian apparatus, the following character states exist: upper jaw protractile in many species; pelvic fins, if present, abdominal; mesocoracoid usually present; basisphenoid absent; orbitosphenoid present.

Injuries to the skin release an alarm substance (Schreckstoff) which causes a fright reaction in members of the same species in proximity (Pfeiffer, 1963). This specific type of reaction, with the alarm substance, is limited to species of ostariophysans (both Anotophysi and Otophysi).

Two orders with 57 families and about 5000 species (some authors believe that the number of species is closer to 6000). This group thus contains about 26.5% of the known fish species in the world while accounting for about 73% of the freshwater species. They are present on all continents and major land masses except Antarctica and Greenland (Australia has a few catfishes secondarily derived from marine groups).

Order CYPRINIFORMES.   Parietal, symplectic, subopercular, and intermuscular bones present; vomerine teeth absent; heavy bony plates never present on body; branchiostegal rays 3–5.

In this book the siluriforms (catfishes) are placed in a separate order. Roberts (1973a), however, does not feel that there is any evidence to suggest that characoids and cyprinoids are more closely related to one another than either is to the siluriforms. He therefore accords all three equal status (subordinal) and places them in the order Cypriniformes. Gosline (1973) also places all three in the Cypriniformes and, as in most recent works, believes that the cypriniform ancestor was related to the gonorynchiform fishes but goes on to suggest a possible clupeiform affinity. If it is accepted that the Ostariophysi have some clupeiform affinity or if it is accepted that the Protacanthopterygii are closer to the

Neoteleostei than are the Ostariophysi, the order of taxa in a new classification proposed by Rosen (1973) would best be utilized to express the relationships. Under his cohort Euteleostei (here a division) he first lists his division Ostariophysi and then his newly proposed division Neognathi (containing the subdivisions Protacanthopterygii and Neoteleostei).

Twenty-six families with about 3000 species (perhaps 600 or so more). In terms of species this is the second largest order of fishes.

Suborder CHARACOIDEI

Superfamily Characoidae.   The classification of this group has been greatly split by Greenwood et al. (1966). Among others, Bailey (1960), Bailey in Bailey and Cavender (1971), Gosline (1971), and Weitzman (1962) recognized the single family, Characidae, whereas Regan (1911), Jordan (1923), and Berg (1940) recognized six families (Characidae, Gasteropelecidae, Xiphostomidae, Anostomidae, Hemiodontidae, and Citharinidae) compared with the 16 listed here (from Greenwood et al., 1966). The group may be oversplit, but the present scheme does emphasize the enormous morphological and ecological diversity which is greater than that which exists between many perciform families. Convergent evolution is common. The group is thought to have been restricted to Africa and South America since its origin (except for a recent invasion north into southern United States), and its distribution can best be explained by continental drift. Much information on the group has been derived from Weitzman (1954, 1960, 1962, 1964, personal communication, 1972) and Roberts (1969, 1971a).

Pelvic fins present (with 5–12 rays); anal fin short to moderately long (fewer than 45 rays); body fusiform to compressed; anal opening well behind head; teeth usually well developed (most are carnivores); adipose fin usually present; body almost always scaled (*Gymnocharacinus bergi* of Argentina is an exception); lateral line often decurved; mouth not truly protractile; seven hypural plates with 19 principal caudal fin rays.

Characoids are small and often extremely colorful (many are silvery); they are popular as tropical aquarium fish. It is the most primitive living group in the Otophysi and has about 1050 living species (about 30 genera with 150 species in Africa and 250 genera with 900 species in Mexico and Central and South America).

Family CHARACIDAE—Characins.   Freshwater; southwestern Texas, Mexico, Central and South America, and Africa (see map on p. 331).

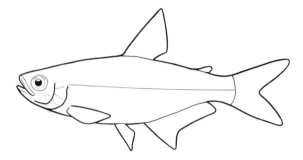

This is a large and diversified family. In it are the potentially dangerous Amazon piranhas (*Serrasalmus*), the South American tetras (e.g., *Hemigrammus* and *Hyphessobrycon*), a blind cave-fish in Mexico (forms of *Astyanax mexicanus,* formerly *Anoptichthys jordani*) and Brazil (*Stygichthys typhlops*), and a species that has dispersed into the southwestern United States (*Astyanax mexicanus* = *A. fasciatus mexicanus*). Within *A. mexicanus* there are eyed surface fish (with relatively high genic variability) and eyeless cave forms (with relatively low genic variability); in at least one cave the two forms interbreed (Avise and Selander, 1972). Some characins lack the adipose fin. The omnivorous *Brycon* grows to about 90 cm.

This and the osteoglossids are the only completely freshwater fish families indigenous to both Africa and South America (some nandids enter brackish water and cyprinodontids and cichlids have a few members that enter marine water). Species of characids on the two continents appear to deserve placement in different subfamilies. In Africa two subfamilies are recognized (both endemic), the Alestiinae with *Alestes, Bryconaethiops, Micralestes,* and *Phenacogrammus,* and the Hydrocyninae with one genus, *Hydrocynus*.

Some South American genera that represent different trends within the family or type genera of proposed subfamilies are *Acestrorhynchus, Catoprion, Characinus, Colossoma, Creagrutus, Crenuchus, Glandulocauda, Metynnis, Myleus, Salminus, Serrasalmus, Tetragonopterus, Triportheus,* and *Xenurobrycon*.

Family ERYTHRINIDAE. Freshwater; South America.

Gape long, extending beyond anterior margin of orbit; five branchiostegal rays; adipose fin absent; anal fin with 10–12 rays; dorsal fin in front of anal fin, usually over pelvic fins; scales relatively large, 30–45 in longitudinal series.

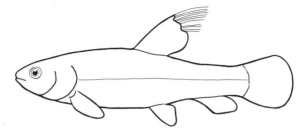

Three genera, *Erythrinus, Hoplerythrinus* (=*Pseuderythrinus*), and *Hoplias* with about five species.

Family CTENOLUCIIDAE (Xiphostomidae)—Pike-Characids. Freshwater; Central and South America.

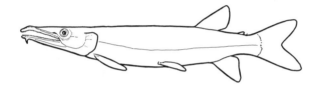

Elongate pikelike body; carnivorous; dorsal and anal fins set far back on body; scales ctenoid; pelvic fin with eight rays.

Includes *Boulengerella* (=*Luciocharax*) and *Ctenolucius.*

Family HEPSETIDAE. Freshwater; tropical Africa.

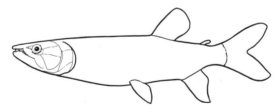

Elongate pikelike body; long snout and large mouth with a few large canines and smaller pointed teeth; dorsal fin with nine rays placed before origin of anal fin which has 11 rays; pelvic fin with nine rays; lateral line scales 49–60, cycloid.

One species, *Hepsetus odoe.* It is most closely related to the ctenoluciids and is considered, at least by Roberts (1969), to be the most primitive known characoid.

Family CYNODONTIDAE. Freshwater; South America.

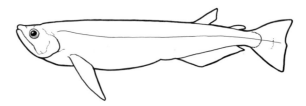

Compressed, elongate body; predaceous with very long canine teeth in the anterior parts of the jaws.

Three genera, *Cynodon*, *Hydrolycus*, and *Rhaphiodon*.

Family LEBIASINIDAE. Freshwater; South America.

Gape short, usually not reaching orbit; three or four branchiostegal rays; adipose fin present or absent; anal fin with 8–14 rays; dorsal fin in front of anal fin, usually over pelvic fins (often behind in the Pyrrhulinini which also have an elongate upper caudal fin lobe); scales large, 18–30 in longitudinal series.

SUBFAMILY LEBIASININAE. Includes two genera, *Lebiasina* and *Piabucina*, and about eight species.

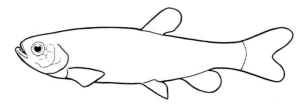

SUBFAMILY PYRRHULININAE. Two tribes are recognized: Pyrrhulinini with about 18 species in *Copeina*, *Copella*, and *Pyrrhulina*, and Nannostomini, which contains about eight species of pencilfishes, *Nannostomus* and *Poecilobrycon*.

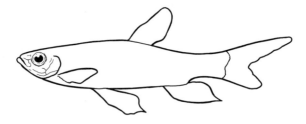

Family PARODONTIDAE. Freshwater; South America.

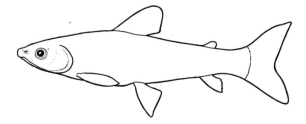

Peculiar fishes with ventral mouths and teeth modified for scraping rock surfaces.

Three genera, *Apareiodon, Parodon,* and *Saccodon.*

Family GASTEROPELECIDAE—Freshwater Hatchetfishes. Freshwater; South America and Panama.

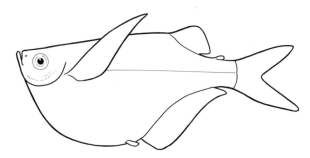

Strongly compressed head and body with protruding muscular breast region; lateral line extremely short, extending to tail, or curved downward to approach origin of anal fin; dorsal fin rays 8–17; anal fin rays 22–44; four or five branchiostegal rays; adipose fin present or absent; posttemporal and supracleithrum fused into a single bone; cleithra of each side fused.

These fishes are capable of making short flights out of the water and are the only fish known to "fly" with a propulsive force while in the air.

Three genera, *Carnegiella, Gasteropelecus, Thoracocharax,* with nine species.

Family PROCHILODONTIDAE. Freshwater; South America.

Superficially resembles the cyprinid *Labeo.*

Three genera, *Ichthyoelephas, Semaprochilodus,* and *Prochilodus,* with about 30 species (Roberts, 1973b).

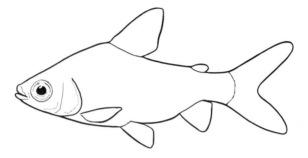

Family CURIMATIDAE. Freshwater; South America.

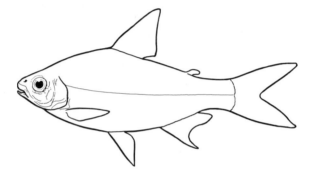

Mulletlike fishes without teeth in the jaws.

Includes *Curimatus* and *Anodus* and several other genera with several species.

Family ANOSTOMIDAE. Freshwater; South America.

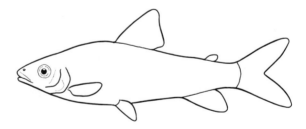

Mouth small, nonprotractile; lateral line straight.

Several genera include *Abramites, Anostomus, Leporinus, Leporellus,* and *Rhytiodus.*

Family HEMIODONTIDAE. Freshwater; tropical South America.

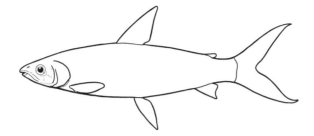

Gill membranes free; lateral line scales 50–125; pectoral fin rays 18–23. Maximum length about 30 cm.

SUBFAMILY HEMIODONTINAE. One genus, *Hemiodus*, with numerous species.

SUBFAMILY BIVIBRANCHIINAE. Three genera, *Argonectes, Atomaster*, and *Bivibranchia*, with about five species.

SUBFAMILY MICROMISCHODONTINAE. One species, *Micromischodus sugillatus*.

Family CHILODONTIDAE. Freshwater; South America.

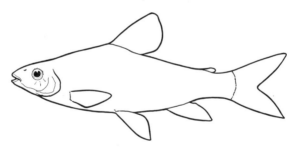

Gill membranes attached to isthmus; lateral line scales about 25–30; pectoral fin rays 13–16. Highly modified pharyngeal apparatus. Often swim in oblique head-down position. May bear a close relationship to Anostomidae. Maximum length 15 cm.

Two genera, *Caenotropus* (=*Tylobranchus*) and *Chilodus*.

Family DISTICHODONTIDAE. Freshwater; Africa.

This family which is closely related to the Citharinidae contains five genera: *Distichodus, Paradistichodus, Nannocharax, Hemigrammocharax*, and *Neolebias*.

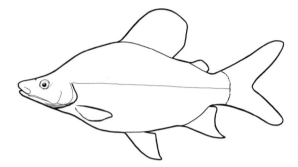

Family CITHARINIDAE. Freshwater; Africa.

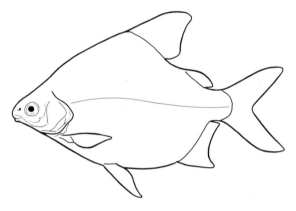

Ctenoid scales; lateral line straight. Some workers combine the disticho-
dontids and ichthyborids into this family.

Two genera: *Citharinus* and *Citharidium.*

Family ICHTHYBORIDAE. Freshwater; Africa.

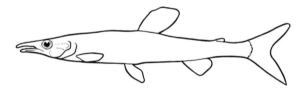

Peculiar elongate fishes with movable premaxillary bone. Some are known
to eat scales and fins of other fishes.

Contains the following genera: *Gavialocharax, Phagoborus, Ichthyborus,
Hemistichodus, Mesoborus, Belonophago, Phago, Paraphago,* and *Eugnath-
ichthys.*

Superfamily Gymnotoidae (see map on p. 332).   Body eellike (compressed or rounded); pelvic fins absent; rayed dorsal fin absent (filamentous "fin" present in some); anal fin extremely long (more than 140 rays) and employed in forward and backward movements; caudal fin absent or greatly reduced; restricted gill openings; anal opening under head or pectorals; basal pterygiophores to anal fin with only one section (radial) and a hemispherical cartilaginous head that articulates the fin rays (allowing them to move in a circular motion); electric organs present; suboperculum and palatine absent; maxillae rudimentary. They are undoubtedly derived from the characoids and probably arose in the Neotropical region. Like catfishes and unlike most of the members of the order, gymnotoids are nocturnal.

About 16 genera and 42 species.

Family GYMNOTIDAE—Knife-Eel or Naked-Back Fishes.   Freshwater; Central and South America.

Scales small; dorsal and caudal fins absent; weak electrical charge. Maximum length 60 cm.

One genus, *Gymnotus,* with three species (Miller, 1966). *G. carapo* is the most widespread; the other two occur in the northern portion of the families' range.

Family ELECTROPHORIDAE—Electric Eels.   Freshwater;   South   America (Orinoco and Amazon).

Scales absent; dorsal fin absent; anal fin united with the caudal fin; large electric organs producing lethal charges for killing prey. Length up to 2.3 m.

One species, *Electrophorus electricus.*

Family APTERONOTIDAE (Sternarchidae).   Freshwater; South America.

Scales small; long filamentous dorsal "fin" without rays in some; small caudal fin which is not united to the anal fin; weak electrical charge.

About 10 genera; for example, *Sternarchella*, *Sternarchus*, and *Apteronotus*.

Family RHAMPHICHTHYIDAE—Knife Fishes. Freshwater; South America.

Scales small; dorsal and caudal fins absent; weak electrical charge.

About four genera: *Sternopygus*, *Eigenmannia*, *Hypopomus*, and *Rhamphichthys*.

Suborder Cyprinoidei. Mouth usually protractile and always toothless; adipose fin absent (except in some cobitids); head scaleless.

Six families, 338 genera, and about 1900 species; the greatest diversity is in southeastern Asia.

Family CYPRINIDAE—Minnows or Carps. Freshwater; North American (northern Canada to Mexico), Africa, and Eurasia (see map on p. 332).

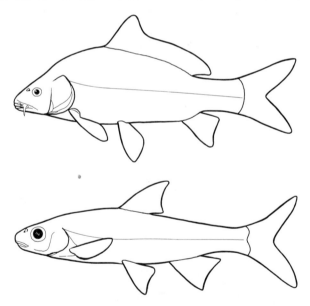

Pharyngeal teeth in one to three rows, never more than eight teeth in any one row; lips usually thin, not with plicae or papillae; upper jaw usually bordered only by premaxillae; spinelike rays in dorsal fin in some.

This is the most abundant family in most areas within its distribution. They are absent from South America, where the characins dominate, and from Madagascar and Australia. About 10 subfamilies are usually recognized, but, in general, the relationships within this large family are poorly known. In the Old World the dominant genera are *Rasbora* and *Barbus; Notropis* dominates in North America.

About 275 genera and about 1600 species (thus it contains more species than any other family of fishes, with gobiids second with about 800).

North American genera include (total of 36 genera with 199 native species) *Couesius, Gila, Hybognathus, Hybopsis, Nocomis, Notropis* (101 species), *Phoxinus* (also in Eurasia), *Pimephales, Rhinichthys,* and *Semotilus.* European genera include *Abramis, Alburnus, Barbus* (barbels), *Gobio* (gudgeons), *Idus, Leuciscus, Rhodeus* (bitterlings), *Rutilus* (roach), and *Scardinius* (rudd). Asian genera include *Barbus, Brachydanio, Carassius, Ctenopharyngodon, Cyprinus, Garra, Gobio, Labeo, Rasbora, Rhodeus, Schizothorax, Xenocypris,* and *Zacco.* The subfamilies that may be recognized tentatively are Cyprininae, Leuciscinae (which includes all North American minnows, except *Notemigonus,* and some Old World members); Abramidinae (includes *Notemigonus*), Barbinae, Rhodeinae, Gobioninae (Gobioinae, Gobiobotiinae), Chondrostominae, Hypophthalmichthyinae, Schizothoracinae, Rasborinae (Danioinae), and Cultrinae (includes *Xenocypris;* most with three rows of pharyngeal teeth).

Family GYRINOCHEILIDAE—Suckerbelly Loaches. Freshwater; Southeast Asia.

Pharyngeal teeth absent; ventral mouth modified into a sucking organ for attaching onto objects; inhalent aperture above gill opening entering into gill chamber; no barbels. Feeds exclusively on algae. Size up to 25 cm.

One genus, *Gyrinocheilus,* with three species.

Family PSILORHYNCHIDAE. Freshwater streams; India and Burma.

Mouth small, subterminal; no barbels; dorsal and anal fin bases short.

One genus, *Psilorhynchus,* with two species.

Family CATOSTOMIDAE—Suckers. Freshwater; China, northeast Siberia, North America (see map on p. 333).

One row of 16 or more pharyngeal teeth; lips usually thick and fleshy with plicae or papillae; upper jaw usually bordered by premaxillae and maxillae. Maximum length about 1.0 m, less than 60 cm for most species.

Twelve genera with 58 species (38 species placed in the genera *Catostomus* and *Moxostoma*).

Subfamily Myxocyprininae.   Twelve to 14 anal rays; 52–57 dorsal rays; 47–55 lateral line scales.

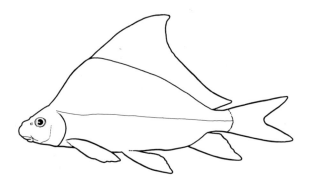

One species, *Myxocyprinus asiaticus* in Yangtse Kiang, China.

Subfamily Cycleptinae.   Seven anal rays; 30–37 dorsal rays; 51–59 lateral line scales; southern United States and Mexico.

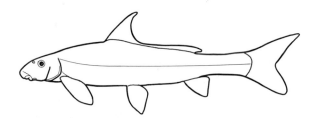

One species, *Cycleptus elongatus*.

Subfamily Ictiobinae.   Seven anal rays; 22–32 dorsal rays; 33–43 lateral line scales. Canada to Guatemala (absent from Pacific drainages). Northernmost species is *Carpiodes cyprinus* (North Saskatchewan and Red Deer rivers, Alberta); southernmost is *Ictiobus meridionalis* (Guatemala).

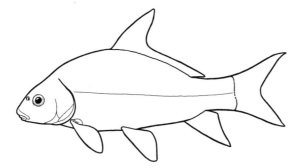

Two genera, *Carpiodes* and *Ictiobus,* with six species.

SUBFAMILY CATOSTOMINAE.   Seven anal rays; 10–18 dorsal rays; 30–120 lateral line scales. Northeastern Siberia, Alaska, and northern Canada to Mexico. Northernmost species is *Catostomus catostomus* (rivers adjacent to Arctic coastline); southernmost is probably *Moxostoma congestum* (northeastern Mexico).

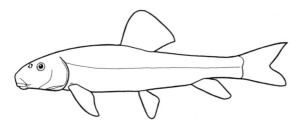

Various species of sucker are known to hybridize as do species of many other families (Schwartz, 1972), primarily ones in north temperate freshwaters. C. L. Hubbs in numerous papers has contributed the most to our knowledge of the extent of this hybridization. Nelson (1968) discusses isolating mechanisms and problems of identifying hybrids in a study of hybridization under natural environmental conditions in two species of *Catostomus.*

TRIBE ERIMYZONTINI.   Lateral line incomplete or absent.

Two genera, *Erimyzon* and *Minytrema,* with four species, in eastern and southern United States.

TRIBE MOXOSTOMATINI.   Lateral line present; fewer than 50 lateral line scales.

Most of the species live in eastern North America. One, *M. macrolepi-*

dotum, which is particularly widespread, extends from easternmost United States to Alberta. *Lagochila* is undoubtedly extinct.

Three genera, *Lagochila, Moxostoma,* and *Hypentelium,* with 22 species.

TRIBE CATOSTOMINI. Lateral line present; more than 50 lateral line scales.

Most of the species live in western North America. Two are particularly widespread, *Catostomus catostomus* (longnose sucker) extends from New York to eastern Siberia and *C. commersoni* (white sucker) extends from Georgia to British Columbia.

Three genera, *Catostomus* (with the subgenera *Catostomus* and *Pantosteus*), *Chasmistes,* and *Xyrauchen,* with 24 species.

Family HOMALOPTERIDAE—Hillstream Loaches. Freshwater; India, Malaya, Borneo, China, and Formosa.

Three or more pairs of barbels present; pelvic fins separate or united under belly; gill opening restricted or not.

Occupy torrential and swift streams from low to high altitudes (Alfred, 1969).

SUBFAMILY HOMALOPTERINAE. Twelve genera (e.g., *Balitora, Bhavania, Hemimyzon, Homaloptera,* and *Sinogastromyzon*) and about 55 species.

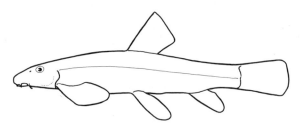

SUBFAMILY GASTROMYZONTINAE. Sixteen genera (e.g., *Beaufortia, Glaniopsis, Gastromyzon, Progastromyzon,* and *Protomyzon*) and about 32 species.

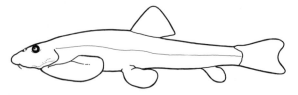

Family COBITIDAE—Loaches. Freshwater; Eurasia, Morocco, and Ethiopia (see map on p. 333).

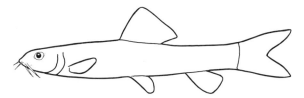

Three or more pairs of barbels present; some with an adipose fin; some with a spine near the eye which can be erected. Greatest diversity in southern Asia; length up to 30 cm; bottom dwellers with wormlike or fusiform bodies. Includes the wormlike coolie loaches (*Acanthophthalmus*), the robust bodied *Botia* and *Noemacheilus,* and the weather fishes, *Misgurnus.*

SUBFAMILY BOTIINAE. Two genera, *Botia* and *Leptobotia,* with about 10 species.

SUBFAMILY COBITINAE. Fifteen genera (e.g., *Acanthophthalmus, Acanthopsis, Cobitis,* and *Misgurnus*) with about 25 species.

SUBFAMILY NOEMACHEILINAE. About four genera with about 110 species.

Order SILURIFORMES (Nematognathi). Parietal, symplectic, suborpercular, and intermuscular bones absent; vomer usually toothed (as is the pterygoid and palatine); adipose fin usually present; spines often present at the front of the dorsal and pectoral fins; body either naked or covered with bony plates; maxillae rudimentary (except in Diplomystidae), supporting a barbel on each side; principal caudal fin rays 18 or fewer (most with 17); caudal skeleton varying between having six separate hypural plates to complete fusion of caudal elements (Lundberg and Baskin, 1969); eyes usually small (barbels are important in detecting food); air-breathing organs in Clariidae and Heteropneustidae. The Weberian apparatus of catfishes is described in detail by Alexander (1964) and Chardon (1968).

Several species of the catfish order are known to be venomous (Halstead, 1970). They can inflict severe wounds with their spines (primarily those of the pectoral fin) and inject a poison produced by glandular cells in the epidermal tissue covering the spines. Most species are passive stingers (e.g., *Noturus*), and presumably the toxicity of their stings has developed as a protective device in response to predation pressure (Birkhead, 1972). Some, such as *Heteropneustes fossilis* of India, which has a painful and potentially dangerous sting, have an aggressive behavior with records of attacks on humans and other fishes. Stings from *Plotosus lineatus* may result in death.

In many areas catfishes are a popular sports fish and a valued food item.

The largest catfish is *Silurus glanis,* the European catfish or wels, which attains a maximum length of at least 3.3 m (weighing 256 kg); reports have been made of 5 m (330 kg) (most populations probably do not contain individuals that approach these lengths). This species, native in Europe east of the Rhine and also occurring in brackish water and in inland saline seas, is the longest fish that lives primarily in fresh water; the longest fish confined to fresh water is *Arapaima gigas.* Many catfishes have a maximum length of less than 12 cm.

There are about 2000 species [of which about 1200 are South American; Gosline (1942) estimated that 1076 valid species were recognized in South America by 1941 but stressed the backward state of knowledge of the fishes on that continent] placed in between 400 and 500 genera. Two families, Ariidae and Plotosidae, consist largely of marine species (about 50 in all) but have representatives that are frequently found in brackish and coastal fresh waters. Other catfishes are freshwater (although some can invade brackish water). The most primitive members exist as relicts in South America. Much early work on the South American catfishes has been done by Carl Eigenmann (e.g., Eigenmann and Eigenmann, 1890; Eigenmann, 1917, 1925).

Chardon (1967) discusses the zoogeography of catfishes and Chardon (1968), largely on the basis of a study of the Weberian apparatus, presents a new classification. The following is the arrangement he proposes.

Suborder Diplomystoidei—Family Diplomystidae
Suborder Siluroidei—Family Helogeneidae, Siluridae, and
     Amblycipitidae
Suborder Malapteruroidei—Family Malapteruridae
Suborder Bagroidei
   Superfamily Bagroidae—Family Bagridae, Pimelodidae, Ictaluridae,
     Ariidae, and Olyridae
   Superfamily Plotosoidae—Family Plotosidae
   Superfamily Schilbeoidae—Family Schilbeidae
   Superfamily Pangasioidae—Family Pangasiidae
   Superfamily Chacoidae—Family Chacidae
   Superfamily Doradoidae—Family Mochokidae, Auchenipteridae,
     Doradidae, and Ageneiosidae
   Superfamily Sisoroidae—Family Amphiliidae and Sisoridae

Superfamily Akysoidae—Family Akysidae
Superfamily Clarioidae—Family Uegitglanididae, Clariidae, and
    Heteropneustidae
Suborder Cetopsoidei—Family Cetopsidae
Suborder Hypophthalmoidei—Family Hypophthalmidae
Suborder Loricarioidei
    Superfamily Aspredinoidae—Family Aspredinidae
    Superfamily Trichomycteroidae—Family Trichomycteridae
    Superfamily Loricarioidae—Family Astroblepidae, Loricariidae, and
    Callichthyidae.

This classification differs in several major respects with the arrangement
in this book (following Greenwood et al., 1966).

Family DIPLOMYSTIDAE—Diplomystid Catfishes. Freshwater; southern South
America, Chile and Argentina.

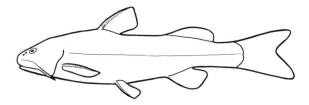

The only catfish family with well-developed teeth on the maxilla; only
maxillary barbels present.
    One genus, *Diplomystes*, with two species.

Family ICTALURIDAE (Ameiuridae)—North American Freshwater Catfishes.
Freshwater; North America (southern Canada to Guatemala) (see map on p. 334).

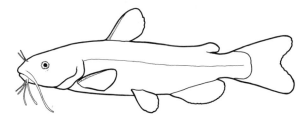

Eight barbels on head (two nasal, two maxillary, four chin); skin naked;
dorsal and pectoral fins with spine on leading edge. Two species of unrelated blind (eyeless) catfish are known from Artesian wells near San An-
tonio, Texas. *Satan eurystomus* is probably allied to *Pylodictis olivaris*,

whereas *Trogloglanis pattersoni* is probably derived from *Ictalurus* (Hubbs and Bailey, 1947).

Maximum length about 1.6 m, atained in *Ictalurus furcatus* and *Pylodictis olivaris*.

Five genera, *Ictalurus* [11 species—catfishes with deeply forked caudal fin and bullheads (placed in the genus *Ameiurus* at one time) which lack a distinctly forked caudal fin], *Noturus* (23 species—stonecat and madtoms which have a poison gland at base of pectoral spine), *Pylodictis* (one species—flathead catfish), and eyeless subterranean *Satan* and *Trogloglanis* of Texas, each with one species.

Family BAGRIDAE—Bagrid Catfishes.   Freshwater; Africa and Asia (see map on p. 334).

Dorsal fin preceded by a spine; adipose fin present, often large.

Many genera (e.g., *Auchenoglanis, Bagrus, Chrysichthys, Leiocassis, Leptoglanis, Macrones, Mystus, Pseudobagrus,* and *Rita*) with numerous species.

Family CRANOGLANIDIDAE.   Freshwater; Asia.

Placed in Bagridae in Berg (1940).

Dorsal fin short, six (rarely five) branched rays and one spine; anal fin with 35–41 rays; pectoral with a spine; caudal fin deeply forked; body naked; rough bony plates on top of head; four pairs of barbels. Similar to *Pseudobagrus*.

Three species, *Cranoglanis sinensis, C. multiradiatus,* and *C. bouderius* (Nichols, 1943; Lundberg and Baskin, 1969).

Family SILURIDAE—Eurasian Catfishes. Freshwater; Europe and Asia (see map on p. 335).

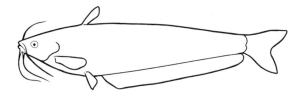

Dorsal fin usually with fewer than seven rays, sometimes absent, not preceded by a spine; adipose fin absent; pelvic fins small, sometimes absent; anal fin base very elongate (up to 90 anal rays).

Many genera [e.g., *Kryptopterus* (glass catfish), *Ompok, Silurus,* and *Wallago*] with numerous species.

Family SCHILBEIDAE—Schilbeid Catfishes. Freshwater; Africa and India.

Adipose fin present or absent; two to four pairs of barbels; anal fin base long; dorsal fin sometimes absent.

Many genera [e.g., *Clupisoma, Eutropius, Physailia* (African glass catfish), and *Schilbe*] with about 40 species.

Family PANGASIIDAE. Freshwater; southeast Asia.

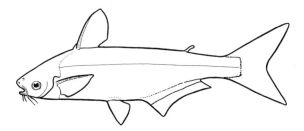

This family is included in the Schilbeidae by many authors. Nasal barbels absent, one pair of chin barbels; adipose fin present.

About eight genera (e.g., *Pangasius* and *Pteropangasius*) with about 25 species.

Family AMBLYCIPITIDAE—Torrent Catfishes.   Freshwater; China, East Indies, and southern Japan.

Small fish inhabiting swift streams.
   Two genera, *Amblyceps* and *Liobagrus,* with several species.

Family AMPHILIIDAE.   Freshwater; Africa.

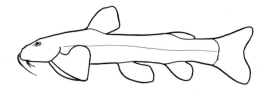

Body elongate; three pairs of barbels; dorsal and anal fin bases short; dorsal and pectoral fins without spines; pelvic fins forming a feeble sucking disc.
   Seven genera (e.g., *Amphilius, Doumea,* and *Phractura*) with about 55 species.

Family AKYSIDAE—Stream Catfishes.   Freshwater; southern Asia.

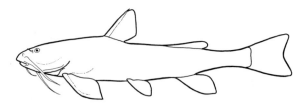

Dorsal fin preceded by a spine; adipose fin usually present; body with longitudinal row of tubercles.
   Several genera (e.g., *Acrochordonichthys, Akysis,* and *Breitensteinia*) and several species.

Family SISORIDAE (Bagariidae)—Sisorid Catfishes.   Freshwater;   southern and western Asia.

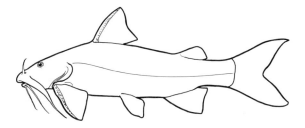

Four pairs of barbels, adipose fin large. Mostly small forms occurring in mountain rapids.

About six genera (e.g., *Bagarius*, *Gagata*, *Glyptothorax*, and *Sisor*) with several species.

Family CLARIIDAE—Airbreathing Catfishes.   Freshwater;   Africa, Syria, and southern and western Asia (Philippines to Java) (see map on p. 335).

Four pairs of barbels; air-breathing labyrinthic organ arising from gill arches (see Greenwood, 1961); dorsal fin usually with more than 30 rays, not preceded by a spine.

Some members of this family can move short distances over land. One species of walking catfish, *Clarias batrachus* (which is found almost throughout the range of the family), has been introduced into southern Florida waters, where it thrives. Members of three African genera (*Gymnallabes*, *Channallabes*, and *Dolichallabes*) have a marked burrowing habit and have small eyes and reduced or absent pectoral and pelvic fins. *Uegitglanis* of Somali Republic, *Horaglanis* of India, and one species of *Clarias* in South-West Africa, are blind (Menon, 1951a,b).

About 15 genera (e.g., *Clarias*, *Dinotopterus*, *Heterobranchus*, *Horaglanis*, and *Uegitglanis*) with about 100 species.

Family HETEROPNEUSTIDAE (Saccobranchidae)—Airsac Catfishes.   Freshwater; India, Ceylon, and Burma.

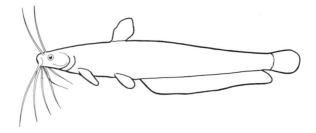

Body elongate, compressed; head greatly depressed; four pairs of barbels; long air sac, serving as a lung, extends posteriorly from the gill chamber; dorsal fin short, without a spine; adipose fin absent or represented as a low ridge.

One genus, *Heteropneustes,* with two species, *H. fossilis* and *H. microps* (Hora, 1936).

Family CHACIDAE—Squarehead Catfish. Freshwater; India to Borneo.

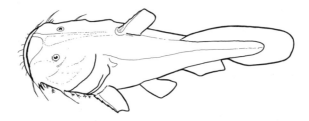

Body strongly depressed anteriorly, compressed posteriorly; mouth wide; rounded caudal fin extends far forward on dorsal surface; no adipose fin.

One species, *Chaca chaca* (Jayaram and Majumbar, 1964).

Family OLYRIDAE. Freshwater; India and Burma.

Body elongate, naked; four pairs of barbels; eyes small and subcutaneous; dorsal fin without spine, with seven or eight soft rays; anal fin with 16–23 rays; adipose fin low; vertebrae 48–53.

One genus, *Olyra,* with 1–3 species (Hora, 1936).

Family MALAPTERURIDAE—Electric Catfishes. Freshwater; tropical Africa and Nile.

No dorsal fin, adipose fin far back. Produce strong stunning electrical currents.

Two species, *Malapterurus electricus* of the Congo and Nile basins and adjacent areas and *M. microstoma* of the Congo basin (Poll and Gosse, 1969).

Family MOCHOKIDAE (Synodidae)—Upside-down Catfishes. Freshwater; Africa.

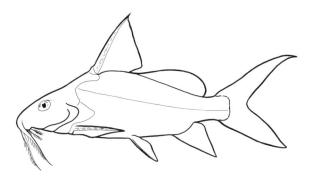

Ossified rays in adipose fin; anal fin with fewer than 10 rays.

About 10 genera (e.g., *Chiloglanis, Euchilichthys,* and *Synodontis*) with about 150 species.

Family ARIIDAE [Tachysuridae, including Berg's (1940) Doiichthyidae with one species endemic to New Guinea]—Sea Catfishes. Mainly marine; tropical and subtropical.

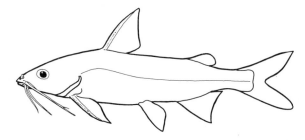

Caudal fin forked; adipose fin present; three pairs of barbels (no nasal barbels, *Batrachocephalus mino* has minute barbels); some bony plates on head and near dorsal fin origin. *Bagre* and *Arius* (=*Galeichthys*) occur in marine waters of southern United States. Many species enter freshwater.

Numerous genera (e.g., *Arius*, *Bagre*, *Hexanematichthys*, *Netuma*, *Potamarius*, *Tachysurus*, and *Doiichthys*) with numerous species.

Family DORADIDAE—Thorny Catfishes. Freshwater; South America.

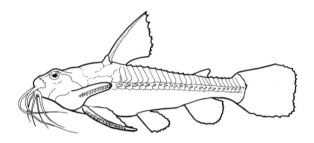

Body with a row of bony plates, most with spines; three pairs of barbels (no nasals); adipose fin usually present.

Several genera (e.g., *Doraops*, *Anadoras*, *Doras*, and *Hemidoras*) with many species. This and the auchenipterids are sometimes placed in the same family; together they have 45 genera and about 130 species.

Family AUCHENIPTERIDAE. Freshwater; tropical South America (to Argentina) and Panama.

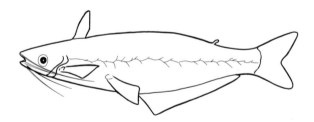

Body naked; maxillary barbels and one or two pairs of chin barbels; adipose fin small.

Several genera (e.g., *Auchenipterus*, *Centromochlus*, *Tatia*, *Trachelyopterus*, and *Trachycorystes*) with about 55 species.

Family ASPREDINIDAE—Banjo Catfishes. Freshwater (some brackish); tropical South America.

Body naked except for large tubercles; no adipose fin; body depressed anteriorly. Maximum length about 42 cm, attained in *Aspredo aspredo;* most species less than 15 cm.

Myers (1960a) reviews the family. Eight genera with about 25 species.

SUBFAMILY BUNOCEPHALINAE. Anal fin with 12 or fewer rays; always freshwater.

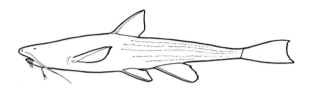

Five genera, *Agmus* (two species), *Amaralia* (one species), *Bunocephalus* (about 15 species), *Hoplomyzon* (two species), and *Xyliphius* (one species), with about 21 species.

SUBFAMILY ASPREDININAE. Anal fin with 50 or more rays; fresh- and brackish water in the Guiana Mangrove province (perhaps rarely extending into marine water).

Three genera, *Aspredinichthys* (one species), *Aspredo* (two species), and *Chamaigenes* (one species), with four species.

Family PLOTOSIDAE—Plotosids or Catfish Eels. Marine, brackish, and freshwater; Indian Ocean and eastern Pacific from Japan to Australia (see map on p. 336).

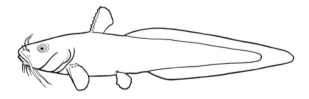

Body eellike, tail pointed or bluntly rounded; usually four pairs of barbels; no adipose fin; two dorsal fins, the second elongate and joined with the caudal (as is the anal fin); branchiostegal rays 9–13. As with some other catfish, these members can inflict painful wounds.

About seven genera (e.g., *Copidoglanis*, *Euristhmus*, *Neosilurus*, *Paraplotosus*, *Plotosus*, and *Tandanus*) with 25–30 species (per comm. G. J. Nelson). Slightly more than half the species are freshwater.

Family PIMELODIDAE—Fat or Long-whiskered Catfishes. Freshwater; Central and South America (north to southernmost Mexico) (see map on p. 336).

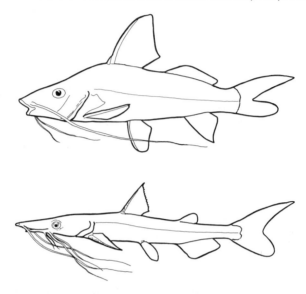

Body naked; adipose fin present; three pairs of barbels.

About 56 genera (e.g., *Calophysus, Heptapterus, Pimelodus, Pimelodella, Pseudopimelodus, Rhamdia, Sorubim, Zungaro,* and *Luciopimelodus*) and about 285 species.

Family AGENEIOSIDAE—Barbel-less Catfishes. Freshwater; tropical South America (to Argentina) and Panama.

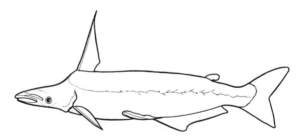

Only maxillary barbels present (which are sometimes rudimentary); adipose fin very small; 14 branchiostegal rays.

Two genera (e.g., *Ageneiosus*) with about 25 species.

Family HYPOPHTHALMIDAE—Low-eyed Catfish. Freshwater; tropical South America.

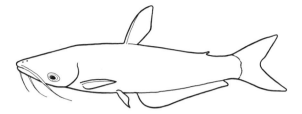

Body naked; three pairs of barbels; adipose fin small.
  One species, *Hypophthalmus edentatus.*

Family HELOGENEIDAE. Freshwater; tropical South America.

Dorsal with five soft rays and no spine; adipose fin very small; anal fin with
about 42 rays.
  One species, *Helogenes marmoratus.*

Family CETOPSIDAE—Whalelike Catfishes. Freshwater; South America.

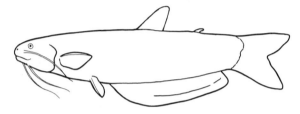

Body naked; three pairs of barbels (no nasals); no adipose fin; swim bladder highly reduced and enclosed in bony capsule.
  Four genera, *Cetopsis, Cetopsogiton, Hemicetopsis,* and *Pseudocetopsis,* with
about 12 species.

Family TRICHOMYCTERIDAE (Pygidiidae)—Parasitic Catfishes. Freshwater;
South America, Panama, and Costa Rica.

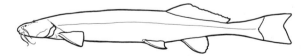

Body naked and elongate; chin barbels usually absent, usually two pairs of maxillary barbels; no adipose fin.

About 27 genera (e.g., *Pygidium, Trichomycterus, Hatcheria, Homodiaetus, Branchioica,* and *Stegophilus*) with about 185 species. Some members pierce the skin of living fish or other animals and gorge themselves on blood. *Branchioica* and *Vandellia* live on blood within the gill cavities of other fish. In addition, individuals of *Vandellia* (a candiru) of Brazil are known to enter the urethra of humans with serious consequences (Eigenmann, 1917; Norman and Greenwood, 1963; Masters, 1968).

Family CALLICHTHYIDAE—Callichthyid Armored Catfishes.   Freshwater; South America and Panama.

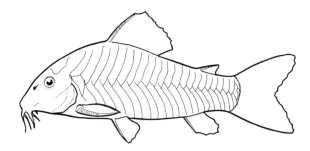

Body with bony plates; swim bladder encased in bone; spine at anterior border of adipose fin. Some species can move short distances on land, by utilizing air in vascular hindgut.

Eight genera [e.g., *Callichthys, Aspidoras, Corydoras* (with about 100 species), and *Hoplosternum*] with about 130 species.

Family   LORICARIIDAE—Armored   Catfishes.   Freshwater;   South   America, Panama, and Costa Rica.

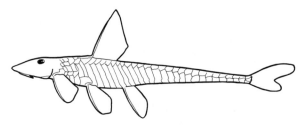

Body with bony plates, rarely naked; mouth ventral without noticeable barbels; ventral lip papillose; adipose fin, when present, with a spine at anterior border; relatively long intestine; 23–38 vertebrae.

About 49 genera (e.g., *Ancistrus, Chaetostoma, Farlowella, Hypostomus,*

Loricaria, Otocinclus, Plecostomus, Sturisoma, and *Xenocara*) with about 410 species.

Family ASTROBLEPIDAE (Argidae).   Freshwater; South America and Panama.

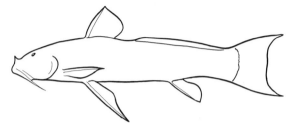

Body naked; relatively short intestine; 34 vertebrae (17 abdominal and 17 caudal).

Placed in the Loricariidae by Berg (1940) and some other workers. Freihofer and Neil (1967) describe an interesting situation in which some members of Astroblepidae and Loricariidae have commensal chironomid larvae on parts of their body. The midges are thought to gain some feeding advantage.

One genus, *Astroblepus,* with about 35 species.

The following three superorders are placed in the same taxon, superorder Neoteleostei, by Nelson (1969a), which is of equivalent rank to his Protacanthopterygii and Ostariophysi [Rosen and Patterson (1969) refer to the "neoteleostean" grade]. A possible arrangement here, though not adopted, would be to place the Protacanthopterygii and Ostariophysi in the same or different cohorts and recognize the three superorders as belonging to the cohort Neoteleostei. As mentioned earlier, the stomiatoids and giganturoids may also be better placed here than in the salmoniforms.

Rosen (1973) has suggested a new classification for euteleosteans, with many new categories and names, that reflect his interpretation of relationships. Under his subdivision Neoteleostei he places the sections Stenopterygii (with the order Stomiatiformes) and Eurypterygii. In the latter he recognizes two subsections, Cyclosquamata (with the order Aulopiformes, which contains two suborders, Aulopoidei and Alepisauroidei) and Ctenosquamata. In the latter are two septs, Scorpelomorpha (Myctophiformes, which in Rosen's classification contains only the Myctophidae, Neoscopelidae, and a few Cretaceous species and thus is markedly different than that presented here) and Acanthomorpha (and the superorders Paracanthopterygii and Acanthopterygii).

Superorder SCOPELOMORPHA (Iniomi, in part)

The premaxillae form the gape of the mouth (maxillae excluded); the upper jaw is not protrusible; adipose fin is usually present; photophores often present; caudal fin usually forked; pelvic fins usually abdominal, with 8–12 rays (eight or nine in most families); usually 19 principal caudal fin rays; branchiostegal rays 6–26; swim bladder, when present, closed (physoclistic); vertebrae 39 or more. Several families have species that are hermaphrodites (with self-fertilization).

The first 10 families belong to the myctophoid line, whereas the last six families belong to the alepisauroid line (Paxton, 1972). However, the classification of this group is subject to much change and suborders and superfamilies are therefore not recognized here. The alepisauroids are pelagic and bathypelagic, whereas the myctophoids are benthic except for the pelagic or bathypelagic families Neoscopelidae, Myctophidae, and Notosudidae.

About 73 genera with 390 species.

Order MYCTOPHIFORMES

Family AULOPODIDAE—Aulopus.   Marine; tropical and subtropical waters except eastern Pacific.

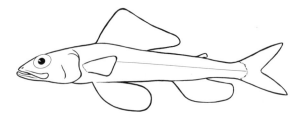

Body slender; fulcral scales on caudal peduncle; dorsal fin origin in front third of body, fin with 14–21 rays; anal fin rays 9–13; pelvic fin thoracic, nine rays; pectoral fin lateral, 11–14 rays; scales in head and body, cycloid or ctenoid; vertebrae 41–53.

The family is considered to be the basal stock to the rest.

One genus, *Aulopus* (includes *Hime* and *Latropiscis*), with eight species.

Family SYNODONTIDAE—Lizardfishes.   Marine; Atlantic, Indian, and Pacific.

Head usually depressed; head and body with scales; scales along lateral line not enlarged; dorsal fin rays 9–14; anal fin rays 8–16; dorsal adipose fin absent in only one species.

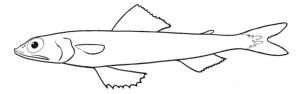

Four genera, *Saurida, Synodus, Trachinocephalus,* and *Xystodus,* with about 34 species.

Family BATHYSAURIDAE.   Marine; Atlantic, Indian, and Pacific.

Head and body with scales; scales along lateral line enlarged; dorsal fin rays 15–18; anal fin rays 11–14; dorsal adipose present in only one species.

One genus, *Bathysaurus,* with three species.

Family HARPADONTIDAE—Bombay Ducks.   Marine and brackish water; Indo-Pacific.

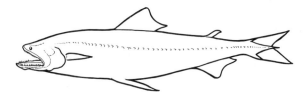

Head compressed; eyes anteriorly placed and directed forward; head and body naked (except for scales along the lateral line and on part of posterior half); trilobed caudal fin; no maxillae.

One genus, *Harpadon,* with three species.

Family CHLOROPHTHALMIDAE—Greeneyes.   Marine; Atlantic, Indian, and Pacific.

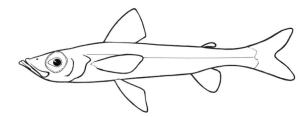

Scales on head and body (cycloid or ctenoid); dorsal fin rays 9–13; anal fin rays 7–11; pectoral fin rays 15–17.

Three genera, *Bathysauropsis, Chlorophthalmus,* and *Parasudis,* with about 20 species.

Family BATHYPTEROIDAE.   Marine; Atlantic, Indian, and Pacific.

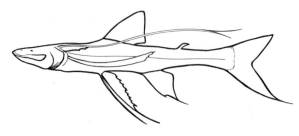

Either pectoral fin divided into two distinct parts with uppermost ray greatly prolonged *or* outer pelvic and lower caudal rays greatly elongated; eye minute, directed laterally, usually over middle of upper jaw; adipose fin present or absent; scales on cheek and body; dorsal fin origin behind pelvics, dorsal rays 11–15; anal fin rays 8–11.

Two genera, *Bathypterois* and *Benthosaurus,* with eight species.

Family IPNOPIDAE.   Marine; Atlantic, Indian, and Pacific.

Eye large, directed dorsally, and lensless (*Ipnops*) or minute, directed laterally, and over middle of upper jaw; no adipose fin; scales on head and body (cycloid and ctenoid); dorsal fin origin behind pelvics, dorsal rays 9–13; anal fin rays 13–16; pectoral fin rays 9–16; vertebrae 51–80.

Three genera, *Bathymicrops, Bathytyphlops,* and *Ipnops,* with about five species.

Family SCOPELOSAURIDAE (Notosudidae).   Marine: Atlantic, Indian, and Pacific.

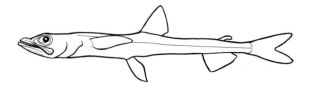

Dorsal fin rays 9–14; anal fin rays 16–21; pectoral fin rays 10–15; no swim bladder; no photophores.

One genus, *Scopelosaurus*, with about five species.

Family MYCTOPHIDAE—Lanternfishes.   Marine; all oceans, Arctic to Antarctic.

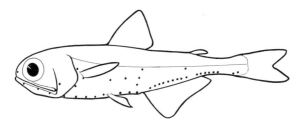

Snout compressed; supramaxillae absent; anal fin relatively far forward; scales cycloid or ctenoid; small photophores arranged in groups and rows on head and body.

About 32 genera with about 220 species. Paxton (1972) presents a detailed analysis of the family.

SUBFAMILY MYCTOPHINAE.   Fourteen genera (e.g., *Protomyctophum, Hierops, Myctophum, Loweina, Tarletonbeania,* and *Gonichthys*).

SUBFAMILY LAMPANYCTINAE.   Eighteen genera (e.g., *Notolychnus, Lampanyctus, Diaphus, Scopelopsis,* and *Gymnoscopelus*).

Family NEOSCOPELIDAE.   Marine; Atlantic, Indian, and Pacific.

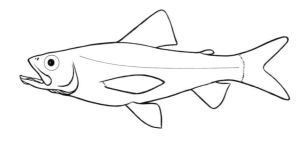

Snout compressed; supramaxillae present; photophores present or absent; swim bladder present.

Three genera, *Neoscopelus, Scopelengys,* and *Solivomer,* with five species.

Family PARALEPIDIDAE—Barracudinas.   Marine; all oceans, Arctic to Antarctic.

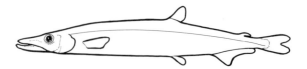

Dorsal fin origin in middle of trunk, fin rays 7–16; anal fin base long, with 20–50 rays; pectoral fin rays 11–17; no swim bladder. Superficially resemble sphyraenids.

Eleven genera (e.g., *Lestidium, Paralepis, Stemonosudis,* and *Sudis*) with 50 species.

Family OMOSUDIDAE.   Marine; Atlantic and Indian.

No scales; an enormously enlarged fang on each dentary; no body pores; dorsal fin rays 9–12; anal fin rays 14–16; pectoral fin rays 11–13; no swim bladder.

One species, *Omosudis lowei.*

Family ALEPISAURIDAE—Lancetfishes.   Marine; Atlantic and Pacific.

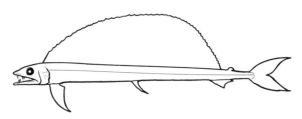

Body slender, covered with pores; scales and light organs absent; dorsal fin high and extending along most of body (originating over opercle and with 36–48 rays); anal fin low with 13–18 rays; pelvics abdominal with 8–10 rays; mouth large; teeth well developed, palatines especially long; vertebrae 50; swim bladder absent. Length up to 2 m.

One genus, *Alepisaurus,* with three species.

Family ANOTOPTERIDAE—Daggertooth.   Marine; Antarctic, Atlantic, and Pacific.

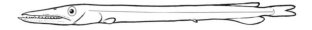

No dorsal fin (adipose fin well developed); no scales; no photophores; pelvic fins minute; anal fin rays 14–16; pectoral fin rays 12–15.

One species, *Anotopterus pharao*.

Family EVERMANNELLIDAE—Sabertooth Fishes.   Marine; Atlantic, Indian, and Pacific.

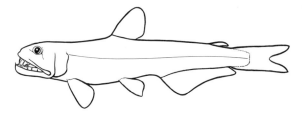

No scales; dorsal fin rays 11–13; anal fin rays 25–36; pectoral fin rays 11–13; no swim bladder.

Three genera, *Coccorella, Evermannella,* and *Odontostomops,* with six species.

Family SCOPELARCHIDAE—Pearleyes.   Marine; Antarctic, Atlantic, Indian, and Pacific.

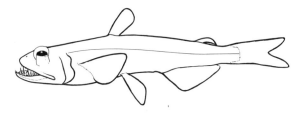

Hooked teeth on tongue; dorsal fin rays 7–9; anal fin rays 18–27; pectoral fin rays 17–27; no swim bladder.

Five genera (e.g., *Benthalbella, Neoscopelarchoides,* and *Scopelarchus*), with 18 species.

Superorder PARACANTHOPTERYGII

The modifications of Greenwood et al. (1966) in the higher classification of this group suggested by Rosen and Patterson (1969) are accepted here with the further modification of removing the Gobiesociformes and including the Indostomiformes.

The 966 or so living species are placed in about 250 genera, 31 families, and six orders.

Series POLYMIXIOMORPHA

Order POLYMIXIIFORMES. Two suborders may be recognized: the Polymixioidei with the extinct (Upper Cretaceous) Sphenocephalidae and the extant Polymixiidae (with such Upper Cretaceous genera as *Berycopsis* and *Omosoma*); the extinct (Upper Cretaceous) Dinopterygoidei with the four families Dinopterygidae, Pycnosteroididae, Aipichthyidae, and Pharmacichthyidae (Patterson, 1964; McAllister, 1968). There appears to be a close relationship between the early percopsiforms and polymixiiforms (Rosen and Patterson, 1969:454).
One extant family.

Family POLYMIXIIDAE—Beardfishes. Marine; tropical and subtropical Atlantic, Indian (primarily off Natal), and western Pacific.

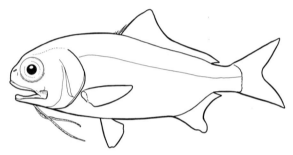

Body moderately elongate and compressed; pair of hyoid barbels; dorsal fin continuous, with 4–6 spines and 26–38 soft rays; anal fin long, with a few short spines; pelvic fins subabdominal, with one spinelike ray and six soft rays; 16 branched caudal rays; four branchiostegal rays; 11–21 gillrakers; three epurals. Beardfishes usually occur between 180–640 m.
This family is placed in the Beryciformes in Berg (1940), Greenwood et al. (1966), and Gosline (1971).
One genus, *Polymixia*, with three species (Lachner, 1955). *P. nobilis* and *P. lowei* are known primarily from the Atlantic, whereas *P. japonica* is known only from the western Pacific (but not from Indo-Australian waters).

Series SALMOPERCOMORPHA

Order PERCOPSIFORMES. Premaxillae form the entire margin of upper jaw, nonprotractile; ectopterygoid and palatine with teeth; pelvic fins, if present, behind pectorals and with 3–8 soft rays; spines (normally weak) usually present in dorsal fin; many species with ctenoid scales; six branchiostegal rays; orbitosphenoid and basisphenoid absent; vertebrae 28–35.

Three families and eight species.

The Sphenocephalidae, known only from fossils and apparently ancestral to the living freshwater groups, were marine.

Suborder Percopsoidei. Adipose fin present; anus in front of anal fin; lateral line complete; vomer toothless.

Family PERCOPSIDAE—Trout-Perches. Freshwater; northern North America (see map on p. 337).

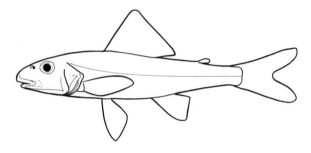

Ctenoid and cycloid scales; head naked; dorsal fin with one or two spines and 9–12 soft rays; anal fin with one or two spines and six or seven soft rays; pelvic fin subthoracic, with eight rays. Maximum length 20 cm, attained in *Percopsis omiscomaycus.*

Two species, the widespread *Percopsis omiscomaycus* and *P.* (= *Columbia*) *transmontana* of Columbia River drainage.

Suborder Aphredoderoidei. Adipose fin absent; anus between gill membranes in adults; lateral line absent or incomplete; vomer toothed.

Family APHREDODERIDAE—Pirate Perch. Freshwater; eastern United States (see map on p. 337).

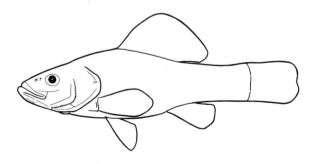

Ctenoid scales; sides of head scaly; eyes normal; dorsal fin with three or four spines and 10 or 11 soft rays; anal fin with two or three spines and 5–7 soft rays; pelvic fin subthoracic, with seven rays.

The anus is in the normal position in juveniles, just ahead of the anal fin, and moves forward during the growth of the fish. Also, in young pirate perch the third anal ray becomes transformed from a soft ray to a spine during growth. Young individuals thus appear to have two spines and eight soft rays; adults have three spines and seven soft rays (Mansueti, 1963). Maximum length about 13 cm.

One species, *Aphredoderus sayanus*.

Family AMBLYOPSIDAE—Cavefishes.   Freshwater; southern and eastern United States (see map on p. 338).

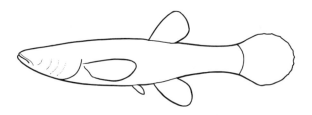

Cycloid scales; head naked; eyes small to rudimentary; dorsal fin with 0–2 spines and 7–12 soft rays; anal fin with 0–2 spines and 7–11 soft rays; pelvic fins usually absent (present only in *Amblyopsis spelaea* where they are small, abdominal, and with 0–6 rays); sensory papillae in rows on the head, body, and tail. Rosen (1962) compares the Amblyopsidae with *Aphredoderus* and the Cyprinodontoidei (with which they were formerly thought to be related).

All the species, except *Chologaster cornuta* of the Atlantic coastal plains, usually live in caves in limestone formations. *C. cornuta* and *C. agassizi* are the only species with functional eyes. The other three species are blind. Maximum length about 9 cm.

Three genera, *Amblyopsis, Chologaster,* and *Typhlichthys,* with five species (Woods and Inger, 1957).

Order GADIFORMES.   Elongate body, usually with long dorsal and anal fins; pelvic fins, if present, below or in front of pectorals; cycloid scales except in macrourids; ectopterygoid toothless; posterior vertebral reduction results in posterior dorsal and anal pterygiophores exceeding the number of caudal vertebrae.

Five suborders, 10 families, 168 genera, and about 684 species.

Members of the first two suborders are commonly referred to as the anacanthine fishes.

Suborder Muraenolepoidei. Caudal fin connected with anal and second dorsal fins; gill openings narrow, extending upward only to level of pectoral bases; pectoral radials 10–13; pelvic fin in front of pectoral; fin spines absent; swim bladder without pneumatic duct; basisphenoid, orbitosphenoid, and myodome absent; 6–8 branchiostegal rays.

Family MURAENOLEPIDIDAE.   Marine; Southern Hemisphere.

Two dorsal fins (the first with only one ray) and one anal fin; chin barbel present; head of vomer toothless; no pyloric caeca.

One genus, *Muraenolepis,* with three species.

Suborder Gadoidei. Caudal fin separate from dorsal and anal fins, only rarely partly connected; gill openings wide, extending above base of pectoral fins; pectoral radials 4–6; pelvic fin in front of pectoral; fin spines absent; swim bladder without pneumatic duct; basisphenoid, orbitosphenoid, and myodome absent; 6–8 branchiostegal rays.

Svetovidov (1948) gives a good review of the group.

About 45 genera and 148 species.

Family MORIDAE (Eretmophoridae)—Morid Cods.   Marine, deep-water; all seas.

One or two, rarely three dorsal fins; one or two anal fins; chin barbel present or absent; head of vomer toothless or with minute teeth; swim bladder in contact with auditory capsules (otophysic connection).

What appears to be a remarkable case of disjunct distribution occurs in *Halargyreus,* in which individuals of what may be the same species have been collected in New Zealand and the North Atlantic (Templeman, 1968).

About 17 genera (e.g., *Antimora, Halargyreus, Laemonema, Lepidion, Lotella, Mora, Physiculus, Salilota,* and *Tripterophycis*) with about 70 species (some based on only one specimen).

Family MELANONIDAE—Melanonids. Marine; southern Atlantic and southern Pacific.

Two dorsal fins, the second united with the pointed caudal; barbel absent; moridlike in most features but lacks otophysic connection.

One genus, *Melanonus*, with three species.

Family BREGMACEROTIDAE—Codlets. Marine; tropical and subtropical seas.

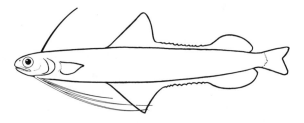

Two dorsal fins and one long anal fin (first dorsal fin on nape and consisting of one elongate ray, second dorsal and anal fins with large notch in middle); no chin barbel; relatively large scales, 40–89 along side; head of vomer toothed; pelvic fins with five rays, outer three are elongate free filaments; lateral line adjacent to second dorsal fin, reported as absent in some works; a few pyloric caeca; swim bladder not in contact with auditory capsules; 43–59 vertebrae. Maximum length about 12 cm.

One genus, *Bregmaceros* (=*Auchenoceros*) with seven species (d'Ancona and Cavinato, 1965).

Family GADIDAE—Cods. Marine with one Holarctic freshwater species; Arctic, Atlantic, and Pacific (see map on p. 338).

First dorsal fin posterior to head; head of vomer toothed; swim bladder not connected with auditory capsules. Maximum length about 1.8 m, attained by the Atlantic *Gadus morhua*.

About 55 species.

SUBFAMILY GADINAE (CODS AND HADDOCK). Three dorsal fins and two anal fins; chin barbel usually present; caudal fin truncate or slightly forked.

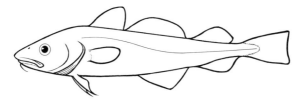

Twelve genera (e.g., *Arctogadus, Boreogadus, Eleginus, Gadus, Melano-grammus, Microgadus,* and *Theragra*) with about 25 species.

SUBFAMILY LOTINAE (HAKES AND BURBOT). One or two dorsals and one anal fin; chin barbel always present; caudal fin rounded.

Nine genera (e.g., *Gaidropsarus, Lota, Molva, Phycis, Raniceps,* and *Uro-phycis*) with about 30 species. *Lota lota* is the only freshwater member of the family.

Family MERLUCCIIDAE—Merluccid Hakes. Marine; Atlantic, eastern Pacific, Tasmania, and New Zealand.

Two dorsal fins (one in *Lyconodes*) and one anal fin (second dorsal and anal fins with a notch posteriorly); no chin barbel; head of vomer with teeth; first principal dorsal ray is spinous; mouth terminal (in *Merluccius* the lower jaw projects forward), large, and with long teeth; 7–9 pelvic rays; seven branchiostegal rays; no pyloric caeca.

The membership of this family follows Marshall (1966b). Most workers have placed the Merlucciinae in Gadidae and some genera of the Macruroninae were formerly placed in the Macrouridae.

SUBFAMILY MACRURONINAE. Long tapering tail; dorsal and anal fins confluent with caudal fin or with each other.

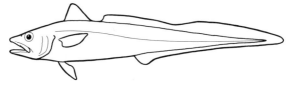

Four genera, *Lyconodes, Lyconus, Macruronus,* and *Steindachneria* (anus is between the pelvic fins; urogenital opening is close to anal fin), and about six species.

SUBFAMILY MERLUCCIINAE. Caudal fin truncate, not confluent with dorsal and anal fins; no fanglike teeth.

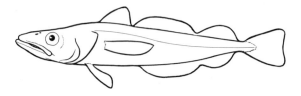

One genus, *Merluccius,* with about seven species.

Suborder Macrouroidei. Okamura (1970) reviews the Japanese forms and recognizes two families, Macrouroididae (with only two genera, *Macrouroides* and *Squalogadus,* which lack the first, short dorsal fin) and Macrouridae.

Family MACROURIDAE (Coryphaenoididae)—Grenadiers or Whiptails. Marine; deep-water, Arctic to Antarctic.

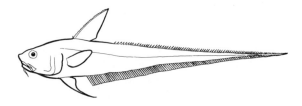

Second dorsal and anal fins continuous with tail, which tapers to a sharp point; no true fin spines (first dorsal fin ray may be spinous); chin barbel usually present; pelvic fins under, behind, or in front of pectoral fin base; small scales. Length normally up to 0.8 m.

About 15 genera (e.g., *Bathygadus, Chalinura, Coelorhynchus, Coryphaenoides, Gadomus, Lepidorhynchus, Lionurus, Macrouroides, Macrourus, Malacocephalus, Nematonurus, Nezumia, Squalogadus,* and *Trachyrhynchus*) with about 250 species.

Suborder Ophidioidei. Pelvic fins, when present, far forward, (mental or jugular) and with a spine; dorsal and anal fin rays numerous (fins may be united to caudal fin).

Gosline (1968, 1971) prefers placing this group in the Perciformes and furthermore includes the Gadopsidae (which appear morphologically intermediate between the percoids and ophidioids) in the Ophidioidei.

Family OPHIDIIDAE—Brotulas and Cusk-Eels.   Marine, rarely freshwater; Atlantic, Indian, and Pacific.

Long tapering fishes with head broader than body; dorsal, caudal, and anal fins often united to form a continuous fin; pelvic and caudal fins usually present; anus behind head; mouth usually protractile.

    Gosline (1971) recognizes three families here: Brotulidae, Aphyonidae, and Ophidiidae.

    Maximum length 1.5 m, attained in South Africa by *Genypterus capensis.*

SUBFAMILY BROTULINAE (BROTULAS).   Pelvics jugular (absent in some). Some are viviparous. Two species of *Lucifuga* (=*Stygicola*) live in freshwater caves in Cuba and are blind; a third, with small eyes, is known from a limestone sink in the Bahamas (Cohen and Robins, 1970). A specimen of *Bassogigas* has been dredged at a depth of about 7 km in the Sunda trench, near Java, which is the deepest definite record of a captured fish.

    About sixty one genera (e.g., *Aphyonus, Brosmophycis, Brotula, Oligopus, Porogadus,* and *Sirembo*) and about 155 species.

SUBFAMILY OPHIDIINAE (CUSK-EELS).   Pelvics mental (under lower jaw).

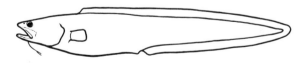

    About 10 genera (e.g., *Brotuloides, Genypterus, Lepophidium, Ophidion, Otophidium, Parophidion,* and *Rissola*), with perhaps more than 35 species.

Family CARAPIDAE—Carapids.   Marine; Atlantic, Indian, and Pacific.

Larvae with a vexillum.

Subfamily status was recommended for the pyramodontids, rather than family status, by Robins and Nielsen (1970).

Subfamily Carapinae (Fierasferidae)—pearlfishes. Marine; tropical and temperate seas.

Body elongate; dorsal and anal fins long; pelvic and caudal fins absent; anus on throat; body with small scales or naked; mouth nonprotractile. The three species of *Encheliophis* lack pectoral fins.

Many species have the interesting habit of hiding in living animals. Some live in sea cucumbers and actually eat the cucumber's internal organs in a parasitic fashion. Pearlfishes pass through two distinct larval stages in their early life. The first larval, or vexillifer, stage is pelagic; the second larval, or tenuis, stage is benthic.

Arnold (1956) describes their life history and gives keys to the genera and species.

Maximum length about 30 cm, attained by *Echiodon drummondi* and *Carapus bermudensis*.

Six genera, *Carapus, Disparichthys* (one species of which occurs in freshwater in New Guinea), *Echiodon, Encheliophis, Jordanicus*, and *Onuxodon*, with about 25 species.

Subfamily Pyramodontinae—pyramodontines. Marine; few localities in tropical Atlantic, Indian, and Pacific (near Japan and New Zealand).

Body elongate and scaleless; anus below middle or anterior part of pectoral fin; pectoral fins nearly as long as head.

Two genera, *Pyramodon* (pelvics present) and *Snyderidia* (pelvics absent), with three species.

Suborder Zoarcoidei

Family ZOARCIDAE—Eelpouts. Marine; Arctic to Antarctic.

Body elongate; dorsal and anal fins long and confluent with caudal fin; mouth subterminal; pelvics, when present, small and in front of pectorals (jugular); gill membranes joined to isthmus; vertebrae 90–150. Some are viviparous. Length up to about 1 m in *Macrozoarces americanus*.

Placed in the Blennioidei by most workers, including Gosline (1968, 1971). Gosline (1971) considered them closely related to the Bathymasteridae. Its placement here in Gadiformes, following Greenwood et al. (1966) and Rosen and Patterson (1969), rather than its retention in Perciformes, is questionable. *Derepodichthys* is often put in its own family, Derepodichthyidae (e.g., Gosline, 1971; Hart, 1973), and is known only from a single specimen taken in 1890 from off British Columbia at a depth of about 2904 m.

At least 28 genera (e.g., *Aprodon*, *Bothrocara*, *Derepodichthys*, *Gymnelis*, *Lycenchelys*, *Lycodapus*, *Lycodes*, *Lycodopsis*, *Macrozoarces*, *Maynea*, *Melanostigma*, and *Zoarces*) and at least 65 species. Information on some of these genera may be found in Andriashev (1955), McAllister and Rees (1964), Nielsen (1968), and Yarberry (1965).

Order BATRACHOIDIFORMES (Haplodoci).   Body usually scaleless (small cycloid scales in some); head large with eyes more dorsal than lateral; mouth large and bordered by premaxillae and maxillae; pore (foramen) in axil of pectoral fin in some; pelvic fins jugular (in front of pectorals), with one spine and two or three soft rays; three pairs of gills; gill membrane broadly joined to isthmus; branchiostegal rays six; four or five pectoral radials; swim bladder present; upper hypurals with peculiar intervertebrallike basal articulation with rest of caudal skeleton; no ribs, epiotics, or intercalars; no pyloric caeca.

Some members can produce audible sounds with the swim bladder and can live out of water for several hours. Most are drab colored.

Family BATRACHOIDIDAE—Toadfishes.   Marine (primarily coastal benthic; rarely entering brackish waters, two species confined to fresh water); Atlantic, Indian, and Pacific.

Three subfamilies and about 55 species.

Subfamily Batrachoidinae.   Off coasts of the Americas, Africa, Europe, southern Asia, and Australia.

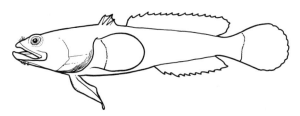

Three solid dorsal spines and solid opercular spine, no venom glands; subopercular spines present; body with or without scales (cycloid); no photophores; axillary gland at pectoral base present or absent; canine teeth absent; usually one or three lateral lines.

The composition of this subfamily is based primarily on Smith (1952a), Greenfield and Greenfield (1973), and D. W. Greenfield (per. comm. 1973).

The following eight genera (with an estimated 21 species) have completely scaleless bodies (the pectoral axillary foramen is absent in the first four and present in the last four): *Amphichthys* (two), *Batrichthys* (three), *Halophryne* (two), *Triathalassothia* (two), *Austrobatrachus* (one), *Batrachomoeus* (three), *Opsanus* (four), and *Sanopus* (four). Six genera (with an estimated 11 species) have scaled bodies (the first four lack the pectoral axillary foramen): *Chatrabus* (two), *Barchatus* (one), *Tharbacus* (two, each known from a single specimen thrown up in a storm in South Africa), *Batrachoides* (four). *Riekertia* (one-most of body naked, known only from a few South African specimens), and *Halobatrachus* (one).

SUBFAMILY PORICHTHYINAE.   Eastern Pacific and western Atlantic.

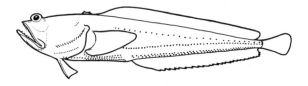

Two solid dorsal spines and solid opercular spine, no venom glands; no subopercular spines; body scaleless; photophores present or absent; axillary gland absent; canine teeth present; several lateral lines.

Two genera with about 12 species.

Aphos: lacks photophores. One southeastern Pacific (Peru and Chile) species.

Porichthys (midshipmen): numerous photophores (this is one of the few shallow-water fishes that possess photophores). Eleven species (includes *Nautopaedium*) (Gilbert, 1968), six along the eastern Pacific (southeastern Alaska to Colombia) and five along the western Atlantic (Virginia to Argentina, but generally absent from the West Indies).

SUBFAMILY THALASSOPHRYNINAE.   Eastern Pacific and western Atlantic.

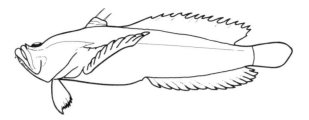

Two hollow dorsal spines and hollow opercular spine (serving as a venom-injecting apparatus capable of producing extremely painful wounds, shown in Halstead, 1970) connecting with venom glands; body scaleless; no photophores; no canine teeth; lateral line single or absent.

Two genera with 11 species (Collette, 1966, 1973).

Daector: second dorsal rays 22–33; anal rays 21–30; distinct glands present between bases of uppermost pectoral fin rays. Four tropical eastern Pacific marine species and *D. quadrizonatus* from fresh water, Colombia (Atrato basin, Atlantic drainage).

Thalassophryne: second dorsal rays 17–22; anal rays 16–20; no distinct glands present on pectoral fin (they are located distally on the upper pectoral rays). Five western Atlantic marine species (Panama and South America) and *T. amazonica,* known only from the Amazon River.

Order LOPHIIFORMES (Pediculati)–Anglerfishes. First ray of spinous dorsal (if present) on head and transformed into illicium [line and bait (esca) device for attracting prey to mouth]; pelvic fins, if present, in front of pectorals and with one spine and five soft rays; gill opening small, at or behind base of pectoral fin; five or six branchiostegal rays; no ribs; pectoral radials 2–4; swim bladder physoclistic.

Fifteen families with about 215 species. All are marine.

Most species occur in deep water.

Suborder Lophioidei. Pelvic fins present; pseudobranch present; body scaleless; frontals united.

Family LOPHIIDAE—Goosefishes. Marine; Atlantic, Indian, and western Pacific.

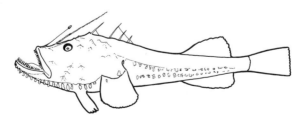

Huge, wide, flattened head; teeth well developed; fringe of small flaps extending around lower jaw and along sides of head onto the body.

The movable "fishing pole" device has a flap of flesh at its tip which acts like a flag, apparently attracting prey within easy reach of its large mouth. Size up to 1.2 m.

Five genera, *Chirolophius, Lophiodes, Lophiomus, Lophius,* and *Sladenia,* with at least 12 species.

Suborder Antennarioidei. Pelvic fins present; pectorals usually muscular and armlike; pseudobranch vestigial or absent; body usually scaleless; frontals not united. Most species are benthic; some are pelagic surface.

Family BRACHIONICHTHYIDAE—Warty Anglers. Marine; Australia.

Body balloon-shaped; skin covered with denticles; second and third dorsal spines united by a membrane; gill opening behind base of pectoral.

One genus, *Brachionichthys* (=*Sympterichthys*), and about three species.

Family ANTENNARIIDAE—Frogfishes. Marine; all tropical and subtropical seas.

Body balloon-shaped, covered with loose skin, naked or with denticles; first three dorsal spines separate (one or two illicia, the third spine may be ornamented or inconspicuous); gill opening below base of pectoral. Species pelagic; its unusual prehensile pectoral fin is used for "clasping" or moving on algal mats.

The "fishing pole" of frogfishes, a modication of the first dorsal fin, is particularly pronounced and highly variable between species. Maximum length 36 cm, some only 3 cm.

Reviewed by Schultz (1957).

SUBFAMILY ANTENNARIINAE. Deep-bodied; eyes lateral.

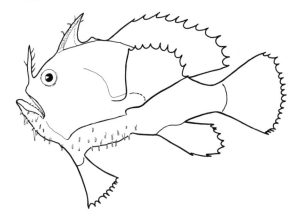

Eight genera (e.g., *Antennarius, Histiophryne,* and *Histrio*) with about 60 species.

SUBFAMILY TETRABRACHIINAE. Body elongate; eyes superior.
One species, *Tetrabrachium viellatum,* of Indian Ocean-Australian region.

Family CHAUNACIDAE—Sea Toads. Marine; Atlantic, Indian, and Pacific.

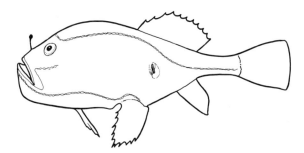

Body balloon-shaped; illicium but no other spinous dorsal rays; mouth oblique; gill opening behind base of pectoral.
One genus, *Chaunax,* with about four species.

Family OGCOCEPHALIDAE—Batfishes. Marine; Atlantic, Indian, and Pacific.

Body usually much depressed; illicium but no other spinous dorsal rays; mouth nearly horizontal; gill opening in or above pectoral base; two or two and one-half gills; well-developed tuberclelike scales.
Batfishes walk about on the bottom on their large armlike pectoral fins

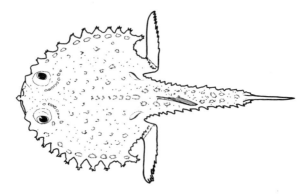

and smaller pelvic fins. They are awkward swimmers. Size normally 20 cm; up to 40 cm in *Ogcocephalus nasutus*.

Nine genera (e.g., *Dibranchus, Halieutaea, Halieutichthys, Ogcocephalus*, and *Zalieutes*) with about 55 species.

Suborder Ceratioidei. Pelvic fins absent; pseudobranch absent; body scaleless (prickles, spines, or plates may be present); frontals not united; lower pharyngeals reduced and toothless; pectoral fin rays 13–30; eight or nine caudal fin rays; only females with illicium, the tip of which usually has a light organ (undoubtedly increasing its function in attracting prey; light organs may also be present elsewhere).

Marked sexual dimorphism is characteristic of the ceratioids. The longest known female in each family is 3 to 13 times longer than the longest known male (within species the difference can be much greater). The adult males of all species in at least four families are parasitic on the larger females. These males actively seek out females after metamorphosis into the parasitic stage, attach to their bodies, and feed on their blood (a vascular connection may exist in all such parasitic relationships). Males are generally different in appearance than females (which are pictured in the family descriptions), although dorsal and anal fin ray counts are the same.

Larval life is spent in the upper food-rich oceanic layer; adults are bathypelagic (usually occurring between 1500 and 2500 m). Ceratioids extend from the subarctic to the subantarctic but are absent from the Mediterranean Sea.

In the past males, females, and larva of the same species have been described as different species. The number of recognized species has been reduced by recent work, but many species are still known only from males, females, or larva and often from only a few specimens (Bertelsen, 1951).

Maximum size in most species is seldom longer than 8 cm; however, the largest specimen is a 1.2 m *Ceratias holboelli*.

Ten families with about 80 species.

Family CAULOPHRYNIDAE. Marine; Atlantic, Indian, and Pacific.

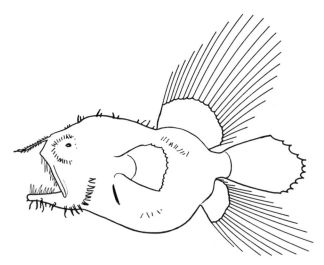

No distal bulb with light organ on illicium; mature males parasitic on females; pelvic fins in larvae (only ceratioid with pelvics at some stage); two pectoral radials (all other ceratioids have 3–5); dorsal fin with 14–22 normal rays and anal fin rays 13–19 (all other ceratioids have 13 or fewer anal fin rays). Bertelsen (1951) notes many similarities between caulophrynids and ogcocephalids.

One species, *Caulophryne jordani*.

Family MELANOCETIDAE. Marine; Atlantic, Indian, and Pacific.

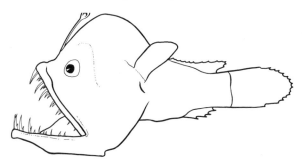

Dorsal fin with 12–17 rays and three or four anal fin rays.
One genus, *Melanocetus*, with nine species.

Family DICERATIIDAE.   Marine; Atlantic and Indian.

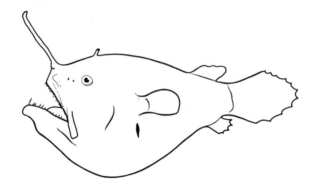

Only ceratioid with second cephalic ray well developed; dorsal fin with
five or six rays and four anal fin rays.

Three genera, *Diceratias, Laevoceratias* (description of males which may
be conspecific with females in the next genus), and *Paroneirodes*, with
four species.

Family HIMANTOLOPHIDAE—Footballfishes.   Marine; Atlantic, Indian, and
Pacific.

Females with some bony plates, each with a median spine, over body;
dorsal fin with five or six rays and four or five anal fin rays.

One genus, *Himantolophus*, with four species.

Family ONEIRODIDAE. Marine; Atlantic, Indian, and Pacific.

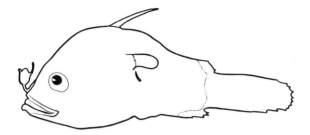

Skin naked or with short spines in some females; dorsal fin with 4–8 rays and 4–7 anal fin rays.

Fifteen genera with at least 33 species.

SUBFAMILY ONEIRODINAE. Jaws equal anteriorly.

Twelve genera (e.g., *Chaenophryne, Dolopichthys, Lophodolus, Microlophichthys,* and *Oneirodes*).

SUBFAMILY THAUMATICHTHYINAE. Upper jaw extending far beyond lower jaw. Given family status by Pietsch (1972).

Three genera, *Amacrodon, Lasiognathus,* and *Thaumatichthys.*

Family GIGANTACTINIDAE. Marine; Atlantic, Indian, and Pacific.

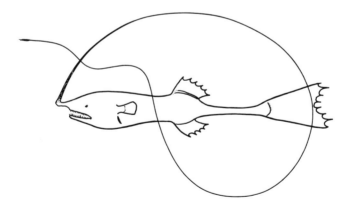

Body elongate in females; illicium almost as long as or longer than body; dorsal fin with 3–10 rays and 3–8 anal fin rays; five pectoral radials.

Two genera, *Gigantactis* and *Rhynchactis,* with about five species.

Family NEOCERATIIDAE. Marine; Atlantic, Indian, and Pacific.

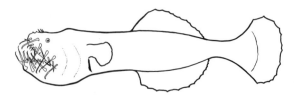

Illicium absent; long movable teeth outside jaws in females; mature males parasitic on females; dorsal fin with 11–13 rays and 10–13 anal rays.
   One species, *Neoceratias spinifer.*

Family CENTROPHRYNIDAE—Deep-Sea Anglerfish. Marine; Atlantic, Indian, and Pacific.

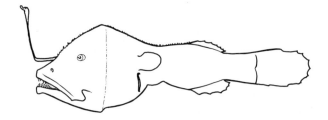

Small hyoid barbel present in young; skin with numerous small spines; dorsal fin with 5–7 rays and five or six anal fin rays.
   One species, *Centrophryne spinulosa.*

Family CERATIIDAE—Seadevils. Marine; Atlantic, Indian, and Pacific.

Females with two or three rays modified into caruncles (low fleshy appendages) in front of soft dorsal fin; mature males parasitic on females; dorsal and anal fin soft-rays usually four, rarely five.
   Two species, *Cryptopsaras couesi* and *Ceratias holboelli.*

Family LINOPHRYNIDAE. Marine; Atlantic, Indian, and Gulf of Panama.

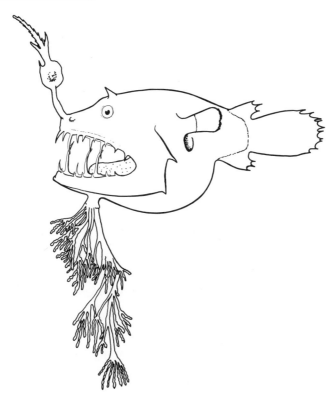

Mature males parasitic on females; dorsal and anal fin soft-rays usually three; hyoid barbel in female *Linophryne*.

Five genera, *Acentrophryne*, *Borophryne*, *Edriolychnus*, *Linophryne*, and *Photocorynus*, with about 20 species.

Order INDOSTOMIFORMES. Banister (1970) removed the Indostomidae from the Gasterosteiformes and placed it in the Paracanthopterygii. He believed it to have some affinity with the batrachoid-lophiidgobiesocid lineage. Its position in classification is particularly weak, and more work is required before convincing arguments can be presented on its evolutionary relationships.

Family INDOSTOMIDAE. Freshwater; Upper Burma in Lake Indawgyi.

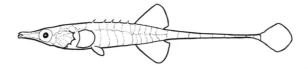

Body slender and covered with bony scutes; upper jaw not protrusible; opercle with six spines; dorsal and anal fins each with six rays, five isolated spines preceding the dorsal fin; 23 pectoral fin rays; pelvic fin with four soft rays, no spine; five branchiostegal rays; no ribs; usually 21 vertebrae; swim bladder physoclistic. Maximum length of Banister's (1970) specimens was 2.7 cm.

One species, *Indostomus paradoxus*.

Superorder ACANTHOPTERYGII

Greenwood et al. (1966) gave equal rank to the Atherinomorpha and Acanthopterygii (= present Percomorpha); Rosen and Patterson (1969) combined them under the category Acanthopterygii.

Fourteen orders and 245 families.

Series ATHERINOMORPHA

Opercular and preopercular margin without spines or serrations; ctenoid scales rare; branchiostegal rays 4–15; no orbitosphenoid; ligamentous support of pectoral skeleton (Baudelot's ligament) to basicranium; four cuboidal pectoral actinosts; caudal skeleton usually with two large triangular hypural plates, never more than four; swimbladder physoclistic.

Generally surface-feeding fish, mostly freshwater.

Our concept of the interrelations of the groups placed in this series has undergone much change. The present scheme follows Rosen (1964), Greenwood et al. (1966), and Rosen and Patterson (1969). The families included were placed by Berg (1940) in the orders Beloniformes (= Exocoetoidei), Cyprinodontiformes (excluding Amblyopsidae), Mugiliformes (only Atherinidae), and Phallostethiformes. Gosline (1971) follows a markedly different scheme. He recognizes, as orders, the Beloniformes and Cyprinodontiformes to be intermediate teleostean groups and places members of the Atherinoidei recognized here in the Perciformes, a higher teleostean group.

One order with 16 families, 167 genera, and about 827 species.

Order ATHERINIFORMES

Suborder Exocoetoidei (Synentognathi, Beloniformes). Dorsal, anal, and pelvic fins placed far back on the body; no spines in fins; single dorsal fin; pelvic fin with six rays; caudal fin with 13 branched rays; lateral line usually low on the body; narial opening single; branchiostegal rays 9–15; upper jaw bordered by premaxilla only; parietals absent.

About 31 genera and 138 species.

Family EXOCOETIDAE—Flyingfishes and Halfbeaks. Marine and freshwater; Atlantic, Indian, and Pacific.

Scales large (usually 38–60 in lateral line); mouth opening small; no isolated finlets; dorsal and anal fins usually with 8–16 rays each; teeth small.

SUBFAMILY EXOCOETINAE (FLYINGFISHES). Marine.

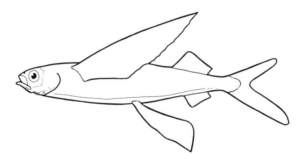

Jaws relatively short and equal in length (lower jaw produced in some juveniles); exceptionally large pectoral fins (gliding flights can be made out of water with the pectorals spread like wings); pelvic fins exceptionally large in some species (thus two-winged and four-winged types can be recognized); lower lobe of caudal fin longer than dorsal lobe (fin deeply forked); juveniles of many have a pair of long, flaplike whiskers. Maximum length 45 cm (attained in *Cypselurus californicus*); most species are less than 30 cm.

Eight genera, *Cypselurus, Danichthys, Exocoetus, Fodiator, Hirundichthys, Oxyporhamphus* (shows many intermediate characters between flyingfish and halfbeaks), *Parexocoetus,* and *Prognichthys,* with about 48 species.

SUBFAMILY HEMIRAMPHINAE (HALFBEAKS). Marine and freshwater.

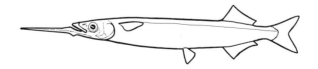

Upper jaw much shorter than lower (lower jaw elongate in most); pectoral and pelvic fins short; some species with lower lobe of caudal fin longer than upper lobe (fin rounded, truncate, or forked). Maximum length about 45 cm.

Eleven genera [e.g., *Chriodorus, Dermogenys* (a freshwater halfbeak with internal fertilization; gives birth to live young), *Euleptorhamphus* (with about 20 dorsal and anal fin rays and 105–125 lateral line scales), *Hemiramphus, Hyporhamphus, Nomorhamphus,* and *Zenarchopterus*] with at least 60 species.

Family BELONIDAE—Needlefishes.   Marine; epipelagic tropical and temperate seas; several species in fresh water.

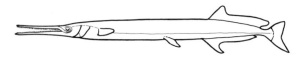

Scales small (usually 130–350 in lateral line); mouth opening large; no isolated finlets; dorsal fin rays usually 10–26; anal fin rays usually 14–23; both upper and lower jaws elongate with numerous needlelike teeth (two South American freshwater species have a short upper jaw, similar to halfbeaks); general body shape superficially resembling *Lepisosteus*. Some species are capable of high jumps out of water. Maximum length about 1.2 m, attained in several species, such as *Stongylura crocodilus* and *S. marina*.

Ten genera (e.g., *Ablennes, Belone, Strongylura,* and *Tylosurus*) with at least 26 species.

Family SCOMBERESOCIDAE—Sauries.   Marine; Atlantic and Pacific.

Scales small; 5–7 finlets after both dorsal and anal fins; jaws relatively short; teeth very small. One species, *Cololabis adocetus*, is neotenic. Maximum size about 35 cm.

Two genera, *Cololabis* and *Scomberesox*, with about four species.

Suborder Cyprinodontoidei (Microcyprini).   Pelvic fins and girdle present or absent; single dorsal fin; no spines in fins; lateral line developed chiefly on head, not on body; narial opening paired; 4–7 branchiostegal rays; upper jaw bordered by premaxillae only, usually protrusible; parietals present or absent.

About 90 genera with 489 species.

Superfamily Adrianichthyoidae. Vomer and supracleithrum absent.

Family ORYZIATIDAE—Medakas. Fresh- and brackish water; India and Japan to Indo-Australian Archipelago.

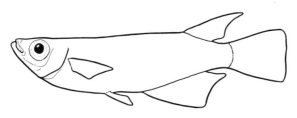

Jaws not tremendously enlarged; almost always egg layers.

One genus, *Oryzias*, with seven species.

Family ADRIANICHTHYIDAE—Adrianichthyids. Freshwater; Celebes Island.

Jaws tremendously enlarged; premaxilla not protrusible; scoop-shovel type mouth; egg layers. Maximum size up to 20 cm.

Two genera, *Adrianichthys* and *Xenopoecilus*, with three species.

Family HORAICHTHYIDAE. Freshwater; India (Bombay Province).

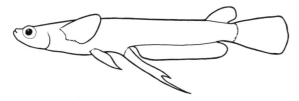

Body thin and translucent; dorsal fin small, near caudal fin; anal fin elongate; right pelvic fin usually absent. Superficially similar to the poeciliid *Tomeurus*. Maximum length about 3 cm.

One species, *Horaichthys setnai*, found in 1937 (Hubbs, 1941).

Superfamily Cyprinodontoidae.   Vomer and supracleithrum present.

Family CYPRINODONTIDAE—Killifishes (Toothcarps).   Fresh- and brackish water, rarely coastal marine; southeastern Canada to South America, Africa, Madagascar, southern Europe, and southern Asia (see map on p. 339).

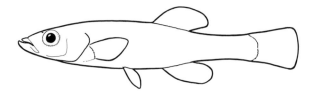

Egg layers, no gonopodium. Some are annual fishes, with eggs that can avoid desiccation, thus carrying the species over dry periods. Ctenoid scales in males of most species. The pelvic fins and girdle are absent in the New World *Crenichthys, Cyprinodon diabolis, Empetrichthys*, and *Megupsilon aporus* (a new species described in 1972 by R. R. Miller and V. Walters) and the Old World *Aphanius apodus*. One species, *Rivulus marmoratus*, has simultaneously functional ovary and testis. Fertilization is internal; then eggs are layed (Harrington, 1961). Maximum size up to 15 cm.

About 50 genera (e.g., *Adinia, Aphanius, Aphyosemion, Crenichthys, Cynolebias, Cyprinodon, Empetrichthys, Fundulus, Lamprichthys, Lucania, Jordanella, Orestias, Pantanodon, Procatopus*, and *Rivulus*) with at least 300 species.

Family GOODEIDAE—Goodeids.   Freshwater; west central Mexico.

Internal fertilization; bear young alive; anterior rays of anal fin in male crowded, shortened, and slightly separated from rest of fin (primitive gonopodium?); males with muscular organ (termed a "pseudophallus")

perhaps functional in insemination; ovaries partly united into a single median organ; embryos and newborn young usually have a placentalike trophotaeniae (ribbonlike extensions from anal region associated with nutrition and respiration). Reviewed by Miller and Fitzsimons (1971).

This family, centered in the Lio Lerma basin, has species of many diverse body forms (deep-bodied to long-bodied) and feeding habits (carnivores to herbivores). Maximum length up to 20 cm.

About 12 genera [e.g., *Ameca, Ataeniobius, Characodon, Ilyodon, Girardinichthys* (=*Lermichthys*), *Skiffia* (=*Neotoca* and *Ollentodon*), and *Xenotoca*] with about 34 species.

Family ANABLEPIDAE—Four-Eyed Fishes. Freshwater, rarely brackish; southern Mexico to northern South America.

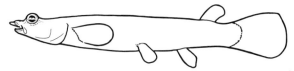

Eye divided (cornea and retina) into upper and lower "eyes"; water line in surface-swimming individuals in center of eye; anterior rays of anal fin modified into tubelike gonopodium for intromission; bear young alive.

In some males the gonopodium can move only to the left; in others, only to the right. In females the genital aperture is open to the right or to the left. In mating a left-handed (sinistral) male must copulate with a right-handed (dextral) female and vica versa. Both sexes are divided equally in dextral and sinistral mating types. Maximum length up to 30 cm, usually somewhat less.

One genus, *Anableps*, with three species.

Family JENYNSIIDAE—Jenynsiids. Freshwater; southern South America.

Tubular gonopodium formed from anal fin rays; bear young alive. Dextral and sinistral mating types occur as in the Anablepidae. Maximum size up to 12 cm.

One genus, *Jenynsia*, with about three species.

Family POECILIIDAE—Livebearers. Fresh- and brackish water; low elevations from eastern United States to northeastern Argentina (see map on p. 339).

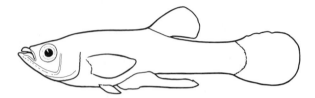

First three anal rays unbranched. Male with elongated anterior anal fin rays (gonopodium) usually with internal fertilization; bear young alive. Reviewed by Rosen and Bailey (1963).

The world-famous guppy, *Poecilia reticulata*, and mosquitofish, *Gambusia affinis*, are popular for aquariums and mosquito control, respectively. All-female forms are known from *Poeciliopsis* (Moore et al., 1970; Schultz, 1973) in northwestern Mexico, whereas in *Poecilia* (=*Mollienesia*) *formosa* virtually all individuals are females. In the latter species (and in some *Poeciliopsis*) the spermatozoan of another species stimulates egg development but does not contribute any genetic material. Maximum size about 18 cm; most species are much smaller.

SUBFAMILY POECILIINAE. About 20 genera (e.g., *Cnesterodon, Gambusia, Girardinus, Heterandria, Poecilia,* and *Xiphophorus*) with 136 species.

SUBFAMILY TOMEURINAE. Gonopodium under pectoral fins; female lays eggs. One species, *Tomeurus gracilus,* in northeastern South America.

SUBFAMILY XENODEXIINAE. One species, *Xenodexia ctenolepis,* in Guatemala.

Suborder Atherinoidei. Lateral line absent or very weak; usually two dorsal fins; the first, if present, with flexible spines; anal fin usually preceded by a spine; narial openings paired; 5–7 branchiostegal rays; parietals present.

Gosline (1971) views the affinity of the five families of this group to be with the members of his suborder Mugiloidei (which includes the polynemids, sphyraenids, and mugilids), the whole group being placed in the Perciformes.

About 46 genera with 200 species.

Superfamily Atherinoidae. Pelvic fins present and abdominal, subabdominal, or thoracic in position, not modified into clasping organ.

Family MELANOTAENIIDAE—Rainbowfishes. Freshwater, some in weak brackish water; Australia, Aru Island, and New Guinea.

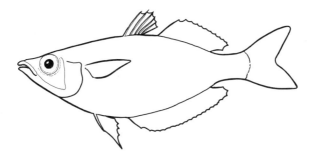

Body deep and compressed; dorsal fins narrowly separated; distance between fins equal to or less than basal length of first dorsal fin; anal fin with one spine and 17–30 soft rays; base is longer than second dorsal fin base; lateral line weakly developed; scales relatively large (28–64 in longitudinal series). Maximum length about 10 cm.

Six genera, *Centratherina, Chilatherina, Glossolepis, Melanotaenia, Nematocentris,* and *Zantecla,* with about 19 species.

Family ATHERINIDAE—Silversides. Marine; tropical to temperate seas; some in fresh water.

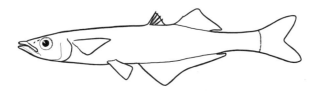

Two widely separated dorsal fins; no lateral line, broad silvery lateral band (black in preserved specimens); pelvic fins usually abdominal; scales relatively large (usually 31–50 in lateral series, more in *Labidesthes*); vertebrae 32–60.

The small grunion, *Leuresthes tenuis,* of southern California has the peculiar adaptation of spawning high on beaches at night during the period of the highest tides, usually from March to August (Walker, 1952). The young hatch out in future high tides.

Most atherinids are marine. There are, however, many species in fresh water; for example, 18 species of *Chirostoma* live in fresh water in the southern portion of the Mexican plateau (Barbour, 1973), whereas *Labidesthes sicculus* is spread across most of the eastern United States. Several species of *Telmatherina* occur in lakes and streams in the Celebes and several species of *Pseudomugil* (and others) occur in fresh water in Australia and New Guinea. Maximum length 60 cm.

About 29 genera (e.g., *Allanetta, Atherinops, Atherion, Bedotia, Chirostoma, Craterocephalus, Labidesthes, Leuresthes, Membras, Menidia, Pranesus, Pseudomugil, Stenatherina,* and *Telmatherina*) with about 156 species.

Family ISONIDAE.   Marine; South Africa, India, Japan, Australia, Hawaii, and Chile.

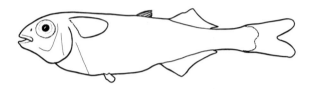

Upper jaw teeth confined to symphyseal portion of premaxillae; pelvis with lateral spur extending upward between pleural ribs almost to vertebral column; epurals absent; autopalatine present.

Two genera with six species: *Iso* with five species, and *Notocheirus hubbsi* (known from Chile).

Superfamily Phallostethoidae.   Body somewhat translucent in life, compressed, and moderately elongate; mouth protractile; muscular and bony copulatory organ (priapium) under throat of male (a complicated internal structure that contains ducts from kidney and gonads as well as terminal parts of intestine); priapium sometimes has a slender anterior, curved bony projection (toxactinium) and one or two posterior projections (ctenactinia) which may be used as claspers; pelvic fins modified to form part of a complex thoracic clasping organ in male (serving to clasp female during copulation; pelvics absent in female); internal fertilization; anus below or in front of pectorals; usually two dorsal fins, the first with one or two tiny spines and the second (completely separated from the first) with 5–10 soft rays; anal fin with one short spine and 11–29 soft rays; caudal fin forked; pectoral fins high, with 10 to 11 rays; two pectoral radials; scales cycloid, 31–58 in lateral series; vertebrae 34–38; no orbitosphenoid; eggs with a filamentous process as in Atherinidae.

Two families with nine genera and 19 species (Bailey, 1936; Herre, 1939, 1953; Roberts, 1971b,c). This group probably originated from the atherinids, the most closely related ones being in the subfamily Taeniomembrasinae (e.g., *Stenatherina*) (Roberts, 1971c).

Family NEOSTETHIDAE.   Brackish and freshwater (rarely coastal marine); Southeast Asia.

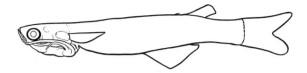

Toxactinium absent; one or two long, curved, nonserrated ctenactinia; usually five branchiostegal rays. Maximum length about 3.7 cm, attained in *Gulaphallus eximus*.

Two subfamilies, seven genera, and 16 species.

SUBFAMILY NEOSTETHINAE. Philippines, Borneo, Malay Peninsula, and adjacent areas. Anterior end of ctenactinium exposed.

Five genera, *Ceratostethus, Solenophallus, Plectrostethus, Neostethus,* and *Manacopus,* with 13 species.

SUBFAMILY GULAPHALLINAE. Luzon, Philippines. Anterior end of ctenactinium fits into a fleshy sheath in the anterior end of the priapium.

Two genera: *Gulaphallus* (two species) and *Mirophallus* (one species).

Family PHALLOSTETHIDAE. Brackish and freshwater; Malaya and Thailand.

Toxactinium present (long bony process projecting from anterior of priapium); ctenactinium single, serrated or not; four branchiostegal rays. Members of this family probably arose from a *Neostethus* lineage. Maximum length about 2.3 cm.

Two genera: *Phallostethus* (with one species, *P. dunckeri*, known only from the four type specimens collected before 1904 from the mouth of the Muar River, Malaya) and *Phenacostethus* (with two species, one from fresh water in Thailand and the other from the Indian Ocean coast of Thailand).

Series PERCOMORPHA

Order LAMPRIDIFORMES. No true spines in fins; premaxillae excludes maxillae from gape; unique type of protrusible upper jaw (maxillae, instead of being ligamentously attached to the ethmoid and palatine, slides in and out with the highly protactile premaxillae in at least the first four suborders); pelvic fins with 0–17 rays; swim bladder, when present, physoclistic; orbitosphenoid present in some.

The scope of this order has been increased over the years. Berg (1940) placed only the first five families in the Lampridiformes (Allotriognathi). Greenwood et al. (1966) added Stylephoridae. The last four families, added by Rosen and Patterson (1969), are retained only provisionally. Rosen's (1973) study suggests that the Mirapinnidae, Eutaeniophoridae, and Megalomycteridae are better placed in the related order Beryciformes. With the Ateleopodidae he finds that their gill-arch structure does not support a lampridiform alignment [indeed, their fragmented pharyngeal tooth plates, which are separated from their endoskeletal support, are similar (secondarily so) to that of elopomorphs and osteoglossomorphs]. In the absence of a more plausible alignment they are retained in the lampridiforms on the basis of having a lampridiform-like upper jaw specialization.

About 18 genera with 35 species.

Suborder Lampridoidei.

Family LAMPRIDIDAE—Opah. Marine; Atlantic and Pacific.

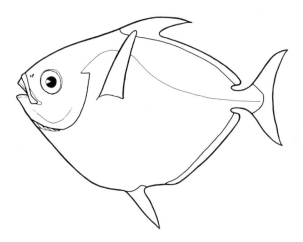

Body oval-shaped and compressed; lateral line arched high in front; dorsal and anal fins long (dorsal usually with 50–55 rays and anal usually with 34–41 rays); pelvic fin rays 15–17; minute cycloid scales. Its food consists primarily of squids, octopuses, and crustaceans. Maximum size up to 1.8 m.

One species, *Lampris guttatus (-regius)*.

Suborder Veliferoidei. Walters (1960) reviews this group.

Family VELIFERIDAE. Marine; Indian and western and mid-Pacific.

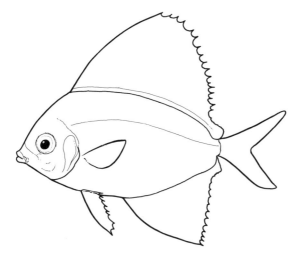

Body deep and compressed; pelvic fins with eight or nine rays; dorsal and anal fins long; swim bladder extending far beyond anus; six branchiostegal rays; vertebrae 33 or 34 (16 abdominal and 17 or 18 caudal).

One genus, *Velifer* (=*Metavelifer*), with two or three species.

Suborder Trachipteroidei. Body very thin and ribbonlike; anal fin short or absent; pelvic fin rays 0–10; six or seven branchiostegal rays; swim bladder, when present, does not extend past the anus; each dorsal fin ray has a lateral spine at its base; suborbital series absent except for the lachrymal and second suborbital (jugal); frontal bones separated by a groove; vertebrae 62–200.

Walters and Fitch (1960) review this group.

Family LOPHOTIDAE—Crestfishes. Marine; most oceans.

Body with small deciduous cycloid scales (sometimes appearing naked); anal fin present (short and posterior); caudal fin normal; pelvic fin, if present, with 1–9 rays; dorsal fin very long with about 220–392 rays and originating above or before tip of snout; swim bladder present; ink sac present which discharges into cloaca. The extinct *Protolophotus* is known from Oligocene deposits in Iran.

Perhaps only two species, *Lophotus capellei* and *L.* (=*Eumecichthys*) *fiski*.

Family TRACHIPTERIDAE—Ribbonfishes. Marine; Arctic, Atlantic (including Mediterranean), Indian, and Pacific.

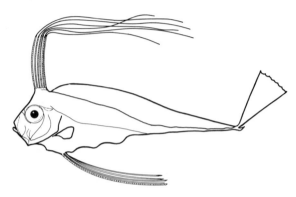

Body naked, with deciduous cycloid scales, or with deciduous modified ctenoid scales (tubercles may also be present); no anal fin; caudal fin long and at a right angle to the body, consisting of upper lobe only, *Desmodema* has the few caudal rays parallel to the caudal peduncle; pelvic fins with 1–10 rays; dorsal fin very long, originating distinctly behind tip of snout; eye large; teeth present; ribs absent; swim bladder rudimentary or absent; vertebrae 62–109. Allometric growth results in various body shapes during growth. Maximum length about 1.7 m, attained in *Trachipterus altivelis*.

Fitch (1964) and Palmer (1961) discuss various members of the group.

Three genera, *Desmodema*, *Trachipterus* (including king-of-the-salmon), and *Zu*, with about seven species.

Family REGALECIDAE—Oarfishes. Marine; all oceans.

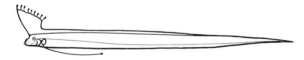

Scales absent; no anal fin; pelvic fin very elongate, slender, with 1–5 rays; dorsal fin very long, originating distinctly behind tip of snout; first few rays are elongate and bright red; eye small; no teeth; swim bladder absent. *Regalecus glesne* (king-of-the-herring) has 40–58 gill rakers; *Regalecus* (=*Agrostichthys*) *parkeri* has about 8–10 gill rakers. This group is probably responsible for many sea-serpent stories. Maximum length up to about 8 m.

One genus, *Regalecus* (=*Agrostichthys*), with two species.

Suborder Stylephoroidei.

Family STYLEPHORIDAE—Tube-Eye or Thread-Tail. Marine abyssal; most oceans.

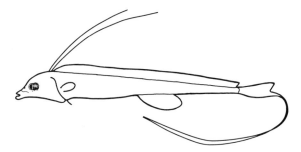

Body ribbonlike; dorsal fin extending from nape to tail, with 110–122 rays; anal fin short, 16 or 17 rays; pectoral fin rays 10 or 11; pelvic fin with only one ray; caudal fin in two parts, upper with five rays and lower with two extremely elongate rays; eyes large, telescopic, may be directed forward or upward; mouth small and protractile; teeth small; no swim bladder. This fish swims in a vertical position, head uppermost. Maximum body size 28 cm.

One species, *Stylephorus chordatus.*

Suborder Ateleopodoidei

Family ATELEOPODIDAE. Marine; Caribbean Sea, eastern Atlantic, and Indo-Pacific.

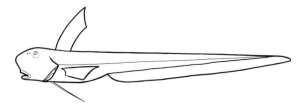

Caudal fin reduced, united with the long anal fin; pelvic fins with two rays (which appear as a single filamentous ray) inserted in front of the pectorals.

Three genera, *Ateleopus, Ijimaia,* and *Parateleopus,* with about 11 species.

Suborder Mirapinnatoidei. No scales; gill membranes separate and free from isthmus; fins without spines; dorsal and anal fins opposite one another; pelvic fins jugular, 4–10 rays; 3–5 branchiostegal rays.

The first specimen of this group was collected in 1911. Bertelsen and Marshall (1956) placed the two families in a new order, Miripinnati, placed here in the order Lampridiformes as advised by Rosen and Patterson (1969). All specimens are immature and 5 cm or less.

Family MIRAPINNIDAE—Hairyfish. Marine; Atlantic.

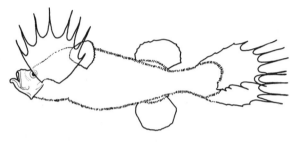

Body moderately elongate, covered with short hairlike pile; two halves of caudal fin overlapping; large, winglike pelvic fins; pectoral fins relatively small and placed high on body.

One species, *Mirapinna esau*.

Family EUTAENIOPHORIDAE (Taeniophoridae)—Tapetails or Ribbonbearers. Marine; Atlantic, Indian, and western Pacific.

Body very elongate, smooth; caudal fin in juveniles with extremely long tapelike streamer (several times body length); dorsal and anal fins near caudal fin; dorsal and anal fins each with 15–31 rays.

Bertelsen and Marshall (1958) give reasons for erecting the name *Eutaeniophorus* to replace *Taeniophorus* and present distributional records.

Two genera, *Eutaeniophorus* and *Parataeniophorus*, with three species.

Suborder Megalomycteroidei. This suborder and the one included family were erected and described by Myers and Freihofer (1966). Five species (Goodyear, 1970).

Family MEGALOMYCTERIDAE—Largenose Fishes. Marine, deep-sea; Atlantic and Pacific.

Olfactory organs exceptionally large; pelvic fin usually absent [present and inserted slightly ahead of the pectorals in *Megalomycter* (three rays) and *Ataxolepis henactis* (one ray)]; fins without spines; dorsal and anal fins near caudal fin; vertebrae 45–52.

Four genera, *Ataxolepis*, with two species (one in the Atlantic and one in the tropical eastern Pacific), and the monotypic *Cetomimoides*, *Megalomycter*, and *Vitiaziella*.

†**Order CTENOTHRISSIFORMES.**   Contains various marine Upper Cretaceous forms (*Aulolepis*, *Ctenothrissa*, *Pateroperca*, and *Patterson-ichthys*). There is much diversity between these forms and the group may not be monophyletic. Only the anatomy of the first two genera is known well enough to include them together as ctenothrissiforms with any certainty. The group is placed in the Acanthopterygii following Rosen (1971). Rosen (1973), however, considers it possible that they are a "primitive sister group of the paracanthopterygian-acanthopterygian assemblage" and classifies them with that assemblage under the category of Sept Acanthomorpha.

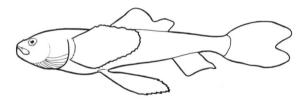

The family Macristiidae, with two marine Atlantic species, *Macristium chavesi* and *Macristiella perlucens* (shown above), which are based on three specimens, one now lost and two larvae (Marshall, 1961; Berry and Robins, 1967), was formerly placed in this order. Rosen (1971) presents evidence that these "species" may be larval or juvenile scopelomorphs.

Order BERYCIFORMES.   The composition of this order has been markedly changed from that given in Greenwood et al. (1966), largely on the work of Rosen and Patterson (1969) (see notes under Ceto-mimoidei).

This group may still be polyphyletic. Rosen (1973), in a study based on the pharyngobranchials and caudal skeleton, suggests that beryciforms

are divisable into five groups: (1) the trachichthyoids with Trachichthyidae, Anomalopidae, Monocentridae, Diretmidae, and possibly the
Korsogasteridae, Sorosichthyidae, and Paradiretmidae; (2) the Berycidae; (3) the Holocentridae; (4) the stephanoberycoids with Barbourisiidae, Rondeletiidae, Gibberichthyidae, Cetomimidae, Mirapinnidae,
Eutaeniophoridae, Megalomycteridae, Melamphaeidae, Stephanoberycidae, and Anoplogasteridae; and (5) the Polymixiidae. A relationship to
the zeoids, lampridiforms, and the Cretaceous dinopterygoids (*Dinop-
teryx, Pycnosteroides, Aipichthys,* and *Pharmacichthys*) of southwest Asia is
also suggested.

About 39 genera with about 143 species.

Suborder Stephanoberycoidei (*Xenoberyces, in part*).   Large cavernous
head with mucous areas; platelike deciduous scales.

Species of this suborder attain a maximum length of about 8 cm.

Family STEPHANOBERYCIDAE—Pricklefishes.   Marine; Atlantic Gulf Stream and
Tuamotus.

Dorsal, anal, and pelvic fins without spines; body spiny; pelvic fin
abdominal or subabdominal; no orbitosphenoid; no subocular shelf;
30–33 vertebrae.

Three monotypic genera: *Acanthochaenus, Malacosarcus,* and *Stephano-
beryx.*

Family MELAMPHAEIDAE—Bigscale Fishes.   Marine, bathypelagic; most oceans.

Dorsal fin single but with spines and soft rays; pelvic fin with one spine
and 6–9 soft rays; body elongate and compressed; large deciduous cycloid scales; no lateral line; no opercular spines; no orbitosphenoid; no
subocular shelf; 24–31 vertebrae.

At least four genera, *Melamphaes, Poromitra, Scopeloberyx,* and *Scope-
logadus,* with about 20 species.

Family GIBBERICHTHYIDAE—Gibberfish.   Marine; North Atlantic and Madagascar.

Pelvic fin subabdominal, with one spine and five soft rays; scales large, cycloid; vertical rows of papillae on sides of body (over the vertical lateral
line tubes); 30 or 31 vertebrae.

One species, *Gibberichthys pumilis,* known only from four specimens.

Family KASIDOROIDAE.   Marine, bathypelagic; western Atlantic and western Indian.

Pelvics abdominal, with six simple rays; fins without spines; dorsal fin rays 12–14; anal fin rays 10–12; principal caudal rays 19; nine branchiostegal rays; gill rakers 18–22. Maximum length about 21 mm.

This family was first erected by Robins and de Sylva (1965) for *Kasidoron edom* and further described by Robins (1966). Thorp (1969) described the second species, *K. latifrons,* based on a 21 mm specimen taken in 1965 from the stomach of an *Alepisaurus* in the western Indian Ocean.

Greenwood et al. (1966) placed this family in the Mirapinnatoidei, one of four suborders of their Cetomimiformes. Rosen and Patterson (1969) felt that *Kasidoron* might be only the larva of *Gibberichthys pumilis,* which it closely resembles. Gosline (1971) speculated along similar lines; and Robins (1973) stated that *Kasidoron* is a prejuvenile of *Gibberichthys* (and related the Gibberichthyidae to the stephanoberyciform-cetomimiform-mirapinniform assemblage rather than to the Beryciformes). Certain other provisionally recognized families contain members that may also be only the young of known species placed in another family.

Suborder Berycoidei.   Well-known fossil record from Cretaceous.

The families Sorosichthyidae (with *Sorosichthys*) and Paradiretmidae (with *Paradiretmus*) are not treated here. They were erected by G. P. Whitley of Australia and placed in the Beryciformes by Patterson (1964), McAllister (1968), and Rosen (1973). They are thought to be related to the Trachichthyidae.

About 23 genera and 102 species.

Family TRACHICHTHYIDAE—Slimeheads.   Marine; Atlantic, Indian, and Pacific.

Pelvic fin with one normal spine and six or seven soft rays; dorsal fin spines 3–8; orbitosphenoid present; scales normal.

Five genera, *Gephyroberyx, Hoplostethus* (=*Leiogaster*), *Optivus, Paratrachichthys,* and *Trachichthys,* with about 14 species.

Family DIRETMIDAE.   Marine; Atlantic and Pacific.

No lateral line; sharp edge to abdomen; pelvic fin with laminar spine and five soft rays; orbitosphenoid present.

One species, *Diretmus argenteus.*

Family KORSOGASTERIDAE.   Marine; Atlantic and Pacific.

Body covered with dermal prickles, no scales.

One species, *Korsogaster nanus*. Known only from two specimens, one taken in 1927 from the Bahamas, and one in 1968 from the central Pacific (Johnson, 1970). These specimens are probably young *Hoplostethus*, and therefore the family name should probably be regarded as a junior synonym of the Trachichthyidae.

Family ANOPLOGASTERIDAE—Fangtooth.   Marine oceanic.

Body short and deep; numerous long fanglike teeth on jaws; scales small or minute; no orbitosphenoid; no subocular shelf.

One species, *Anoplogaster* (=*Caulolepis*) *cornuta*.

Family BERYCIDAE—Alfonsinos.   Marine; Atlantic, Indian, and Pacific.

Pelvic fin with one spine and 7–13 soft rays; dorsal fin with 4–7 spines and 12–19 soft rays; orbitosphenoid present; 24 vertebrae.

Two genera, *Beryx* and *Centroberyx* (=*Hoplopteryx*), with about 10 species.

Family MONOCENTRIDAE—Pinecone Fishes.   Marine; Indo-Pacific.

Pelvic fin with one large spine and three small soft rays; dorsal fin spines alternating from side to side; heavy platelike scales over body; two phosphorescent light organs under lower jaw; orbitosphenoid present.

One genus, *Monocentris*, with two species.

Family ANOMALOPIDAE—Lanterneye Fishes.   Marine; scattered warm-water localities, primarily Indo-Pacific.

Pelvic fin with one spine and five soft rays; light organs beneath eye with varied "shutter" arrangements which allow them to be turned off at will; orbitosphenoid present. This family contains, along with *Porichthys,* the few shallow-water fishes with luminous organs.

Three monotypic genera: *Anomalops, Kryptophanaron,* and *Photoblepharon.*

Family HOLOCENTRIDAE—Squirrelfishes. Tropical marine; Atlantic, Indian, and Pacific.

Pelvic fin with one spine and 5–8 (usually seven) soft rays; long dorsal fin with spiny portion (10–13 spines) and soft-rayed portion divided by a notch; caudal fin forked, with 18 or 19 principal rays; scales large and ctenoid (extremely rough); eyes large; opercle with spiny edge; orbitosphenoid present; color usually reddish.

Squirrelfishes are mostly nocturnal, usually hiding in crevices or beneath ledges of reefs in the daytime (along with cardinalfishes, bigeyes, and sweepers). Unlike most beryciforms, which are deep-sea, most species occur between the shoreline and 100 m. Adults tend to remain close to the bottom (the very young are planktonic). Maximum length about 60 cm, attained in *Holocentrus spinifer.*

Nine genera with about 70 species.

SUBFAMILY HOLOCENTRINAE (SQUIRRELFISHES). A strong spine present at angle of preoperculum (sometimes a toxin is associated with this spine); longest anal spine usually longer than or equal to longest dorsal spine; swim bladder tubular, extending entire length of body (contacting the skull in a few species).

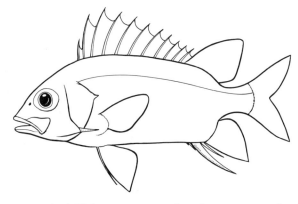

The circumtropical *Holocentrus* contains the most species in this subfamily.

Three genera: *Holocentrus, Adioryx,* and *Flammeo.*

SUBFAMILY MYRIPRISTINAE (SOLDIERFISHES). No enlarged preopercular spine; longest anal spine usually shorter than longest dorsal spine; swim bladder constricted in anterior third to form two more or less separate chambers (anterior section with two anterolateral projections).

In this subfamily, *Myripristis* with 16 species, is the largest genus. As in many other circumtropical genera most species occur around the Indo-Australian Archipelago. The genus is absent from the Mediterranean, and the most wide-ranging species, *M. murdjan,* extends from the Galapagos Islands to the Red Sea (Greenfield, 1968).

Six genera: *Beanea, Myripristis, Ostichthys, Plectrypops, Holotrachys,* and *Corniger.*

Suborder Cetomimoidei (*Cetunculi, Xenoberyces, in part*). Body whale-shaped; mouth very large and stomach highly distensible; eyes well-developed to degenerate; lateral line made up of enormous hollow tubes; luminous tissue on body; no fin spines; no swim bladder; color usually orange and red on a black body. Bathypelagic.

Greenwood et al. (1966) placed a heterogeneous assemblage of poorly known oceanic fish together in their order Cetomimiformes of the superorder Protacanthopterygii. Gosline (1971) recognized a different composition in the order (he excluded the giganturoids and included the megalomycterids and gibberichthyids) but acknowledged its composite origin. Here, Rosen and Patterson (1969) are followed in placing three families in a suborder of the Beryciformes. Other members of the order Cetomimiformes (given by Greenwood et al., 1966) were placed by them in the Lampridiformes or elsewhere in the Beryciformes as I have done here. Size up to 15 cm.

Seven genera and about 13 species (all rare). Harry (1952) and Rofen (1959) discuss the families.

Family RONDELETIIDAE—Redmouth Whalefishes. Marine; oceanic.

Box-shaped head with bony protuberances; skin smooth; lateral line system composed of as many as 20 vertical mucous tubes outlined with papillae; pelvics subabdominal; three epurals and six hypurals; vertebrae 27.

Two species, *Rondeletia bicolor* and *R. loricata.*

Family BARBOURISIIDAE. Marine; Atlantic and Madagascar.

Pelvic fins present, subabdominal; skin spiny; vertebrae 42.
   One species, *Barbourisia rufa*.

Family CETOMIMIDAE—Flabby Whalefishes.   Marine; oceanic.

Pelvic fins absent; skin naked; eyes reduced or rudimentary; three or four
gills; vertebrae 51 or 52.
   Five genera (e.g., *Cetomimus, Cetostomus, Ditropichthys,* and *Gyrinomimus*)
and 10 species.

Order ZEIFORMES.   No orbitosphenoid; pelvic fin with one spine and
5–9 soft rays; simple posttemporal fused to skull; more or less distinct
spinous anal fin with 1–4 spines; body usually thin and deep; jaws
usually greatly distensible.
   The membership in families is based largely on Mead (1957), Myers
(1937, 1960b), and Smith (1960). The Pacific genera, *Capromimus* and
Cyttomimus, are of uncertain position. The classification of this order is
particularly weak. Most are deep-sea forms. The zeids, however, tend to
be midwater.
   About 25 genera and about 50 species.

Family PARAZENIDAE—Parazen.   Marine; Japan and Cuba.

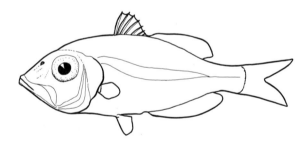

Body compressed and elongate; premaxillaries extremely protractile; two
lateral lines, uniting behind the soft dorsal fin; two dorsal fins, the first
with eight spines, second with 26–30 soft rays; anal fin with one spine
and 31 soft rays; pectoral fin with 15 or 16 rays; pelvic fins thoracic, with
one unbranched ray and six branched rays; principal caudal rays 11;
scales weakly ctenoid; three and one-half gills, 34 vertebrae.
   One species, *Parazen pacificus.* Mead (1957) stated, however, that the
Japanese and Cuban populations are probably specifically or subspeci-
fically distinct.

Family MACRUROCYTTIDAE. Marine.

SUBFAMILY MACRUROCYTTINAE. Luzon (Philippines).

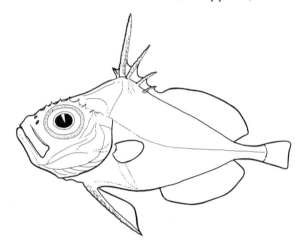

Spinous dorsal elevated, with five spines; anal fin without spine, only 22 soft rays; pectoral rays 15.

One species, *Macrurocyttus acanthopodus,* described by Fowler (1933).

SUBFAMILY ZENIONTINAE. Two genera, *Cyttula* and *Zenion.*

Family ZEIDAE—Dories. Marine; Atlantic and Pacific.

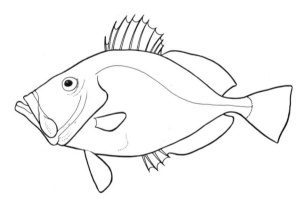

Small spines or bucklers at base of dorsal and anal fin rays; eight or nine spinous plates along abdomen; some with large round black spot surrounded by a yellow ring in center of body; long trailing filaments extending from the 10 or so spines in adults.

Contains seven genera in three groups (which may deserve subfamily status): *Zeus* and *Zenopsis* in the first, *Cyttus* and *Cyttoidops* in the second, and *Cyttopsis*, *Zen*, and *Stethopristes* in the third.

Family OREOSOMATIDAE—Oreos.   Marine; Antarctic, Atlantic, Indian, and Pacific. Known primarily from off South Africa and southern Australia.

Body very deep and compressed; mouth upturned, protractile; scales small, cycloid or ctenoid; young with conical scutes on parts of body; pelvic fin with a spine.

Six genera, *Allocyttus* (two species), *Cyttosoma* (two species), *Neocyttus* (two species), *Pseudocyttus* (southern Brazil and South Africa), *Oreosoma* (described in 1839 and not positively taken since; the type probably represents the young of some member of the family), and *Xenocyttus* [known from one specimen taken from the stomach of an Antarctic whale, described by Abe (1957)]. Karrer (1968) gives locality records for the above species.

Family GRAMMICOLEPIDIDAE—Grammicolepids.   Marine; deep-sea; South Africa, western Pacific, southwestern Atlantic, and Carribean Sea.

Scales vertically elongate; mouth small, nearly vertical; pelvic fin with one spine and six soft rays; 46 vertebrae.

Three genera with four species are tentatively recognized here. The group has been reviewed by Myers (1937) and Smith (1960). A number of problems remain with the group. *Grammicolepis brachiusculus* is known from the Caribbean (Cuba). *Vesposus egregius*, based on one specimen brought to the surface in a lava flow in 1919 in Hawaii (Gosline and Brock, 1960), was thought by Myers (1937) also to belong to this species (but this remains open to question). *Daramattus* contains two species, *D. armatus* from South Africa and possibly Japan and *D. americanus* from the western Atlantic. *Xenolepidichthys dagleishi* is recorded from southern Brazil, the Caribbean, South Africa, the Philippines, and Japan.

Family CAPROIDAE—Boarfishes.   Marine; Atlantic, Indian, and Pacific.

Body covered with small ctenoid scales; dorsal fin spines 7–9; two or three anal fin spines; pelvic fin with one spine and five soft rays; caudal fin rounded; vertebrae 21–23.

Subfamily Antigoniinae.   Red colored fishes with extremely deep and slim bodies (rhomboid shape); dorsal fin with eight or nine spines and 26–38 soft rays; three anal spines, separate from the anal soft rays.

In the western Atlantic they range from the northern United States to southern Brazil between approximately 70–600 m (Berry, 1959). Both Berry and Fraser-Brunner (1950a) have studied *Antigonia*.

One genus, *Antigonia,* with five species.

SUBFAMILY CAPROINAE.   Similar to Zeidae except that there are no abdominal spinous plates.

One species, *Capros aper.*

Order SYNGNATHIFORMES (Solenichthys).   Mouth small, at end of tube-shaped snout; tufted lobelike gills; pelvic fins, when present, abdominal; postcleithrum present; upper jaw not protractile; circumorbital bones, except for the lachrymal, absent; aglomerular kidney.

Many workers combine the Syngnathiformes and Gasterosteiformes either under the former (e.g., Gosline, 1971) or the latter (e.g., Greenwood et al., 1966; Bailey and Cavender, 1971) ordinal names. Monophyly has not been established and McAllister (1968) has the two groups on different lineages. Until their relationships are clarified it seems best to place them in separate orders.

Forty-four genera and about 200 species.

Suborder Aulostomoidei.   Teeth small or absent; lateral line well developed to absent; four or five branchiostegal rays; gills comblike.

Superfamily Aulostomoidae.   Anterior four vertebrae elongate; ribs absent; three median, well-developed bones dorsally behind head (nuchal plates); usually six pelvic rays.

Family AULOSTOMIDAE—Trumpetfishes.   Tropical marine; Atlantic and Indo-Pacific.

Body compressed, elongate, and scaly; fleshy barbel at tip of lower jaw; series of 8–12 isolated dorsal spines followed by a normal dorsal fin of 23–28 soft rays; anal rays 25–28; caudal fin rounded; anus far behind pelvics; lateral line well developed; abdominal vertebrae with two transverse processes of equal size (or a divided process); body musculature with a network of bony struts that forms an interwoven pattern (observed in *Aulostomus chinensis* from Easter Island).

Trumpetfishes are usually seen on reefs with their body at odd angles,

often vertical with head downward. Maximum length up to 80 cm.
One genus, *Aulostomus*, with four species.

Family FISTULARIIDAE—Cornetfishes. Tropical marine; Atlantic, Indian, and Pacific.

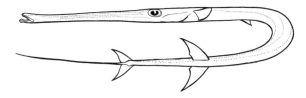

Body depressed, elongate, and naked or with minute prickles and linear series of scutes (no scales); no barbel on jaw; no dorsal spines; anal and dorsal fins each with about 13–17 soft rays; caudal fin forked with middle ray elongate; anus shortly behind pelvics; lateral line well developed; abdominal vertebrae with two transverse processes but the posterior ones very reduced. The long tubular snout, which functions as a pipette, is an excellent adaptation for feeding among reefs. Maximum length up to 1.8 m, attained in *Fistularia tabacaria*.
One genus, *Fistularia*, with four species.

Superfamily Centriscoidae. Anterior five or six vertebrae elongate.

Family MACRORHAMPHOSIDAE—Snipefishes. Tropical and subtropical marine; Atlantic, Indian, and Pacific.

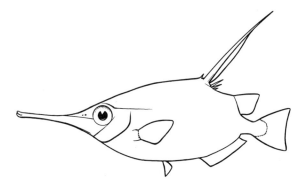

Body compressed, deep, and usually with bony plates on each side of back; no barbel on jaw; 4–8 dorsal spines, second spine very long, all joined by a membrane; second dorsal fin has about 11–19 soft rays; lateral line present or absent. Maximum length up to 30 cm.

Three genera, *Centriscops*, *Macrorhamphosus*, and *Notopogon*, with 11 species.

Family CENTRISCIDAE—Shrimpfishes. Marine; Indo-Pacific.

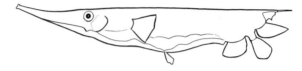

Extremely compressed, razorlike body with sharp ventral edge; body almost entirely encased by thin bony plates which are expansions of the vertebral column; first dorsal spine long and sharp at extreme end of body, followed by two shorter spines; soft dorsal fin and caudal fin displaced ventrally; no lateral line; mouth toothless. Swimming is in a vertical position, snout downwards. Maximum length up to 15 cm.

Two genera, *Aeoliscus* and *Centriscus*, with four species.

Suborder Syngnathoidei (Lophobranchii). No teeth; no lateral line; branchiostegal rays 1–3; gills lobed.

Family SOLENOSTOMIDAE—Ghost Pipefishes. Marine; tropical Indo-Pacific.

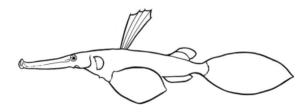

Body short, compressed and with large stellate bony plates; two separate dorsal fins, the first with five long feeble spines and the second with 18–23 soft rays on an elevated base; pelvic fins relatively large, with one spine and six soft rays, opposite spinous dorsal; gill openings moderately large; females with brood pouch formed by the pelvics. Maximum length up to 16 cm.

One genus, *Solenostomus* (=*Solenichthys* and *Solenostomatichthys*), with five species.

Family SYNGNATHIDAE—Pipefishes and Seahorses. Marine; rarely fresh water; Atlantic, Indian, and Pacific.

Body elongate and encased in a series of bony rings; one dorsal fin, usually with 15–60 soft rays; no pelvic fins; gill openings very small; anal fin very small, usually with 2–6 rays; pectoral fin rays usually 10–23; caudal fin absent in some; tail (caudal peduncle) may be prehensile and employed for holding onto objects.

Syngnathids are usually confined to shallow water. Males care for the eggs which are attached to them by the female on the undersurface of the trunk or tail or in a pouch. Genera such as *Amphelikturus* and *Acentronura* are to a certain extent morphological intermediates, if not evolutionary links, between pipefishes and seahorses.

Subfamily Syngnathinae (pipefishes).   Marine and brackish water; some in freshwater.

Thirty-four genera (e.g., *Amphelikturus, Acentronura, Bombonia, Corythoichthys, Dermatostethus, Doryichthys, Doryrhamphus, Micrognathus, Nerophis, Oostethus, Solegnathus, Syngnathoides,* and *Syngnathus*) with about 150 species.

Subfamily Hippocampinae (seahorses).   Marine.

Two genera, *Hippocampus* and *Phyllopteryx,* with about 25 species.

Order GASTEROSTEIFORMES (Thoracostei). Upper jaw protractile, ascending process of premaxillae well developed; postcleithrum absent; circumorbital bones, in addition to lachrymal, present; nasals and parietals present.

Seven genera with about 10 species. Banister (1970) gives reasons for not including Indostomidae in this order, as done by Berg (1940) and Greenwood et al. (1966). See notes under Syngnathiformes.

Family AULORHYNCHIDAE—Tubesnouts. Coastal marine; North Pacific.

Body elongate, with lateral bony scutes; series of 24–26 very short isolated dorsal spines, followed by a normal dorsal fin with about 10 soft rays; pelvic fin with one spine and four soft rays; caudal fin with 13 rays; four branchiostegal rays; circumorbital ring complete posteriorly; epipleurals absent; vertebrae 52–56. Maximum length 16 cm, attained in *Aulorhynchus flavidus*.

Two species, *Aulichthys japonicus* and *Aulorhynchus flavidus* (Nelson, 1971).

Family GASTEROSTEIDAE—Sticklebacks. Marine, brackish, and freshwater; Northern Hemisphere (see map on p. 340).

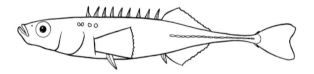

Body elongate or not, with lateral bony scutes or naked; series of 3–16 well-developed isolated dorsal spines (very rarely fewer than three) followed by a normal dorsal fin with 6–14 rays; pelvic fin (rarely absent) with one spine and one or two soft rays; caudal fin usually with 12 rays; three branchiostegal rays; circumorbital ring incomplete posteriorly; epipleurals present; vertebrae 28–42.

This family is famous for the numerous studies made of its species, especially by ethologists and physiologists. The mating behavior and nest-building activity of the males has attracted much attention.

The recognition of only eight species in this family fails to account for the enormous genetic diversity and biological species that exist (but form taxonomic problems) in the *Gasterosteus aculeatus* complex and perhaps in the *Pungitius pungitius* complex (e.g., see Hagen and McPhail, 1970; Nelson, 1971). Five genera with about eight species.

Spinachia spinachia (fifteenspine stickleback): marine; Atlantic Europe (Norway to France).

Apeltes quadracus (fourspine stickleback): usually marine and brackish water (rarely freshwater); Atlantic North America (Newfoundland to Virginia).

Gasterosteus wheatlandi (blackspotted stickleback): marine (rarely freshwater); Atlantic North America (Newfoundland to Massachusetts).

Gasterosteus aculeatus complex (threespine stickleback): anadromous and freshwater; Atlantic and Pacific coastal areas of northern North America and Eurasia, throughout much of Europe, along part of the Arctic coastline. Seldom above 100 m elevation.

Pungitius pungitius complex (ninespine stickleback): anadromous and freshwater; Atlantic, Pacific, and Arctic coastal areas of North America (south to Alaska and New Jersey) and Eurasia (south to Greece and Japan) and across much of above continental areas. Seldom above 600 m elevation.

Pungitius platygaster: fresh- and brackish water; Black Sea to Aral Sea and Balkash Lake area.

Pungitius timensis: freshwater; Japan.

Culaea inconstans (brook stickleback): freshwater; North America. Up to about 1670 m elevation.

Order SYNBRANCHIFORMES (Symbranchii).   Body eellike; gill openings confluent, restricted above; dorsal and anal fins confluent with the small caudal; no rays in dorsal and anal fins; no pectoral fins; pelvics minute and jugular or absent; anus in anterior half of body; no swim bladder; no ribs.

Liem (1968) does not believe that the two suborders are at all related. Seven genera with about 13 species.

Suborder Alabetoidei.

Family ALABETIDAE—Singleslit Eels.   Marine; Australia (including Tasmania).

Dorsal and anal fins well developed; small pelvic fins present behind gill opening (jugular), each with two rays; mouth small; about 75 vertebrae.
One genus, *Alabes* (=*Cheilobranchus*), with four species.

Suborder Synbranchoidei. Dorsal and anal fins vestigial (reduced to a ridge); no pelvic fins; mouth moderately large; vertebrae 100–188.

Family SYNBRANCHIDAE—Swamp-Eels. Tropical fresh- and brackish waters with one marine species; Africa, Asia, Indo-Australian Archipelago, Central and South America (see map on p. 340).

No lunglike air sac (capable of air breathing, however); body naked; pectoral and pelvic fins absent; one or two small gill openings under head or throat (the marine *Macrotrema caligans* of southeastern Asia has normal size gill openings continuous with each other under throat); three or four gills.

Blind cave species are known from Yucatan (*Furmastix infernalis*, known from a single 32 cm specimen) and Liberia (*Typhlosynbranchus boueti*). One species, the burrowing nocturnal *Synbranchus marmoratus*, has an exceptionally large range that extends from Mexico to Argentina and includes some of the Antillean islands (Rosen and Rumney, 1972). Maximum length up to 1.5 m.

Five genera, *Macrotrema, Monopterus* (=*Fluta*), *Furmastix* (=*Pluto*), *Synbranchus*, and *Typhlosynbranchus*, with about eight species.

Family AMPHIPNOIDAE—Cuchia. Fresh- and brackish water; India, Burma, and Queensland.

Two separate lunglike air sacs connecting with gill cavity; body scaled.
One species, *Amphipnous cuchia*.

Order SCORPAENIFORMES. (Cataphracti in part, Scleroparei in part, Pareioplitae, Loricati, Sclerogeni, Cottomorphi, Perciformes in part). This order contains the "mail-cheeked" fishes, distinguished by the suborbital stay, a posterior extension of the third suborbital bone (counting the lachrymal), which extends across the cheek to the pre-operculum. Head and body tend to be spiny or bony plated; pectoral fin usually rounded, membranes between lower rays often incised; caudal fin rarely forked.

Twenty-one families with about 260 genera and very approximately 1000 species.

Suborder Scorpaenoidei. Contains the world's most venomous fishes. Usually brightly colored. The placement of genera in families differs in some works.

Family SCORPAENIDAE—Scorpionfishes (Rockfishes). Marine; all tropical and temperate seas.

Body compressed; head usually with ridges and spines (usually with two opercular and five preopercular spines); suborbital stay usually securely fastened to preopercle (no attachment in some); scales, when present, usually ctenoid; dorsal fin usually single (often with a notch), usually with 11–17 spines and 8–18 soft rays; anal fin with 1–3 spines (usually three) and 3–9 soft rays (usually five); pelvic fin with one spine and 2–5 soft rays (usually five); pectoral fin well developed (usually with 15–25 rays), rarely with one free lower ray; gill membranes free from isthmus; swim bladder absent in some; vertebrae 24–40. Venom gland in dorsal, anal, and pelvic spines. Most have internal fertilization and are live bearers. One of the rare egg layers, *Scorpaena guttata,* is reported to have a gelatinous egg balloon that may be as much as 20 cm in diameter. Many species are commercially important.

About 60 genera with about 330 species. Most species are in the Indian and Pacific oceans; only 58 species in 11 genera recognized from the Atlantic Ocean (Eschmeyer, 1969). Other taxa are recognized in this family by some workers. Matsubara (1943) and Eschmeyer and Rao (1973) include the Synanceidae; Eschmeyer, Hirosaki, and Abe (1973:307) include the Congiopodidae (as a subfamily). These groups, as in Greenwood et al. (1966), are given family status here. Several sub-families can be recognized [see Matsubara (1943) and Eschmeyer (1969)]. A provisional listing follows. The first three and the last one are Indo-Pacific only.

SUBFAMILY APISTINAE. For example, *Apistus.*

SUBFAMILY PTEROIDICHTHYINAE. For example, *Rhinopias.* Eschmeyer, Hirosaki, and Abe (1973) discuss this group.

SUBFAMILY PTEROINAE.   For example, *Pterois* (highly venomous lion-fishes and turkeyfishes).

SUBFAMILY SCORPAENINAE

   About 12 genera (e.g., *Idiastion, Neomerinthe, Phenacoscorpius, Pontinus, Scorpaena, Scorpaenodes,* and *Trachyscorpia*).

SUBFAMILY SEBASTOLOBINAE.   One North Pacific genus: *Sebastolobus,* with 15–17 dorsal spines and 27–30 vertebrae. *Trachyscorpia* shows some affinity with this subfamily (Eschmeyer, 1969:47).

SUBFAMILY SEBASTINAE.   Four genera: *Helicolenus, Sebastes* (=*Sebastodes*), *Hozukius,* and *Sebastiscus.* The first two occur in all oceans, whereas the latter two occur only in the western Pacific. The live-bearing genus *Sebastes* is the largest in the family with about 100 species (almost all of them occurring in the North Pacific).

SUBFAMILY SETARCHINAE.   Three genera (e.g., *Setarches* and *Ectreposebastes*) with four species. This subfamily is treated in detail by Eschmeyer and Collette, 1966).

SUBFAMILY TETRAROGINAE (SAILBACK SCORPIONFISHES)

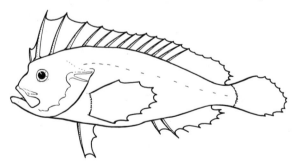

Several genera (e.g., *Paracentropogon, Tetraroge,* and *Vespicula*). This group shows some resemblance to the Aploactinidae.

Family SYNANCEIIDAE (Synancejidae). Tropical marine (rarely brackish and fresh-water); coastal Indo-Pacific (including the Red Sea), South Africa east to Japan, Society Islands, and Australia.

Body scaleless, usually covered with skin glands; head large; swim bladder usually absent; venom glands present near base of hypodermiclike dorsal fin spines. The neurotoxin of these fishes is the most deadly of the fish venoms and can be fatal to man (Halstead, 1970; Munro, 1967). The fish is particularly dangerous because it usually rests in a half-buried position, looking much like a rock. Maximum length about 32 cm.

Nine genera with about 20 species. Eschmeyer and Rao (1973) place the following three subfamilies as subfamilies of the Scorpaenidae.

SUBFAMILY SYNANCEIINAE (STONEFISHES). No free pectoral rays; skin glands present (appearing as "warts" in most species) and usually scattered over the body; dorsal fin with 11–17 spines and 4–14 soft rays; anal fin with 2–4 spines and 4–14 soft rays; pelvic fin with one spine and 3–5 soft rays; pectoral fin rays 11–19; vertebrae 23–30.

Six genera and about 10 species.

TRIBE SYNANCEIINI. Mouth vertical or superior; eyes dorsal, directed outward and upward or only upward. Some species known from rivers.

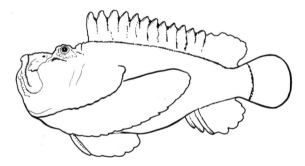

Four genera, the monotypic *Pseudosynanceia, Leptosynanceia,* and *Trachicephalus* and *Synanceia* with five species.

TRIBE EROSINI. Mouth terminal and slightly oblique; eyes lateral, directed outward.

Two species, *Erosa erosa* (Japan to Australia) and *Dampierosa daruma* (northwestern Australia).

SUBFAMILY INIMICINAE (PELORINAE).   Two (*Inimicus*) or three (*Choridactylus*) free pectoral rays in each fin; skin glands concentrated in a widely spaced row above the lateral line and in a patch behind the head.

Two genera, *Inimicus* (=*Pelor*) and *Choridactylus* (=*Choridactylodes*).

SUBFAMILY MINOINAE.   One free lower pectoral ray in each fin; skin glands absent (body smooth); dorsal fin with 9–12 spines and 10–12 soft rays; anal fin with 9–13 soft rays; pelvic fin with one spine and five soft rays.

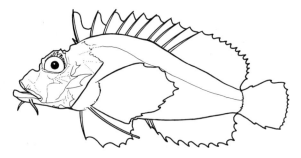

One genus, *Minous*, with about five species.

Family TRIGLIDAE—Searobins.   Marine; all tropical and temperate seas.

Two separate dorsal fins; casquelike, bony head; lower two or three pectoral rays enlarged and free, used for detecting food. Benthic habitat. Triglids are good sound producers. Maximum length up to 1 m.

SUBFAMILY TRIGLINAE (UNARMORED SEAROBINS).   Body with scales or covered in long plates; preorbitals usually produced forward, with spines; barbels sometimes present. Benthic in habitat.

Ten genera (e.g., *Bellator, Lepidotrigla, Prionotus,* and *Trigla*) with about 70 species.

SUBFAMILY PERISTEDIINAE (ARMORED SEAROBINS). Body entirely encased in heavy spine-bearing plates; preorbitals each with a forward projection; barbels on lower jaw.

About four genera (e.g., *Peristedion*) with several species (perhaps 15).

Family CARACANTHIDAE—Orbicular Velvetfishes.   Marine; Indo-Pacific.

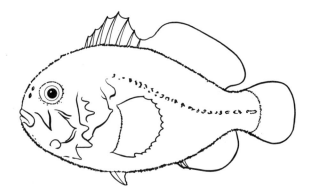

Body oval, extremely compressed, and scaleless but covered with small rough papillae; mouth small and terminal; one dorsal fin with a notch, origin on nape, with 6–8 spines and 11–13 soft rays; anal fin with two spines and 11–14 soft rays; pelvic fins inconspicuous; gill openings restricted to sides. Maximum length only 5 cm.

One genus, *Caracanthus*, with about three species.

Family APLOACTINIDAE—Velvetfishes.   Marine; coastal western Pacific.

Body scaleless, covered with papillae (giving a velvety appearance); origin of dorsal fin far forward, above eye or almost so; anterior 3–5 spines usually divergent, either elevated or largely devoid of connecting membrane; anal spines rudimentary or absent; pelvic fin with fewer than four rays; gill openings, usually reduced to a small aperture, may appear to be wide; four barbels usually present; interorbital area sunken; head armed with long knoblike preorbital and preopercular spines.

SUBFAMILY APLOACTININAE.   Japan to Australia.

About nine genera (e.g., *Adventor, Aploactis, Aploactisoma, Cocotropus, Kanekonia,* and *Paraploactis*) with many species.

Subfamily Bathyaploactinae. Queensland.   Dorsal fin continuous but with two small notches, the first seven spines forming a distinct fin and followed by seven or eight spines and about eight soft rays; anal fin with 11 soft rays. A varient subspecies is reported from Western Australia (T. C. Marshall, 1965). Maximum length about 6.3 cm.
   One species, *Bathyaploactis curtisensis.*

Family PATAECIDAE.   Marine; Australia.

Body scaleless (smooth or with tubercles or papillae).

Subfamily Pataecinae (prowfishes).   No pelvic fins; very long continuous dorsal fin, extending from head to tail (connected with or free from caudal fin).

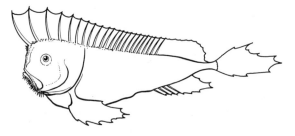

   About three genera, *Aetapcus, Neopataecus,* and *Pataecus,* with several species.

Subfamily Gnathanacanthinae (red velvetfish).   Pelvic fins present, with one spine and five soft rays; two separate dorsal fins of about equal length, the first with seven spines, the second with three spines and 10 or 11 soft rays; anal fin with three spines and eight or nine soft rays.

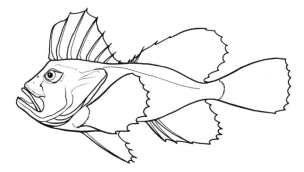

One species, *Gnathanacanthus goetzeei.*

Suborder Hexagrammoidei

Family ANOPLOPOMATIDAE—Sablefishes.   Marine; North Pacific.

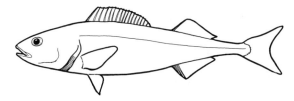

Head without spines, ridges, or cirri; two dorsal fins; anal fin with three weak spines and 11–19 soft rays; pelvic fins with one spine and five soft rays; two well-developed nostrils on each side; gill membranes attached to isthmus; lateral line single. Maximum length about 1.8 m, attained in *Erilepis zonifer* (the skilfish).

Two species, *Anoplopoma fimbria* (with well-separated dorsal fins and 17–22 spines in first dorsal) and *Erilepis zonifer* (with closely spaced dorsal fins and 12–14 spines in first dorsal). Both species range from California to Japan.

Family HEXAGRAMMIDAE—Greenlings.   Marine; North Pacific.

Head with cirri but without ridges or spines; lateral lines one or five; scales cycloid or ctenoid; one dorsal fin (but with a notch) with 16–27 spines and 11–24 soft rays; pelvic fin with one spine and five soft rays; well-developed anterior nostril on each side, posterior nostril (if present) reduced to a small pore; anal fin with 0–3 spines followed by soft rays; six or seven branchiostegal rays; swim bladder absent. Maximum length up to 1.5 m, attained in *Ophiodon elongatus;* most other species less than 45 cm.

This is the richest family endemic to the North Pacific. Most species are primarily littoral.

Four subfamilies, five genera, and 11 species. The following classification is based on Rutenberg (1962), except that family status is given to *Zaniolepis* (the combfishes), following Greenwood et al. (1966).

SUBFAMILY HEXAGRAMMINAE. Dorsal fin divided approximately in the middle by a notch into an anterior spinous portion and a posterior soft portion; anal fin without spines; head covered with scales; caudal fin rounded, truncate, or slightly emarginate; no large ridges on skull; vertebrae 47–56; single lateral line in *Agrammus* and five in *Hexagrammos*.

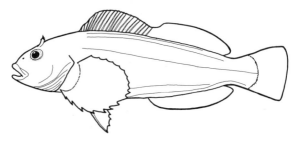

Two genera, *Agrammus* (with one species, *A. agrammus*) of Japan, Korea, and North China, and *Hexagrammos* of western and eastern coasts of Pacific with six species.

SUBFAMILY PLEUROGRAMMINAE. Dorsal fin without a notch but with 47–51 hard rays; anal fin without spines (24–30 soft rays); scales partly covering head; caudal fin forked; strongly developed ridges on upper surface of skull; vertebrae 59–62; five lateral lines on body. Primarily pelagic.

One genus, *Pleurogrammus*, with two species in the northwestern Pacific and southern Bering Sea.

SUBFAMILY OPHIODONTINAE. Dorsal fin divided into two parts by a deep notch, first portion with 24–27 spines and second portion with 21–24 soft rays; anal fin without spines but first three rays are nonsegmented; head not covered with scales; only member with cycloid scales on body, others may have cycloid scales on head; caudal fin truncate or slightly emarginate; 57 vertebrae; single lateral line; mouth large; jaws with small teeth interspersed with large fanglike teeth; feeds primarily on fishes, crustaceans, and squids and is extremely voracious.

One species, *Ophiodon elongatus* (lingcod), of eastern Pacific from southern Alaska to Mexico.

SUBFAMILY OXYLEBINAE. Dorsal fin divided by a shallow notch; anal fin usually with three large spines, of which the second is longest; scales covering the head; caudal fin rounded; one lateral line.

One species, *Oxylebius pictus,* of eastern Pacific from southern British Columbia to California.

Family ZANIOLEPIDIDAE—Combfishes. Marine; eastern North Pacific.

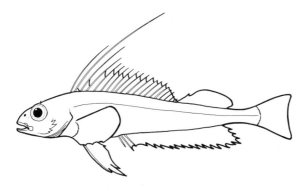

Dorsal fin with deep incision in posterior third of fin; first three spines elongate, the second greatly prolonged; ctenoid scales; first two pelvic fin rays thickened and extending past origin of anal fin; one lateral line. This group is placed in the hexagrammids by most workers. Primarily benthic. Maximum length about 30 cm.

Two species, *Zaniolepis latipinnis* and *Z. frenata,* found from California to British Columbia.

Suborder Platycephaloidei

Family PLATYCEPHALIDAE—Flatheads. Marine (some brackish); Indo-Pacific.

Body elongate and cylindrical; head depressed, usually with ridges and spines; mouth large, lower jaw projecting forward; ctenoid scales covering body; two dorsal fins, the first with 6–9 spines and second with 11–14 soft rays; anal fin with 11–14 soft rays; gill openings wide; pelvic fins widely separated, with one spine and five soft rays; pectoral fins without free rays; no swim bladder; 27 vertebrae.

SUBFAMILY BEMBRINAE. Head moderately depressed; pelvics below pectoral base; spinous dorsal fin not preceded by an isolated spine. Most are small red fishes.

About four genera (e.g., *Bembras* and *Parabembras*) with several species.

SUBFAMILY PLATYCEPHALINAE.   Head extremely depressed; pelvics behind pectoral base; spinous dorsal fin preceded by a single short isolated spine. Benthic habitat, often burying into the bottom.

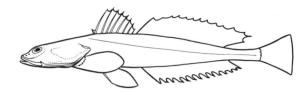

About 18 genera (e.g., *Cociella, Onigocia, Platycephalus, Suggrundus*, and *Thysanophrys*) and numerous species.

Suborder Hoplichthyoidei

Family HOPLICHTHYIDAE (Oplichthyidae)—Ghost Flatheads.   Marine; Indo-Pacific.

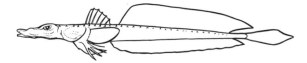

Body elongate; head depressed and very wide, with spines and ridges; no scales, row of spiny scutes along side; lower pectoral rays (three or four) free; pelvic fins widely separated, with one spine and five soft rays; no anal spines; 26 vertebrae (eight abdominal and 18 caudal).

One genus, *Hoplichthys*, with several species.

Suborder Congiopodoidei

Family CONGIOPODIDAE—Racehorses (Pigfishes).   Marine; Southern Hemisphere (to Antarctica).

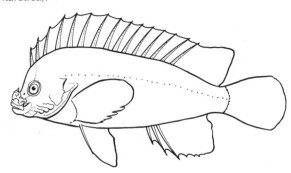

Snout relatively long; body without scales, skin sometimes granular; only one nostril on each side; gill opening reduced, above pectoral base; lateral line well developed; anal spines present or absent. One species in South Africa is reported to cast its skin, like reptiles.

Four genera, *Alertichthys, Congiopodus* (=*Agriopus*), *Perryena,* and *Zanclorhynchus,* with seven species (Moreland, 1960).

Suborder Cottoidei.   Several of the following families are usually lumped with Cottidae. Jordan (1923), on the other hand, split the present family Cottidae into several families.

A number of changes in the following classification, which is basically adopted from Greenwood et al. (1966), may be desirable. The first family, Icelidae, should perhaps be included with the Cottidae as a subfamily; also, several genera other than those mentioned here have usually been associated with it. Members of the family Psychrolutidae share many features (often in a mosaic fashion) with *Neophrynichthys,* the two genera placed in Cottunculidae, and a few other genera, considered here to be cottids; all could well be placed in Psychrolutidae. The similarities could be a result of convergent evolution or of taxa arising from a common cottid ancestor, and it is not certain which of the two hypotheses is more probable, although the latter seems more reasonable for at least some of the genera in question.

Family ICELIDAE.   Marine; Arctic, North Atlantic, and North Pacific.

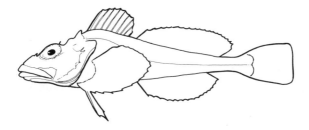

Subfamily Icelinae.   No free pectoral fin rays; upper preopercular spine with two or three prongs.

North America and Japan; one genus, *Icelus,* with three species.

Subfamily Ereuninae. Four lower pectoral fin rays free; body with spinous ctenoid scales.

Western Pacific; at least two species, *Marukawichthys ambulator* (with pelvic fins) and *Ereunias grallator* (without pelvic fins).

Family COTTIDAE—Sculpins. Marine and freshwater; Northern Hemisphere and near New Zealand, eastern Australia, and Argentina.

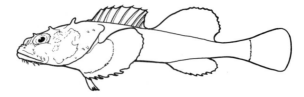

Body often appearing naked, commonly with scales or prickles (never completely encased in heavy bony armor); eye usually large and placed high on the head; lateral line present, single; pelvic fins (absent in one species) with one spine and 2–5 soft rays; no spines in anal fin; adults without swim bladder. Maximum length about 78 cm (e.g., *Scorpaenichthys marmoratus*).

Detailed studies on this family include those by Bolin (1947- and reference therein to his 1944 review) and Watanabe (1960). Regional studies such as Hart (1973) also give a good account of many species.

Most species are marine with the greatest diversity occurring along the North Pacific coastline. About 130 species are known from fresh and marine waters in North America and about 75 species are known from Japan. At least two cottids are known from the Southern Hemisphere; four specimens of *Antipodocottus galatheae* and one of *A. megalops* have been taken in the New Zealand region (DeWitt, 1969). In addition, *Neophrynichthys* is placed in this family by Greenwood et al. (1966). Most workers, however, have placed it in the Psychrolutidae. One species (=*Besnardia*) occurs off Argentina, one is known along the east coast of New Zealand, and one has been described from off southeastern Australia.

About 67 genera [e.g., *Artediellus*, *Artedius*, *Ascelichthys* (lacks pelvics), *Blepsias*, *Ceratocottus*, *Clinocottus*, *Cottus* (a large circumpolar, freshwater group), *Dasycottus*, *Enophrys*, *Gymnocanthus*, *Hemilepidotus*, *Hemitripterus*, *Icelinus*, *Jordania*, *Myoxocephalus*, *Oligocottus*, *Pseudoblennius*, *Radulinus*, *Rhamphocottus*, *Scorpaenichthys*, *Synchirus*, and *Triglops*] with probably as many as 300 species.

Family COTTOCOMEPHORIDAE. Freshwater; primarily Lake Baikal (USSR); some species in other USSR drainages.

Postcleithra reduced or absent. Some species are pelagic.

The taxonomy and biology of this and the next family are discussed by Taliev (1955) and briefly reviewed by Kozhov (1963), both of whom

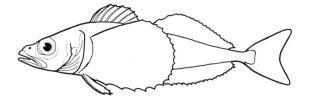

placed the following two subfamilies in the Cottidae. In the present classification all sculpins in Lake Baikal are placed in this and the following family and account for 26 of its 50 known fish species. Maximum length about 18 cm.

SUBFAMILY ABYSSOCOTTINAE. Three genera, *Abyssocottus, Asprocottus,* and *Cottinella,* with about 12 species. Species formerly placed in *Limnocottus* are now placed in the first two genera.

SUBFAMILY COTTOCOMEPHORINAE. Five genera, *Batrachocottus, Cottocomephorus, Metacottus, Paracottus* (similar to *Cottus*), and *Procottus,* with about 12 species.

Family COMEPHORIDAE—Baikal Oilfishes. Freshwater; Lake Baikal (USSR).

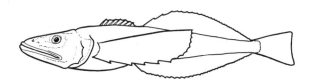

Body naked; pectoral fins very long; no pelvic fins (pelvic bones present); postcleithra absent; body glassy—dull and translucent in living fish; body usually high in fat content; vertebrae 48–50; viviparous. Maximum length about 20 cm.

One genus, *Comephorus,* with two species.

Family NORMANICHTHYIDAE. Marine; off Chile.

Body covered with ctenoid scales; head unarmed; pelvic fin with one spine and five soft rays; no ribs.

One species, *Normanichthys crockeri,* described by Clark (1937).

Family COTTUNCULIDAE. Marine; North Atlantic and off South Africa, Japan, and Argentina.

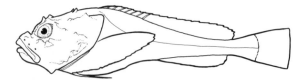

Dorsal fins not separated but forming a single, low, skin-covered fin. Most species have prickles on skin, conspicuous bony protuberances on head, and vomerine teeth.

Two genera, *Cottunculoides* and *Cottunculus,* with about six species.

Family PSYCHROLUTIDAE.   Marine; North Pacific.

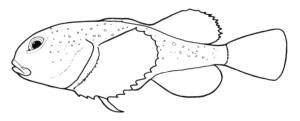

Dorsal fins not separated but forming a single, low, skin-covered fin; no bony protuberances on head.

One endemic eastern Pacific species, *Psychrolutes paradoxus,* one genus, *Gilbertidia,* with one western Pacific species and one eastern Pacific species, and two endemic western Pacific species, *Eurymen gyrinus* and *Ebinania vermiculata.* See comments under Cottoidei.

Family AGONIDAE—Poachers.   Marine; North Atlantic, North Pacific, and southern South America.

Body usually elongate and covered with bony plates; pelvic fins thoracic, each with one spine and two soft rays; one or two dorsal fins.

About 20 genera and 49 species.

SUBFAMILY ASPIDOPHOROIDINAE (ALLIGATORFISHES).   One dorsal fin.

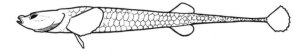

Two genera, *Anoplagonus* and *Aspidophoroides.*

SUBFAMILY AGONINAE.   Two dorsal fins.

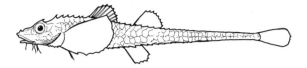

About 18 genera (e.g., *Agonopsis*, *Agonus*, *Asterotheca*, *Bathyagonus*, *Bothragonus*, *Hypsagonus*, *Occella*, *Odontopyxis*, *Pallasina*, *Sarritor*, *Stellerina*, and *Xeneretmus*).

Family CYCLOPTERIDAE—Lumpfishes and Snailfishes.   Marine; Antarctic, Arctic, Atlantic, and Pacific.

Pelvic fins, when present, modified into a sucking disc, thoracic; lateral line usually absent; gill opening usually small.

SUBFAMILY CYCLOPTERINAE (LUMPFISHES OR LUMPSUCKERS).   Cooler regions of Northern Hemisphere.

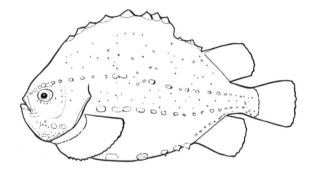

Body globose, usually covered with tubercles; usually two short dorsal fins, the first spinous, the second soft rayed (the spinous is "absent" in some), never confluent with caudal; anal fin short. Maximum length up to 60 cm.

The following classification is based on Ueno (1970) who recognized its tribes as subfamilies. Among its members *Cyclopterus* shows some affinity to the Cottidae and Psychrolutidae, whereas *Aptocyclus* is the most closely related to the Liparinae.

TRIBE CYCLOPTERINI.   First dorsal fin projecting above the upper profile of the back; skin with large conical bony tubercles or dermal cirri or warts (skin naked in *Lethotremus* which has long dermal tubes on underside of head).

Five genera, *Cyclopterus, Eumicrotremus, Cyclopteropsis, Cyclopsis,* and *Lethotremus,* with 24 species.

TRIBE APTOCYCLINI.   First dorsal fin embedded under thick skin, not visible without dissection; skin without bony or dermal appendages.

Two species, *Aptocyclus ventricosus* and *Pelagocyclus vitiazi.* The latter leads a pelagic life and has a rudimentary sucking disk

SUBFAMILY LIPARINAE (SNAILFISHES).   Northern   Hemisphere   and Antarctic.

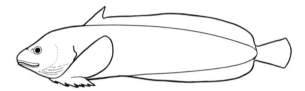

Body elongate, scaleless (small prickles in some) and skin jellylike; dorsal and anal fins long, confluent, or nearly so, with caudal fin; pelvic fin absent in some. Maximum length up to 30 cm.

About 13 genera (e.g., *Careproctus, Cyclogaster, Liparis, Paraliparis, Polypera,* and *Psednos*) and about 115 species.

SUBFAMILY RHODICHTHYINAE.   North Atlantic; one genus, *Rhodichthys.*

Order DACTYLOPTERIFORMES

Family DACTYLOPTERIDAE (Cephalacanthidae)—Flying Gurnards. Marine tropical; Indo-Pacific and Atlantic.

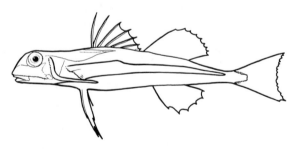

Large, blunt, bony head (with spines and keels); body covered with scutelike scales; tremendously enlarged pectoral fins with inner rays free (supposedly capable of gliding short distances); two free spines (the first

may be on the nape) before the two dorsal fins; pelvic fins thoracic, each with one spine and four soft rays; no lateral line; 22 vertebrae.

These benthic fishes, which superficially resemble triglids, produce sounds by stridulation by utilizing the hyomandibular bone and "walk" on the sea floor by alternately moving the pelvic fins.

About four genera (e.g., *Dactyloptena*, *Dactylopterus*, and *Daicocus*) and about four species.

Order PEGASIFORMES (Hypostomides)

Family PEGASIDAE—Seamoths.   Marine; Indo-Pacific.

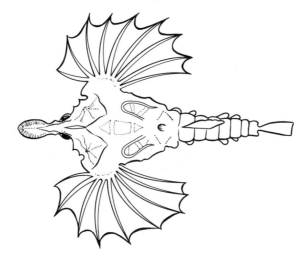

Body oddly shaped (broad and depressed), encased in bony rings; small mouth beneath a long flattened rostrum; gill cover with a single bone; dorsal and anal fins short (usually five rays in each), of soft rays only; pectorals relatively large, with 8–10 unbranched rays; pelvics abdominal, with one spine and 1–3 soft rays; caudal peduncle quadrangular; no swim bladder. Maximum size about 13 cm.

Two genera, *Pegasus* and *Zalises*, with five species.

Order PERCIFORMES.   (Percomorphi in part, Acanthopterygii in part, Labyrinthici in part, Jugulares in part, Beryciformes in part, and many more).

The order Perciformes is the most diversified of all fish orders. Indeed, it is the largest vertebrate order. Perciformes dominate in vertebrate ocean life and are the dominant fish group in many tropical and subtropical fresh waters. They are the basal evolutionary group from which numerous other groups are believed to have been derived (all the following orders).

Although they are a morphologically and ecologically diverse group, with secondary losses and gains, the level of evolution reached, as contrasted with "typical" lower teleosts (Protacanthopterygii and Ostariophysi), can be generalized as follows (many exceptions to these generalizations occur; for example, the bodies of some perciforms are covered mainly by cycloid scales).

	Lower teleosts	Perciformes
Spines in fins	Absent	Present
Dorsal fin number	One, adipose fin may also be present	Two, never an adipose fin
Scales	Cycloid	Ctenoid or absent
Pelvic fin position	Abdominal	If present, thoracic or jugular
Pelvic fin rays	Six or more soft rays	One spine and five soft rays, sometimes fewer
Pectoral fin base	Ventral and horizontal	Lateral and vertical
Upper jaw bordered by	Premaxilla and maxilla	Premaxilla
Swim bladder	Duct present (physostomes)	Duct absent (physoclists)
Orbitosphenoid	Present	Absent
Mesocoracoid	Present	Absent
Intermuscular bones	Present	Absent
Bone cells in bone of adult	Present	Absent
Principal caudal fin ray number	Often 18 or 19	Never more than 17, often fewer

The classification of this order is controversial and some workers would include other groups (e.g., Scorpaeniformes) while excluding others (e.g., Mugiloidei). Monophyly for the group is by no means certain. The basic classification of the order employed here follows Greenwood et al. (1966). Gosline (1968) disagrees with Greenwood's removal of some groups from Regan's Percomorphi. Gosline's work has been useful in defining many of the groups. Most families in many suborders are basically similar but lack unique features and are not diagnosed here.

The Perciformes contain 18 suborders, 147 families, about 1257 genera, and about 6880 species. Four suborders, Percoidei, Labroidei, Blennioidei, and Gobioidei, account for about 6340 of the species (92%). The five largest families of this, the largest, fish order are Gobiidae (800), Cichlidae (680), Labridae (400), Serranidae (370), and Blenniidae (276). Together they have about 2526 species, which constitute more than one-third of the number of species in the order. The 10 largest families have about 50% of the species. About three-fourths of all Perciformes are marine shore fishes. The rest are oceanic or freshwater.

Suborder Percoidei. This, the largest, suborder of the Perciformes contains 72 families, 595 genera, and about 3935 species. Among the 72 families 11 have 100 or more species, four contain only two species, and nine are monotypic. The seven largest families contain more than 50% of the species. Cichlidae, with about 680 species, has the most within the suborder (and is the fourth largest fish family); Serranidae is second with 370. This suborder contains many highly colorful fishes.

Superfamily Percoidae. Most of the families are very similar and poorly separated from one another. Drastic changes in the classification may be required in the future.

Family CENTROPOMIDAE—Snooks. Marine (often brackish); Atlantic, Indian, and Pacific, some in fresh water (especially in Africa).

Lateral line extending onto tail; scaly process usually in pelvic axis; dorsal fin in two portions, the first with 7–9 spines and the second with one spine and 9–15 soft rays; anal fin with three spines and 6–17 soft rays; pelvic fin with one spine and five soft rays.

Nine genera [e.g., *Ambassis, Centropomus, Chanda* (Asiatic glassfishes), *Lates* (large freshwater African fish, the Nile perch) and *Psammoperca*] with about 30 species.

Family PERCICHTHYIDAE—Temperate Basses.   Marine, brackish, and freshwater; tropical and temperate regions of world.

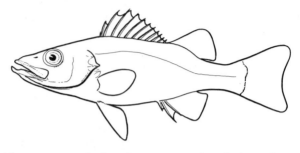

Opercle with two rounded spines—no spine below the main spine (except in *Niphon,* which has three); lateral line complete and continuous; caudal fin usually forked; no scaly process in pelvic axis; pelvic fin with one spine and five soft rays; not hermaphroditic, sexes separate.

This family, which is one of the most generalized percoids, was erected from the family Serranidae by Gosline (1966).

About 17 genera: the marine *Acropoma* (has light organs), *Doderleinia, Malakichthys, Neoscombrops, Niphon, Polyprion,* and *Stereolepis;* the freshwater *Morone* (=*Roccus*) (North America, Europe, and North Africa), *Percichthys* and *Percilia* (South America), *Ctenolates, Macquaria, Maccullochella,* and *Percalates* (Australia), and *Coreoperca, Lateolabrax,* and *Siniperca* (Asia); about 40 species. In addition, Fraser (1972) refers several other genera with three anal spines, previously placed in Apogonidae, to this family. *Acropoma* is retained in a separate family here (p. 228–229).

Family SERRANIDAE—Sea Basses.   Marine (a few freshwater); tropical and temperate seas.

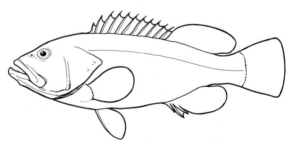

Opercle with three spines—the main spine with one above it and one below it (the lower opercular spine is also found in Grammistidae and *Niphon*); scales usually ctenoid, cycloid in some; lateral line complete and continuous; caudal fin usually rounded, truncate, or lunate (rarely forked); no scaly axillary pelvic process; pelvic fin with one spine and five soft rays; three anal fin spines; seven branchiostegal rays; usually 24 or 25 vertebrae; hermaphroditic, although the two sexes usually do not develop at the same time (most *Serranus* and their immediate relatives are functional hermaphrodites). Maximum length up to about 3 m (and weight up to about 400 kg); some species, however, grow no longer than 10 cm.

Numerous genera [e.g., *Alphestes, Anthias, Caesioperca, Centropristis, Cephalopholis, Dermatolepis, Diplectrum, Epinephelus* (groupers), *Gonioplectrus, Hemanthias, Hypoplectrus* (hamlets), *Liopropoma, Mycteroperca* (groupers), *Ocyanthias, Paralabrax, Paranthias, Pikea, Promicrops, Pteranthias,* and *Serranus*] and about 370 species.

Genera of uncertain position but with serranid or other percoid affinities include the following:

Callanthias: usually placed in Serranidae (Subfamily Anthiinae). It lacks many serranid specializations and may have a pseudochromid affinity.

Centrogenys: placed in its own family but bears a superficial resemblance to the cirrhitids.

Ostracoberyx: this genus, with a relatively small oblique mouth and a prominent spine extending backward from the preopercle, was placed in its own family in Beryciformes by Berg (1940). It may be related to *Niphon.*

Symphysanodon: this genus has often been considered a serranid but is more probably allied to the lutjanids. Contains five species found in the western Atlantic, western Pacific, and Hawaii.

Family GRAMMISTIDAE—Soapfishes.   Marine; Atlantic and Indo-Pacific.

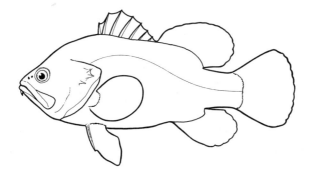

Dorsal fin with 2–9 spines and 12–27 soft rays; anal fin with two or three short spines or none at all and 8–17 soft rays; lower jaw projecting and chin usually with terminal appendage; opercle with three distinct spines (two in one species); pelvic fins inserted below or slightly in front of pectoral base; innermost pelvic ray attached to abdomen by a membrane; scales mainly ctenoid and not embedded or cycloid and often embedded, small with about 75–140 rows along the single complete lateral line; body mucus can create a soapsudslike effect (with toxin grammistin); vertebrae 24 or 25. Maximum length about 30 cm.

Six genera, *Aulacocephalus, Diploprion, Grammistes, Grammistops, Pogonoperca,* and *Rypticus,* with about 17 species (Randall et al., 1971).

Family PSEUDOCHROMIDAE—Dottybacks.   Marine; Indo-Pacific.

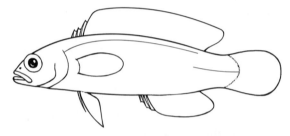

Dorsal fin with three or fewer spines; anal fin with three spines and about 13 or 14 soft rays; lateral line usually interrupted or divided into upper and lower portions; scales on head; 17 or more pectoral rays.

Norman (1957) placed this and the next two families in the subfamily Pseudochromidinae of the family Serranidae. Genera include *Pseudochromis* and *Labracinus* and probably *Dampieria, Nesiotes,* and *Nematochromis.*

Family PSEUDOGRAMMIDAE.   Marine; West Africa, Indo-Pacific, both coasts of tropical America.

Seven dorsal fin spines; anal fin with three spines and about 16 or 17 soft rays; lateral line usually interrupted or divided into upper and lower portions; 26–28 vertebrae.

Some species, as in a few other families, are hermaphroditic (Smith and Atz, 1969). Maximum length about 10 cm.

Genera include *Pseudogramma* (=*Rhegma*), *Aporops,* and *Suttonia,* with about six species.

Family GRAMMIDAE—Basslets.   Marine; tropical West Atlantic and Indo-Pacific.

Lateral line on body interrupted or absent; pelvic fin with one spine and five soft rays; dorsal fin with 11–13 spines.

About six genera with nine species; includes *Gramma* and *Lipogramma* (each with two species in the West Indies), *Stigmatonotus australis* (of western Australia), and possibly *Pseudochromichthys riukianus* (Japan) and *Pseudocrenilabrus natalensis* (coast of Natal).

Family PLESIOPIDAE—Roundheads.   Marine; Indo-Pacific, south to Tasmania.

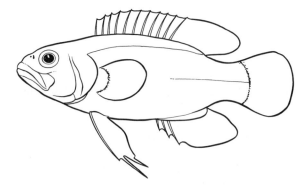

Pelvic fins with one spine and four soft rays; three anal spines; lateral line in two parts.

Four genera: *Assessor, Paraplesiops, Plesiops,* and *Trachinops.*

Family PSEUDOPLESIOPIDAE.   Marine; Indo-Australia.

Pelvic fins with a small spine and four soft rays; pelvic fins long, usually extending past anal fin origin; dorsal and anal fin spines absent; lateral line on body interrupted or absent; head scaly.

Two genera: *Pseudoplesiops* (Indo-Australian Archipelago) with several species and *Chlidichthys johnvoelckeri* (southeastern Africa).

Family ANISOCHROMIDAE.   Marine; western Indian off Kenya.

Pelvic fin with one weak spine and five soft rays, inserted markedly anterior to pectorals; 14 pectoral fin rays; anal fin with one weak spine and 16 or 17 soft rays; dorsal fin with one weak spine and 24 or 25 branched rays; single distinct lateral line along base of dorsal fin; head naked.

The sexes in this exceptionally small species are strikingly different and both are extremely colorful. Maximum size 2.7 cm.

One species: *Anisochromis kenyae* (first described by Smith, 1954).

Family ACANTHOCLINIDAE.   Marine; New Zealand, India, and Queensland.

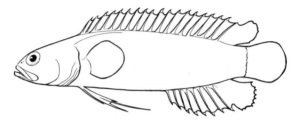

Pelvic fin with one spine and two soft rays; more than three anal spines; 1–4 lateral lines. Maximum length about 7 cm.

Three genera, *Acanthoclinus, Acanthoplesiops,* and *Belonepterygion,* and about five species.

Family GLAUCOSOMIDAE.   Marine; western Pacific (Japan to Australia).

Dorsal fin with eight graduated spines and 12–14 soft rays; anal fin with three spines and 12 soft rays; maxillae scaled; lateral line nearly straight and extending to tail; caudal fin lunate.

One genus, *Glaucosoma,* with five species.

Family THERAPONIDAE (Teraponidae)—Tigerperches.   Marine coastal (some in fresh water), Indo-Pacific.

Body oblong to oblong-ovate, somewhat compressed; opercle with one or two spines; dorsal fin with a small notch, 12–14 spines, and 8–14 soft rays; anal fin with three spines and 7–12 soft rays; pelvics inserted behind base of pectorals; caudal fin rounded, truncate, or emarginate; lat-

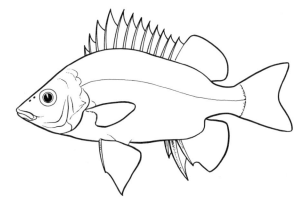

eral line continuous and complete; longitudinal bands often present on body. Theraponids are carnivorous. Maximum length about 28 cm.

Three genera, *Helotes*, *Pelates*, and *Therapon*, with at least 15 species.

Family BANJOSIDAE.   Marine; coasts of China, southern Japan, and Korea.

Body deep, strongly compressed; head with steep, nearly straight profile; opercle spineless; dorsal fin with 10 flattened spines and 12 soft rays; anal fin with three spines, the second much longer than other anal rays, and seven soft rays; pelvics inserted behind base of pectorals; caudal fin slightly emarginate; lateral line continuous and complete; color brownish or olive with eight faint longitudinal darkish bands. This fish closely resembles the pomadasyids. Maximum length about 30 cm.

One species; *Banjos banjos* (=*typus*) (Fowler, 1972:485).

Family KUHLIIDAE—Aholeholes. Marine and freshwater; Indo-Pacific.

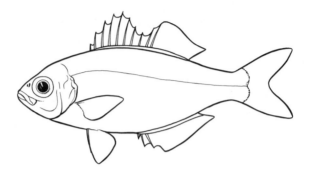

Dorsal and anal fins each with a well-developed scaly sheath; no scaly pelvic axillary process; anal fin with three spines. Maximum length up to 45 cm.

Three genera, the marine *Kuhlia* (=*Dules*) and the poorly known freshwater Australian *Nannatherina* and *Nannoperca,* with about 12 species.

Family CENTRARCHIDAE—Sunfishes. Freshwater; North America (see map on p. 341).

Three or more anal spines; pseudobranch small and concealed; branchiostegal rays 5–7; gill membranes separate.

Most sunfishes are nest builders. The male hollows out a small depression with his tail and then guards the eggs. Centrarchids are an important sports fish and have been introduced into many areas beyond their native range. Some, such as *Lepomis macrochirus,* the bluegill, have been used in physiological and ecological experimental work. Maximum length about 83 cm, attained in *Micropterus salmoides* (largemouth bass). At the other extreme species of *Elassoma* are not known to exceed 4 cm.

Nine genera with 30 species.

SUBFAMILY CENTRARCHINAE (SUNFISHES). Suborbital bones present in addition to the lachrymal; dentary and angular penetrated by lateral line; lateral line present on body, sometimes incomplete; anal fin spines usually three (or fewer) or five (or more); dorsal fin usually with 5–13 spines (most with about 10).

The 20 species typically with three anal spines are placed in *Enneacanthus, Lepomis* (upper figure), and *Micropterus* (basses) (lower figure). The seven species typically with more than three anal spines (usually

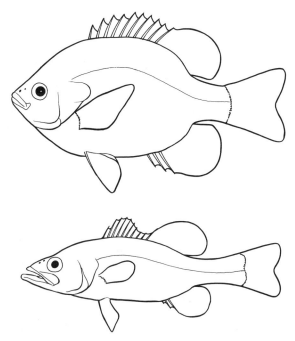

five) are placed in *Acantharchus*, *Ambloplites*, *Archoplites* (one species, the Sacramento perch, is the only living centrarchid native west of the Rocky Mountains), *Centrarchus*, and *Pomoxis* (crappies).

SUBFAMILY ELASSOMATINAE (ELASSOMINAE) (PYGMY SUNFISHES). No suborbitals, except the lachrymal; dentary and angular not penetrated by lateral line; no lateral line on body; anal fin with three spines and 4–8 soft rays; dorsal fin with 3–5 spines and 8–13 soft rays.

The pygmy sunfishes are placed in their own family by some workers (e.g., Branson and Moore, 1962).

One genus, *Elassoma*, with at least three species.

Family PRIACANTHIDAE—Bigeyes (Catalufas).   Marine; tropical and subtropical; Atlantic, Indian, and Pacific.

Very large eyes; mouth oblique; anal fin with three spines; caudal fin with 16 principal rays (14 branched); scales strongly ctenoid; membrane present connecting the inner rays of the pelvic fin to the body; color usually bright red.

Bigeyes are usually carnivorous and nocturnal. The tapetum lucidum, in at least one species, lies in the chorioid as it does in many "lower" fishes, whereas in all other teleosts investigated it lies, when present, in the retina (Nicol et al., 1973). Maximum length up to 60 cm.

Three genera, *Cookeolus*, *Priacanthus*, and *Pristigenys* (=*Pseudopriacanthus*), with about 18 species.

Family APOGONIDAE—Cardinalfishes. Marine; Atlantic, Indian, and Pacific, some brackish water; a few in streams on tropical Pacific Islands.

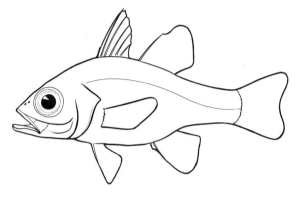

Two separated dorsal fins, the first with 6–8 spines and the second with one spine and 8–14 soft rays; anal fin with two spines and 8–18 soft rays; scales usually ctenoid, but cycloid in several groups and absent in *Gymnapogon;* seven branchiostegal rays; 24 or 25 vertebrae (10 abdominal and 14 or 15 caudal). Many of the species are mouthbreeders; it is suspected that in some only the males incubate the eggs, whereas in others it is only the females. Maximum length 20 cm, most less than 10 cm.

A confusing synonymy exists in this family in that the names Amiidae and *Amia* are used in some works (e.g., Fowler, 1959).

Fraser (1972) recognizes three subfamilies and gives a detailed review of the shallow-water forms. He places several genera previously contained in this family in other families, primarily in the Percichthyidae (not named in this work), but *Dinolestes* with one anal spine is given family status (Dinolestidae).

About 20 genera (e.g., *Amiichthys*, *Apogon*, *Apogonichthyoides*, *Astrapogon*, *Cheilodipterus*, *Epigonus*, *Gymnapogon*, *Paramia*, *Phaeoptyx*, *Pseudamia*, and *Siphamia*) with about 170 species. Fraser (1972) estimates slightly more genera and species.

Family ACROPOMATIDAE. Marine; Indo-Pacific.

Two separated dorsal fins, the first with 7–9 weak spines; anal fin with three spines; anus anterior, near pelvic base (the only other perciform with an anterior anus is the serranid *Bullisichthys*); two opercular spines; lateral line straight and extending beyond caudal base; luminous organs present; 25 vertebrae.

One genus, *Acropoma*, with three species.

Family PERCIDAE—Perches.   Freshwater; Northern Hemisphere (see map on p. 341).

Two dorsal fins, separate or narrowly joined (broadly joined in *Zingel*); one or two anal spines, if two, the second is usually weak; pelvic fins thoracic, with one spine and five soft rays; premaxillae protractile or nonprotractile; branchiostegal rays 5–8; the membrane is not joined to isthmus (may be united or not); pseudobranchiae well developed to rudimentary; vertebrae 32–50. Maximum size up to 90 cm, attained in *Stizostedion vitreum* (walleye); most species much smaller.

Nine genera with 126 species. Collette (1963) recognizes two subfamilies, as shown here, whereas some other workers recognize three by giving subfamily status to the Etheostomatini.

SUBFAMILY PERCINAE.   Anteriormost interhaemal bone greatly enlarged; anal spines usually well developed; lateral line usually not extending onto tail.

Six genera with 117 species.

TRIBE PERCINI.   Preopercle strongly serrate; usually seven or eight branchiostegal rays; body compressed; anal spines prominent; swim bladder well developed.

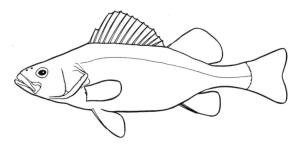

Three genera: the circumpolar *Perca* with three species, the European and western Asian *Gymnocephalus* (=*Acerina*) with three species, and *Percarina demidoffi* of the northern Black Sea area.

TRIBE ETHEOSTOMATINI.   Preopercle margin smooth or partly serrate; usually five or six branchiostegal rays; body slightly compressed or fusiform; anal spines moderately prominent; swim bladder reduced or absent. Seldom over 11 cm.

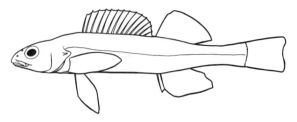

Three genera of North American darters: *Ammocrypta* with five species, *Etheostoma* with 80 species, and *Percina* with 25 species.

SUBFAMILY LUCIOPERCINAE. Anteriormost interhaemal no larger than posterior ones; anal spines weak; lateral line extending onto tail.

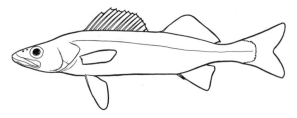

Contains four species of European darterlike fish [*Romanichthys* and *Zingel* (=*Aspro*)] without swim bladder and five species of European (including the Caspian and Aral seas) and North American pikeperches [*Stizostedion* (=*Lucioperca*)] with well-developed swim bladder.

Family SILLAGINIDAE—Smelt-Whitings. Marine and brackish water; Indo-Pacific.

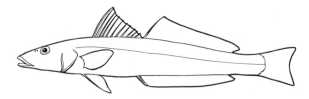

Body elongate; mouth small; two dorsal fins (little or no interspace), first with 9–12 spines and second with 16–26 soft rays; anal fin with two spines and 15–27 soft rays. Maximum length about 35 cm.

Three genera, *Sillaginodes*, *Sillaginopsis*, and *Sillago*, with about six species.

Family BRANCHIOSTEGIDAE—Tilefishes.   Marine; Atlantic, Indian, and Pacific.

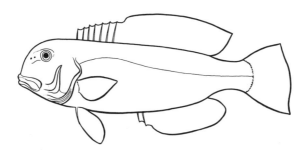

Long, single dorsal fin with spines and soft rays; mouth nearly horizontal; pelvic fin with one spine and five soft rays; anal fin long, with one or two weak spines; 24–27 vertebrae.

Six genera, *Branchiostegus*, *Caulolatilus*, *Hoplolatilus*, *Lopholatilus*, *Malacanthus*, and *Prolatilus*, and about 24 species.

Family LABRACOGLOSSIDAE.   Marine; western Pacific.

Single dorsal fin, with spines and soft rays; soft-rayed portion of dorsal and anal fins covered with scales; jaws without canine teeth.

Three genera, *Bathystethus*, *Evistius*, and *Labracoglossa*, with about five species.

Family LACTARIIDAE—False Trevallies.   Marine; Indo-Pacific.

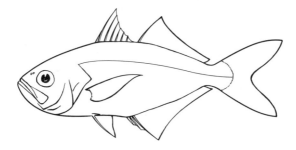

Dorsal fins separate; soft-rayed portion of dorsal and anal fins covered with scales (all scales easily shed); each jaw with two small canine teeth at front.

One genus, *Lactarius*, with two species.

Family POMATOMIDAE—Bluefishes.   Marine; Atlantic, Indian, and Pacific.

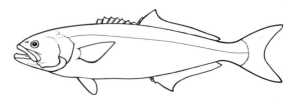

Dorsal fins separate; soft dorsal and anal fins covered with scales; preoperculum with a membrane flap over the suboperculum; black blotch at
base of pectoral.

   Pomatomus saltatrix is described as being extremely bloodthirsty, killing
more fish than it can consume.

   Two genera, *Pomatomus* and *Scombrops,* with about three species.

Family RACHYCENTRIDAE—Cobia.   Marine; Atlantic and Indo-Pacific.

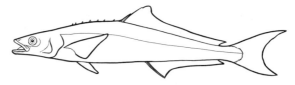

Body elongate, head depressed; 6–9 short free spines ahead of the long
dorsal fin (1–3 spines and 26–33 soft rays); anal fin long, with two or
three spines and 22–28 soft rays; three dark stripes on side of body.
Maximum length up to 1.5 m.

   One species: *Rachycentron canadum.*

Family ECHENEIDAE—Remoras.   Marine; Atlantic, Indian, and Pacific.

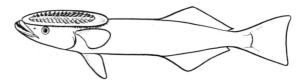

Body elongate, head flattened; sucking disc on head (developed from a
transformed spinous dorsal fin, the spines of which are split to form
10–28 transverse movable lamina inside a fleshy margin). The remora
presents the disc against other fish and creates a partial vacuum by
operating the movable disc ridges like the slats in a Venetian blind,
thereby causing the sucking action which permits it to obtain rides on
larger animals. Remoras are found on sharks, bony fishes, sea turtles,
and marine mammals; some species show considerable host specificity.

Maximum length about 1.0 m attained in *Echeneis naucrates*. The smallest species is 17 cm.

This family is given ordinal status by Berg (1940) and Gosline (1971).

Seven genera, *Echeneis, Phtheirichthys, Remilegia, Remora, Remorina, Remoropsis,* and *Rhombochirus,* with seven or eight species (Strasburg, 1964).

Family CARANGIDAE—Jacks and Pompanos.   Marine (rarely brackish), Atlantic, Indian, and Pacific.

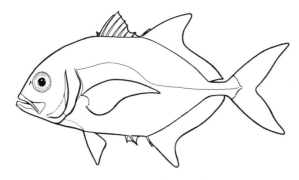

Body compressed and with small cycloid scales (those on the lateral line are modified into spiny scutes in many species), naked areas variously developed; usually three anal spines with the first two detached from the rest of the fin; detached finlets sometimes behind dorsal and anal fins; caudal fin widely forked; caudal peduncle slender; one species (*Parona signatus*) lacks pelvic fins.

Carangids occur in a wide range of body shapes, from the shallow-bodied *Decapterus* to the extremely thin and deep-bodied *Selene.* The family contains some important food species.

About 24 genera (e.g., *Caranx, Chloroscombrus, Decapterus, Nematistius, Oligoplites, Scomberoides, Selar, Selene, Seriola, Trachinotus, Trachurus, Uraspis,* and *Vomer*) with about 200 species.

Family CORYPHAENIDAE—Dolphins.   Marine; Atlantic, Indian, and Pacific.

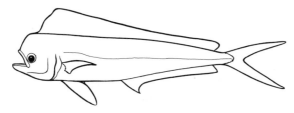

Dorsal fin originating on head, with 48–65 rays; no spines in dorsal and anal fins; caudal fin deeply forked; forehead prominent (steep and high) in adult males of the largest of the two species; color in life exceedingly beautiful; vertebrae 30–34. Maximum length 1.5 m, attained in *Coryphaena hippurus.*

One genus, *Coryphaena,* with two species.

Family FORMIONIDAE.   Marine; Indo-Pacific.

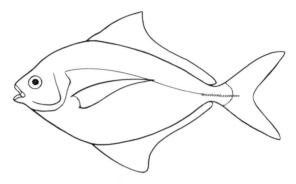

No pelvic fins in adult; dorsal fin with 2–6 rudimentary spines and 42–46 soft rays; anal fin with two rudimentary spines and 35–40 soft rays; a few enlarged scutes at end of lateral line. Maximum length about 75 cm.

One species: *Formio* (=*Apolectus*) *niger.*

Family MENIDAE—Moonfish.   Marine; Indo-Pacific.

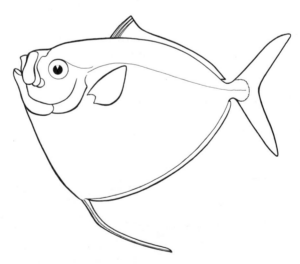

Body disclike, with sharp breast; dorsal contour nearly horizontal; dorsal fin with 43–45 soft rays, no spines; anal fin with 30–33 soft rays, no spines; first pelvic ray in adult prolonged.

One species, *Mene maculata* (=*anno-carolina*).

Family LEIOGNATHIDAE—Slimys, Slipmouths, or Ponyfishes. Marine and brackish water; Indo-Pacific.

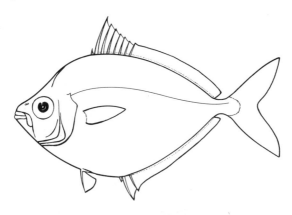

Body greatly compressed and slimy, with small scales; head naked, upper surface with bony ridges; gill membranes united with isthmus; mouth small and highly protrusible; no pseudobranchiae; single dorsal fin, the anterior portion usually with eight or nine spines that are more or less elevated; anal fin with three spines; both dorsal and anal fins fold into a basal scaly sheath.

Leiognathus klunzingeri, a former Red Sea endemic, is one of the 24 known species of fishes which since the Suez Canal was opened in 1869 have passed from the tropical Red Sea, through the highly saline Great Bitter Lake, to the subtropical Mediterranean Sea; it is common in parts of the eastern Mediterranean and is the only leiognathid known to have dispersed through the Suez (Ben-Tuvia, 1966).

Berg (1940) and Norman (1957) lumped the family Gerreidae with this one.

Three genera, *Gazza, Leiognathus* (=*Equula*), and *Secutor*, with about 18 species.

Family BRAMIDAE—Pomfrets. Marine; oceanic, Atlantic, Indian, and Pacific.

Single dorsal fin (extending length of body in some) with unbranched anterior spines. *Eumegistus* is thought to be the most primitive genus. Maximum length 85 cm, attained in *Taractichthys longipinnis.*

Six genera with 18 species (Mead, 1972).

SUBFAMILY BRAMINAE.   Dorsal and anal fins of adults with scales and not wholly depressable; pelvic fins thoracic.

Four genera, *Brama, Eumegistus, Taractes,* and *Taractichthys,* with about 13 species.

SUBFAMILY PTERACLINAE.   Dorsal and anal fins high, scaleless, and completely depressable; pelvic fins often jugular or nearly so.

Two genera, *Pteraclis* and *Pterycombus,* with about five species.

Family CARISTIIDAE—Manefishes.   Marine; oceanic.

Pelvic fin with one spine and five soft rays; 15 branched caudal rays; pelvics in advance of pectorals in some species, beneath in others.

Berg (1940), Norman (1957), McAllister (1968), and Gosline (1971) placed this poorly known family in the Beryciformes. Placement in Perciformes by Greenwood et al. (1966) and Scott et al. (1970) is accepted here.

One genus, *Caristius* (=*Elephenor, Platyberyx*), with about four species.

Family ARRIPIDAE—Australian Salmon.   Marine; South Pacific (southern Australia and New Zealand region).

Three anal spines; gill membranes free from isthmus; anal fin much shorter than the soft dorsal.

One genus, *Arripis,* with two species.

Family EMMELICHTHYIDAE—Bonnetmouths.   Marine; Atlantic, Indian, and South Pacific.

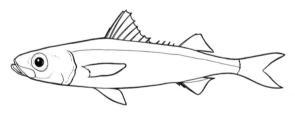

Mouth toothless or nearly so, very protractile; anal fin with three spines; caudal fin forked with the two lobes folding in scissorlike fashion.

SUBFAMILY CENTRACANTHINAE (MAENINAE).   Mediterranean, eastern Atlantic, and Indian.

Five genera, *Centracanthus, Coleosmaris, Merolepis, Pterosmaris,* and *Spicara,* with nine species.

Subfamily Emmelichthyinae. Indo-Pacific, South Pacific, eastern Atlantic, and Caribbean Sea.

Five genera, *Dipterygonotus, Emmelichthys, Erythrocles, Inermia,* and *Plagiogeneion,* with eight species.

Family LUTJANIDAE—Snappers. Marine (rarely in estuaries); Atlantic, Indian, and Pacific.

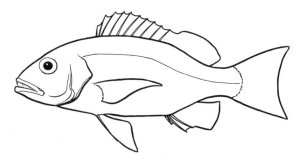

Dorsal fin continuous or with a shallow notch; three anal fin spines; pelvics below or slightly behind pectoral base; most with enlarged canine teeth on jaws; palatines usually with teeth; maxillae slips beneath preorbital when mouth closed; usually 24 vertebrae.

Snappers are important food fishes but are sometimes responsible for ciguatera, the tropical fish poisoning disease. Maximum length about 1.0 m.

About 23 genera (e.g., *Aphareus, Apsilus, Caesio, Etelis, Hoplopagrus, Lutjanus, Ocyurus, Rhomboplites,* and *Verilus*) and about 230 species.

Family NEMIPTERIDAE—Threadfin Breams. Marine; Indo-Pacific.

Palatine and vomer toothless; dorsal fin continuous, with 10 spines and 8–11 soft rays; anal fin with 3 spines and 6–8 soft rays; caudal fin in some with filament off upper lobe; 24 vertebrae.

Three genera, *Nemipterus, Parascolopsis,* and *Scolopsis,* with numerous species.

Family LOBOTIDAE—Tripletails. Marine, brackish, and freshwater; most warm seas.

Palatine and vomer toothless; caudal fin rounded; profile similar to centrarchids; rounded lobes on second dorsal and anal fins giving fish the appearance of having three tails.

The very young can camouflage themselves by turning sideways and floating like leaves. Maximum length about 1.0 m, attained in *Lobotes surinamensis*.

Two genera, *Datnioides* (fresh- and brackish water from India to Malay Archipelago) and *Lobotes* (marine), with about four species.

Family GERREIDAE—Mojarras.   Marine (occasionally brackish and rarely in fresh water); most warm seas.

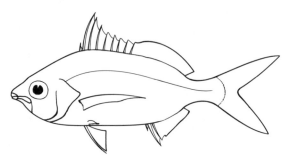

Mouth highly protrusible; head scaly, upper surface smooth; scaly sheath along bases of dorsal and anal fins; gill membranes free from isthmus; tail deeply forked.

The former family name Gerridae is preoccupied by the water striders of the insect order Hemiptera. Emmendation of the orthography to Gerreidae to eliminate homonymy follows Böhlke and Chaplin (1968). Berg (1940) and Norman (1957) included this family with the Leiognathidae. Maximum length 35 cm.

Seven genera, *Diapterus, Eucinostomus, Gerres, Parequula, Pentaprion* (with five or six spines in anal fin), *Ulaema,* and *Xystaema,* with about 40 species.

Family POMADASYIDAE—Grunts.   Marine (some in brackish water, rarely in fresh water); Atlantic, Indian, and Pacific.

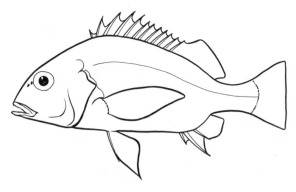

Dorsal fin continuous or with shallow notch; three anal spines; canine teeth on jaws and teeth on vomer absent; vertebrae 26 or 27.

Grunts make sounds, as their common name suggests, by grinding their pharyngeal teeth. The sound is amplified by the adjacent swim bladder.

Twenty-one genera (e.g., *Anisotremus, Conodon, Haemulon, Orthopristis, Pomadasys, Xenichthys,* and *Xenistius*) with about 175 species.

Family LETHRINIDAE—Scavengers or Emperors. Marine coastal; west Africa and Indo-Pacific.

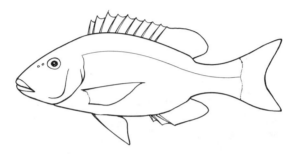

Dorsal fin continuous, with 10 spines and 8–9 soft rays; three anal fin spines; gill membranes broadly united; lips thick and fleshy; preoperculum and top of head scaleless.

Two genera, *Lethrinus* and *Neolethrinus,* with about 21 species.

Family PENTAPODIDAE—Large-eye Breams. Marine coastal; Indo-Pacific.

Dorsal fin continuous with 10 spines and 9–11 soft rays; three anal fin spines; gill membranes broadly united; preoperculum and rest of head behind eyes scaled.

Four genera, *Gnathodentex, Gymnocranius, Monotaxis,* and *Pentapodus,* with about nine species.

Family SPARIDAE—Porgies. *Marine (very rarely brackish); Atlantic, Indian, and Pacific.*

Three anal spines; distal end of premaxillae overlapping the maxillae externally; lateral teeth low molariforms; palate toothless. Maximum length about 1.2 m.

Twenty-nine genera (e.g., *Archosargus, Boops, Calamus, Chrysophrys, Dentex, Diplodus, Pagellus, Pagrus, Paradicichthys, Pimelepterus, Sparus,* and *Stenotomus*) with about 100 species.

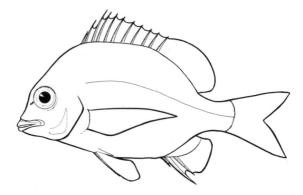

Family SCIAENIDAE—Drums (Croakers).   Marine, brackish, and freshwater (particularly in South America); Atlantic, Indian, and Pacific.

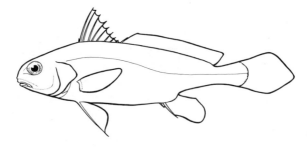

Dorsal fin almost completely divided; anal fin with one or two (usually weak) spines; lateral line extending to end of caudal fin; caudal fin rounded or truncate; single barbel or a patch of small barbels on chin of some species; swim bladder (rarely absent) with many branches; otoliths exceptionally large.

Sciaenids can produce sound, using the swim bladder as a resonating chamber. Some are important food fishes.

Twenty-eight genera [e.g., *Aplodinotus* (freshwater, North America), *Bairdiella, Cynoscion, Equetus, Larimus, Menticirrhus, Micropogon, Otolithes, Sciaena, Seriphus,* and *Umbrina*] with about 160 species.

Family MULLIDAE—Goatfishes.   Marine (rarely brackish water); Atlantic, Indian, and Pacific.

Body elongate; two widely separated dorsal fins, the first with 6–8 spines; soft dorsal fin shorter than anal fin; anal fin with one or two small spines; two long chin barbels (used in detecting food); caudal fin forked; 23 or 24 vertebrae.

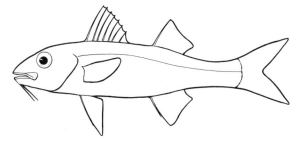

Goatfishes are important as a food fish. Many are brightly colored. Maximum length up to 60 cm.

Six genera, *Mulloidichthys*, *Mullus*, *Parupeneus*, *Pseudupeneus*, *Upeneichthys*, and *Upeneus*, with 55 species.

Family MONODACTYLIDAE—Moonfishes (Fingerfishes). Marine and brackish water (sometimes entering fresh water); west Africa and Indo-Pacific.

Body strongly compressed and deep (deeper than long in some); pelvic fins usually small or vestigial; dorsal fin single and with a long base, covered with scales and 5–8 short graduated spines; anal fin with three spines, long base; scales cycloid or ctenoid.

Moonfishes are occasionally sold as aquarium fishes. They are often of a silvery color.

Three genera, *Monodactylus*, *Psettias*, and *Schuettea*, with five species. Most authors place *Schuettea* (with two species in New South Wales and Western Australia) in the Monodactylidae but Tominaga (1968) recommends placement in a family of its own. It differs from other monodactylids in a few characters (e.g., normally developed pelvic fins, cycloid scales, teeth absent from endopterygoid and ectopterygoid) but it is provisionally retained in the family as a conservative measure.

Family PEMPHERIDAE—Sweepers. Marine and brackish water; western Atlantic, Indian, and Pacific.

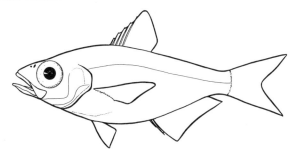

Body compressed and deep; maxillae not reaching beyond center of eye; preorbital smooth; eye large, without adipose lid; one short dorsal fin, originating before middle of body, with 4–7 graduated spines and 7–12 soft rays; anal fin with two (very rarely) or three spines and 17–45 soft rays; lateral line scales usually 40–82; tubes of lateral line usually short and wide; gill rakers long and usually 25–31; luminescent organs in a few species; pyloric caeca 9 or 10; swim bladder absent in one species (*Pempheris poeyi*); 25 vertebrae (10 abdominal and 15 caudal).

Tominaga (1968) presents a detailed description of their morphology and gives reasons for removing *Leptobrama* from this family. Maximum length about 30 cm.

Two genera: *Parapriacanthus* with about five species and *Pempheris* (=*Priacanthopsis*) with about 20 species.

Family LEPTOBRAMIDAE—Beachsalmon. Marine and brackish water (occasionally entering rivers); coasts of southern New Guinea, Queensland, and Western Australia.

Body compressed and deep; maxillae reaching far behind eye; preorbital serrate; eye relatively small, with adipose lid; one short dorsal fin behind middle of body (above anal fin), with four spines and 16–18 soft rays; anal fin with three spines and 26–30 soft rays; lateral line scales about 75-77; tubes in lateral line long and narrow; gill rakers short, usually 10.

This family was included with the Pempheridae by such workers as Norman (1957) and Greenwood et al. (1966) but Tominaga (1965, 1968) has shown it to have no particular affinity with the pempherids. Maximum length about 30 cm.

One species: *Leptobrama muelleri*.

Family BATHYCLUPEIDAE. Marine oceanic; Indian, western Pacific, and Gulf of Mexico.

One dorsal fin in posterior half of body, without spines; anal fin long, with one spine; dorsal and anal fins covered with scales; premaxillae and maxillae bordering mouth; usually 31 vertebrae (10 abdominal and 21 caudal).

Berg (1940) placed this family in its own order, Bathyclupeiformes, between the Clupeiformes and Galaxiiformes.

One genus, *Bathyclupea*, with about four species.

Family TOXOTIDAE—Archerfishes. Marine coastal, brackish, and freshwater; from India to Philippines and Australia and Polynesia (see map on p. 342).

Body deep and compressed; eye large; dorsal spines strong, 4–6, followed by 11–14 soft rays; anal fin with three spines and 12–18 soft rays; length of soft dorsal much shorter than soft portion of anal; mouth large, terminal (lower jaw protruding), and highly protractile; lateral line scales about 23–45; seven branchiostegals; 24 vertebrae (10 abdominal and 14 caudal).

These fishes are capable of forcefully ejecting squirts of water from their mouths and downing insects.

One genus, *Toxotes*, with about four species.

Family CORACINIDAE—Galjoen Fishes. Marine coastal and brackish water; South Africa and Madagascar.

Body relatively deep; mouth small; dorsal fin with 10 spines and usually 18–23 soft rays; anal fin with three spines and usually 13 or 14 soft rays; gill membranes fused with isthmus; some teeth incisiform.

One genus, *Coracinus* (=*Dichistius*), with about three species.

Family KYPHOSIDAE—Sea Chubs. Marine; Atlantic, Indian, and Pacific.

Three anal fin spines. Most are plant-feeding fishes usually found near shore.

Fifteen genera with 31 species.

SUBFAMILY GIRELLINAE (NIBBLERS). Some incisiform teeth present; maxillae concealed beneath suborbital bones. Pacific (primarily Philippines to Australia).

Six genera (e.g., *Girella*) with 10 species.

SUBFAMILY KYPHOSINAE (CYPHOSINAE) (RUDDERFISHES). Some incisiform teeth; maxillae exposed. Atlantic, Indian, and Pacific.

Three genera, *Hermosilla*, *Kyphosus*, and *Sectator*, with 10 species.

SUBFAMILY SCORPINAE (SCORPIDINAE) (HALFMOONS). No incisiform teeth; pelvics well behind pectorals. Indo-Pacific and California.

Six genera (e.g., *Atypichthys*, *Medialuna*, *Parascorpis*, and *Scorpis*) with 11 species.

Family EPHIPPIDAE—Spadefishes. Marine; Atlantic, Indian, and Pacific.

Three anal fin spines; gill membranes united to isthmus; body deep and laterally compressed; mouth small; spinous portion of dorsal fin distinct from soft-rayed portion (except in *Platax*).

Young with about five or six vertical bands extending around body which are lost with growth.

SUBFAMILY DREPANINAE.   Mouth protractile; pectoral fins longer than head; maxillae distally exposed; subocular shelf absent. Indo-Pacific and west Africa.

One genus, *Drepane,* with two species.

SUBFAMILY EPHIPPINAE (CHAETODIPTERINAE).   Mouth not protractile or scarcely so; pectoral fins shorter than head; maxillae distally hidden; subocular shelf usually present. Atlantic, Indian, and Pacific.

Six genera (e.g., *Chaetodipterus, Ephippus, Platax,* and *Tripterodon*) with 12 species. Separate subfamily status may be warranted for *Platax* (whose young have very elongate dorsal and anal fins).

Family SCATOPHAGIDAE—Scats.   Marine and brackish water; Indo-Pacific (see map on p. 342).

Four anal fin spines; first dorsal spine procumbent; caudal fin with 16 principal rays; mouth not protractile.

Two genera, *Prenes* and *Scatophagus,* with about three species.

Family RHINOPRENIDAE—Threadfin Scat.   Marine and brackish water; Gulf of Papua, New Guinea.

Body deep and compressed, quadrangular in outline; mouth small and inferior; second dorsal spine, fourth pectoral ray, and first pelvic ray greatly prolonged into free filaments which reach tail base or beyond; anal fin with three spines and 16 or 17 soft rays.

One species: *Rhinoprenes pentanemus* (Munro, 1964, 1967).

Family CHAETODONTIDAE—Butterflyfishes. Marine; Atlantic, Indian, and Pacific (primarily Indo-Pacific).

Thin, deep, discus-shaped body; mouth small, with comblike teeth; caudal fin with 17 principal rays (15 branched); mouth protractile; vertical fins densely scaled; single continuous dorsal fin; caudal fin emarginate to rounded; 24 vertebrae.

Chaetodontids form one of the most colorful elements of coral reefs. The young are often colored differently from the adults. W. E. Burgess has recently presented evidence suggesting that butterflyfishes and angelfishes be placed in separate families.

SUBFAMILY CHAETODONTINAE (BUTTERFLYFISHES). No strong spine at angle of preopercle; well-developed pelvic axillary process.

Eleven genera (e.g., *Chaetodon, Heniochus, Microcanthus,* and *Prognathodes*) with about 160 species.

SUBFAMILY POMACANTHINAE (ANGELFISHES). Strong spine at angle of preopercle; no well-developed pelvic axillary process.

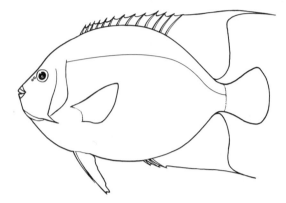

Seven genera (e.g., *Centropyge, Holacanthus,* and *Pomacanthus*) with about 30 species.

Family ENOPLOSIDAE.   Marine; Celebes and southern and eastern Australia.

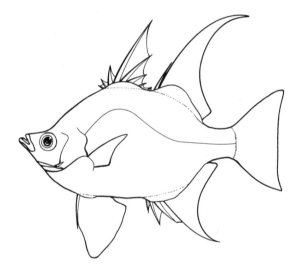

Pelvic fins unusually large, each with a strong spine; external bones of head not rough; supramaxillae present; two sharp spines on lower angle of preoperculum.

One species: *Enoplosus armatus.*

Family PENTACEROTIDAE (Histiopteridae)—Armorheads or Boarfishes.   Marine; Indo-Pacific.

Body strongly compressed; pelvic fins unusually large, with one long, strong spine and five soft rays; head encased in exposed rough bones; no supramaxillae; single dorsal fin with 4–14 strong spines and 9–29 soft rays; anal fin with 2–5 strong spines and 8–13 soft rays; scales small.

Five genera in two subfamilies: *Histiopterus, Zanclistius,* and *Paristiopterus* in Histiopterinae and *Pentaceropsis* and *Pentaceros* (=*Pseudopentaceros* and *Quinquarias*) in Pentacerotinae, with a total of about 12 species.

Family NANDIDAE—Leaffishes. Freshwater (occasionally brackish water); northeast South America, West Africa, and Southern Asia (see map on p. 343).

Head usually large; mouth usually large and highly protrusible; dorsal fin continuous; caudal fin rounded; lateral line incomplete or absent; pelvic fin without scaly axillary process. Many are vicious predators. At rest, most look deceptively like drifting leaves.

As with many families, this one has been split in various ways by past authors. Recently Barlow et al. (1968), in a detailed and comprehensive study, erected a new family for *Badis badis* and concluded that it descended from a proto-anabantoid stock. Gosline (1971) recognized three families—Badidae, Nandidae, and Pristolepidae—and placed them at the start of his Percoidei. He believed them to be related to the Anabantoidei and perhaps even deserving of placement with them. Liem (1970), in a detailed myological and osteological study with a functional analysis of the feeding apparatus, argues convincingly that nandids (Nandinae here) and anabantoids show no phylogenetic affinity and considers ·

nandids to resemble relatively advanced Percoidei. He also places *Badis* and *Pristolepis* in separate families and does not believe that they bear any close affinity to his Nandidae [he apparently agrees with Barlow et al. (1968) that *Badis* and anabantoids may be related]. Here, although acknowledging the diversity of the group, the Nandinae, *Badis,* and *Pristolepis* are tentatively placed in the same family. Maximum length about 21 cm, attained in *Pristolepis fasciata.*

Seven genera with about 10 species.

SUBFAMILY NANDINAE

TRIBE NANDINI.   Tropical west Africa, India, and southeast Asia (to Borneo).

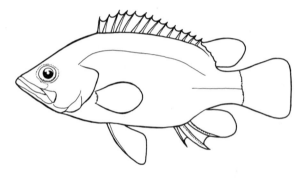

Anal fin with three spines in *Nandus* spp., four in *Afronandus sheljuzhkoi,* and 9–12 in *Polycentropsis abbreviata.* Maximum length about 20 cm, usually much smaller.

Three genera, *Afronandus* (springs in Ivory Coast), *Nandus* (India to Borneo), and *Polycentropsis* (West Africa), with four species.

TRIBE POLYCENTRINI.   Northeast South America. Dorsal fin with 16–18 spines, plus a soft-rayed portion; anal fin with 12 or 13 spines, plus a soft-rayed portion. Maximum length about 10 cm.

Two species: *Monocirrhus polyacanthus* (Guiana and the Amazon lowlands) and *Polycentrus schomburgki* (Trinidad to Guiana).

SUBFAMILY PRISTOLEPINAE.   Small area of peninsular India and Ceylon, southeast Asia, and parts of Malay Archipelago (e.g., Sumatra, Java, and Borneo).

Mouth relatively small and only slightly protrusible; suborbital shelf present. The most widespread species, *Pristolepis fasciata,* has dorsal fin with 13–16 spines and 14–16 soft rays; anal fin with three spines and eight or nine soft rays; lateral line scales 26–28.

One genus, *Pristolepis*, with about three species.

SUBFAMILY BADINAE.   India.

Mouth relatively small and only slightly protrusible; no suborbital shelf; dorsal fin with six or seven spines and 6–10 soft rays; anal fin with three spines and 6–8 soft rays; lateral line scales 26–33.

This is a colorful fish, which can change its color quite rapidly. Its behavior has been studied in considerable detail by Dr. G. W. Barlow and others. Maximum length about 8 cm.

One species: *Badis badis*.

Family OPLEGNATHIDAE—Knifejaws.   Marine; Japan, western Australia, Tasmania, Hawaii, Galapagos, and South Africa.

Teeth in adult united to form a parrotlike beak (as in Scaridae); spinous dorsal fin low.

One genus, *Oplegnathus* (=*Hoplegnathus*), with about four species.

Family EMBIOTOCIDAE—Surfperches.   Coastal marine (rarely in fresh water); North Pacific.

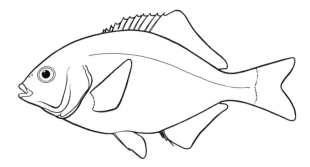

Anal fin with three spines and 15–35 soft rays; scales cycloid. Viviparous (impregnation by the male is aided by the thickened forward end of the anal fin). Maximum length about 45 cm, attained in *Rhacochilus toxotes*.

About 20 genera [e.g., *Amphistichus, Brachyistius, Cymatogaster, Ditrema, Embiotoca, Hyperprosopon, Hysterocarpus* (with one species, *H. traski*, in streams in California), *Micrometrus, Phanerodon, Rhacochilus*, and *Zalembius*] and about 23 species.

Family CICHLIDAE—Cichlids.   Fresh- and brackish water; Central and South

America (one species extending north to Texas), West Indies, Africa, Madagascar, Syria, and coastal India (see map on p. 343).

Single nostril on each side; lateral line interrupted; three or more anal fin spines; no subocular shelf.

As in many families, there is much variability in body shape between some species. Most cichlids have a moderately deep and compressed body similar to *Cichlasoma* shown in the above figure. However, the body can be discshaped and have extremely high, saillike fins as in *Pterophyllum* (angelfishes) or low fins as in *Symphysodon* (discus fishes); it can also be elongate as in *Crenicichla* (pike cichlids).

Cichlids form an important group of relatively large aquarium fishes. They have highly organized breeding actions and some are mouthbreeders. Female discus fish secrete a whitish milklike substance from the skin to "nurse" their young.

A wealth of information on the biology, adaptive radiation, and speciation of African cichlids is provided by Fryer and Iles (1972). Endemic cichlids make up most of the fish fauna in the three African lakes which contain the most species of fish of any lake in the world. Lake Malawi has more than 200 cichlids (all but four endemic; total of 42 non-cichlids), Lake Victoria has at least 170 (all but six endemic; total of 38 noncichlids), and Lake Tanganyika has 126 (all endemic; total of 67 noncichlids). These cichlids exhibit a vast diversity of feeding habits. New species are still being described and Axelrod (1973), in a book with hundreds of excellent color photos, estimates that there are about 250 species of cichlids in Malawi and 150 species in Tanganyika. About 76 species of *Cichlasoma* (one of which, *C. cyanoguttatum,* ranges into Texas) are known from Mexico and Central America (Miller, 1966); other species occur in South America. Maximum length about 80 cm attained in *Boulengerochromis microlepis* of Lake Tanganyika.

About 85 genera; for example, *Aequidens, Apistogramma, Astronotus, Cichlasoma, Crenicichla, Geophagus, Pterophyllum,* and *Symphysodon* from

Central and South America, *Haplochromis, Hemichromis, Pelmatochromis,* and *Tilapia* (ranges to Syria and widely introduced elsewhere) from Africa, and *Etroplus* from India and Ceylon) with at least 680 species [Fryer and Iles (1972) estimate at least 700 species]. It is the second largest family in the Perciformes.

Superfamily Pomacentroidae

Family POMACENTRIDAE—Damselfishes. Marine (rarely brackish); all tropical seas (primarily Indo-Pacific).

Single nostril (rarely two) on each side; body high (rarely terete) and compressed; mouth small; lateral line incomplete or interrupted; anal fin with two spines (three in the rare *Zabulon*); subocular shelf present; palate toothless; single continuous dorsal fin with 9–14 spines (rarely more) and usually 11–18 soft rays (but base of spinous portion longer than soft). Maximum length about 35 cm.

Damselfishes present many problems to the taxonomist because of the many species complexes and color patterns which vary with individuals and between localities in a species. Considerable morphological diversity exists in currently recognized genera, many of which are being revised (Allen and Emery, 1973).

About 23 genera with about 230 species.

SUBFAMILY PREMNINAE. Transverse scale rows 68–78; dorsal fin with 10 spines and 17 or 18 soft rays; caudal fin rounded; suborbital spine reaching to operculum. Body color deep reddish-brown with three white transverse bands.

One species, *Premnas biaculeatus* (sabrecheeked tomato clownfish), which lives among tentacles of sea anemones from the northeastern Indian Ocean to the Philippines and northern Queensland.

SUBFAMILY AMPHIPRIONINAE. Transverse scale rows usually 50–65 (most members of the following two subfamilies have fewer than 40); dorsal fin usually with 10 spines, rarely 9 or 11 (most members of the following two subfamilies have 12–14 spines) and usually 14–20 soft rays; caudal fin rounded, truncate, or emarginate.

These fish live in coral reefs and show a commensal relationship with sea anemones, living about and within them for protection (they probably have a factor in the skin inhibiting nematocyst discharge).

One genus, *Amphiprion* (anemonefishes or clownfishes) with about 26 species in coastal tropical Indo-Pacific (Allen, 1972).

Subfamily Pomacentrinae. Teeth more or less compressed, incisor-like; upper and lower edges of caudal peduncle without spiny caudal rays; caudal fin usually forked.

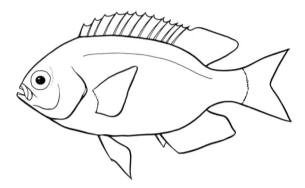

tribe pomacentrini. Margin of preoperculum finely serrated to denticulate.

About six genera (e.g., *Pomacentrus* and *Eupomacentrus*).

tribe abudefdufini (sergeant-majors). Margin of preoperculum entire or nearly so.

About 10 genera (e.g., *Abudefduf*, *Glyphisodon*, *Hypsypops*, and *Microspathodon*).

Subfamily Chrominae. Teeth conical or villiform; upper and lower edges of caudal peduncle usually with short spiny caudal rays; caudal fin usually forked. *Dascyllus* is "commensal" with coral and sea anemones.

Five genera (e.g., *Chromis* and *Dascyllus*) and about 60 species.

Superfamily Gadopsoidae

Family GADOPSIDAE—Blackfish. Freshwater; eastern Australia and Tasmania.

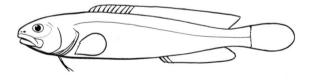

Body elongate and rounded; single long dorsal fin with 10–12 spines and 25–28 soft rays; anal fin with three small spines and 17–19 soft rays; pelvic fin with one ray in front of pectorals; body with small cycloid scales. Length up to 0.6 m.

One species, *Gadopsis marmoratus* (Lake, 1971, recognized the larger Tasmanian form as a separate species).

Rosen and Patterson (1969) feel that this species is perhaps more related to the Trachinoidei and Blennioidei than its present position in the Percoidei would suggest. Gosline (1968) felt that it should be placed in the Ophidioidei which he, in turn, felt should be in the Perciformes. It is placed in its own order by Scott (1962).

Superfamily Cirrhitoidae. Pelvics rather far behind pectorals; lower 5–8 rays of pectorals unbranched, usually thickened, and sometimes separate from one another; anal fin usually with three spines.

Five families and about 68 species.

Family CIRRHITIDAE—Hawkfishes. Marine; tropical western and eastern Atlantic, Indian, and Pacific (majority are Indo-Pacific).

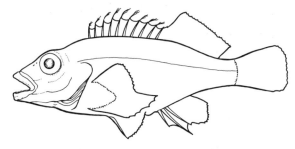

Dorsal fin continuous with 10 spines and 11–17 soft rays; cirri on interspinous membrane; anal fin with 5–7 soft rays; scales cycloid or ctenoid; vertebrae 26–28.

Hawkfishes are usually small and richly colored fishes that live in rocky and coral habitats. They have many features in common with the scorpaenids.

Ten genera (e.g., *Amblycirrhitus*, *Cirrhitus*, and *Paracirrhites*) with about 34 species (Randall, 1963).

Family CHIRONEMIDAE—Kelpfishes. Marine; coastal Australia and New Zealand.

Dorsal fin with 14 or 15 spines and 16–21 soft rays; anal fin with 6–8 soft rays; vomer with teeth, palatines without teeth; jaw teeth conical or villiform. Maximum length about 40 cm.

Two genera, *Chironemus* and *Threpterius*, with about four species.

Family APLODACTYLIDAE (Haplodactylidae). Coastal marine; southern Australia, New Zealand, Peru, and Chile.

Dorsal fin with 14–23 spines and 16–21 soft rays; anal fin with 6–8 soft rays; vomer with teeth; jaw teeth incisiform, lanceolate, or tricuspid.

Three genera, *Aplodactylus*, *Crinodus*, and *Dactylosargus*, with about five species.

Family CHEILODACTYLIDAE—Morwongs. Marine; parts of the Southern Hemisphere in Atlantic, Indian, and Pacific and in the Northern Hemisphere off coasts of China and Japan and reported from the Hawaiian Islands.

Dorsal fin with 14–22 spines and 21–39 soft rays; anal fin with 7–19 soft rays; vomer toothless; lower pectoral fin rays in adults usually produced and detached (free of rest of fin). Maximum length about 1.0 m attained in *Palunolepis grandis* of South Africa.

Six genera, *Cheilodactylus*, *Chirodactylus*, *Goniistius*, *Nemadactylus*, *Palunolepis*, and *Sciaenoides*, with about 15 species.

The nominal species *Gregoryina gygis* is tentatively assigned to this family. It is known from a single 5 cm specimen described in 1924 and obtained at Laysan Island (northwestern portion of the Hawaiian Islands), to which a white tern had brought it to a nest (Gosline and Brock, 1960). This unusual specimen has 15 spines and 24 soft rays in the dorsal fin, three spines and seven soft rays in the anal fin, and is keeled ventrally. Norman (1957) considered it to be synonymous with a cheilodactylid of the genus *Goniistius*, Berg (1940) thought it might be best placed in the Kyphosidae, whereas Gosline and Brock (1960) and Greenwood et al. (1966) thought it best to consider it as the sole member of a distinct family, the Gregoryinidae (the latter workers thought it might be based on a young cheilodactylid). Rather than assign family status to this small specimen it seems best to place it here until further specimens suggest another placement to be better.

Family LATRIDAE—Trumpeters. Marine; coastal southern Australia, New Zealand, and Chile.

Dorsal fin with 14–23 spines and 23–40 soft rays; anal fin with 18–35 soft rays; vomer with or without teeth. Trumpeters form an important sport fishery and are known for their fine taste.

Three genera, *Latridopsis*, *Latris*, and *Mendosoma*, with about 10 species.

Superfamily Cepoloidae

Family OWSTONIIDAE. Marine deepwater; Indo-Pacific.

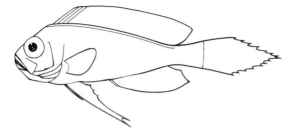

Body elongate and compressed; cycloid scales; caudal fin elongate; lateral line along base of dorsal fin.

Two genera, *Owstonia* and *Parasphenanthias*, with about six species. *Sphenanthias,* included by some workers in the family Serranidae (subfamily Anthiinae), probably belongs here.

Family CEPOLIDAE—Bandfishes.   Marine; eastern Atlantic (off Europe and in Mediterranean) and Indo-Pacific (including New Zealand).

Body elongate, gradually tapering to tail, and highly compressed; scales minute; dorsal and anal fins very long and connected with caudal fin, without spines; lateral line along base of dorsal fin; vertebrae 65–100. Maximum length 70 cm attained in *Cepola rubescens* of Europe.

Two genera, *Acanthocepola* and *Cepola,* with about seven species.

Suborder Mugiloidei.   Berg (1940) placed the three families Atherinidae, Mugilidae, and Sphyraenidae in the order Mugiliformes at the subperciform level. Gosline (1968, 1971) considered the suborder Mugiloidei as a perciform and included the families Polynemidae, Sphyraenidae, Mugilidae, Melanotaeniidae, Atherinidae, Isonidae, Neostethidae, and Phallostethidae [unlike Greenwood et al., (1966), followed here, who gave subordinal status to the first three families and placed the latter five in the preacanthopterygian order Atheriniformes]. Gosline also considered his suborders Mugiloidei and Anabantoidei to be early perciform offshoots and listed them first in his perciform classification. He did this largely on the basis that all mugiloids and some anabantoids lack any direct articulation between the pelvic girdle and the cleithra (whereas in most other perciforms they are attached). It is not certain whether the lack of a pelvic-cleithral articulation is a primitive condition or whether it represents a secondary loss. Such information, however, would still leave the value of the characters in relation to the other characters in determining phylogenetic relationships open to question. McAllister (1968) placed Sphyraenidae and Mugilidae in Mugiloidei and Polynemidae in its own suborder and considered them all as perciforms, whereas he considered the Anabantoidei and its closest relatives (Luciocephalidae and Channidae) as preperciforms.

The next three families, which contain about 148 species, probably bear a closer relationship to one another than they do to any other family. It may eventually prove desirable to place them in the same suborder but in different infraorders or superfamilies.

Family MUGILIDAE—Mullets.   Coastal marine and brackish water (some are freshwater); all tropical and temperate seas.

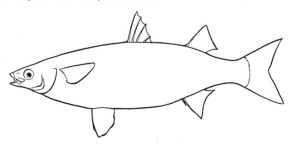

Widely separated spiny-rayed (with four spines) and soft-rayed dorsal fins; pelvic fins subabdominal, with one spine and five branched soft rays; lateral line absent or very faint; mouth moderate in size; teeth small or absent; gill rakers long; stomach muscular and intestine exceedingly long; vertebrae 24–26. Maximum length about 0.9 m.

Ten genera (e.g., *Agonostomus, Cestraeus, Chaenomugil, Joturus, Liza, Mugil, Myxus, Rhinomugil,* and *Valamugil*) with about 95 species. Thomson (1964), in his bibliography of the mugilids, recognizes 13 generic names and 70 valid species (with 32 more of doubtful status) from a list of 281 nominal species.

Suborder Sphyraenoidei.   See taxonomic notes under Mugiloidei.

Family SPHYRAENIDAE—Barracudas.   Marine; tropical and subtropical Atlantic, Indian, and Pacific.

Body elongate; mouth large, jutting lower jaw with strong fanglike teeth; upper jaw not protrusible (a secondary modification adapting the fish to feeding on large prey); lateral line well developed; gill rakers obsolete; pectoral fins relatively low; two widely separated dorsal fins, the first with five spines and the second with one spine and nine soft rays; 24 vertebrae.

Barracudas are known to attack humans and are feared more than sharks in some areas. Maximum length normally to 1.8 m but said to reach somewhat longer lengths.

One genus, *Sphyraena*, with 18 species.

Suborder Polynemoidei. Berg (1940) placed the one family Polynemidae in its own order, Polynemiformes, and considered it to be a subperciform. See also taxonomic notes under Mugiloidei.

Family POLYNEMIDAE—Threadfins. Marine and brackish water (some in rivers); all tropical and subtropical seas.

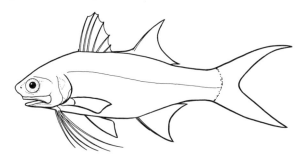

Mouth subterminal; pectoral fin divided into two sections, the upper with rays attached and the lower with 4–7 long unattached rays; two widely separated dorsal fins (one spiny and one soft rayed); pelvics subabdominal, with one spine and five branched soft rays; caudal fin deeply forked; 24 vertebrae. Maximum length 1.8 m, attained in *Eleutheronema tetradactylum*.

Seven genera (e.g., *Eleutheronema*, *Polydactylus*, and *Polynemus*) with about 35 species.

Suborder Labroidei

Family LABRIDAE—Wrasses. Marine; Atlantic, Indian, and Pacific.

Mouth protractile; jaw teeth mostly separate, usually projecting outward; dorsal fin spines 8–21; anal fin usually with three spines and 7–18 soft rays; scales cycloid; lateral line interrupted in many; vertebrae 23–41.

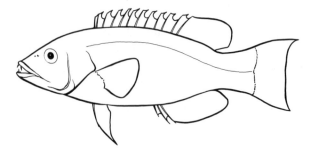

This family is one of the most diversified of all fish families in shape and size. Most species bury themselves in sand at night. Some small species clean larger fishes of their ectoparasites. In a few species females are known to change to males under certain conditions (e.g., see Robertson, 1972). Maximum size 3 m, although many species reach only about 6 cm.

Fifty-eight genera (e.g., *Anampses, Bodianus, Cheilinus, Clepticus, Coris, Epibulus, Halichoeres, Hemipteronotus, Julichthys, Labrus, Neolabrus, Pseudodax, Pseudojulis, Tautoga,* and *Thalassoma*) with perhaps about 400 species. Several subfamilies are recognized.

Family ODACIDAE. Coastal marine; Australia and New Zealand.

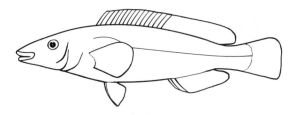

Mouth nonprotractile; jaw teeth coalesced (parrotlike teeth); dorsal fin with 14–24 spines; pelvics each with one spine and four soft rays; scales usually small or moderate. Five genera, *Coridodax* of New Zealand and *Haletta, Neoodax, Odax,* and *Siphonognathus* of Australia, with about eight species.

Family SCARIDAE (Callyodontidae)—Parrotfishes. Marine (mainly tropical); Atlantic, Indian, and Pacific.

Mouth nonprotractile; jaw teeth coalesced (parrotlike teeth); dorsal fin with nine spines and 10 soft rays; anal fin with three spines and nine soft

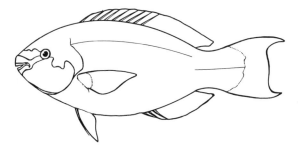

rays; pelvics each with one spine and five soft rays; branched caudal rays 11; scales large and cycloid, usually 22–24 in lateral line; 25 vertebrae; herbivorous.

Some species at night are known to secrete an envelope of mucus in which they rest. The wide diversity of bright colors in the species is shown in Schultz (1969).

Two subfamilies with about 68 species [80 were tentatively recognized in the review by Schultz, (1958); this number was reduced to 68 in Schultz (1969)].

SUBFAMILY SCARINAE. Two to four rows of scales on cheek below eye. Four genera (e.g., *Scarus*) with 53 species.

SUBFAMILY SPARISOMATINAE. Single row of scales on cheek below eye. Seven genera (e.g., *Cryptotomus, Nicholsina,* and *Sparisoma*) and 15 species.

Suborder Blennioidei. In this suborder are three infraorders which were given subordinal rank in Greenwood et al. (1966).

Includes 35 families, 245 genera, and about 925 species.

Infraorder Trachinoidea. Gosline's (1968) classification differs quite markedly from that of Greenwood et al. (1966). Gosline placed four families, Trachinidae, Uranoscopidae, Leptoscopidae, and Dactyloscopidae under the superfamily Trachinoidae which was one of five placed in the suborder Blennioidei. The arrangement of families in the following scheme differs somewhat from Greenwood et al. (1966). The first four families were placed in the suborder Percoidei in Gosline's (1968) work.

Sixteen families with about 56 genera and 181 species.

Family TRICHODONTIDAE—Sandfishes. Marine; North Pacific.

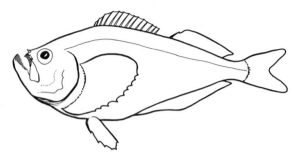

Mouth nearly vertical, with fringed lips; preopercle with five sharp spines; body scaleless; dorsal spines 10–15. Normal habitat is lying partly buried in the bottom. Maximum length about 30 cm.

Two species, *Arctoscopus japonicus* (Alaska to Korea) and *Trichodon trichodon* (northern California to Alaska).

Family OPISTHOGNATHIDAE—Jawfishes. Marine; western and central Atlantic, Indian, and Gulf of California region.

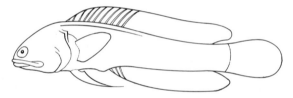

Mouth large; body with cycloid scales; head naked; pelvic fins ahead of pectorals, with one spine and five soft rays; pectoral fin base vertical; dorsal fin continuous; lateral line high, ending near middle of dorsal fin; palate without teeth; moderate canine teeth present on jaws. Males of many of the species are known to practice oral incubation.

About three genera, *Lonchopisthus*, *Lonchistium*, and *Opisthognathus*, with about 30 species.

Family CHAMPSODONTIDAE. Marine; Indo-Pacific.

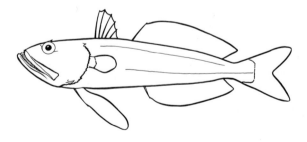

Pelvic fins large, in front of pectorals; pectoral fins small, base oblique; spinous dorsal short, soft dorsal and anal fins long.

Placed in its own division by Norman (1957). One genus, *Champsodon*, with several species.

Family CHIASMODONTIDAE. Marine; oceanic.

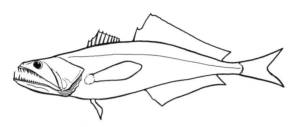

Similar to Percoidei. Premaxilla and maxilla long and slender, firmly united posteriorly.

Placed in its own division by Norman (1957) and in the Percoidei by Gosline (1971). Five genera (e.g., *Chiasmodon, Kali,* and *Pseudoscopelus*) and about 15 species.

Family BATHYMASTERIDAE—Ronquils. Marine coastal; North Pacific.

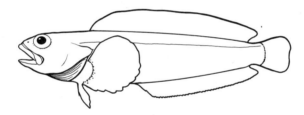

Dorsal fins continuous; pectoral fin base vertical; lateral line high, ending near end of dorsal fin; palate with teeth. Maximum length about 30 cm.

Three genera, *Bathymaster, Rathbunella* and *Ronquilus,* and seven species.

Family PERCOPHIDIDAE. Marine; Atlantic and Indo-Pacific (to Hawaii and New Zealand).

Head depressed; eyes usually large and interorbital narrow; spinous dorsal, if present, separate from soft dorsal; anal fin with or without a single spine.

McKay (1971) gives a key to the 13 genera he recognizes in the family (omitting *Hemerocoetes*). Many of these genera should probably be synonymized and not all are formally recognized here, pending a revision of the family. With the inclusion of all these genera the number of species in the family would be approximately 27 rather than the 17 I have recognized. Most species occur in deepish water.

The following three subfamilies have usually been accorded family status by past authors.

SUBFAMILY BEMBROPSINAE. Atlantic and Indo-Pacific. Dorsal fins with six spines and 14–18 soft rays; anal fin usually with 15–20 soft rays; lower jaw projecting past upper; caudal fin with 10 or 11 branched rays.

Two genera, *Bembrops* and *Chrionema* (=*Chriomystax*), with at least seven species.

SUBFAMILY HEMEROCOETINAE. Western Pacific in Oceania and Japan to Australia. Caudal fin with seven or eight branched rays. Median barbel at tip of snout and spine at anterior end of each maxilla in some.

Three genera, *Acanthaphritis* (= *Pteropsaron*, which some past authors have given family status—Pteropsaridae), *Enigmapercis*, and *Hemerocoetes*, with about nine species. The first two genera have separate dorsal fins; the latter New Zealand endemic has a continuous spineless fin. The nominal genera *Branchiopsaron*, *Cirrinasus*, *Matsubaraea*, *Osopsaron*, and *Spinapsaron*, which occur in the western Pacific and eastern Indian oceans, probably also belong here.

SUBFAMILY PERCOPHIDINAE. Tropical western Atlantic. Dorsal fins with eight or nine spines and about 31 soft rays; anal fin with one spine and about 38–42 soft rays; lower jaw projecting past upper; caudal fin with 13 branched rays.

One species, *Percophis brasiliensis*

Family MUGILOIDIDAE (Parapercidae and Pinguipedidae)—Sandperches.
Marine; Atlantic coast of South America and Africa, Indo-Pacific (to New Zealand and Hawaii), and off Chile.

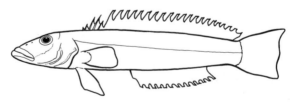

Pelvic fins below or slightly in front of pectorals; mouth protractile and terminal; caudal fin truncate to deeply crescentic, with 13 or 15 branched rays; dorsal fin continuous, with four or five short spines and 19–26 soft rays; anal fin with 17–25 rays, first one or two may be spinelike; lateral line continuous; gill membranes united, free from isthmus.

Three genera, *Mugiloides, Parapercis* (= *Neopercis*), and *Pinguipes*, with about 25 species.

Family TRICHONOTIDAE—Sanddivers.   Marine; most warm seas.

Snout pointed and extending in front of lower jaw; gill openings extending far forward; pelvic fins in most, each with one spine and five branched rays; some species with lateral line running along base of anal fin.

These small fishes dive into the sand and disappear at the least provocation.

The following genera may belong in this "catch-all" family: *Chalixodytes, Crystallodytes, Lesuerina, Trichonotops,* and *Trichonotus.* In all, there are probably about nine genera and 19 species.

Family CHEIMARRHICHTHYIDAE (Cheimarrichthyidae).   Freshwater (young are known from the sea); rivers of New Zealand.

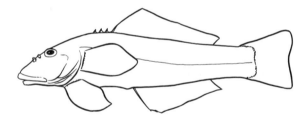

Pelvic fins well in front of pectorals, wide apart; mouth nonprotractile and inferior; caudal fin with 13–15 branched rays; dorsal fin usually has four or five spines and 19 or 20 soft rays, the anterior three or four spines are short and stout and separated from the remainder of the continuous fin; anal fin with one or two spines and 15 soft rays; 15 pectoral rays; about 50 scales along lateral line; vertebrae 31–33. Maximum length about 15 cm.

McDowall (1973b) provides an osteological description and because of the similarity with *Parapercis colias* favors assigning *Cheimarrichthys* to the Mugiloididae.

One species, *Cheimarrichthys fosteri.*

Family CREEDIIDAE.   Marine coastal; South Africa and Australia.

Dorsal and anal fins without spines; mouth protractile, usually slightly subterminal; lower jaw lined with cirri; most lateral line scales trilobed. Maximum length about 9 cm.

This family shows many similarities with the Limnichthyidae. Three species, *Apodocreedia vanderhorsti* (lacks pelvic fins), *Creedia haswelli* (= *clathrisquamis*), and *Squamicreedia obtusa*.

Family LIMNICHTHYIDAE.   Marine coastal; Indo-Pacific (primarily Australia and Oceania).

Dorsal and anal fins without spines; origin of anal fin usually in front of dorsal origin; upper jaw and palate with villiform teeth. Maximum length about 7 cm.

Three genera, the monotypic *Schizochirus* of eastern Australia and *Tewara* of New Zealand and *Limnichthys* with four species from Australia, New Zealand, Japan, midwestern Pacific, and Indian Ocean.

Family OXUDERCIDAE.   Marine; China Sea.

No pelvic fins; dorsal fin with six spines and 24 soft rays; anal fin with six spines and 21 soft rays; 18 pectoral rays; about 72 lateral scales; head scaleless; mouth wide and long; lateral line not evident.

One species, *Oxuderces dentatus* (Fowler, 1972: 989).

Family TRACHINIDAE—Weeverfishes.   Marine; eastern Atlantic, Black Sea, and off Chile.

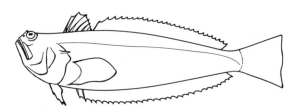

Body elongate; anal and second dorsal fins long; pelvic fins in front of pectorals; poisonous glands associated with gill cover spine and first dorsal spines. Have habit of burying in sand.

One genus, *Trachinus*, with four species.

Family URANOSCOPIDAE—Stargazers.   Marine; Atlantic, Indian, and Pacific.

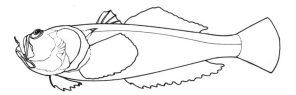

Head large and cuboid; body naked or covered with small smooth scales; mouth extremely oblique; lips fringed; eyes dorsal or nearly so; lateral line on upper part of side; pelvic fins narrowly separated, with one spine and five soft rays and located under the throat; dorsal and anal fins moderately long, spinous dorsal absent in many; some with small wormlike filament extending from floor of mouth used to lure prey fish; two large, double-grooved poison spines, with a venom gland at each base, just above the pectoral fin and behind the opercle; 24–26 vertebrae.

One genus, *Astroscopus,* has internal nares used during inspiration and electric organs derived from portions of eye muscle.

Eight genera (e.g., *Astroscopus, Gnathagnus, Ichthyscopus, Kathetostoma, Pleuroscopus,* and *Uranoscopus*) and 25 species.

Family LEPTOSCOPIDAE.   Marine; Australia and New Zealand.

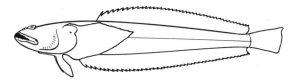

Mouth moderately oblique; lips fringed; eyes dorsal or nearly so; lateral line on middle of side; body with scales; pelvic fins widely separated; dorsal and anal fins long.

Two genera, *Crapatulus* and *Leptoscopus,* with at least three species.

Family DACTYLOSCOPIDAE—Sand Stargazers.   Marine (rarely brackish); tropical America in Atlantic and Pacific and off Chile.

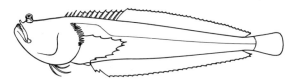

Mouth extremely oblique; lips fringed; upper free edge of gill cover subdivided into fingerlike elements; pelvic fins with one spine and three soft rays (tips largely free of membrane), jugular; eyes small, usually on top of head, often stalked; dorsal fin long, continuous or divided.

Sand stargazers frequently bury themselves in sand bottoms, similar to uranoscopids. However, they are unique to other teleosts, which normally pump water over the gills by alternately expanding and contracting the buccal and opercular cavities, in having developed a branchiostegal pump which replaces the opercular pump (other benthic fish have both). Fingerlike labial and opercular fimbriae probably function to prevent particles from clogging the branchial chamber.

Five genera, *Dactylagnus, Dactyloscopus, Gillellus, Leurochilus,* and *Myxodagnus,* with about 20 species.

Infraorder Notothenioidea.   Pelvic fins each with one spine and five branched rays; one nostril on each side; three pectoral actinosts; primarily Antarctic in distribution.

Gosline (1968) gave this group superfamily status, Notothenioidae, included Mugiloididae, Trichonotidae, and Cheimarrichthyidae, and placed it in the suborder Blennioidei.

Four families with about 96 species.

Family BOVICHTHYIDAE (Bovictidae).   Marine; southern Australia, New Zealand, and southern South America regions and freshwater southeastern Australia and Tasmania.

Gill membranes free from isthmus, extending far forward; mouth protractile; spinous dorsal fin present; snout not produced.

Four genera, *Aurion, Bovichthys, Cottoperca,* and *Pseudaphritis,* with about six species.

Family NOTOTHENIIDAE—Cod Icefishes.   Marine; coastal Antarctic and southern South America.

Gill membranes united; mouth protractile; spinous dorsal fin present; some species without red blood cells.

Some species live at an average temperature of $-1.9°C$ and have a glycoprotein in their blood which lowers the freezing point.

SUBFAMILY HARPAGIFERINAE.   Body naked; gill membranes broadly united to isthmus; all but *Harpagifer* have a chin barbel.

Five genera, *Artedidraco, Dolloidraco, Histiodraco, Pogonophryne,* and *Harpagifer,* with about 11 species.

SUBFAMILY NOTOTHENIINAE. Body scaled; gill membranes form a fold across the isthmus.

Five genera (e.g., *Notothenia, Pleuragramma,* and *Trematomus*) with about 48 species.

Family BATHYDRACONIDAE. Marine, Antarctic.

Gill membranes united; mouth usually nonprotractile; no spinous dorsal fin.

Eight genera, *Bathydraco, Cygnodraco, Gerlachea, Gymnodraco, Parachaenichthys, Prionodraco, Psilodraco,* and *Racovitzia,* with 15 species (Andriashev, 1965).

Family CHANNICHTHYIDAE (Chaenichthyidae)—Crocodile Icefishes. Marine; Antarctic and southern South America.

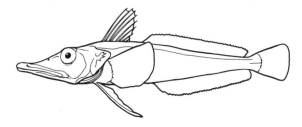

Gill membranes united; mouth nonprotractile; snout produced and depressed; spinous dorsal fin present.

Most or all species are without red blood cells. Survival is probably permitted by the fish living in extremely cold, well-oxygenated water and having a large volume of blood circulation and skin respiration.

Nine genera (e.g., *Chaenocephalus, Channichthys, Cryodraco,* and *Pagetopsis*) with 16 species.

Infraorder Blennioidea. Pelvic fins with fewer than five soft rays, often minute or absent, ahead of pectorals when present.

Fifteen families with about 648 species, of which about 84% belong to the three tropical families Tripterygiidae, Clinidae, and Blenniidae.

Family XENOCEPHALIDAE—Armored Blenny. Marine; New Ireland.

Large truncated head, armed with plates and spines; dorsal fin single, with seven soft rays, weakly separated from the large caudal; anal fin with 10 soft rays. The position of this family is questionable. Its morphology is poorly known.

One species, *Xenocephalus armatus* (Munro, 1967).

Family CONGROGADIDAE—Eelblennies.   Marine (rarely brackish); Indo-Pacific.

Body elongate to eellike; body with small cycloid scales; mouth protractile; gill membranes united; pelvics present (jugular and with one or two rays) or absent; dorsal and anal fins long. Maximum length about 50 cm.

Six genera with about eight species.

SUBFAMILY CONGROGADINAE.   Mouth large, maxillae extending to hind margin of eye or past; palate toothless; opercle spineless; fins without spines (pelvics absent); caudal fin barely differentiated from dorsal and anal fins; single lateral line.

One genus, *Congrogadus* (East Africa to Japan and Australia) with one or two species.

SUBFAMILY HALIOPHINAE.   Mouth moderate, maxillae not extending past eye; teeth on vomer; opercle with long retrorse spine on upper margin; one spine before dorsal fin; pelvics, if present, have small spine (pelvics present only in *Halidesmus* and *Blennodesmus*); caudal fin distinctly differentiated from dorsal and anal fins (membrane joined to greater or lesser degrees); one or three lateral lines, fully or partly complete.

J. L. B. Smith (1952b) reviewed this group but gave it family status.

Five genera, *Congrogadoides* (with three western Pacific species; Philippines to Australia) and four monotypic genera, *Haliophis* (Red Sea to Madagascar), *Halimuraena* (East Africa), *Halidesmus* (southern Africa), and *Blennodesmus* (northeastern and northwestern Australia).

Family NOTOGRAPTIDAE.   Primarily marine; New Guinea (Fly River) and Australia.

Body with small cycloid scales; dorsal fin with spines; dorsal and anal fins confluent with the caudal; pelvics reduced to a single bifed ray; short central barbel on lower jaw.

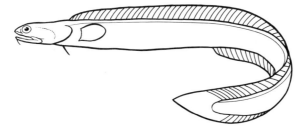

Two genera, *Notograptus* and *Sticharium,* with three species.

Family PERONEDYSIDAE.   Marine; South Australia.

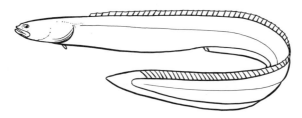

Body eel-shaped; pectoral fins absent; pelvics with three small rays; dorsal fin mostly of spines; dorsal and anal fins confluent with the caudal; lateral line single and short (although some authors state it has three). A poorly known group with doubtful affinities and only provisionally placed here. Maximum length about 10 cm.

One species, *Peronedys anguillaris.*

Family OPHICLINIDAE—Snakeblennies.   Marine; southern Australia and New Zealand.

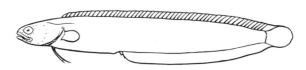

Body eel-shaped; most fin rays spinous.

Springer (1970) suggests that this family might be included in the Clininae.

Three genera, *Breona, Ophiclinops,* and *Ophiclinus,* with about five species.

Family TRIPTERYGIIDAE—Threefin Blennies.   Marine (primarily tropical); Atlantic, Indian, and Pacific.

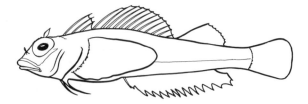

Dorsal fin divided into three distinct segments, the first two composed of spines; anal fin with two spines; pelvics jugular; branchiostegal rays six or seven; no cirri on nape; scales usually ctenoid; first gill arch attached to the opercle.

Fifteen genera (e.g., *Enneanectes*, *Trianectes*, and *Tripterygion*), with about 95 species.

Family CLINIDAE—Clinids.   Marine (primarily tropical); Atlantic, Indian, and Pacific.

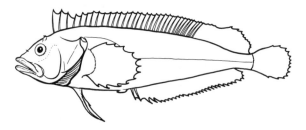

Patches of fixed conical teeth; cirri usually on nape; scales cycloid or absent; dorsal fin with more spines than soft rays; no branched rays in pectoral fin; many males with an intromittant organ: some viviparous species. Maximum length about 60 cm, attained in *Heterostichus rostratus;* most much smaller.

About 40 genera with about 175 species.

SUBFAMILY CLININAE.   Scales with radii on all margins; scales frequently small and embedded.

Includes *Clinus*, *Gibbonsia*, *Heterostichus*, and *Myxodes*.

SUBFAMILY LABRISOMINAE.   Scales with radii only on anterior margin; scales never small and embedded. An entirely American group, mostly tropical.

Includes *Exerpes*, *Labrisomus*, *Malacoctenus*, *Mnierpes*, and *Starksia*.

SUBFAMILY CHAENOPSINAE (PIKEBLENNIES OR FLAGBLENNIES).   Body naked and no lateral line. Warm seas of America and Japan. This group is very close to the clinids and is placed with it by many workers (e.g.,

Bailey et al., 1970), as is done here, but retained as a separate family by Greenwood et al. (1966) and Gosline (1968, 1971).

Ten genera (e.g., *Acanthemblemaria, Chaenopsis, Coralliozetus, Emblemaria, Neoclinus,* and *Stathmonotus*) with about 40 species.

Family BLENNIIDAE—Combtooth Blennies. Marine (rarely fresh- or brackish water, primarily tropical and subtropical);

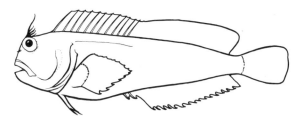

Body naked or with vestigial scales; head usually blunt; pelvic fins present (in all but *Plagiotremus spilistius*), anterior to the pectorals, and with one short spine and 2–4 segmented rays; palate usually toothless; jaws with comblike teeth, fixed or freely movable; dorsal fin with 3–17 flexible spines and 9–119 segmented rays; pectoral rays not branched, 10–18; anal fin with two spines (the first is buried beneath genital tissue in females); vertebrae usually 28–44 (up to 134 in *Xiphasia*).

Many species of blenniids are involved in mimetic associations with other fishes, being similar in external appearance to the other species (Springer and Smith-Vaniz, 1972a). Elements of Mullerian, Batesian, and aggressive mimicry are involved.

Classification of the family is based largely on Springer (1968, 1972), Springer and Smith-Vaniz (1972b), and Smith-Vaniz and Springer (1971).

Forty-six genera with about 276 species.

SUBFAMILY BLENNIINAE. Basisphenoid present; adults without swim bladder.

TRIBE BLENNIINI. Marine (rarely fresh- and brackish water). Caudal fin rays branched; five circumorbital bones; three or four segmented pelvic fin rays.

About 10 genera (e.g., *Blennius, Chasmodes, Hypleurochilus,* and *Hypsoblennius*) and approximately 65 species.

TRIBE SALARIINI. Marine. Caudal fin rays branched or not; two, four, or five circumorbital bones; three or four segmented pelvic fin rays.

Twenty-four genera (e.g., *Ecsenius, Alticus, Praealticus, Istiblennius, Cirripectes, Ophioblennius, Entomacrodus, Salarias,* and *Antennablennius*) with about 155 species.

TRIBE OMOBRANCHINI.   Marine (rarely fresh- and brackish water). Caudal fin rays not branched; two segmented pelvic fin rays; 15–27 segmented dorsal fin rays.

Six genera (e.g., *Enchelyurus, Omobranchus,* and *Parenchelyurus*) with about 25 species.

TRIBE PHENABLENNIINI.   Fresh- and brackish water; Sumatra and Cambodia. All fin rays simple; three segmented pelvic fin rays; 14 segmented dorsal fin rays; postcleithrum single (other blenniids have two postcleithra or 1–3 fragments); body similar in appearance to the Omobranchini.

One species, *Phenablennius heyligeri.*

SUBFAMILY NEMOPHIDINAE.   Basisphenoid absent; adults of most species with swim bladder.

TRIBE NEMOPHIDINI.   Marine (rarely brackish water). Caudal fin rays unbranched; three or four circumorbital bones; three segmented pelvic rays.

Five genera (e.g., *Nemophis, Meiacanthus, Plagiotremus,* and *Xiphasia*) with about 30 species.

Family STICHAEIDAE—Pricklebacks.   Marine; primarily North Pacific, a few in North Atlantic.

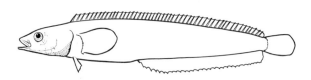

At least some spinous rays in dorsal fin (entirely spinous in most species); dorsal fin long; pelvic fin rays, if present, branched; ribs present; distance from snout to anal origin usually equal to or less than distance from anal origin to caudal fin.

Each of the following eight tribes, placed in three subfamilies, was given subfamily status by Makushok (1958) from whom much of the following information is taken.

Thirty-one genera with about 57 species.

SUBFAMILY STICHAEINAE. Pelvic fins with one spine and three or four soft rays (*Gymnoclinus* has only two soft rays); pectoral fins large; vertebrae 46–71.

TRIBE STICHAEINI. North Pacific (primarily along the Asiatic coast) and northwestern Atlantic.

Five genera, *Ernogrammus, Eumesogrammus, Stichaeopsis, Stichaeus,* and *Ulvaria,* with about 11 species.

TRIBE CHIROLOPHINI. North Pacific with one species endemic to Atlantic.

Four genera, *Bryozoichthys, Chirolophis, Soldatovia,* and *Gymnoclinus,* with about 13 species.

SUBFAMILY LUMPENINAE. Pelvic fins with one spine and three soft rays to absent (fins and girdle absent in *Kasatkia*); pectoral fins large; vertebrae 53–94; lateral line usually indistinct or absent.

TRIBE LUMPENINI. North Pacific, North Atlantic, and Arctic.

Six genera, *Acantholumpenus, Anisarchus, Leptoclinus, Lumpenella, Lumpenus,* and *Poroclinus,* with about nine species.

TRIBE OPISTHOCENTRINI. Sea of Japan to Bering Sea and eastern North Pacific.

Six genera, *Allolumpenus, Ascoldia, Kasatkia, Lumpenopsis, Opisthocentrus,* and *Plectobranchus,* with about nine species.

SUBFAMILY XIPHISTERINAE. Pectoral fins small; pelvic fins absent; vertebrae 62–81 (first two tribes) or greater than 100 (last two tribes).

TRIBE ALECTRIINI. North Pacific.

Four genera, *Alectrias, Alectridium, Pseudalectrias,* and *Anoplarchus,* with about five species.

TRIBE XIPHISTERINI. North Pacific. Three or four lateral lines present in *Phytichthys* and *Xiphister*.

Four genera, *Dictyosoma, Cebidichthys, Phytichthys,* and *Xiphister* (= *Epigeichthys*), with about seven species.

TRIBE AZYGOPTERINI. Kuril Islands.

One species, *Azygopterus corallinus*.

TRIBE EULOPHIINI. Sea of Japan.
One genus, *Eulophias,* with two species.

Family CRYPTACANTHODIDAE—Wrymouths. Marine; northwest Atlantic and northern Pacific.

Pelvic fins absent; mouth very oblique; lateral line obsolete.
The wrymouths were placed in the Stichaeidae in Greenwood et al. (1966) but are recognized as a separate family in most works (e.g., Makushok, 1958; Gosline, 1968; Bailey et al., 1970).
Four monotypic genera, *Cryptacanthodes, Cryptacanthoides, Delolepis,* and *Lyconectes.*

Family PHOLIDIDAE (Pholidae)—Gunnels. Marine; North Atlantic and North Pacific.

Dorsal fin with 75 to 100 spines, about twice as long as the anal fin; pectoral fins small, rudimentary, or absent; pelvic fins rudimentary (one spine and one soft ray in *Pholis*) or absent (along with pelvic girdle); vertebrae 84–107; ribs absent; distance from snout to anal origin usually more than distance from anal origin to caudal fin; lateral line short or absent.
Gunnels are small littoral fishes that, like some pricklebacks, are often found under rocks or in tide-pools at low tide.
Four genera with about 13 species.

SUBFAMILY PHOLINAE. Most are North Pacific, a few North Atlantic.
One genus, *Pholis,* with about 10 species.

SUBFAMILY APODICHTHYINAE. Pacific coast of North America.
Three monotypic genera: *Apodichthys, Xererpes,* and *Ulvicola.*

Family ANARHICHADIDAE—Wolffishes. Marine; North Atlantic and North Pacific.

Body naked or with minute cycloid scales; no lateral line; gill membranes attached to isthmus; dorsal fin with spines only; pectoral fins large; pelvic fins absent (rudiments of girdle retained); caudal fin small or pointed; jaws with strong conical canines anteriorly and with large molariform teeth laterally; vertebrae 72–89 to more than 250. Maximum length about 2.5 m.
Two genera, *Anarhichas* (= *Lycichthys*) with six species (North Atlantic and Pacific) and *Anarrhichthys ocellatus* (Alaska to California).

Family PTILICHTHYIDAE—Quillfish.   Marine; Pacific North America (Puget Sound to northwestern Alaska).

Body extremely elongate and slender; caudal fin absent; pelvics absent; body naked; dorsal fin with 90 isolated low spines and 137–145 high soft rays; anal fin with 185–196 high soft rays; no lateral line; extremely elongate body; vertebrae about 238–240. Maximum length 33 cm.

One species, *Ptilichthys goodei.*

Family ZAPRORIDAE—Prowfish.   Marine; North Pacific (California to Alaska and Hokkaido).

No pelvic fins; gill membranes united; small cycloid scales on body; no lateral line; pectoral rays 24 or 25; dorsal fin long, with 54–57 spines; anal fin short, with three weak spines and 24–27 soft rays; large pores on head; vertebrae 61 or 62 (24–26 abdominal); pyloric caeca about 36. Maximum length 88 cm.

One species, *Zaprora silenus* (McAllister and Krejsa, 1961).

Family SCYTALINIDAE—Graveldiver.   Marine; Pacific coast North America (southern California to northwestern Alaska).

No pelvic fins; gill membranes united; eyes very small and placed high on head; no scales; no lateral line; dorsal and anal fins on posterior half of back and confluent with caudal fin. Maximum length 15 cm.

One species, *Scytalina cerdale.*

Suborder Icosteoidei (Malacichthyes).   The one included family and species are placed in their own order, Icosteiformes, by Berg (1940) and Gosline (1971).

Family ICOSTEIDAE—Ragfish.   Marine; Pacific coast North America.

Body elliptical, highly compressed, and limp; skeleton largely cartilaginous; no spines in fins; no scales in adult; pelvic fins loosely attached in young, lost in adults; 70 vertebrae. Maximum length 2 m.

One species, *Icosteus aenigmaticus*.

Suborder Schindlerioidei

Family SCHINDLERIIDAE.   Marine; oceanic.

Small neotenic fishes that show no adult characteristics. Some of the larval characteristics found in sexually mature individuals include functional pronephros, transparent body, and large opercular gills. Other characteristics are 15–20 dorsal fin rays, 11–17 anal fin rays, 15–17 pectoral fin rays, 13 principal rays in caudal fin, five short branchiostegal rays, 33–39 vertebrae, and rodlike terminal section on vertebral column.

Gosline (1959) placed this family in its own suborder in the Perciformes, as is done here. Its relationships are highly speculative, although there is a possible relationship with the ammodytoids (Gosline 1963b, 1971).

One genus, *Schindleria*, with two species.

Suborder Ammodytoidei.   Body elongate; premaxillae protractile; caudal fin forked; dorsal and anal fin spines absent; lower jaw projecting forward beyond upper jaw; no swim bladder.

Family AMMODYTIDAE—Sand Lances.   Marine; Atlantic, Indian, and Pacific.

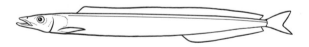

Scales cycloid, minute; pelvic fins usually absent (jugular and with one spine and three soft rays in *Embolichthys*); lateral line high, close to dorsal fin; no teeth; single long dorsal fin usually with 40–65 soft rays; seven branchiostegal rays; gill membranes separate. Length up to 30 cm.

Three genera, *Ammodytes* (=*Gymnammodytes* and *Hyperoplus*), *Bleekeria*, and *Embolichthys*, with about 12 species.

Family HYPOPTYCHIDAE—Sand Eel. Marine; Japan and Korea to Sea of Okhotsk.

Scales absent; pelvic fins absent; lateral line along middle of side; dorsal and anal fins about equal in length, both usually with 20 soft rays; four branchiostegal rays; gill membranes united and free from isthmus. Length up to 8.5 cm.

Retained in separate family by Gosline (1963b, 1971) and Greenwood et al. (1966) but reduced to subfamily status in Ammodytidae in Berg (1940), Fowler (1972:1195), and Robins and Böhlke (1970).

One species, *Hypoptychus dybowskii.*

Suborder Gobioidei. Parietals absent; infraorbitals unossified or absent; lateral line absent; swim bladder usually absent; gill membranes usually joined to isthmus; barbels on head in some; no pyloric caeca; spinous dorsal, when present, with 1–8 flexible spines; pelvic fins below pectorals, with one spine and four or five soft rays, often united; vertebrae 25-35 (exceptions to some characters occur in *Microdesmidae).*

Some authors have given ordinal status to this group.

Seven families, about 234 genera, and very approximately 1012 species.

Family ELEOTRIDAE—Sleepers. Marine, brackish, and freshwater; most tropical and subtropical areas.

Pelvic fins separate (no sucking disc), bases close together or united (there is considerable variation in the degree of union or separation of the pelvic fins and sleepers and gobies cannot always be neatly separated on the basis of this character alone); mouth never inferior; spinous dorsal with 2–8 flexible spines; scales cycloid or ctenoid; vertebrae 25–28. Maximum length about 60 cm, attained in *Dormitator maculatus.*

About 40 genera (e.g., *Dormitator, Eleotris, Erotelis, Gobiomorphus, Gobiomorus,* and *Philypnodon),* with about 150 species.

Family GOBIIDAE—Gobies. Marine, brackish, and occasionally freshwater; most tropical and subtropical areas.

Pelvic fins, when well developed, united, usually forming an adhesive or sucking disc; spinous dorsal, when present, separate from soft dorsal and with 2–8 flexible spines; scales cycloid or ctenoid (rarely absent).

This is the largest family of marine fishes; they are often the most abundant fish in fresh water on oceanic islands. A few species are known even in the headwaters of rivers in mountains (Smith, 1945). Some species that occur in fresh water spawn in the ocean and are thus catadromous like the anguillids. Together with clinids and blennies, they form the dominant element in the small-fish fauna of benthic habit in tropical reefs. Some gobies live in close association with other animals (e.g., sponges, shrimps, and sea urchins). Some species of *Gobiosoma* feed on ectoparasites of other fishes. Several gobies live on wet beaches and may spend several days out of water. In at least one of these species, *Periophthalmus vulgaris,* the opercular chambers, which serve as a storehouse for the respiratory air in aerial respiration, are highly modified into saclike structures bounded by highly vascularized and folded epithelium (Singh and Datta Munshi, 1969). *Gillichthys mirabilis,* which usually remains in the water, comes to the surface, however, when the water is low in oxygen and gulps air which is held in the highly vascularized buccopharynx for respiratory exchange. Some of the land gobies, such as the mudskippers (e.g., *Periophthalmus*), can move along with considerable speed. Their eyes, placed on top of the head on short stalks and may be elevated or retracted, are well adapted for vision in air.

Maximum length usually only about 10 cm. This family contains the world's smallest fishes (and vertebrates). *Pandaka pygmaea,* a colorless freshwater fish of Luzon, Philippines, reaches about 12 mm (and matures at 6 mm); some species of *Mistichthys* are almost as small. *Eviota zonura,* a 16 mm goby of the Marshall Islands, probably the smallest marine fish, is in great contrast with the world's largest fish, the whale shark (*Rhincodon*), which in the late embryonic stages in the 30 cm egg case is about 35 cm long. The largest adult specimens are estimated to have been about 18 m long.

About 170 genera (e.g., *Amblygobius, Apocryptes, Bathygobius, Benthophilus, Bollmannia, Clevelandia, Coryphopterus, Eucyclogobius, Gillichthys, Go-*

bionellus, Gobiosoma, Gobius, Lebetus, Lepidogobius, Lethops, Lythrypnus, Microgobius, Periophthalmus, Pipidonia, Pomatoschistus, Quietula, Sicydium, Tridentiger, and *Typhlogobius*), with about 800 species. Several subfamilies can be recognized (see, for example, Fowler, 1972:1227) (e.g., Apocrypteinae, Benthophilinae, Gobiinae, Gobiodontinae, and Periophthalminae).

Family RHYACICHTHYIDAE—Loach Gobies. Freshwater streams; Indo-Australian Archipelago (e.g., Java, Celebes, and New Guinea), Philippines, China, and Solomon Islands.

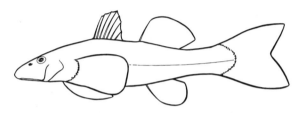

Head depressed, tail compressed; mouth inferior with fleshy upper lip; eyes small; pelvic fins widely separated; pectoral fins very broad, with 21 or 22 rays; lower surface of head and anterior part of body, with the paired fins, form an adhesive disc; dorsal fins well separated, first with seven feeble spines and second with one spine and eight or nine soft rays; anal fin with one feeble spine and eight or nine soft rays; lateral line scales (ctenoid) about 35–40; caudal fin lunate. This fish superficially resembles the homalopterids in appearance and habit. Maximum length about 32.5 cm.

One genus, *Rhyacichthys* (=*Platyptera*), with perhaps only one species (*R. aspro*) (Herre, 1953; Munro, 1967; Fowler, 1972:1457).

Family KRAEMERIIDAE—Sandfishes or Sand Gobies. Marine (rarely brackish or freshwater); Indo-Pacific (to Hawaii).

Body elongate; tongue bilobed at tip; lower jaw protruding forward with enlarged chin; eyes small; body usually naked; dorsal and anal fins free of caudal; dorsal fin usually single with 4–6 feeble spines and usually 13–18 soft rays; pelvics with one spine and five soft rays, usually separate.

These fishes generally inhabit sandy shallow waters. Many species burrow into the sand with only the head protruding. Maximum length about 7 cm.

Four genera with about 10 species (Norman, 1957, recognized only the wide ranging *Kraemeria samoensis* in the family): *Kraemeria* (=*Psammichthys*) with about seven species; *Kraemericus chapmani* (in which the spiny and soft-rayed portion of the dorsal fins are separated and the body is scaled); *Gobitrichinotus radiocularis* [with fused pelvics, known from the Malabang River, Mindanao, Philippines (Herre, 1953) and Tahiti]; and *Parkraemeria ornata* (with the opercular opening restricted to side of head) (Gosline, 1955; Matsubara and Iwai, 1959; Schultz et al., 1966).

Family GOBIOIDIDAE—Eellike Gobies. Marine, brackish, and freshwater; coastal tropical west Africa, Indo-Pacific, and both coasts of tropical America.

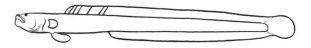

Body eellike; eyes very small; body naked or with cycloid scales; spinous and soft portions of dorsal fin confluent, the latter united or nearly so with the caudal; pelvic fins usually forming an adhesive disc; anal fin with 15–52 rays; no pouchlike cavity in opercular region.

Many authors combine this and the next family (Trypauchenidae) under the family name Taenioididae, recognizing the two lineages at the subfamily level (e.g., Fowler, 1972:1400). Family status with the names accepted here is given by Herre (1953) and Greenwood et al. (1966).

Eight genera (e.g., *Brachyamblyopus*, *Caragobius*, *Gobioides*, *Nudagobioides*, *Odontamblyopus*, *Taenioides*, and *Tyntlastes*) with about 18 species.

Family TRYPAUCHENIDAE—Burrowing Gobies. Marine, brackish, and freshwater; Indo-Pacific region (Natal, Persian Gulf, India to southern Japan and Philippines).

Body eellike; eyes very small to virtually absent; body naked or with cycloid scales; spinous and soft portions of dorsal fins confluent, the latter united or nearly so with the caudal; pelvic fins usually form an adhesive disc; pouchlike cavity in opercular region on each side.

These fish, like the closely related gobioids, live in shallow waters and often burrow in muddy bottoms. Some are virtually blind (e.g., *Ctenotrypauchen microcephalus* of the East Indies and the Philippines).

Five genera (e.g., *Amblyotrypauchen*, *Ctenotrypauchen*, and *Trypauchen*) with 10 species.

Family MICRODESMIDAE(Cerdalidae)—Wormfishes.   Marine (rarely brackish); tropical waters.

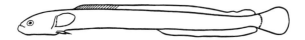

Body elongate to eellike; tongue simple at tip; body naked or with small embedded scales; dorsal fin extending along most of body, confluent with the caudal as is the anal (except in one species); pelvic fins with one spine and 3–5 soft rays; lower jaw heavy and protruding; vertebrae 42–62.

These fishes burrow in sand and mud and are usually found in shallow waters. Their greatest recorded depth is about 40 m. Maximum length 30 cm.

The type genus, *Microdesmus* (includes *Cerdale*), with about 16 species (11 in the eastern Pacific and five in the Atlantic), is known from both coasts of tropical America and West Africa. *Paragobioides grandoculis,* known from the Marshall and Christmas islands, is referred to the microdesmids by some but others feel it to be closer to the Ammodytidae and Trichonotidae. However, at least three other genera with five species may be placed in this family (*Clarkichthys bilineatus* may also belong here): *Gunnellichthys* with three Indo-Pacific species, *Pholidichthys leucotaenia* (which is given family status by some), and *Allomicrodesmus dorotheae* (dorsal and anal fins are free from caudal), known from the Marshall Islands area of the central Pacific (Gosline, 1955; Gilbert, 1966; Schultz et al., 1966; Dawson, 1968).

Suborder Kurtoidei

Family KURTIDAE—Nurseryfishes.   Brackish and freshwater (rarely marine); in Indo-Malay area and parts of Australia.

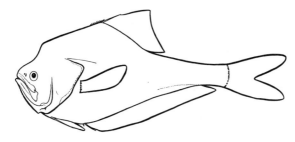

Males with occipital hook, used for carrying eggs; scales small and cycloid; lateral line short and rudimentary; mouth large; dorsal fin single, with spines and soft rays; anal fin with two spines and 31–47 soft rays; pelvic fins with one spine and five soft rays; caudal fin deeply forked; ribs expanded, partly enclosing the anterior portion of the swim bladder and entirely enclosing the posterior portion.

Tominaga (1968) gives additional features for the group and compares it with the beryciforms and perciforms. Maximum length 59 cm, attained in *Kurtus gulliveri.*

One genus, *Kurtus,* with two species. *K. gulliveri* has 44–47 soft rays in anal fin and is found in southern New Guinea and northern Australia; *K. indicus* has 31 or 32 soft rays in anal fin and is found in the Indo-Malay area (India, China, Borneo, etc.).

Suborder Acanthuroidei. Body deeply compressed; mouth small; swim bladder large; elongate nasal bones give a high-headed appearance; dorsal fin single, with spines and soft rays; gill openings restricted; caudal fin lunate; 22 or 23 vertebrae.

All are herbivorous, feeding mostly on algae. They pass through a planktonic larval stage, termed the acronurus stage, in which their bodies are transparent.

Twelve genera and about 87 species.

Family ACANTHURIDAE—Surgeonfishes. Marine; all tropical seas.

Subfamily Acanthurinae (Hepatidae, Teuthidae). One or more spines on caudal peduncle (which, when extended, can form a formidable weapon); premaxillae not protractile.

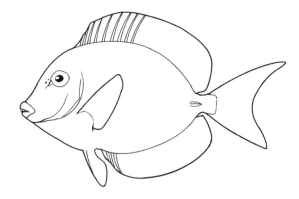

Nine genera with about 75 species. Three tribes can be recognized (regarded as subfamilies in Smith, 1966): the Acanthurini (all tropical seas) with four genera (e.g., *Acanthurus* and *Zebrasoma*) and about 53

species; Prionurini (Pacific), with *Prionurus* and *Xesurus* and six species; and Nasini (Indo-Pacific) (the unicornfishes), with *Axinurus, Callicanthus,* and *Naso* and 16 species.

Subfamily Zanclinae (moorish idols).   Caudal peduncle unarmed; premaxillaries protractile; spine at corner of mouth in juveniles and protuberances in front of eyes in adults.

Moorish idols are found in tropical regions of the Indian and Pacific oceans.

One genus, *Zanclus,* with two species.

Family SIGANIDAE—Rabbitfishes.   Marine; Indo-Pacific and eastern Mediterranean.

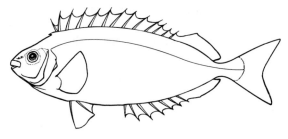

Pelvic fins each with two spines and three soft rays between them; dorsal with 13 strong spines and 10 soft rays; anal fin with seven spines and nine soft rays; spines venomous.

Two genera, *Lo* and *Siganus* (=*Teuthis*), with about 10 species.

Suborder Scombroidei. Premaxillae fixed [nonprotrusible upper jaw (except in *Scombrolabrax* and *Luvarus*)].

This suborder includes species that are probably the world's fastest swimming fish. Sailfish, swordfish, and bluefin tuna have had speeds between 60 and 100 km/hr attributed to them (for short periods of time).

Gosline (1968) recognizes two suborders in this group: the Xiphioidei (recognized here as a superfamily) and the Scombroidei.

Six families with 36 genera and about 94 species.

Superfamily Trichiuroidae. Thirty or more vertebrae; protruding lower jaw; teeth very long.

Family GEMPYLIDAE—Snake Mackerels. Marine, tropical and subtropical seas, often in very deep water.

Body oblong or elongate; maxillae exposed; pectorals low on body; pelvics reduced or absent; isolated finlets usually present behind dorsal and anal fins; caudal fin present. *Lepidocybium* has many scombrid characters. *Scombrolabrax* has a protrusible upper jaw and is of uncertain position.

Ten genera (e.g., *Epinnula, Gempylus, Lemnisoma, Lepidocybium, Ruvettus,* and *Scombrolabrax*) with about 20 species.

Family TRICHIURIDAE—Cutlassfishes. Marine; Atlantic, Indian, and Pacific.

Body very elongate; dorsal fin extremely long based, with spines and soft rays; maxillae concealed by preorbitals; fanglike teeth usually present; pectorals low on body and pelvics reduced or absent.

SUBFAMILY LEPIDOPINAE. Caudal fin small.
Four genera, *Aphanopus, Assurger, Benthodesmus,* and *Lepidopus,* with about 12 species.

SUBFAMILY TRICHIURINAE. Caudal fin absent, tail tapering to a point.
Two genera, *Eupleurogrammus* and *Trichiurus,* with about five species.

Superfamily Scombroidae. Thirty or more vertebrae.

Family SCOMBRIDAE—Mackerels and Tunas.   Marine; tropical and subtropical seas.

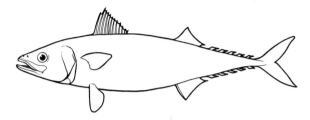

Two dorsal fins (depressible into grooves) with finlets behind second dorsal and anal fins; first dorsal fin origin well behind head; pectoral fins inserted high on body; pelvic fins with six rays, placed beneath the pectorals; gill membranes free from isthmus; scales cycloid and small; slender caudal peduncle with one or two keels; specialized subcutaneous vascular system in *Thunnus* and its close relatives.

The body temperature of large tunas is warmer than the surrounding water because of their high metabolic rate. These fast-swimming fish constitute a popular sport and valuable commercial fisheries. Length up to 4.2 m, attained by *Thunnus thynnus.*

The placement of certain of the tunas in a separate order by Berg (1940) seems ill advised.

Fifteen genera with about 45 species.

The following classification is based on information from Gibbs and Collette (1967). Fraser-Brunner (1950b) gives a good review of the group.

SUBFAMILY GASTEROCHISMATINAE.   Scales moderate in size, about 80 in lateral series.

One species, the aberrant *Gasterochisma melampus* (resembles the bramids), of the Southern Hemisphere.

SUBFAMILY SCOMBRINAE.   Scales minute.

TRIBE SCOMBRINI (MACKERELS).   Five genera, *Scomber, Rastrelliger, Scomberomorus, Grammatorcynus* (resembles the gempylids), and *Acanthocybium,* with up to 24 species.

TRIBE THUNNINI (BONITOS AND TUNAS).   Nine genera (the first four form one line and the other five form a second line): *Gymnosarda, Orcynopsis, Sarda, Cybiosarda, Allothunnus, Auxis, Euthynnus, Katsuwonus,* and *Thunnus,* with about 20 species.

Superfamily Xiphioidae.   Vertebrae 23–26; dorsal fin origin over back of head except in *Luvarus;* pectorals inserted low on body; pelvics reduced (three rays or fewer) or absent; mouth inferior except in *Luvarus;* two anal fins except in *Luvarus,* in which one is present.

   Luvaridae probably bears little or no affinity with xiphioids and is only provisionally retained with them because of the few similarities and lack of a sound basis for placing it elsewhere.

Family XIPHIIDAE—Swordfish.   Marine; tropical and subtropical seas.

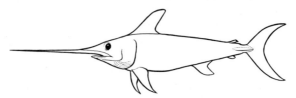

Premaxillae and nasal bones elongated to form a long, pointed, depressed rostrum; gill membranes free from isthmus; scales absent in adult; pelvic fins and girdle absent; jaws toothless in adult; caudal peduncle in adult with single median keel on each side; 26 vertebrae.

   Swordfish are a valuable commercial species. Length up to 4.5 m. One species, *Xiphias gladius.*

Family LUVARIDAE—Louvar.   Marine; tropical and subtropical seas.

Premaxillae protrusible—no long pointed rostrum (snout blunt); gill membranes broadly joined to isthmus; dorsal fin origin in juvenile well forward, moving back with growth; 22 vertebrae, last two fused. Bolin (1940) gives a detailed description of one specimen.

   These fish have an enormous egg production; a 1.7 m individual had an estimated 47.5 million eggs, characteristic of nonschooling oceanic fish. Length up to 1.8 m.

   One species, *Luvarus imperialis.*

Family ISTIOPHORIDAE (Histiophoridae)—Billfishes.   Marine; most tropical and subtropical seas.

Premaxillae and nasal bones elongated to form a long, pointed, rounded rostrum; gill membranes free from isthmus; scales present; pelvic fins elongate; jaws with teeth; caudal peduncle in adult with two keels on each side; dorsal fin with very long base, sometimes saillike, depressible into groove; lateral line retained throughout life; 24 vertebrae.

The bill is used to stun prey fish by slashing back and forth. Billfishes are an extremely popular sportfish. Length up to 4 m.

Three genera with about 10 species.

Istiophorus (sailfishes)—first dorsal fin sail-shaped and distinctly taller than body depth; rays of pelvic fin very long. Two species.

Tetrapturus (spearfishes)—forward portion of first dorsal fin about as high as body is deep. Six species.

Makaira (marlins)—forward portion of first dorsal fin not so high as body is deep (shown in figure). Two species.

Suborder Stromateoidei (see map on p. 344). Toothed saccular outgrowths in gullet behind last gill arch; lacrymal bone covering most of maxillae; scales usually cycloid, weakly ctenoid in some; branchiostegal rays 5–7; hypural plates 2–6; caudal fin with 15 branched rays; vertebrae 25–60. Length up to 1.2 m.

Six families, 15 genera, and about 60 species. All are marine. Classification based on Haedrich (1967) and modifications by Haedrich and Horn (1972).

Family AMARSIPIDAE.   Marine; tropical Indian and Pacific, close to the equator.

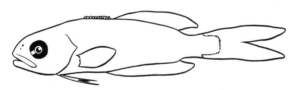

Pelvic fins present, jugular, their origin well before the pectoral fins; body translucent, no color pattern; pharyngeal sacs absent; dorsal fin with 10–12 short spines and 22–27 longer soft rays; anal fin with 28–32 soft rays, no spines; pectoral fin with 17–19 rays; vertebrate 45–47. No adults of this pelagic fish are known.

One species, *Amarsipus carlsbergi*, described in 1969.

Family CENTROLOPHIDAE—Medusafishes.   Marine; tropical to temperate, all seas except most of mid-Indian and mid-Pacific.

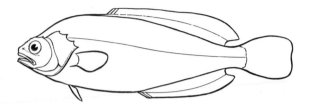

Pelvic fins present in adult; dorsal fin continuous [spines either 0–5, weakly developed and graduating into the soft rays (as in the above illustration and in the first three genera listed below) or 5–9, stout, and considerably shorter than and generally not graduating into the soft rays (in the last three genera listed below)]; total anal fin rays 15–41 (usually three spines).

Centrolophus is the only stromateoid in the far North Atlantic (to Iceland), whereas Icichthys is the only stromateoid in the far North Pacific (to Alaska) (both genera are also in southern oceans).

Six genera, Centrolophus, Icichthys, Schedophilus, Hyperoglyphe, Psenopsis, and Seriolella, with about 22 species.

Family NOMEIDAE—Driftfishes. Marine; tropical and subtropical seas.

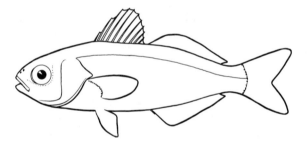

Pelvic fins present in adult; two dorsal fins, the first with 9–12 slender spines and the second with 0–3 spines and 15–32 soft rays; anal fin with 1–3 spines and 14–30 soft rays.

The 10 cm Nomeus gronovii (man-of-war fish) is circumtropical and usually found with the Portuguese man-of-war (Physalia). The fish swims unharmed among the stinging tentacles.

Three genera, Cubiceps, Nomeus, and Psenes, with about 15 species.

Family ARIOMMIDAE—Ariommids. Marine; deep water, tropical and subtropical coastlines of eastern North and South America, Africa, Asia, Kermadec Islands, and Hawaii.

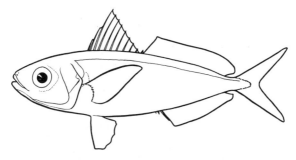

Pelvic fins present in adult; two dorsal fins, the first with 10–12 slender spines and the second with 14–18 soft rays; anal fin with three short spines and 13–16 soft rays; pectoral fin with 20–24 rays; caudal peduncle with two low, fleshy, lateral keels on each side; vertebrae 30–32.

One genus, *Ariomma*, with about six species.

Family TETRAGONURIDAE—Squaretails. Marine; tropical and subtropical seas.

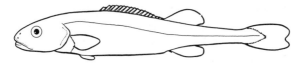

Body elongate; pelvic fins present in adult; two dorsal fins, the first with 10–20 short spines and the second with 10–17 soft rays; anal fin with one spine and 10–16 soft rays; caudal peduncle with a single keel on each side; lateral scales 73–114; vertebrae 40–58. Individuals are thought to feed almost exclusively on coelenterates and ctenophores.

One genus, *Tetragonurus*, with three species. This is the most widely distributed of all the stromateoid genera.

Family STROMATEIDAE—Butterfishes. Marine; coastal North and South America, western Africa, and southern Asia (Indo-Pacific).

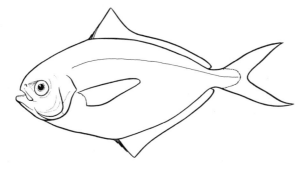

Body usually very deep; pelvic fins absent in adult (present in some young—pelvic bones present); dorsal fin continuous; anal fin usually with 2–6 spines and 30–50 soft rays.

Three genera, *Pampus*, *Peprilus*, and *Stromateus*, with about 13 species.

Suborder Anabantoidei (see map on p. 344). A suprabranchial organ present, usually labyrinthine, formed by expansion of first epibranchial; dorsal and anal fins with spines; gill membranes scaly and broadly united; pelvic fins thoracic, usually with one spine and five soft rays; five or six branchiostegal rays; swim bladder divided posteriorly, extending into caudal region; vertebrae 25–31.

The suprabranchial organ is an auxiliary breathing apparatus. Air taken in through the mouth passes through the labyrinth where capillaries absorb oxygen. As air is taken in at various intervals, old air is forced out of the labyrinth through the gill covers. This organ has enabled many species to occupy submarginal or even anoxic waters.

In most anabantoids the male builds a nest of floating bubbles. Eggs are deposited in the bubbles and the male exhibits parental care.

This and the next two suborders, Luciocephaloidei and Channoidei, have been variously classified. Under some schemes (e.g., Jordan, 1923) members of the three suborders were placed together in a separate order, the Labyrinthici. Liem (1963) attributed the possession in all three of a suprabranchial organ to convergent evolution and not phylogenetic relationship. Certainly the first epibranchial becomes variously modified to form the suprabranchial organ. Greenwood et al. (1966), in a fashion similar to Berg (1940), placed on the anabantoids and luciocephalids in separate suborders and placed the channids in their own order between Gasterosteiformes and Synbranchiformes, considering them as preperciforms. Gosline (1968, 1971) placed all three in the same suborder, the Anabantoidei, and, like his suborder Mugiloidei, considered it a "protopercoid" in the perciformes. Here all three are recognized as separate suborders and placed consecutively. All are freshwater and indigenous to Africa and southern Asia.

Gosline (1971) believes that the group is an early perciform offshoot with some affinity with the Nandidae (which he suggests may best be placed in the Anabantoidei).

Four families, 15 genera, and about 70 species.

Family ANABANTIDAE—Climbing Gouramies. Freshwater (rarely brackish); Africa and India to Philippines.

Jaws, prevomer, and parasphenoid with fixed conical teeth; mouth relatively large; upper jaw only weakly protrusile; one genus, *Sandelia*, only with cycloid scales, not ctenoid; gill rakers few and diet generally carnivorous.

Three genera, *Anabas*, *Ctenopoma*, and *Sandelia*, with perhaps 40 species.

Family BELONTIIDAE (Polyacanthidae)—Gouramies. Freshwater; west Africa and India to Malay Archipelago and Korea.

Prevomer and palatine without teeth; upper jaw protrusile; lateral line vestigial or absent; dorsal fin never with more than 10 soft rays; many species with an elongate pelvic ray on each side.

Ten genera with perhaps 28 species.

Liem (1963) established the following three subfamilies, which represent the three major evolutionary lines of the family.

SUBFAMILY BELONTIINAE (COMBTAIL GOURAMIES).   One genus, *Belontia*, with perhaps two species.

SUBFAMILY MACROPODINAE (SIAMESE FIGHTING FISHES, PARADISEFISHES, ETC.)

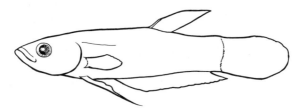

Five genera, *Betta* (shown in figure), *Trichopsis*, *Macropodus*, *Parosphromenus*, and *Malpulutta*, with perhaps 14 species.

SUBFAMILY TRICHOGASTERINAE (GOURAMIES, ETC.).

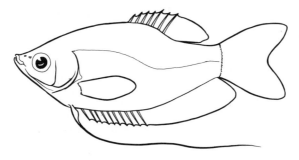

Four genera, *Sphaerichthys, Parasphaerichthys, Colisa,* and *Trichogaster* (shown in figure), with about 12 species.

Family HELOSTOMATIDAE—Kissing Gourami.   Freshwater; Thailand to Malay Archipelago.

Premaxillae, dentaries, palatine, and pharynx devoid of teeth; two lateral lines, the lower commencing below the end of the upper; dorsal fin with 16–18 spines and 13–16 soft rays; anal fin with 13–15 spines and 17–19 soft rays; lateral line scales 43–48; scales on top of head cycloid, others ctenoid. Numerous gill rakers form an elaborate filter apparatus on the gill arches which adapts the fish to filter feeding (horny teeth on the lips also enable the fish to scrape algae off surfaces). Liem (1967a) describes the functional morphology of the head region. Maximum length about 30 cm.
    One species, *Helostoma temmincki.*

Family OSPHRONEMIDAE—Giant Gourami.   Freshwater; Thailand to Malay Archipelago.

Prevomer and palatine devoid of teeth; one lateral line, complete and continuous; all scales ctenoid; dorsal fin with 11–13 spines and 11–13 soft rays; anal fin with 9–12 spines and 16–22 soft rays. Maximum length about 60 cm.
    One species, *Osphronemus goramy.*

Suborder Luciocephaloidei.   See notes under Anabantoidei for taxonomic placement of this group.

Family LUCIOCEPHALIDAE—Pikehead.   Freshwater; Malay Peninsula and Archipelago.

Suprabranchial organ for air breathing present; no dorsal or anal spines; dorsal fin inserted posteriorly, with 9–12 rays; anal fin with a deep notch and 18 or 19 rays; pelvic fin with one spine and five soft rays (one of which is produced into a threadlike ray); caudal fin rounded; lateral line scales about 40–42; mouth very protractile; gill membranes not united;

median gular element present; no swim bladder. Liem (1967b) gives a detailed description of the species. Maximum length about 18 cm. One species, *Luciocephalus pulcher*.

Suborder Channoidei (Ophiocephaliformes). See notes under Anabantoidei for taxonomic placement of this group.

Family CHANNIDAE—Snakeheads. Freshwater; tropical Africa and southern Asia (see map on p. 345).

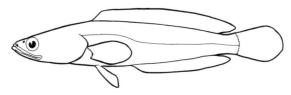

Body elongate; long dorsal and anal fins; no fin spines; cycloid or ctenoid scales; lower jaw protruding beyond upper; suprabranchial organ for air breathing present. Maximum length about 1.2 m (attained in *Ophicephalus marulius*); the smallest species (*O. guacha*) reaches about 15 cm.

Two genera, *Ophicephalus* (six soft rays in subabdominal pelvic fins) with about 10 species and *Channa asiatica* (no pelvic fins).

Suborder Mastacembeloidei (Opisthomi). Body elongate (eellike); no pelvic fins; dorsal and anal fins continuous to or continuous with the small caudal fin; pectoral arch (supracleithrum) attached to the vertebral column by a ligament; no air duct to swim bladder (physoclistic); no posttemporal bone; 70–95 vertebrae.

This group, a perciform derivative, is placed in its own order by many workers.

Family MASTACEMBELIDAE—Spiny Eels. Freshwater; tropical Africa; through Syria to Malay Archipelago and China (see map on p. 345).

Dorsal fin preceded by a series of isolated spines (usually 14–35); anal fin usually with two or three spines and 30–130 soft rays; fleshy rostral appendage present; body covered with small scales; no basisphenoid.

Two genera, *Macrognathus* and *Mastacembelus*, with about 50 species.

Family CHAUDHURIIDAE. Freshwater; Burma.

No dorsal spines; no rostral appendage; body naked; basisphenoid present.
One species, *Chaudhuria caudata.*

Order GOBIESOCIFORMES. Head and body scaleless; branchiostegal rays 5–7; no circumorbital bones behind the lachrymal; articular processes of premaxillae either fused with the ascending processes or absent; no swim bladder. Most species are shallow-water bottom-dwelling fishes.

Greenwood et al. (1966) placed this order in the Paracanthopterygii and, like other workers, accommodated only the Gobiesocidae in it. Gosline (1970) felt that the Gobiesocidae, Callionymidae, and Draconettidae evolved from the notothenioids and placed the three families together in the order Gobiesociformes, after the Perciformes, as I have done here.

About 42 genera with 144 species in three families.

Suborder Gobiesocoidei (Xenopterygii)

Family GOBIESOCIDAE—Clingfishes. Marine; primarily shallow water or intertidal; few in fresh water; Atlantic, Indian, and Pacific.

Pelvic fins modified into a thoracic sucking disk (permitting fish to adhere to substrate); each fin with one small spine and four or five soft rays; single dorsal fin without spines; no basibranchials; vertebrae 25–54; lateral line confined to head; two postcleithra; hypurals fused into a single plate. Length normally 7 cm; up to 30 cm.

About 33 genera [e.g., *Arcos, Aspasma, Chorisochismus, Diademichthys, Diplecogaster, Gobiesox* (four species of which occur in freshwater streams in Central America), *Haplocylix, Lepadogaster, Rimicola, Tomicodon,* and *Trachelochismus*] with about 100 species. Briggs (1955) recognized eight subfamilies identifiable by the following character states: sucking disk single or double; gill arches three or three and one-half; gill membranes free or attached to isthmus.

Suborder Callionymoidei. Pelvic fins with one spine and five soft rays, not modified into a sucking disk; spinous dorsal fin present (except *Draculo*); basibranchials present; vertebrae 21–23.

Family CALLIONYMIDAE—Dragonets. Marine; all warm seas, primarily Indo-Pacific.

Gill opening reduced to a small opening on upper side of head; preoperculum with a strong spine, operculum and suboperculum spineless; lateral line continued on body; three radials in pectoral skeleton; usually no basisphenoid or posttemporal; paired nasal bones; two postcleithra; hypurals fused into a single plate; dorsal fin spines usually four and soft rays 6–11; anal fin with 4–10 soft rays. Maximum length about 20 cm.

About eight genera (e.g., *Callionymus, Draculo, Pogonymus, Synchiropus,* and *Yerutius*) with about 40 species.

Family DRACONETTIDAE. Marine; Japan to Hawaii and western Atlantic.

Gill opening comparatively broad; operculum and suboperculum each with a strong straight spine, preoperculum spineless; lateral line confined to head; four radials in pectoral skeleton; basisphenoid and posttemporal present; no nasal bone; one postcleithrum; two separate hypurals; three dorsal fin spines and 12–15 soft rays; anal fin with 12 or 13 soft rays.

One genus, *Draconetta,* with four species (Briggs and Berry, 1959).

Order PLEURONECTIFORMES (Heterosomata). Adults not bilaterally symmetrical; body highly compressed, somewhat rounded on eyed side and flat on blind side; dorsal and anal fins usually long; usually six or seven branchiostegal rays, rarely eight; body cavity small; adults almost always without swim bladder; scales cycloid, ctenoid, or tuberculate.

This is a very distinctive group. Young flatfishes are bilaterally symmetrical and swim upright, but early in their development one eye migrates across the top of the skull to lie adjacent to the eye on the other side. They then lie and swim on the eyeless side. The change involves a complex modification of skull bones, nerves, and muscles and leaves one side of the fish blind (lower side) and the other side with two eyes (upper side). The upper side is also pigmented, whereas the under side is usually white. Asymmetry may also be reflected in other characters such as dentition, squamation, and paired fins. Most species have both eyes on the right side and lie on the left side (dextral) or both eyes on the left side and lie on the right side (sinistral). In some species both dextral ("right-handed") and sinistral ("left-handed") individuals may occur. Flatfishes are benthic and carnivorous. Maximum length almost 3 m in the halibuts; much smaller in most groups.

Common names for flatfishes include flounder, halibut, sole, plaice, dab, and turbot, which often apply to species in different families. Many species are important in commercial fisheries and are valued as a food source.

About 520 extant species are contained in approximately 117 genera and six families [seven familes are recognized by Greenwood et al. (1966)]. Norman (1934) and Hubbs (1945) have dealt with the classification of the order. About 63% of the species are placed in two families, Bothidae and Soleidae. This group has probably had more than one origin from a percoid form (Amaoka, 1969).

Suborder Psettodoidei.   Dorsal fin not extending onto head (to or past eye); anterior dorsal and anal rays spinous; palatine with teeth; basisphenoid present; 24 or 25 vertebrae.

Family PSETTODIDAE—Psettodids.   Marine; west Africa and Indo-Pacific.

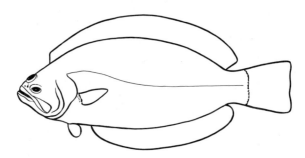

Pelvic fins nearly symmetrical, with one spine and five soft rays; mouth large; eyes sinistral or dextral; preopercular margin distinct, not covered with skin.

One genus, *Psettodes*, with two species [*P. belcheri* from tropical west Africa (eastern Atlantic) and *P. erumei* from eastern Africa and the Red Sea to the western Pacific]. Stauch and Cadenat (1965) recognized two west African species, *P. benneti* (coastal Senegal and Mauritania) and *P. belcheri* (coastal Ghana to Angola).

Suborder Pleuronectoidei. Dorsal fin extending onto head at least to eyes; dorsal and anal fins without spines; palatine without teeth; no basisphenoid; vertebrae 26–70, 10 or more are abdominal; preopercular margin distinct, not covered with skin; one or two postcleithra; optic nerve of migrating eye always dorsal (may be dorsal or ventral in other flatfishes).

Family CITHARIDAE—Citharids. Marine; Mediterranean, Indian Ocean, and Japan to Australia.

Pelvic fins with 1 spine and 5 soft rays; pelvic fin bases short; branchiostegal membranes separated from each other.

Four genera with 5 species.

SUBFAMILY BRACHYPLEURINAE. Eyes dextral.
Two monotypic genera, *Brachypleura* and *Lepidoblepharon*.

SUBFAMILY CITHARINAE. Eyes sinistral.

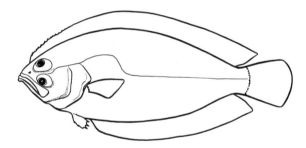

Two genera, *Citharoides* and *Citharus* (=*Eucitharus*), with three species.

FAMILY BOTHIDAE—Lefteye Flounders. Marine; Atlantic, Indian, and Pacific.

Eyes sinistral; pelvic fins without a spine; branchiostegal membranes connected; egg with a single oil globule in the yolk.
Thirty-six genera with about 212 species.

SUBFAMILY BOTHINAE. Pelvic fin base on blind side shorter than on eyed side; pectoral and pelvic fin rays not branched.
Thirteen genera (e.g., *Arnoglossus, Bothus, Chascanopsetta, Engyprosopon,* and *Taeniopsetta*) with about 116 species.

SUBFAMILY PARALICHTHYINAE.   Pelvic fin bases short and nearly symmetrical; pectoral and pelvic rays branched.

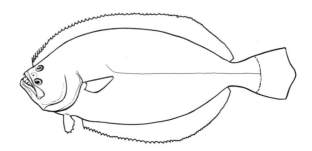

Nineteen genera (e.g., *Ancylopsetta, Citharichthys, Etropus, Gastropsetta, Hippoglossina, Paralichthys, Pseudorhombus, Tarphops,* and *Xystreurys*) with about 86 species.

SUBFAMILY SCOPHTHALMINAE.   Both pelvic fin bases elongate. This group, confined to the north Atlantic and Mediterranean Sea, is given family status in Greenwood et al. (1966).
    Four genera (e.g., *Scophthalmus*) with 10 species.

FAMILY PLEURONECTIDAE—Righteye Flounders.   Marine (occasionally in brackish water, rarely in fresh water); Arctic, Atlantic, and Pacific.

Eyes almost always dextral; no oil globule in yolk of egg.
    Forty-one genera with about 99 species.

SUBFAMILY PLEURONECTINAE.   Origin of dorsal fin above the eyes; lateral line well developed on both sides; pelvic fins symmetrical.

    TRIBE HIPPOGLOSSINI.   Mouth large and symmetrical; maxillae extending to or behind pupil of eyes; teeth well developed on both sides of jaws. The commercially important and large halibuts belong to this group.
    Ten genera (e.g., *Atheresthes, Eopsetta, Hippoglossoides, Hippoglossus, Lyopsetta, Psettichthys,* and *Reinhardtius*) with about 18 species.

    TRIBE PLEURONECTINI.   Mouth small and asymmetrical; maxillae usually not extending to pupil of eye; teeth chiefly on blind side of jaw.

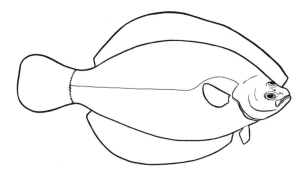

Sixteen genera (e.g., *Embassichthys, Glyptocephalus, Hypsopsetta, Isopsetta, Lepidopsetta, Limanda, Liopsetta, Microstomus, Parophrys, Platichthys, Pleuronectes, Pleuronichthys,* and *Pseudopleuronectes*) with about 42 species.

SUBFAMILY POECILOPSETTINAE. Origin of dorsal fin above the eyes; lateral line rudimentary on blind side; pelvic fins symmetrical.
    Three genera (e.g., *Poecilopsetta*) with 13 species.

SUBFAMILY RHOMBOSOLEINAE. Pelvic fins asymmetrical (one on the eyed side may be joined to anal fin); lateral line equally developed on both sides; pectoral radials absent. A South Pacific group, occurring primarily around Australia and New Zealand.
    Eight genera (e.g., *Ammotretis, Peltorhamphus,* and *Rhombosolea*) with 12 species.

SUBFAMILY SAMARINAE. Origin of dorsal fin in front of eyes; lateral line well developed or rudimentary; pelvic fins symmetrical. An Indo-Pacific group.

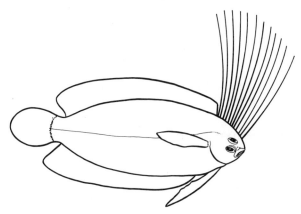

Four genera (e.g., *Paralichthodes*, *Samaris*, and *Samariscus*) with 14 species.

Suborder Soleoidei. Preopercular margin not entirely free, covered by skin; vertebrae usually 24–50—10 or fewer are abdominal; no post-cleithrum; no basisphenoid; pectoral fins usually absent in adult—right pectoral fin well developed in some; ribs absent.

FAMILY SOLEIDAE—Soles. Marine (some freshwater); tropical to temperate seas.

Eyes dextral.
Thirty-one genera with about 117 species.

SUBFAMILY ACHIRINAE. Amphi-American, many in fresh water. Margin of preoperculum represented by a superficial groove; dorsal and anal fins free from caudal fin; right pelvic fin joined to anal fin.

Nine genera (e.g., *Achirus*, *Gymnachirus*, and *Trinectes*) with about 28 species.

SUBFAMILY SOLEINAE. Primarily Europe to Australia and Japan. Margin of preoperculum completely concealed; dorsal and anal fins free from caudal fin or united with caudal; pelvics free from anal fin.

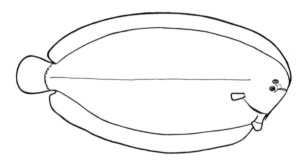

Twenty-two genera (e.g., *Aseraggodes*, *Euryglossa*, *Solea*, *Synaptura*, and *Zebrias*) with about 89 species.

FAMILY CYNOGLOSSIDAE—Tonguefishes. Marine (some freshwater); tropical and subtropical seas.

Eyes sinistral; dorsal and anal fins confluent with the pointed caudal fin; usually only left pelvic fin developed; pectorals absent (a fine membrane in *Symphurus*); eyes very small and usually close together; mouth asymmetrical. Maximum length for almost all species is less than 30 cm. Four genera with at least 86 species.

SUBFAMILY CYNOGLOSSINAE. Snout well-hooked; mouth inferior and notably contorted; lateral line(s) well developed, at least on eyed side.

Three genera, *Cynoglossus* (=*Cynoglossoides*), *Arelia*, and *Paraplagusia*.

SUBFAMILY SYMPHURINAE. Snout slightly hooked; mouth nearly terminal and almost straight; lateral line absent.

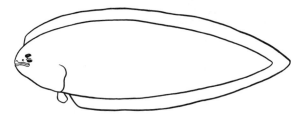

One genus, *Symphurus*.

Order TETRAODONTIFORMES (Plectognathi). No parietals, nasals, infraorbitals, or lower ribs; posttemporal, if present, simple and fused with pterotic of skull; hyomandibular and palatine firmly attached to skull; gill openings restricted; maxillae usually firmly united or fused with premaxillae; scales usually modified as spines, shields, or plates; lateral line present or absent, sometimes multiple; swim bladder present or absent.

Tetraodontiformes can produce sounds by grinding the jaw teeth or the pharyngeal teeth or by vibrating the swim bladder. The stomach of some tetraodontiforms is highly modified to allow inflation to an enormous size. Fish with this ability, belonging to the two families Diodontidae and Tetraodontidae, are popularly called puffers. Inflation is caused by gulping down water into a ventral diverticulum of the stomach when the fish is frightened or annoyed. Deflation occurs by expelling the water. If the fish is removed from the water, inflation can occur with air. Members of Balistidae and Triodontidae have another mechanism for slightly enlarging their bodies. They do this by expanding a ventral flap supported by a large movable pelvic bone.

Eight families with approximately 65 genera and 320 extant species. Two families, Balistidae and Tetraodontidae, have about 78% of the species.

Additional information can be found in Breder and Clark (1947), Berry and Vogele (1961), Fraser-Brunner (1951), Fuhrman (1967), and Tyler (1968).

Suborder Balistoidei (Sclerodermi). Jaws with distinct teeth (i.e., teeth not fused).

Superfamily Triacanthoidae. Upper jaw slightly protractile (ascending process of premaxillae well developed); pelvic fin with one large spine and up to two soft rays; dorsal fin usually with six spines; caudal fin with 12 principal rays; 2–6 separate hypurals; 20 vertebrae.

Family TRIACANTHODIDAE—Spikefishes. Marine; deepwater benthic; tropical and subtropical western Atlantic and Indo-Pacific.

Dorsal fin rays 12–18; anal fin rays 11–16; caudal fin rounded to truncate.

Fossils include the Eocene *Spinacanthus.*

Subfamily Hollardiinae. Western Atlantic, one species in Hawaii. Two genera, *Hollardia* and *Parahollardia,* with five species.

SUBFAMILY TRIACANTHODINAE. Indo-Pacific, one species in western Atlantic.

Nine genera, *Atrophacanthus, Bathyphylax, Halimochirurgus, Johnsonina, Macrorhamphosodes, Mephisto, Paratriacanthodes, Triacanthodes,* and *Tydemania,* with 14 species.

Family TRIACANTHIDAE—Triplespines.   Marine; shallow benthic; Indo-Pacific.

Dorsal fin rays 20–26; anal fin rays 13–22; caudal fin deeply forked.

Fossils include the Eocene *Protacanthodes* and the balistidlike Oligocene *Cryptobalistes.*

Four genera, *Pseudotriacanthus, Triacanthus, Tripodichthys,* and *Trixiphichthys,* with seven species.

Superfamily Balistoidae

Family BALISTIDAE—Triggerfishes and Filefishes.   Marine; Atlantic, Indian, and Pacific.

Body compressed; no pelvic fins (pelvic spine or tubercle may be present, underlying pelvis present); first dorsal spine with locking mechanism (the small second spine forms the locking mechanism); upper jaw not protractile; upper jaw with two rows of protruding incisorlike teeth; soft dorsal and anal fins usually each with 25–50 rays; in life the eyes can be rotated independently. Maximum length about 1.0 m, attained in *Aluterus scriptus.*

About 120 species.

SUBFAMILY BALISTINAE (TRIGGERFISHES).   Three dorsal spines; all soft fins with branched rays; scales in regular series, platelike; upper jaw usually with eight teeth in outer and six in the inner series.

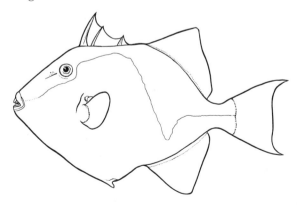

Seven genera, *Balistapus*, *Balistes*, *Canthidermis*, *Melichthys*, *Odonus*, *Rhinecanthus*, and *Xanthichthys*, with about 35 species.

SUBFAMILY MONACANTHINAE (FILEFISHES). Usually two dorsal spines —the second may be small or absent; soft dorsal, anal, and pectoral rays simple; scales small, not in regular series, body prickly or furry to the touch; upper jaw usually with six teeth in outer and four in the inner series.

Twelve genera, *Aluterus* (=*Alutera*), *Amanses*, *Anacanthus*, *Cantherhines*, *Chaetoderma*, *Monacanthus*, *Oxymonacanthus*, *Paraluteres*, *Paramonacanthus*, *Pervagor*, *Pseudalutarius*, and *Stephanolepis*, with about 85 species.

Superfamily Ostraciontoidae (Ostracodermi)

Family OSTRACIONTIDAE (Ostraciidae)—Boxfishes (Cowfish and Trunkfish). Marine; tropical; Atlantic, Indian, and Pacific.

Body encased in a bony carapace; no pelvic skeleton; no spinous dorsal; upper jaw not protractile; vertebrae 14–16. Maximum length about 60 cm.

Some trunkfish are known to discharge a toxic substance, termed ostracitoxin, which will kill other fishes in confined quarters. The substance is also toxic to the trunkfish, but less so than to most other fishes.

SUBFAMILY ARACANINAE. Carapace open behind the dorsal and anal fins; ventral ridge more or less developed.

Six genera (e.g., *Aracana*, *Capropygia*, and *Kentrocapros*) with about nine species.

SUBFAMILY OSTRACIONTINAE. Carapace closed, at least behind the anal fin; no ventral ridge.

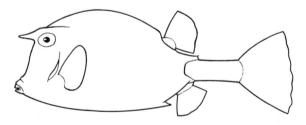

Six genera (e.g., *Acanthostracion*, *Lactophrys*, *Lactoria*, *Ostracion*, and *Tetrosomus*) with about 15 species.

Suborder Tetraodontoidei (Gymnodontes). Jaw "teeth" fused (true teeth are absent—the upper and lower jaws have cutting edges; a similar looking beak is found in the Scaridae); depending on the presence or absence of sutures, there may be two, three, or four such "teeth"; upper jaw not protractile; pelvics (fin and rays) absent.

Superfamily Triodontoidae

Family TRIODONTIDAE—Three-Toothed Puffer. Marine; Indo-Pacific.

Three fused teeth in jaws (upper jaw with a median suture, the lower without); pelvis present; dorsal fin usually with 10 rays and anal fin usually with nine rays.
    One species, *Triodon bursarius*.

Superfamily Tetraodontoidae. Body inflatable.

Family TETRAODONTIDAE—Puffers. Marine (several entering and occurring in brackish and fresh water); tropical and subtropical; Atlantic, Indian, and Pacific.

Body naked or with only small scattered prickles; four fused teeth in jaws (teeth in each jaw fused but separated by a median suture); dorsal and anal fins usually each with 7–12 soft rays.
    The "flesh" (especially the viscera) of some puffers contains the alkaloid poison tetraodotoxin, produced by the fish, which can be fatal. In at least some species the gonads at spawning time contain the highest concentration of this poison; none occurs in the muscle.
    Several species, mostly of *Tetraodon*, occur only in fresh water, primarily in the Congo River and in southern Asia. Maximum length 90 cm; most much less.
    Ten genera with perhaps up to 131 species.

SUBFAMILY TETRAODONTINAE. Body broadly rounded in cross section.

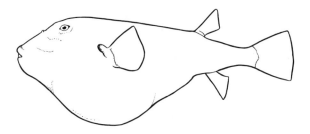

Nine genera (e.g., *Lagocephalus*, *Sphoeroides*, and *Tetraodon*) with numerous species.

SUBFAMILY CANTHIGASTERINAE (SHARPNOSE PUFFERS). Body deeper than broad in uninflated condition.

One genus, *Canthigaster*, with several species.

Family DIODONTIDAE—Porcupinefishes. Marine; Atlantic, Indian, and Pacific.

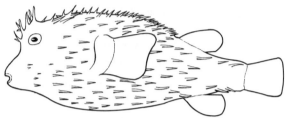

Body covered with well-developed sharp spines (in some species the spines erect only when body is inflated); two fused teeth in jaws (parrotlike); pelvis absent.

Adults inhabit inshore waters while the young are pelagic.

Five genera (e.g., *Chilomycterus* and *Diodon*) with 15 species.

Superfamily Moloidae

Family MOLIDAE—Molas. Marine; tropical and subtropical; Atlantic, Indian and Pacific.

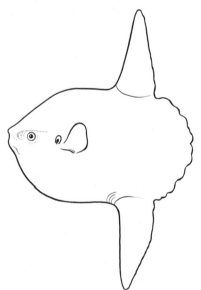

Two fused teeth in jaws; pelvis absent; no spines in dorsal or anal fins; no caudal peduncle; 13 "caudal" rays (gephyrocercal tail fin); no swim bladder; vertebrae 16 or 17.

The major locomotory thrust is provided by the powerful dorsal and anal fins. It has been estimated that up to 300,000,000 eggs can be produced by *Mola mola* (the ocean sunfish), probably making it the most fecund fish species. Maximum length about 3.3 m with weights up to 900 kg.

Three monotypic genera, *Masturus*, *Mola*, and *Ranzania*. The first two are considered by some to be synonymous, the two species being placed in *Mola*.

Appendix I

Checklist of the extant classes (numbered), orders (numbered), suborders (not numbered), and families (numbered).

Class 1 Cephalaspidomorphi
    Order 1. Petromyzoniformes
        Family 1. Petromyzonidae
Class 2 Pteraspidomorphi
    Order 2. Myxiniformes
        Family 2. Myxinidae
Class 3 Chondrichthyes
    Order 3. Heterodontiformes
        Family 3. Heterodontidae
    Order 4. Hexanchiformes
        Family 4. Chlamydoselachidae
        Family 5. Hexanchidae
    Order 5. Lamniformes
        Suborder Lamnoidei
        Family 6. Rhincodontidae
        Family 7. Orectolobidae
        Family 8. Odontaspididae
        Family 9. Lamnidae
        Suborder Scyliorhinoidei

Family 10.   Scyliorhinidae
Family 11.   Carcharhinidae
Family 12.   Sphyrnidae
Order 6.   Squaliformes
Suborder Squaloidei
Family 13.   Squalidae
Family 14.   Pristiophoridae
Suborder Squatinoidei
Family 15.   Squatinidae
Order 7.   Rajiformes
Family 16.   Pristidae
Family 17.   Rhinobatidae
Family 18.   Torpedinidae
Family 19.   Rajidae
Family 20.   Dasyatidae
Family 21.   Potamotrygonidae
Family 22.   Myliobatidae
Family 23.   Mobulidae
Order 8.   Chimaeriformes
Family 24.   Callorhynchidae
Family 25.   Chimaeridae
Family 26.   Rhinochimaeridae
Class 4   Osteichthyes
Order 9.   Ceratodiformes
Family 27.   Ceratodidae
Order 10.   Lepidosireniformes
Family 28.   Lepidosirenidae
Family 29.   Protopteridae
Order 11.   Coelacanthiformes
Family 30.   Latimeriidae
Order 12.   Polypteriformes
Family 31.   Polypteridae
Order 13.   Acipenseriformes
Family 32.   Acipenseridae
Family 33.   Polyodontidae
Order 14.   Semionotiformes
Family 34.   Lepisosteidae
Order 15.   Amiiformes
Family 35.   Amiidae
Order 16.   Osteoglossiformes
Suborder Notopteroidei
Family 36.   Hiodontidae
Family 37.   Notopteridae
Suborder Osteoglossoidei
Family 38.   Osteoglossidae
Family 39.   Pantodontidae

Order 17. Mormyriformes
    Family 40. Mormyridae
    Family 41. Gymnarchidae
Order 18. Clupeiformes
    Suborder Denticipitoidei
    Family 42. Denticipitidae
    Suborder Clupeoidei
    Family 43. Clupeidae
    Family 44. Engraulidae
    Family 45. Chirocentridae
Order 19. Elopiformes
    Suborder Elopoidei
    Family 46. Elopidae
    Family 47. Megalopidae
    Suborder Albuloidei
    Family 48. Albulidae
Order 20. Anguilliformes
    Suborder Anguilloidei
    Family 49. Anguillidae
    Family 50. Heterenchelyidae
    Family 51. Moringuidae
    Family 52. Nemichthyidae
    Family 53. Cyemidae
    Family 54. Xenocongridae
    Family 55. Myrocongridae
    Family 56. Muraenidae
    Family 57. Synaphobranchidae
    Family 58. Simenchelyidae
    Family 59. Dysommidae
    Family 60. Macrocephenchelyidae
    Family 61. Colocongridae
    Family 62. Congridae
    Family 63. Muraenesocidae
    Family 64. Nettastomidae
    Family 65. Serrivomeridae
    Family 66. Ophichthidae
    Family 67. Derichthyidae
    Suborder Saccopharyngoidei
    Family 68. Saccopharyngidae
    Family 69. Eurypharyngidae
    Family 70. Monognathidae
Order 21. Notacanthiformes
    Suborder Halosauroidei
    Family 71. Halosauridae
    Suborder Notacanthoidei
    Family 72. Lipogenyidae

Family 73.   Notacanthidae
Order 22.   Salmoniformes
Suborder Esocoidei
Family 74.   Esocidae
Family 75.   Umbridae
Suborder Salmonoidei
Family 76.   Salmonidae
Family 77.   Retropinnidae
Family 78.   Aplochitonidae
Family 79.   Galaxiidae
Family 80.   Osmeridae
Family 81.   Plecoglossidae
Family 82.   Salangidae
Suborder Argentinoidei
Family 83.   Argentinidae
Family 84.   Bathylagidae
Family 85.   Opisthoproctidae
Family 86.   Alepocephalidae
Family 87.   Searsiidae
Suborder Stomiatoidei
Family 88.   Gonostomatidae
Family 89.   Sternoptychidae
Family 90.   Chauliodontidae
Family 91.   Stomiatidae
Family 92.   Astronesthidae
Family 93.   Melanostomiatidae
Family 94.   Malacosteidae
Family 95.   Idiacanthidae
Suborder Giganturoidei
Family 96.   Giganturidae
Family 97.   Rosauridae
Order 23.   Gonorynchiformes
Suborder Chanoidei
Family 98.   Chanidae
Family 99.   Kneriidae
Family 100.   Phractolaemidae
Suborder Gonorynchoidei
Family 101.   Gonorynchidae
Order 24.   Cypriniformes
Suborder Characoidei
Family 102.   Characidae
Family 103.   Erythrinidae
Family 104.   Ctenoluciidae
Family 105.   Hepsetidae
Family 106.   Cynodontidae
Family 107.   Lebiasinidae

Family 108. Parodontidae
Family 109. Gasteropelecidae
Family 110. Prochilodontidae
Family 111. Curimatidae
Family 112. Anostomidae
Family 113. Hemiodontidae
Family 114. Chilodontidae
Family 115. Distichodontidae
Family 116. Citharinidae
Family 117. Ichthyboridae
Family 118. Gymnotidae
Family 119. Electrophoridae
Family 120. Apteronotidae
Family 121. Rhamphichthyidae
Suborder Cyprinoidei
Family 122. Cyprinidae
Family 123. Gyrinocheilidae
Family 124. Psilorhynchidae
Family 125. Catostomidae
Family 126. Homalopteridae
Family 127. Cobitidae
Order 25. Siluriformes
Family 128. Diplomystidae
Family 129. Ictaluridae
Family 130. Bagridae
Family 131. Cranoglanididae
Family 132. Siluridae
Family 133. Schilbeidae
Family 134. Pangasiidae
Family 135. Amblycipitidae
Family 136. Amphiliidae
Family 137. Akysidae
Family 138. Sisoridae
Family 139. Clariidae
Family 140. Heteropneustidae
Family 141. Chacidae
Family 142. Olyridae
Family 143. Malapteruridae
Family 144. Mochokidae
Family 145. Ariidae
Family 146. Doradidae
Family 147. Auchenipteridae
Family 148. Aspredinidae
Family 149. Plotosidae
Family 150. Pimelodidae
Family 151. Ageneiosidae

Family 152. Hypophthalmidae
Family 153. Helogeneidae
Family 154. Cetopsidae
Family 155. Trichomycteridae
Family 156. Callichthyidae
Family 157. Loricariidae
Family 158. Astroblepidae
Order 26. Myctophiformes
Family 159. Aulopodidae
Family 160. Synodontidae
Family 161. Bathysauridae
Family 162. Harpadontidae
Family 163. Chlorophthalmidae
Family 164. Bathypteroidae
Family 165. Ipnopidae
Family 166. Scopelosauridae
Family 167. Myctophidae
Family 168. Neoscopelidae
Family 169. Paralepididae
Family 170. Omosudidae
Family 171. Alepisauridae
Family 172. Anotopteridae
Family 173. Evermannellidae
Family 174. Scopelarchidae
Order 27. Polymixiiformes
Family 175. Polymixiidae
Order 28. Percopsiformes
Suborder Percopsoidei
Family 176. Percopsidae
Suborder Aphredoderoidei
Family 177. Aphredoderidae
Family 178. Amblyopsidae
Order 29. Gadiformes
Suborder Muraenolepoidei
Family 179. Muraenolepididae
Suborder Gadoidei
Family 180. Moridae
Family 181. Melanonidae
Family 182. Bregmacerotidae
Family 183. Gadidae
Family 184. Merlucciidae
Suborder Macrouroidei
Family 185. Macrouridae
Suborder Ophidioidei
Family 186. Ophidiidae
Family 187. Carapidae

Suborder Zoarcoidei
Family 188. Zoarcidae
Order 30. Batrachoidiformes
Family 189. Batrachoididae
Order 31. Lophiiformes
Suborder Lophioidei
Family 190. Lophiidae
Suborder Antennarioidei
Family 191. Brachionichthyidae
Family 192. Antennariidae
Family 193. Chaunacidae
Family 194. Ogcocephalidae
Suborder Ceratioidei
Family 195. Caulophrynidae
Family 196. Melanocetidae
Family 197. Diceratiidae
Family 198. Himantolophidae
Family 199. Oneirodidae
Family 200. Gigantactinidae
Family 201. Neoceratiidae
Family 202. Centrophrynidae
Family 203. Ceratiidae
Family 204. Linophrynidae
Order 32. Indostomiformes
Family 205. Indostomidae
Order 33. Atheriniformes
Suborder Exocoetoidei
Family 206. Exocoetidae
Family 207. Belonidae
Family 208. Scomberesocidae
Suborder Cyprinodontoidei
Family 209. Oryziatidae
Family 210. Adrianichthyidae
Family 211. Horaichthyidae
Family 212. Cyprinodontidae
Family 213. Goodeidae
Family 214. Anablepidae
Family 215. Jenynsiidae
Family 216. Poeciliidae
Suborder Atherinoidei
Family 217. Melanotaeniidae
Family 218. Atherinidae
Family 219. Isonidae
Family 220. Neostethidae
Family 221. Phallostethidae
Order 34. Lampridiformes

Suborder Lampridoidei
Family 222. Lamprididae
Suborder Veliferoidei
Family 223. Veliferidae
Suborder Trachipteroidei
Family 224. Lophotidae
Family 225. Trachipteridae
Family 226. Regalecidae
Suborder Stylephoroidei
Family 227. Stylephoridae
Suborder Ateleopodoidei
Family 228. Ateleopodidae
Suborder Mirapinnatoidei
Family 229. Mirapinnidae
Family 230. Eutaeniophoridae
Suborder Megalomycteroidei
Family 231. Megalomycteridae
Order 35. Beryciformes
Suborder Stephanoberycoidei
Family 232. Stephanoberycidae
Family 233. Melamphaeidae
Family 234. Gibberichthyidae
Family 235. Kasidoroidae
Suborder Berycoidei
Family 236. Trachichthyidae
Family 237. Diretmidae
Family 238. Korsogasteridae
Family 239. Anoplogasteridae
Family 240. Berycidae
Family 241. Monocentridae
Family 242. Anomalopidae
Family 243. Holocentridae
Suborder Cetomimoidei
Family 244. Rondeletiidae
Family 245. Barbourisiidae
Family 246. Cetomimidae
Order 36. Zeiformes
Family 247. Parazenidae
Family 248. Macrurocyttidae
Family 249. Zeidae
Family 250. Oreosomatidae
Family 251. Grammicolepididae
Family 252. Caproidae
Order 37. Syngnathiformes
Suborder Aulostomoidei
Family 253. Aulostomidae
Family 254. Fistulariidae

Family 255. Macrorhamphosidae
Family 256. Centriscidae
Suborder Syngnathoidei
Family 257. Solenostomidae
Family 258. Syngnathidae
Order 38. Gasterosteiformes
Family 259. Aulorhynchidae
Family 260. Gasterosteidae
Order 39. Synbranchiformes
Suborder Alabetoidei
Family 261. Alabetidae
Suborder Synbranchoidei
Family 262. Synbranchidae
Family 263. Amphipnoidae
Order 40. Scorpaeniformes
Suborder Scorpaenoidei
Family 264. Scorpaenidae
Family 265. Synanceiidae
Family 266. Triglidae
Family 267. Caracanthidae
Family 268. Aploactinidae
Family 269. Pataecidae
Suborder Hexagrammoidei
Family 270. Anoplopomatidae
Family 271. Hexagrammidae
Family 272. Zaniolepididae
Suborder Platycephaloidei
Family 273. Platycephalidae
Suborder Hoplichthyoidei
Family 274. Hoplichthyidae
Suborder Congiopodoidei
Family 275. Congiopodidae
Suborder Cottoidei
Family 276. Icelidae
Family 277. Cottidae
Family 278. Cottocomephoridae
Family 279. Comephoridae
Family 280. Normanichthyidae
Family 281. Cottunculidae
Family 282. Psychrolutidae
Family 283. Agonidae
Family 284. Cyclopteridae
Order 41. Dactylopteriformes
Family 285. Dactylopteridae
Order 42. Pegasiformes
Family 286. Pegasidae
Order 43. Perciformes

Suborder Percoidei
Family 287. Centropomidae
Family 288. Percichthyidae
Family 289. Serranidae
Family 290. Grammistidae
Family 291. Pseudochromidae
Family 292. Pseudogrammidae
Family 293. Grammidae
Family 294. Plesiopidae
Family 295. Pseudoplesiopidae
Family 296. Anisochromidae
Family 297. Acanthoclinidae
Family 298. Glaucosomidae
Family 299. Theraponidae
Family 300. Banjosidae
Family 301. Kuhliidae
Family 302. Centrarchidae
Family 303. Priacanthidae
Family 304. Apogonidae
Family 305. Acropomatidae
Family 306. Percidae
Family 307. Sillaginidae
Family 308. Branchiostegidae
Family 309. Labracoglossidae
Family 310. Lactariidae
Family 311. Pomatomidae
Family 312. Rachycentridae
Family 313. Echeneidae
Family 314. Carangidae
Family 315. Coryphaenidae
Family 316. Formionidae
Family 317. Menidae
Family 318. Leiognathidae
Family 319. Bramidae
Family 320. Caristiidae
Family 321. Arripidae
Family 322. Emmelichthyidae
Family 323. Lutjanidae
Family 324. Nemipteridae
Family 325. Lobotidae
Family 326. Gerreidae
Family 327. Pomadasyidae
Family 328. Lethrinidae
Family 329. Pentapodidae
Family 330. Sparidae
Family 331. Sciaenidae

Family 332. Mullidae
Family 333. Monodactylidae
Family 334. Pempheridae
Family 335. Leptobramidae
Family 336. Bathyclupeidae
Family 337. Toxotidae
Family 338. Coracinidae
Family 339. Kyphosidae
Family 340. Ephippidae
Family 341. Scatophagidae
Family 342. Rhinoprenidae
Family 343. Chaetodontidae
Family 344. Enoplosidae
Family 345. Pentacerotidae
Family 346. Nandidae
Family 347. Oplegnathidae
Family 348. Embiotocidae
Family 349. Cichlidae
Family 350. Pomacentridae
Family 351. Gadopsidae
Family 352. Cirrhitidae
Family 353. Chironemidae
Family 354. Aplodactylidae
Family 355. Cheilodactylidae
Family 356. Latridae
Family 357. Owstoniidae
Family 358. Cepolidae
Suborder Mugiloidei
Family 359. Mugilidae
Suborder Sphyraenoidei
Family 360. Sphyraenidae
Suborder Polynemoidei
Family 361. Polynemidae
Suborder Labroidei
Family 362. Labridae
Family 363. Odacidae
Family 364. Scaridae
Suborder Blennioidei
Family 365. Trichodontidae
Family 366. Opisthognathidae
Family 367. Champsodontidae
Family 368. Chiasmodontidae
Family 369. Bathymasteridae
Family 370. Percophididae
Family 371. Mugiloididae
Family 372. Trichonotidae

Family 373.   Cheimarrhichthyidae
Family 374.   Creediidae
Family 375.   Limnichthyidae
Family 376.   Oxudercidae
Family 377.   Trachinidae
Family 378.   Uranoscopidae
Family 379.   Leptoscopidae
Family 380.   Dactyloscopidae
Family 381.   Bovichthyidae
Family 382.   Nototheniidae
Family 383.   Bathydraconidae
Family 384.   Channichthyidae
Family 385.   Xenocephalidae
Family 386.   Congrogadidae
Family 387.   Notograptidae
Family 388.   Peronedysidae
Family 389.   Ophiclinidae
Family 390.   Tripterygiidae
Family 391.   Clinidae
Family 392.   Blenniidae
Family 393.   Stichaeidae
Family 394.   Cryptacanthodidae
Family 395.   Pholididae
Family 396.   Anarhichadidae
Family 397.   Ptilichthyidae
Family 398.   Zaproridae
Family 399.   Scytalinidae
Suborder Icosteoidei
Family 400.   Icosteidae
Suborder Schindlerioidei
Family 401.   Schindleriidae
Suborder Ammodytoidei
Family 402.   Ammodytidae
Family 403.   Hypoptychidae
Suborder Gobioidei
Family 404.   Eleotridae
Family 405.   Gobiidae
Family 406.   Rhyacichthyidae
Family 407.   Kraemeriidae
Family 408.   Gobioididae
Family 409.   Trypauchenidae
Family 410.   Microdesmidae
Suborder Kurtoidei
Family 411.   Kurtidae
Suborder Acanthuroidei
Family 412.   Acanthuridae

Family 413. Siganidae
Suborder Scombroidei
Family 414. Gempylidae
Family 415. Trichiuridae
Family 416. Scombridae
Family 417. Xiphiidae
Family 418. Luvaridae
Family 419. Istiophoridae
Suborder Stromateoidei
Family 420. Amarsipidae
Family 421. Centrolophidae
Family 422. Nomeidae
Family 423. Ariommidae
Family 424. Tetragonuridae
Family 425. Stromateidae
Suborder Anabantoidei
Family 426. Anabantidae
Family 427. Belontiidae
Family 428. Helostomatidae
Family 429. Osphronemidae
Suborder Luciocephaloidei
Family 430. Luciocephalidae
Suborder Channoidei
Family 431. Channidae
Suborder Mastacembeloidei
Family 432. Mastacembelidae
Family 433. Chaudhuriidae
Order 44. Gobiesociformes
Suborder Gobiesocoidei
Family 434. Gobiesocidae
Suborder Callionymoidei
Family 435. Callionymidae
Family 436. Draconettidae
Order 45. Pleuronectiformes
Suborder Psettodoidei
Family 437. Psettodidae
Suborder Pleuronectoidei
Family 438. Citharidae
Family 439. Bothidae
Family 440. Pleuronectidae
Suborder Soleoidei
Family 441. Soleidae
Family 442. Cynoglossidae
Order 46. Tetraodontiformes
Suborder Balistoidei
Family 443. Triacanthodidae

Appendix II

The following 45 fish distribution maps are based on information from numerous sources, primarily those acknowledged. Parts of the ranges are often based on scattered populations of a single or a few species. The margins are often generalized.

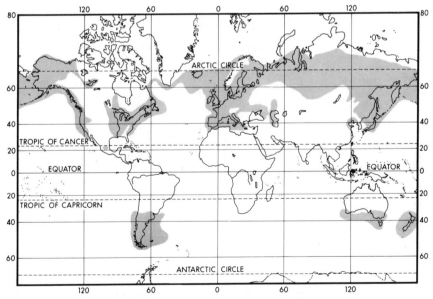

Map 1   Distribution of the family Petromyzonidae, based primarily on Hubbs and Potter (1971).

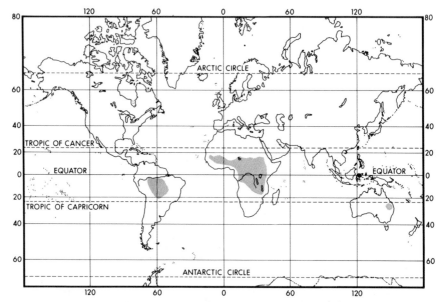

Map 2   Distribution of the subclass Dipneusti, based on Sterba (1966).

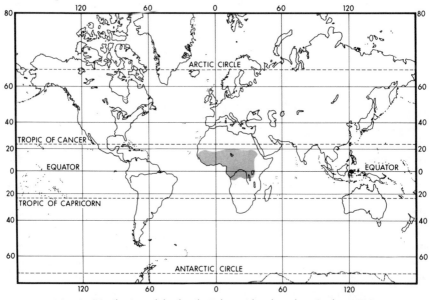

Map 3   Distribution of the family Polypteridae, based on Sterba (1966).

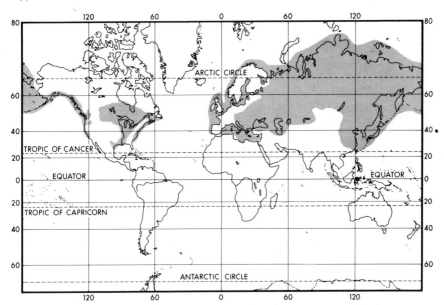

Map 4 Distribution of the family Acipenseridae, based on numerous regional sources.

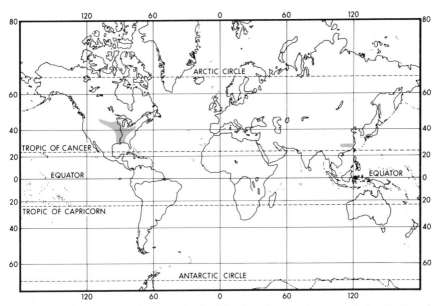

Map 5 Distribution of the family Polyodontidae based primarily on Nichols (1943) and Trautman (1957).

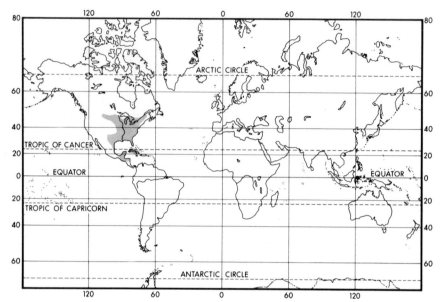

Map 6   Distribution of the family Lepisosteidae, based primarily on Trautman (1957) and Miller (1966).

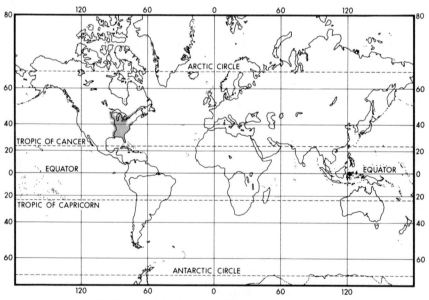

Map 7   Distribution of the family Amiidae, based on Trautman (1957).

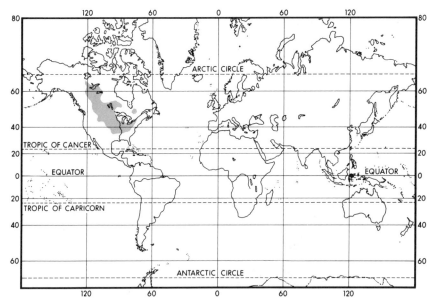

Map 8   Distribution of the family Hiodontidae, based primarily on Trautman (1957) and Mc-Phail and Lindsey (1970).

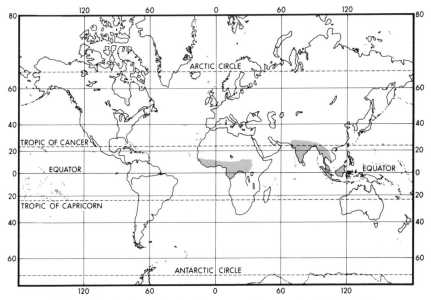

Map 9   Distribution of the family Notopteridae, based on Sterba (1966).

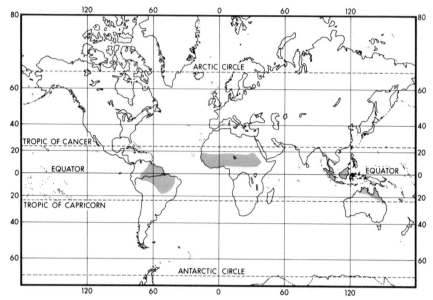

Map 10   Distribution of the family Osteoglossidae, based on Darlington (1957) and Sterba (1966).

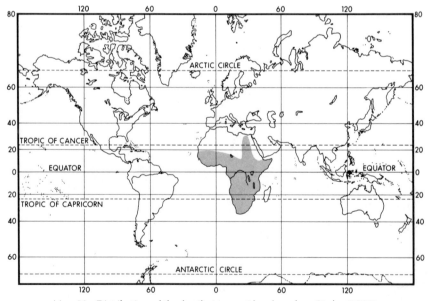

Map 11   Distribution of the family Mormyridae, based on Sterba (1966).

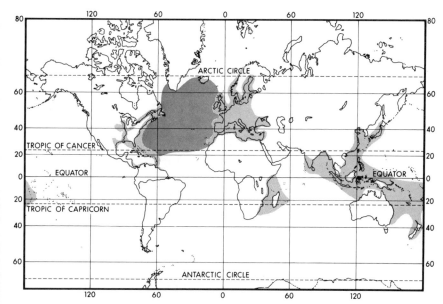

Map 12 Distribution of the family Anguillidae, based on Ege (1939) and regional works (dark zone in the Atlantic denotes area of presumed migration).

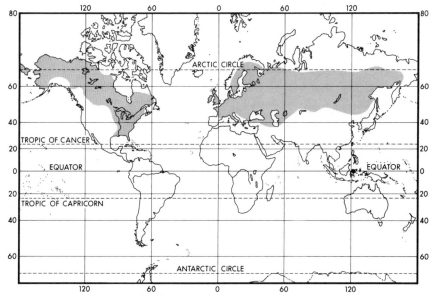

Map 13 Distribution of the family Esocidae, based on Lagler et al. (1962) and McPhail and Lindsey (1970).

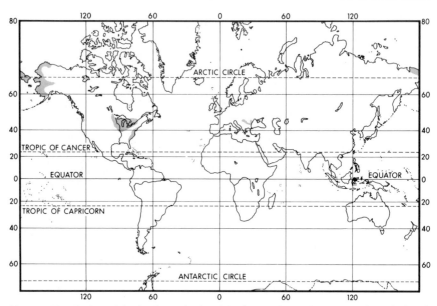

Map 14 Distribution of the family Umbridae, based on Lagler et al. (1962) and McPhail and Lindsey (1970).

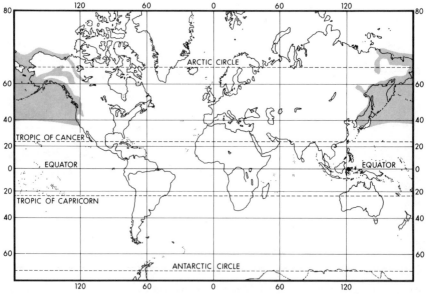

Map 15 Distribution of the genus *Oncorhynchus*, based on numerous sources.

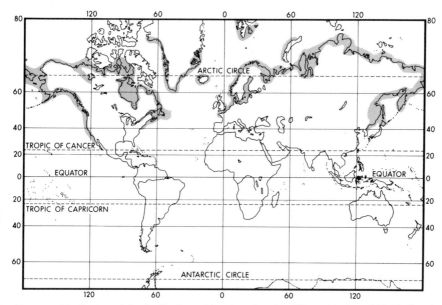

Map 16   Distribution of the family Osmeridae, based on McAllister (1963) and McPhail and Lindsey (1970).

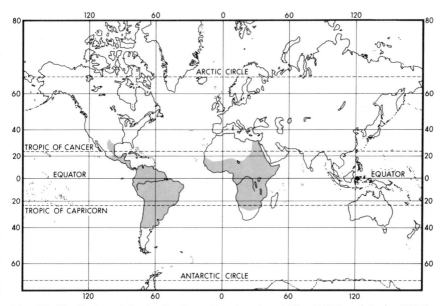

Map 17   Distribution of the family Characidae, based on Miller (1966) and Sterba (1966).

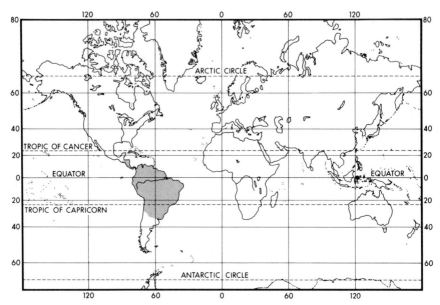

Map 18   Distribution of the superfamily Gymnotoidae, based on Sterba (1966).

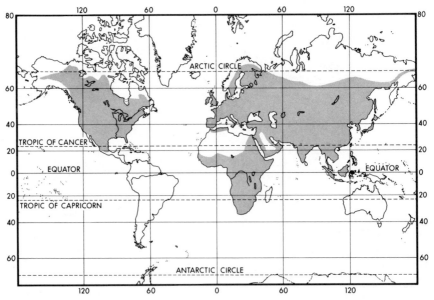

Map 19   Distribution of the family Cyprinidae, based on Lagler et al. (1962).

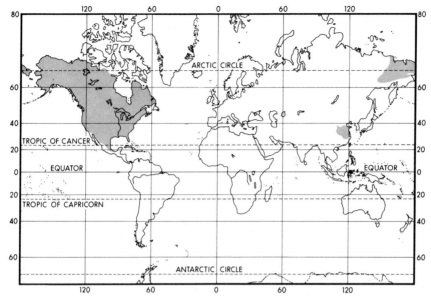

Map 20   Distribution of the family Catostomidae, based on Lagler et al. (1962).

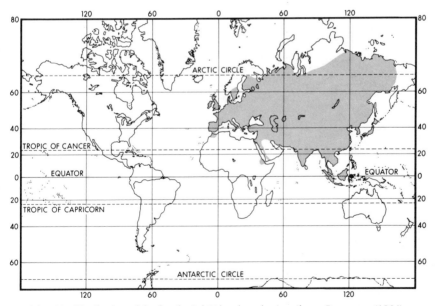

Map 21   Distribution of the family Cobitidae, based primarily on Banarescu (1964).

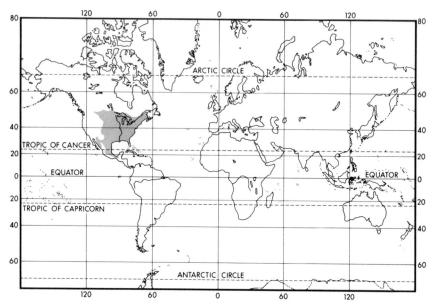

Map 22   Distribution of the family Ictaluridae, based on Miller (1958).

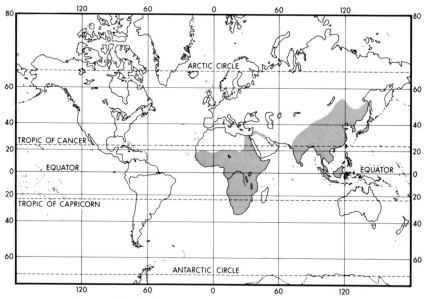

Map 23   Distribution of the family Bagridae, based on Darlington (1957) and Sterba (1966).

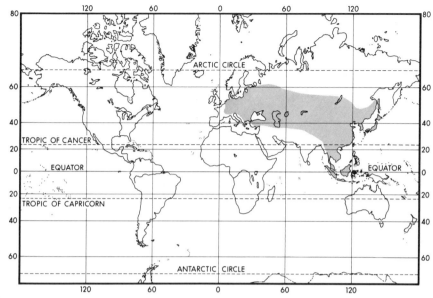

Map 24   Distribution of the family Siluridae, based on several sources.

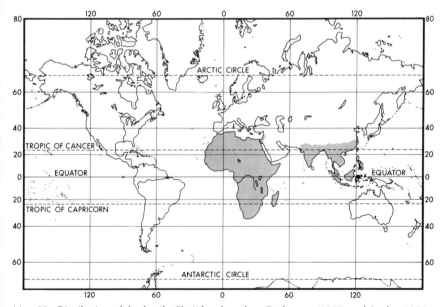

Map 25   Distribution of the family Clariidae, based on Darlington (1957) and Sterba (1966).

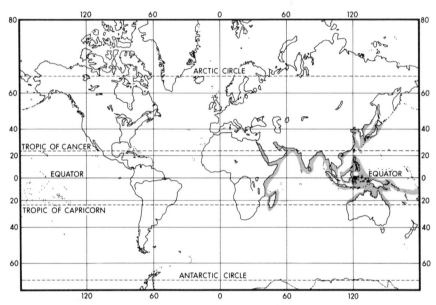

Map 26   Distribution of the family Plotosidae, based primarily on Sterba (1966).

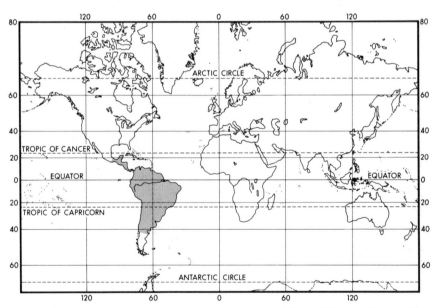

Map 27   Distribution of the family Pimelodidae, based on Miller (1966) and Sterba (1966).

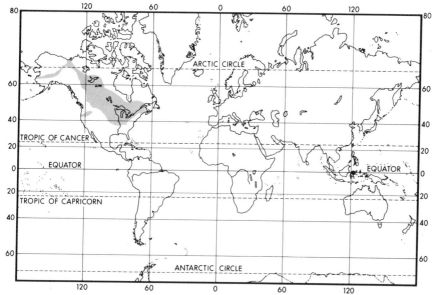

Map 28   Distribution of the family Percopsidae, based on several regional sources.

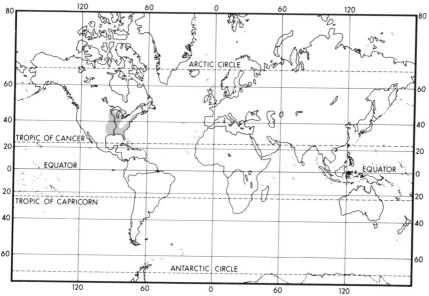

Map 29   Distribution of the family Aphredoderidae, based on Trautman (1957) and Miller (1958).

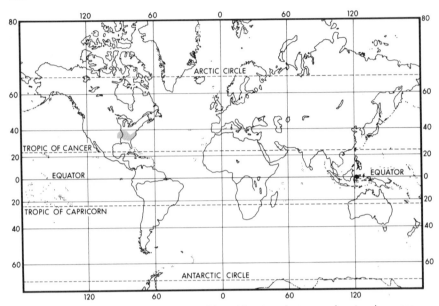

Map 30   Distribution of the family Amblyopsidae, based on several regional sources.

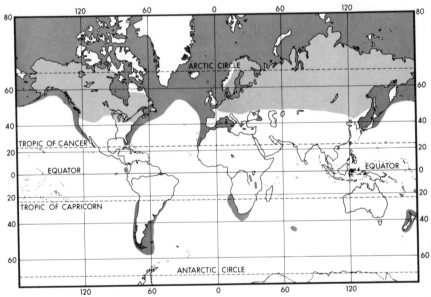

Map 31   Distribution of the family Gadidae, based on Svetovidov (1948) and McPhail and Lindsey (1970) (the light area is the freshwater distribution of *Lota lota*).

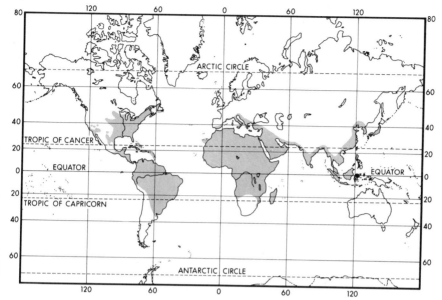

Map 32   Distribution of the family Cyprinodontidae, based on Lagler et al. (1962).

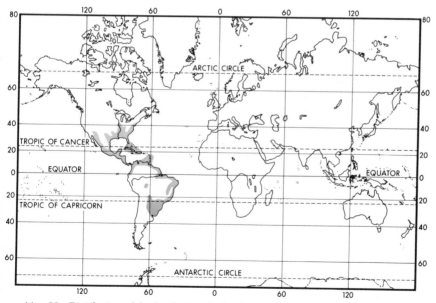

Map 33   Distribution of the family Poeciliidae, based on Rosen and Bailey (1963).

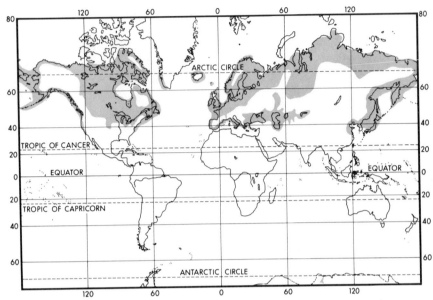

Map 34   Distribution of the family Gasterosteidae, based on numerous regional sources.

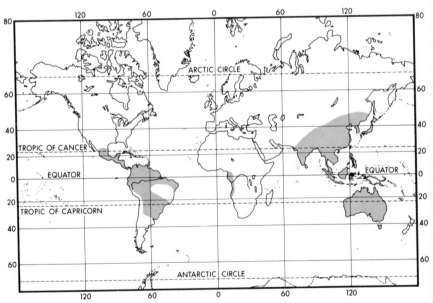

Map 35   Distribution of the family Synbranchidae, based on Sterba (1966) and Rosen and Rumney (1972).

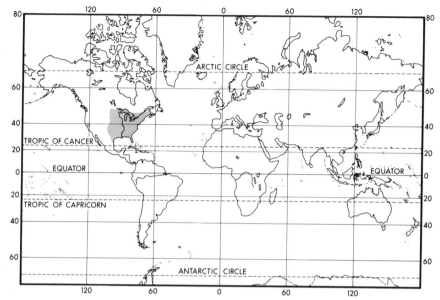

Map 36 Distribution of the family Centrarchidae, based on Miller (1958).

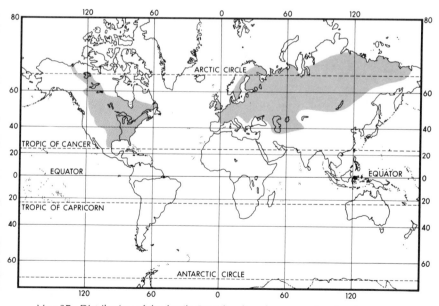

Map 37 Distribution of the family Percidae, based on several regional sources.

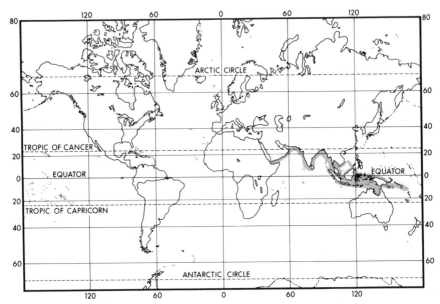

Map 38   Distribution of the family Toxotidae, based on Sterba (1966).

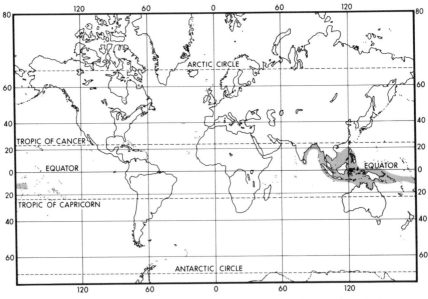

Map 39   Distribution of the family Scatophagidae, based on Sterba (1966).

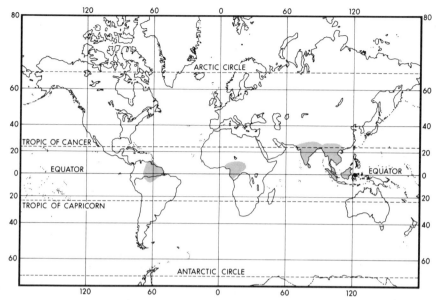

Map 40   Distribution of the family Nandidae, based on Sterba (1966).

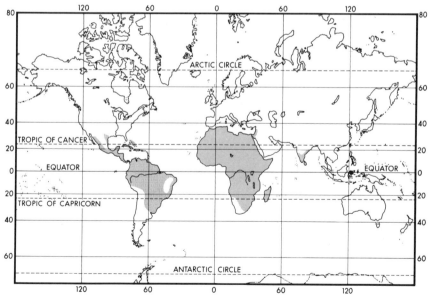

Map 41   Distribution of the family Cichlidae, based on Lagler et al. (1962).

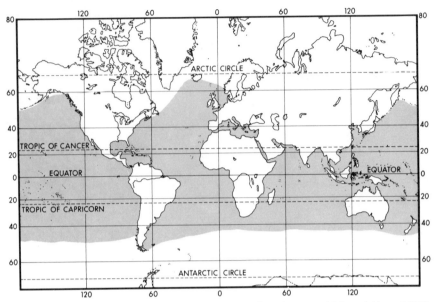

Map 42   Distribution of the suborder Stromateoidei, based on Haedrich and Horn (1972).

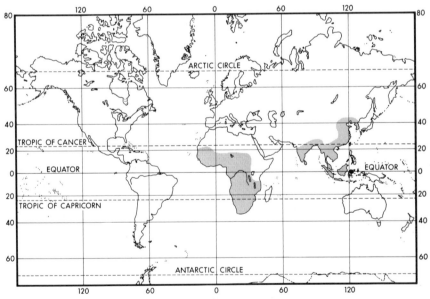

Map 43   Distribution of the suborder Anabantoidei, based on Sterba (1966).

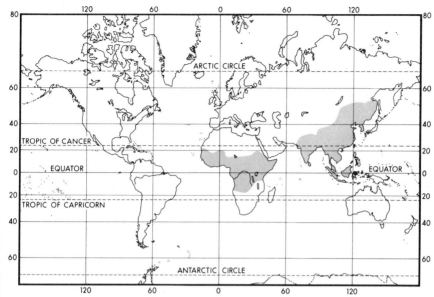

Map 44   Distribution of the family Channidae (Ophicephalidae), based on Sterba (1966).

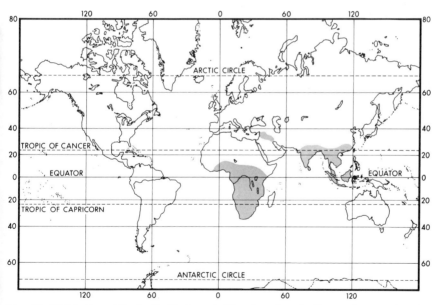

Map 45   Distribution of the family Mastacembelidae, based on Darlington (1957) and Sterba (1966).

Bibliography

Abe, T. 1957. Notes on fishes from the stomachs of whales taken in the Antarctic. I. *Xenocyttus nemotoi*, a new genus and species of zeomorph fish of the subfamily Oreosominae Goode and Bean, 1895. *Sci. Rep. Whales Res. Inst.* **12:**225–233.

Adam, H. and R. Strahan. 1963. Systematics and geographical distribution of myxinoids. In A. Brodal and R. Fänge (Eds.), *The biology of Myxine:* 1–8. Oslo: Universitetsforlaget. 588 pp.

Albuquerque, R. M. 1956. Peixes de Portugal e ilhas and adjacentes. *Separata Portugaliae Acta Biol.*, Serie B, **5.** 1164 pp.

Aleev, Y. G. 1963. *Functional basis of the exterior structure in fish.* Moscow: Akademii Nauk SSSR. 247 pp. Translated from the Russian: Israel Program for Scientific Translations, Jerusalem, 1969.

Alexander, R. McN. 1964. The structure of the Weberian apparatus in the Siluri. *Proc. Zool. Soc. Lond.* **142**(3): 419–440.

Alexander, R. McN. 1967. *Functional design in fishes.* London: Hutchinson. 160 pp.

Alfred, E. R. 1966. The fresh-water fishes of Singapore. *Zool. Verh.* **78.** Leiden: Rijksmus. Nat. Hist. 68 pp.

Alfred, E. R. 1969. The Malayan cyprinoid fishes of the family Homalopteridae. *Zool. Meded., Leiden* **43**(18):213–237.

Allen, G. R. 1972. *The anemonefishes. Their classification and biology.* Neptune City, N. J.: T.F.H. Public. 288 pp.

Allen, G. R. and A. R. Emery. 1973. *Pomacentrus exilis,* a new species of damselfish from the central-west Pacific. *Copeia* **1973:**565–568.

Allis, E. P. 1928. Concerning homologies of the hyomandibula and preoperculum. *J. Anat.* **62**:198–220.

Amaoka, K. 1969. Studies on the sinistral flounders found in the waters around Japan—taxonomy, anatomy, and phylogeny. *J. Shimonoseki Univ. Fish.* **18**(2):1–340.

Ancona, U.D' and G. Cavinato. 1965. The fishes of the family Bregmacerotidae. *Dana Rep.* **64**:1–92.

Andrews, S. M. 1973. Interrelationships of crossopterygians. In P. H., Greenwood, R. S. Miles, and C. Patterson (Eds.), Interrelationships of fishes: 137–177. *J. Linn. Soc. (Zool.)* **53**. Suppl. 1. New York: Academic.

Andrews, S. M. and T. S. Westoll. 1970. The postcranial skeleton of *Eusthenopteron foordi* Whiteaves. *Trans. R. Soc. Edinb.* **68**:207–329.

Andriashev, A. P. 1954. *Fishes of the Northern Seas of the U.S.S.R.* Translated from the Russian, Israel Program for Scientific Translations, Jerusalem, 1964. 565 pp.

Andriashev, A. P. 1955. Observations on the eel-like lycodids (*Lycenchelys* Gill) (Pisces, Zoarcidae) and related forms, in the seas of USSR and neighbouring waters. *Trud. Zool. Inst. Akad. Nauk, SSSR* **18**:349–384. (Partial translation by D. E. McAllister, 1960. *Fish. Res. Bd. Can. Trans.* **278** and *Israel Program for Scientific Translation; Jerusalem,* **1963**:1–36).

Andriashev, A. P. 1965. A general review of the Antarctic fish fauna. In *Biogeography and ecology in Antarctica:* 491–550. *Monogr. Biol.* **15**. The Hague: Dr. W. Junk Publ.

Applegate, S. P. 1967. A survey of shark hard parts. In P. W. Gilbert, R. F. Mathewson, and D. P. Rall (Eds.), *Sharks, skates, and rays:* 37–67 Baltimore: Johns Hopkins.

Arambourg, C. 1958a. Sous-classe des Crossopterygiens. *Trait. Zool.* **13**(3):2541–2552.

Arambourg, C. 1958b. Classe des Osteichthyens. *Trait. Zool.* **13**(3):2068–2069.

Arambourg, C. and L. Bertin. 1958. Super-ordres des Holostéens et des Halecostomes. *Trait. Zool.* **13**(3):2173–2203.

Arambourg, C. and J. Guibe. 1958. Sous-classe des Dipneustes (Dipneusti). *Trait. Zool.* **13**(3):2522–2540.

Arnold, D. C. 1956. A systematic revision of the fishes of the teleost family Carapidae (Percomorphi, Blennioidea), with descriptions of two new species. *Bull. Br. Mus. Nat. Hist. (Zool.)* **4**(6):17–307.

Arnoult, J. 1959. Poissons des eaux douces. Faune de Madagascar. *Publ. l'Instit. Recherche Sci. Tananarive* **10**. 160 pp.

Avise, J. C. and R. K. Selander. 1972. Evolutionary genetics of cave-dwelling fishes of the genus *Astyanax. Evolution* **26**:1–19.

Axelrod, H. R. 1973. *African cichlids of lakes Malawi and Tanganyika.* Neptune City, N. J.: T.F.H. Public. 224 pp.

Axelrod, H. R. and L. P. Schultz. 1955. *Handbook of tropical aquarium fishes.* New York: McGraw-Hill. 718 pp.

Bailey, R. J. 1936. The osteology and relationships of the phallostethid fishes. *J. Morph.* **59**:453–478.

Bailey, R. M. 1960. Forty-five articles on Recent fishes. Reprinted from *McGraw-Hill Encyclopedia of Science and Technology.* New York: McGraw-Hill. 21 pp.

Bailey, R. M. et al. 1970. A list of common and scientific names of fishes from the United States and Canada. *Am. Fish. Soc. Spec. Publ. 6,* 3rd ed. 150 pp.

Bailey, R. M. and T. M. Cavender, 1971. Fishes. Reprinted from *McGraw-Hill Encyclopedia of Science and Technology.* New York: McGraw-Hill. 34 pp.

Baird, R. C. 1971. The systematics, distribution, and zoogeography of the marine hatchet-fishes (family Sternoptychidae). *Bull. Mus. Comp. Zool., Harv.* **142**(1):1–128.

Banarescu, P. 1964. Pisces: Osteichthyes (Pesti Ganoizi si Ososi). *Acad. Republ. Populare Romine, Fauna RPR 13.* 959 pp.

Banister, K. E. 1970. The anatomy and taxonomy of *Indostomus paradoxus* Prashad and Mukerji. *Bull. Br. Mus. Nat. Hist. (Zool.)* **19**(5):179–209.

Barbour, C. D. 1973. A biogeographical history of *Chirostoma* (Pisces: Atherinidae): a species flock from the Mexican plateau. *Copeia* **1973**:533–556.

Bardach, J. E., J. H. Ryther, and W. O. McLarney. 1972. *Aquaculture.* New York: Wiley-Interscience. 896 pp.

Bardack, D. 1965. Anatomy and evolution of chirocentrid fishes. *Paleont. Contr. Univ. Kans.* **40**:1–88.

Bardack, D. and R. Zangerl. 1968. First fossil lamprey: a record from the Pennsylvanian of Illinois. *Science* **1962**:1265–1267.

Bardack, D. and R. Zangerl. 1971. Lampreys in the fossil record. In M. W. Hardisty, and I. C. Potter (Eds.), *The biology of lampreys:* 67–84. London: Academic.

Barlow, G. W., K. F. Liem, and W. Wickler. 1968. Badidae, a new fish family—behavioural, osteological, and developmental evidence. *J. Zool.* **156**:415–447.

Barrington, E. J. W. 1965. *The biology of Hemichordata and Protochordata.* Edinburgh: Oliver and Boyd. 176 pp.

Beamish, R. J., M. J. Merrilees, and E. J. Crossman. 1971. Karyotypes and DNA values for members of the suborder Esocoidei (Osteichthyes: Salmoniformes). *Chromosoma* (Berlin) **34**:436–447.

Bean, T. H. 1882. A preliminary catalogue of fishes of Alaskan and adjacent waters. *Proc. U. S. Natl. Mus.* **4**:239–272, 1881.

De Beaufort, L. F. 1962. *The Fishes of the Indo-Australian Archipelago.* Vol. 11. Leiden: E. J. Brill. 481 pp.

Behnke, R. J. 1968. A new subgenus and species of trout, *Salmo (Platysalmo) platycephalus,* from southcentral Turkey, with comments on the classification of the subfamily Salmoninae. *Mitt. Hamb. Zool. Mus. Inst.* **66**:1–15.

Behnke, R. J. 1970. The application of cytogenetics and biochemical systematics to phylogenetic problems in the family Salmonidae. *Trans. Am. Fish. Soc.* **99**:237–248.

Behnke, R. J. 1972. The systematics of salmonid fishes of recently glaciated lakes. *J. Fish. Res. Bd. Can.* **29**:639–671.

Ben-Tuvia, A. 1966. Red Sea fishes recently found in the Mediterranean. *Copeia* **1966**:254–275.

Bendix-Almgreen, S. E. 1968. The bradyodont elasmobranchs and their affinities; a discussion. In T. Ørvig (Ed.), *Current problems of lower vertebrate phylogeny:* 153–170. New York: Wiley-Interscience.

Bennett, G. W. 1971. *Management of lakes and ponds.* New York: Van Nostrand Reinhold. 2nd ed. 375 pp.

Berg, L. S. 1940. Classification of fishes, both Recent and fossil. *Trav. Inst. Zool. Acad. Sci. URSS,* **5**(2):87–517. Also lithoprint, J. W. Edwards, Ann Arbor, Michigan, 1947.

Berg, L. S. 1955. Classification of fishes both Recent and fossil. *Trud. Zool. Inst. Akad. Nauk, SSSR,* **20**:1–286. 2nd ed. (in Russian).

Berrill, N. J. 1950. *The Tunicata with an account of the British species.* London: The Ray Society. 354 pp.

Berry, F. H. 1959. Boar fishes of the genus *Antigonia* of the western Atlantic. *Bull. Fla. St. Mus.* **4**(7):205–250.

Berry, F. H. 1964. Review and emendation of: Family Clupeidae by Samuel F. Hildebrand. *Copeia* **1964**:720–730.

Berry, F. H. and C. R. Robins. 1967. *Macristiella perlucens,* a new clupeiform fish from the Gulf of Mexico. *Copeia* **1967**(1):46–50.

Berry, F. H. and L. E. Vogele. 1961. Filefishes (Monacanthidae) of the western North Atlantic. *U. S. Fish Wildl. Serv., Fish. Bull. 181,* **61**:61–109.

Bertelsen, E. 1951. The ceratioid fishes. *Dana Rep.* **39**:1–276.

Bertelsen, E. and N. B. Marshall. 1956. The Mirapinnati, a new order of teleost fishes. *Dana Rep.* **42**:1–34.

Bertelsen, E. and N. B. Marshall. 1958. Notes on Miripinnati: (An addendum to Dana Rep. 42). *Dana Rep.* **45**:9–10.

Bertin, L. and C. Arambourg. 1958. Super-ordre des Teleostéens. *Trait. Zool.* **13**(3):2204–2500.

Bertmar, G. 1968. Lungfish phylogeny. In T. Ørvig (Ed.), *Current problems of lower vertebrate phylogeny:* 259–283. New York: Wiley-Interscience.

Bhuiyan, A. L. 1964. Fishes of Dacca. *Asiatic Soc. Pakistan, Publ. 13.* Dacca. 148 pp.

Bigelow, H. B. and W. C. Schroeder. 1948–1953. Fishes of the western North Atlantic. *Mem. Sears Found. Mar. Res.* Vols. 1 and 2.

Bigelow, H. B. and W. C. Schroeder. 1962. New and little known batoid fishes from the western Atlantic. *Bull. Mus. Comp. Zool., Harv.* **128**(4):159–244.

Birkhead, W. S. 1972. Toxicity of stings of ariid and ictalurid catfishes. *Copeia* **1972**:790–807.

Bjerring, H. C. 1973. Relationships of coelacanthiforms. In P. H. Greenwood, R. S. Miles, and C. Patterson (Eds.), Interrelationships of fishes: 179–205. *J. Linn. Soc. (Zool.)* **53.** Suppl. 1. New York: Academic.

Blackwelder, R. E. 1967. *Taxonomy.* New York: Wiley. 698 pp.

Blackwelder, R. E. 1972. *Guide to the taxonomic literature of vertebrates.* Ames: Iowa State University Press. 259 pp.

Böhlke, J. E. 1956. A synopsis of the eels of the family Xenocongridae (including the Chlopsidae and Chilorhinidae). *Proc. Acad. Nat. Sci. Philad.* **108**:61–95.

Böhlke, J. E. 1966. Lyomeri, Eurypharyngidae, Saccopharyngidae. In Fishes of the western North Atlantic, 5. *Mem. Sears Found. Mar. Res.* **1**(5):603–628.

Böhlke, J. E. and C. C. G. Chaplin. 1968. *Fishes of the Bahamas and adjacent tropical waters.* Academy of Natural Sciences of Philadelphia: Wynnewood, Pa.: Livingston. 771 pp.

Böhlke, J. E. and C. L. Hubbs. 1951. *Dysommina rugosa,* an apodal fish from the North Atlantic, representing a distinct family. *Stanford Ichthyol. Bull.* **4**(1):7–10.

Bolin, R. L. 1940. A redescription of *Luvarus imperialis* Rafinesque based on a specimen from Monterey, California. *Calif. Fish and Game* **26**(3):282–284.

Bolin, R. L. 1947. The evolution of the marine Cottidae of California with a discussion of the genus as a systematic category. *Bull. Nat. Hist. Mus., Stanford Univ.* **3**(3):153–168.

Bone, Q. 1960. The origin of the chordates. *J. Linn. Soc. (Zool.)* **44**:252–269.

Botros, G. A. 1971. Fishes of the Red Sea. In H. Barnes (Ed.), *Oceanography and Marine Biology Annual Review* **9**:221–348. London: George Allen and Unwin.

Boulenger, G. A. 1904. Teleostei (Systematic part). In S. F. Harmer, and A. E. Shipley (Eds.), Fishes:539–727. London: *Cambridge Natural History* **7.**

Boulenger, G. A. 1909, 1911, 1915, 1916. *Catalogue of the freshwater fishes of Africa in the British Museum.* London: British Museum, Vol. 1–4. 1882 pp.

Boydan, A. 1973. *Perspectives in zoology.* Vol. 51. Oxford: Pergamon. 288 pp.

Brannon, E. L. 1972. Mechanisms controlling migration of sockeye salmon fry. *Int. Pac. Salmon Fish. Comm. Bull.* **21.** 86 pp.

Branson, B. A. and G. A. Moore. 1962. The lateralis components of the acoustico-lateralis system in the sunfish family Centrarchidae. *Copeia* **1962:**1–108.

Breder, C. M. and E. Clark. 1947. A contribution to the visceral anatomy, development, and relationships of Plectognathi. *Bull. Am. Mus. Nat. Hist.* **88**(5):287–320.

Breder, C. M. and D. E. Rosen. 1966. *Modes of reproduction in fishes.* New York: Natural History Press. 941 pp.

Briggs, J. C. 1955. A monograph of the clingfishes (Order Xenopterygii). *Stanford Ichthyol. Bull.* **6:**1–224.

Briggs, J. C., 1960. Fishes of worldwide (circumtropical) distribution. *Copeia* **1960:**171–180.

Briggs, J. C. and F. H. Berry, 1959. The Draconettidae—A review of the family with the description of a new species. *Copeia* **1959:**123–133.

Brodal, A. and R. Fänge, 1963. *The biology of Myxini.* Oslo: Universitetsforlaget. 588 pp.

Brown, J. H., 1971. The desert pupfish. *Sci. Am.* **225**(5):104–110.

Bullis, H. R., Jr. and J. S. Carpenter, 1966. *Neoharriotta carri*–a new species of Rhinochimaeridae from the southern Caribbean Sea. *Copeia* **1966:**443–450.

Bulman, O. M. B., 1970. Graptolithina with sections on Enteropneusta and Pterobranchia. In C. Teichert (Ed.), *Treatise on invertebrate paleontology:* Part V. Geological Society of America and University of Kansas. 163 pp.

Burgess, W. and H. R. Axelrod, 1972-continuing. *Pacific marine fishes.* Books 1-onward. Neptune City, N. J.: T.F.H. Public.

Caldwell, D. K., 1966. Marine and freshwater fishes of Jamaica. *Bull. Inst. Jamaica,* Sci. Series **17,** 120 pp.

Castex, M. N., 1967. Fresh water venomous rays. In F. E. Russell and P. R. Saunders (Eds.), *Animal toxins:* 167–176. Symposium Publ. Div. Oxford: Pergamon. 428 pp.

Castle, P. H. J., 1961. Deep water eels from Cook Strait, New Zealand. *Zool. Publi. Victoria University, Wellington* **27:**1–30.

Castle, P. H. J., 1967. Two remarkable eel-larvae from off southern Africa. *Spec. Publ. 1, Department of Ichthyology, Rhodes University, South Africa.* 12 pp.

Castle, P. H. J., 1969. An index and bibliography of eel larvae. *Spec. Publ. 7. The J. L. B. Smith Institute of Ichthyology, Rhodes University.* 121 pp.

Castle, P. H. J. 1970. Distribution, larval growth, and metamorphosis of the eel *Derichthys serpentinus* Gill, 1884 (Pisces: Derichthyidae). *Copeia* **1970**(3):444–452.

Castle, P. H. J. 1972. The eel genus *Benthenchelys* (Fam. Ophichthidae) in the Indo-Pacific. *Dana Rep.* **82:**1–31.

Castle, P. H. J., 1973. A giant notacanthiform leptocephalus from the Chatham Islands, New Zealand. *Rec. Dom. Mus.* 8(8):121–124.

Cavender, T. 1966. Systematic position of the North America Eocene fish *"Leuciscus" rosei* Hussakof. *Copeia* **1966:**311–320.

Cavender, T. 1969. An oligocene mudminnow (family Umbridae) from Oregon with remarks on relationships within the Esocoidei. *Occ. Pap. Mus. Zool. Univ. Mich. No. 660.* 33 pp.

Cavender, T. M. 1970. A comparison of coregonines and other salmonids with the earliest known teleostean fishes. In C. C. Lindsey and C. S. Woods (Eds.), *Biology of coregonid fishes:* 1–32. Winnipeg: University of Manitoba Press.

Cervigon, F. 1966. *Los peces marinos de Venezuela.* Estacion de Investigaciones marinas de Margarita, Fundacion La Salle de Ciencias Naturales (Monografias 11 and 12). Vol. 1 and 2. Caracas. 951 pp.

Chapman, W. M. 1948. The osteology and relationships of the Microstomidae, a family of oceanic fishes. *Proc. Calif. Acad. Sci.* **26**(1):1–22.

Chardon, M. 1967. Réflexions sur la dispersion des Ostariophysi à la lumière de recherches morphologiques nouvelles. *Ann. Soc. R. Zool. Belg.* **97**(3):175–186.

Chardon, M. 1968. Anatomie comparée de l'appareil de Weber et des structures connexes chez les Siluriformes. *Mus. R. Afr. Cent. Ann.* (Ser. 8, Zool.) **169**:1–277.

Clark, H. W. 1937. New fishes from the Templeton Crocker Expedition. *Copeia* **1937**:88–91.

Clausen, H. S. 1959. Denticipitidae, a new family of primitive isospondylous teleosts from west African freshwater. *Vidensk. Meddr. Dansk. Naturh. Foren.* **121**:141–156.

Clemens, W. A. and G. V. Wilby. 1961. Fishes of the Pacific Coast of Canada. *Bull. Fish. Res. Bd. Can.* **68**. 443 pp. 2nd ed.

Cohen, D. M. 1958. A revision of the fishes of the subfamily Argentininae. *Bull. Fla. St. Mus.* **3**(3):93–172.

Cohen, D. M., 1970. How many recent fishes are there? *Proc. Calif. Acad. Sci.,* Ser. 4., **38**:341–345.

Cohen, D. M. and C. R. Robins. 1970. A new ophidioid fish (genus *Lucifuga*) from a limestone sink, New Providence Island, Bahamas. *Proc. Biol. Soc. Wash.* **83**(11):133–144.

Collette, B. B. 1963. The subfamilies, tribes and genera of the Percidae (Teleostei). *Copeia* **1963**(4):615–623.

Collette, B. B. 1966. A review of the venomous toadfishes, subfamily Thalassophryninae. *Copeia* **1966**(4):846–864.

Collette, B. B. 1973. *Daector quadrizonatus,* a valid species of freshwater venomous toadfish from the Río Truandó, Colombia with notes on additional material of other species of *Daector. Copeia* **1973**:355–357.

Compagno, L. J. V. 1973. Interrelationships of living elasmobranchs. In P. H. Greenwood, R. S. Miles, and C. Patterson (Eds.), Interrelationships of fishes: 15–61. *J. Linn. Soc.* (*Zool.*) **53,** Suppl. 1. New York: Academic.

Cope, E. D. 1884. The Vertebrata of the Tertiary formations of the West. *Rep. U. S. Geol. Surv. No. 3,* 1009 pp.

Cross, R. S. 1964. *Freshwater fishes of Natal.* Pietermaritzburg: Shuter and Shooter. 167 pp.

Crowson, R. A. 1970. *Classification and biology.* London: Heinemann Educational Books. New York: Atherton. 350 pp.

Cuvier, G. L. C. F. D. and M. A. Valenciennes. 1828–1849. *Histoire Naturelle des poissons.* Paris and Strasbourg. Reprint 1969. 22 vols.

Danil'chenko, P. G. 1964. Superorder Teleostei. In D. B. Obruchev, (Ed.). *Osnovy palentologii.,* 11. Beschelyustne, Ryby. Moscow: Izd. Akademii Nauk SSSR, pp. 396–472.

Darlington, P. J., Jr., 1957. *Zoogeography: the geographical distribution of animals.* New York: Wiley. 675 pp.

David, L. R., 1956. Tertiary anacanthin fishes from California and the Pacific northwest; their paleoecological significance. *J. Paleontol.* **30**:568–607.

Dawson, C. E. 1968. Eastern Pacific wormfishes, *Microdesmus dipus* Günther and *Microdesmus dorsipunctatus* sp. nov. *Copeia* **1968:**512–531.

Day, F., 1875–1878. *The fishes of India, being a natural history of the fishes known to inhabit the seas and fresh waters of India, Burma and Ceylon.* London: Dawson. Vol. 1. Text. 778 pp. Vol. 2. 195 plates. Reprint 1958.

Dean, B. 1895. *Fishes, living and fossil, an outline of their forms and probable relationships.* New York: Macmillan. 300 pp.

Dean, B., 1916–1923. *A bibliography of fishes.* American Museum of Natural History. 3 vols.

Denison, R. H. 1971a. The origin of the vertebrates: A critical evaluation of current theories. *Proc. North American Paleontol. Convention.*, Pt. H., pp. 1132–1146.

Denison, R. H. 1971b. On the tail of Heterostraci (Agnatha). *Forma et Functio* **4:**87–98.

DeWitt, H. H. 1969. A second species of the family Cottidae from the New Zealand region. *Copeia* **1969:**30–34.

Dietz, R. S. and J. C. Holden, 1970. Reconstruction of Pangaea: breakup and dispersion of continents, Permian to Present. *J. Geophys. Res.* **75**(26):4939–4956.

Dillion, L. S. 1965. The hydrocoel and the ancestry of the chordates. *Evolution* **19**(3):436–446.

Eaton, T. H. 1970. The stem-tail problem and the ancestry of chordates. *J. Paleontol.* **44:**969–979.

Ege, V. 1939. A revision of the genus *Anguilla* Shaw, a systematic, phylogenetic and geographical study. *Dana Rep.* **16:**1–256.

Eigenmann, C. H. 1917. Descriptions of sixteen new species of Pygidiidae. *Proc. Am. Phil. Soc.* **56:**691–703.

Eigenmann, C. H. 1925. A review of the Doradidae. *Trans. Am. Phil. Soc.* **22:**280–365.

Eigenmann, C. H. and R. S. Eigenmann. 1890. A revision of the South American Nematognathi or catfishes. *Occ. Pap. Calif. Acad. Sci.* **1**. 508 pp.

Eschmeyer, W. N. 1969. A systematic review of the scorpionfishes of the Atlantic Ocean (Pisces: Scorpaenidae). *Occ. Pap. Calif. Acad. Sci.* **79**. 143 pp.

Eschmeyer, W. N. and B. B. Collette. 1966. The scorpionfish subfamily Setarchinae, including the genus *Ectreposebastes. Bull. Mar. Sci.* **16**(2):349–375.

Eschmeyer, W. N., Y. Hirosaki, and T. Abe. 1973. Two new species of the scorpionfish genus *Rhinopias,* with comments on related genera and species. *Proc. Calif. Acad. Sci.* Ser. 4. **39:**285–310.

Eschmeyer, W. N. and K. V. R. Rao. 1973. Two new stonefishes (Pisces, Scorpaenidae) from the Indo-West Pacific, with a synopsis of the subfamily Synanceiinae. *Proc. Calif. Acad. Sci.* Ser. 4. **39:**337–382.

Fitch, J. E. 1964. The ribbon fishes (Family Trachipteridae) of the eastern Pacific Ocean, with a description of a new species. *Calif. Fish and Game* **50**(4):228–240.

Forey, P. L. 1973a. Relationships of Elopomorpha. In P. H. Greenwood, R. S. Miles, and C. Patterson (Eds.), Interrelationships of fishes: 351–368. *J. Linn. Soc. (Zool.)* **53**. Suppl. 1. New York: Academic.

Forey, P. L. 1973b. A revision of the elopiform fishes, fossil and Recent. *Bull. Br. Mus. Nat. Hist. (Geol.).* Suppl. 10. 222 pp.

Fowler, H. W. 1933. Descriptions of new fishes obtained 1907 to 1910, chiefly in the Philippine Islands and adjacent seas. *Proc. Acad. Nat. Sci. Philad.* **85:**233–367.

Fowler, H. W. 1948. Os peixes de agua doce do Brasil. *Arq. Zool. Est. São Paulo* **6:**1–204.

Fowler, H. W. 1956. *Fishes of the Red Sea and southern Arabia.* Jerusalem: Weizmann Science Press. 240 pp.

Fowler, H. W. 1959. *Fishes of Fiji.* Government of Fiji, Avery Press, New Zealand. 670 pp.

Fowler, H. W. 1964–1973. A catalog of world fishes. *Quart. J. Taiwan Mus.*

1964.17 (3 and 4):125–186.	Vol. 1 (Preface, etc., Branchiostemea to Pteraspidae)
1965.18 (1 and 2):137–202.	Vol. 2 (*Pteraspis* to Astrolepida)
1965.18 (3 and 4):341–397.	Vol. 3 (Microbrachiidae to Climatiida)
1966.19 (1 and 2):75–139.	Vol. 4 (Climatiidae to Cladodontida (Cochliodontidae))
1966.19 (3 and 4):303–371.	Vol. 5 (*Sandalodus* to Edestidae)
1967.20 (1 and 2):79–148.	Vol. 6 (*Edestus* to Scapanorhynchidae)
1967.20 (3 and 4):341–366.	Vol. 7 (*Scapanorhynchus* cont. to Galeocerdinae)
1968.21 (1 and 2):53–78.	Vol. 8 (*Galeocerdo* to Scoliodontinae)
1968.21 (3 and 4):181–211.	Vol. 9 (*Aporomicrodus* to Etmopterinae)
1969.22 (1 and 2):57–84.	Vol. 10 (*Atractophorus* to Rajida)
1969.22 (3 and 4):125–190.	Vol. 11 (Rajina to Dasyatidae)
1970.23 (1 and 2):39–126.	Vol. 12 (*Pastinachus* to Ptychontidae)
1970.23 (3 and 4):151–251.	Vol. 13 (Dipterea to Holoptychiidae)
1971.24 (1 and 2):1–58.	Vol. 14 (Rhizodopsidae to Palaeoniscidae)
1971.24 (3 and 4):365–409.	Vol. 15 (*Palaeoniscum* to Uropterygidae)
1972.25 (1 and 2):1–40.	Vol. 16 (*Proteurynotus* to Saurichthyidae)
1972.25 (3 and 4):157–198.	Vol. 17 (*Gymnosaurichthys* to Caturidae)
1973.26 (1 and 2):1–111.	Vol. 18 (*Neorhombolepis* to Clupeida (Raphiosauridae))
1973.26 (3 and 4):217–346.	Vol. 19 (*Hemielopopsis* . . . Clupeidae and Albulidae . . . to Alepocephalidae (*Anomalopterichthys*))

Fowler, H. W. 1972. *A synopsis of the fishes of China.* Reprint of 1930–1962 publications. Netherlands: Antiquariaat Junk. 2 vols. 1459 pp.

Fraser, T. H. 1972. Comparative osteology of the shallow water cardinal fishes (Perciformes: Apogonidae) with reference to the systematics and evolution of the family. *Ichthyol. Bull. Rhodes Univ.* (34):1–105.

Fraser-Brunner, A. 1950a. Notes on the fishes of the genus *Antigonia* (Caproidae). *Ann. Mag. Nat. Hist.* Ser. 12, **3**:721–724.

Fraser-Brunner, A. 1950b. The fishes of the family Scombridae. *Ann. Mag. Nat. Hist.* Ser. 12, **3**(26):131–163.

Fraser-Brunner, A. 1951. The ocean sunfishes (family Molidae). *Bull. Br. Mus. Nat. Hist.* (*Zool.*) **1**:89–121.

Freihofer, W. C. and E. H. Neil. 1967. Commensalism between midge larvae (Diptera: Chironomidae) and catfishes of the families Astroblepidae and Loricariidae. *Copeia* **1967**:39–45.

Fryer, G. and T. D. Iles. 1972. *The cichlid fishes of the great lakes of Africa.* Edinburgh: Oliver and Boyd. 641 pp.

Fuhrman, F. A. 1967. Tetrodotoxin. *Sci. Am.* **217**(2):60–71.

Gardiner, B. G. 1963. Certain palaeoniscoid fishes and the evolution of the snout in actinopterygians. *Bull. Br. Mus. Nat. Hist.* (*Geol.*) **8**(6):255–325.

Gardiner, B. G. 1966. Catalogue of Canadian fossil fishes. *Contr. R. Ont. Mus.* **68.** University of Toronto Press. 154 pp.

Gardiner, B. G. 1967. The significance of the preoperculum in actinopterygian evolution. *J. Linn. Soc.* (*Zool.*) **47**(311):197–209.

Gardiner, B. G. 1973. Interrelationships of teleostomes. In P. H. Greenwood, R. S. Miles, and C. Patterson (Eds.), Interrelationships of fishes: 105–135. *J. Linn. Soc. (Zool.)* **53**. Suppl. 1. New York: Academic.

Garrick, J. A. F. 1951. The blind electric rays of the genus *Typhlonarke* (Torpedinidae). *Zool. Publ. Victoria University College* No. 14, 6 pp.

Garrick, J. A. F. 1954. Studies on New Zealand Elasmobranchii. Part I. Two further specimens of *Arhynchobatis asperrimus* Waite, (Batoidei) with an account of the skeleton and a discussion on the systematic position of the species. *Trans. R. Soc. N.Z.* **82**:119–132.

Garrick, J. A. F. 1957. Further notes on the affinities of *Arhynchobatis asperrimus* Waite with other rajoids and data on a fourth specimen. *Trans. R. Soc. N.Z.* **85**:201–203.

Garrick, J. A. F. 1960. Studies on New Zealand Elasmobranchii. Part XII. The species of *Squalus* from New Zealand and Australia; and a general account and key to the New Zealand Squaloidea. *Trans. R. Soc. N.Z.* **88**:519–557.

Garrick, J. A. F. 1971. *Harriotta raleighana*, a long-nosed chimaera (Family Rhinochimaeridae), in New Zealand waters. *J. R. Soc. N.Z.* **1**:203–213.

Garstang, W. 1931. The phyletic classification of Teleostei. *Proc. Leeds Phil. Lit. Soc. (Sci.)* **2**(5):240–260.

Gibbs, R. H. and B. B. Collette. 1967. Comparative anatomy and systematics of the tunas, genus *Thunnus*. *U. S. Fish Wildl. Serv., Fish. Bull.* **66**(1):65–130.

Gilbert, C. R. 1966. Two new wormfishes (Family Microdesmidae) from Costa Rica. *Copeia* **1966**:325–332.

Gilbert, C. R. 1967. A revision of the hammerhead sharks (family Sphyrnidae). *Proc. U. S. Natl. Mus.* **119**:1–88.

Gilbert, C. R. 1968. Western Atlantic batrachoidid fishes of the genus *Porichthys*, including three new species. *Bull. Marine Sci.* **18**:671–730.

Gill, T. N. 1891. The characteristics of the Dactylopteroidea. *Proc. U. S. Natl. Mus.* **13**:243–248.

Gill, T. N. 1893. Families and subfamilies of fishes. *Mem. Natl. Acad. Sci.* **6**:127–138.

Ginsburg, I. 1950. Review of the western Atlantic Triglidae (Fishes). *Texas J. Sci.* **2**(4):489–527.

Goody, P. C. 1969. The relationships of certain Upper Cretaceous teleosts with special reference to the myctophoids. *Bull. Br. Mus. Nat. Hist. (Geol.)* Suppl. 7. 255 pp.

Goodyear, R. H. 1970. A new species of *Ataxolepis*, a bathypelagic fish from the Gulf of Panama (Pisces, Lampridiformes, Megalomycteridae). *Steenstrupia* **1**(3):17–20.

Gosline, W. A. 1942. Notes on South American catfishes (Nematognathi). *Copeia* **1942**:39–41.

Gosline, W. A. 1955. The osteology and relationships of certain gobioid fishes, with particular reference to the genera *Kraemeria* and *Microdesmus*. *Pac. Sci.* **9**:158–170.

Gosline, W. A. 1959. Four new species, a new genus, and a new suborder of Hawaiian fishes. *Pac. Sci.* **13**:67–77.

Gosline, W. A. 1960. Contributions toward a classification of modern isospondylous fishes. *Bull. Br. Mus. Nat. Hist. (Zool.)* **6**(6):325–365.

Gosline, W. A. 1961. Some osteological features of modern lower teleostean fishes. *Smithsonian Misc. Coll.* **142**(3):1–42.

Gosline, W. A. 1963a. Considerations regarding the relationships of the percopsiform, cyprinodontiform, and gadiform fishes. *Occ. Pap. Mus. Zool. Univ. Mich.* (629):1–38.

Gosline, W. A. 1963b. Notes on the osteology and systematic position of *Hypoptychus dybowskii* Steindachner and other elongate perciform fishes. *Pac. Sci.* **17**(1):90–101.

Gosline, W. A. 1966. The limits of the fish family Serranidae, with notes on other lower percoids. *Proc. Calif. Acad. Sci.* Ser. 4, **33**(6):91–112.

Gosline, W. A. 1968. The suborders of perciform fishes. *Proc. U. S. Natl. Mus.* **124**:1–78.

Gosline, W. A. 1969. The morphology and systematic position of the alepocephaloid fishes. *Bull. Br. Mus. Nat. Hist. (Zool.)* **18**(6):183–218.

Gosline, W. A. 1970. A reinterpretation of the teleostean fish order Gobiesociformes. *Proc. Calif. Acad. Sci.* Ser. 4, **37**(19): 363–382.

Gosline, W. A. 1971. *Functional morphology and classification of teleostean fishes.* Honolulu: University Press of Hawaii. 208 pp.

Gosline, W. A. 1973. Considerations regarding the phylogeny of cypriniform fishes, with special reference to structures associated with feeding. *Copeia* **1973**:761–776.

Gosline, W. A. and V. E. Brock. 1960. *Handbook of Hawaiian fishes.* Honolulu: University of Hawaii Press. 372 pp.

Gosline, W. A., N. B. Marshall, and G. W. Mead. 1966. Order Iniomi. Characters and synopsis of families. In Fishes of the western North Atlantic. *Mem. Sears Found. Mar. Res.* **1**(5):1–18.

Graham, J. B. 1971. Aerial vision in amphibious fishes. *Fauna* **1**(3):14–23.

Greenfield, D. W. 1968. The zoogeography of *Myripristis* (Pisces: Holocentridae). *Syst. Zool.* **17**:76–87.

Greenfield, D. W. and T. Greenfield. 1973. *Triathalassothia gloverensis,* a new species of toadfish from Belize (=British Honduras) with remarks on the genus. *Copeia* **1973**:560–565.

Greenwood, P. H. 1961. A revision of the genus *Dinotopterus* (Pisces, Clariidae) with notes on the comparative anatomy of the suprabranchiae organs in the Clariidae. *Bull. Br. Mus. Nat. Hist. (Zool.),* **7**(4):215–241.

Greenwood, P. H. 1966. *The fishes of Uganda.* 2nd ed. Kampala: The Uganda Society. 131 pp.

Greenwood, P. H. 1968. The osteology and relationships of the Denticipitidae, a family of clupeomorph fishes. *Bull. Br. Mus. Nat. Hist. (Zool.),* **16**:213–273.

Greenwood, P. H. 1970. On the genus *Lycoptera* and its relationships with the family Hiodontidae (Pisces, Osteoglossomorpha). *Bull. Br. Mus. Nat. Hist. (Zool.)* **19**:257–285.

Greenwood, P. H., R. S. Miles, and C. Patterson (Eds.). 1973. Interrelationships of fishes. *J. Linn. Soc. (Zool.)* **53**. Suppl. 1. New York: Academic. 536 pp.

Greenwood, P. H., G. S. Myers, D. E. Rosen, and S. H. Weitzman. 1967. Named main divisions of teleostean fishes. *Proc. Biol. Soc. Wash.* **80**:227–228.

Greenwood, P. H. and D. E. Rosen. 1971. Notes on the structure and relationships of the alepocephaloid fishes. *Am. Mus. Novit.* **2473,** 41 pp.

Greenwood, P. H., D. E. Rosen, S. H. Weitzman, and G. S. Myers. 1966. Phyletic studies of teleostean fishes, with a provisional classification of living forms. *Bull. Am. Mus. Nat. Hist.* **131**:339–456.

Gregory, W. K. 1933. Fish skulls: a study of the evolution of natural mechanisms. *Trans. Am. Phil. Soc.* (new series) **23**(2):75–481.

Grey, M. 1956. The distribution of fishes found below a depth of 2000 meters. *Fieldiana, Zool.* **36**(2):75–337.

Grey, M. 1960. A preliminary review of the family Gonostomatidae, with a key to the genera and the description of a new species from the tropical Pacific. *Bull. Mus. Comp. Zool. Harv.* **122**(2):57–125.

Gudger, E. W. 1926. A study of the smallest shark-suckers (Echeneididae) on record, with special reference to metamorphosis. *Am. Mus. Novit.* **234**, 26 pp.

Gunther, A. C. L. G. 1859–70. *Catalogue of the fishes of the British Museum.* Vols. 1–8. London: British Museum.

Haedrich, R. 1967. The stromateoid fishes: systematics and a classification. *Bull. Mus. Comp. Zool., Harv.* **135**:31–319.

Haedrich, R. L. and M. H. Horn. 1972. A key to the stromateoid fishes. Technical Rept. WHOI-72-15. Woods Hole Oceanographic Institution. 46 pp. Unpublished manuscript.

Hagen, D. W. and L. G. Gilbertson. 1972. Geographic variation and environmental selection in *Gasterosteus aculeatus* L. in the Pacific Northwest, America. *Evolution* **26**:32–51.

Hagen, D. W. and J. D. McPhail. 1970. The species problem within *Gasterosteus aculeatus* on the Pacific coast of North America. *J. Fish. Res. Bd. Can.* **27**:147–155.

Halstead, B. W. 1967–1970. Poisonous and venomous marine animals of the world. Vols. 2 and 3. *Vertebrates*. Washington, D. C.: U. S. Government Printing Office.

Halstead (Tarlo), L. B. 1969. *The pattern of vertebrate evolution.* San Francisco: Freeman 209 pp.

Hardisty, M. W. and I. C. Potter (Eds.). 1971–1972. *The biology of lampreys.* Vols. 1 and 2. London: Academic.

Harland, W. B. et al. (Eds.). 1967. *The fossil record.* London (Geol. Soc.). 828 pp.

Harrington, R. W. 1955. The osteocranium of the American cyprinid fish, *Notropis bifrenatus,* with an annotated synonomy of teleost skull bones. *Copeia* **1955**(4):267–290.

Harrington, R. W. 1961. Oviparous hermaphroditic fish with internal self-fertilization. *Science* **134**:1749–1750.

Harrisson, C. M. H. 1966. On the first halosaur leptocephalous, from Madeira. *Bull. Br. Mus. Nat. Hist. (Zool.).* **14**:441–486.

Harry, R. R. 1952. Deep-sea fishes of the Bermuda oceanographic expeditions. Families Cetomimidae and Rondeletiidae. *Zoologica* **37**:55–71.

Hart, J. L. 1973. Pacific fishes of Canada. *Bull. Fish. Res. Bd. Can.* **180**. 740 pp.

Heintz, A. 1967. Some remarks about the structure of the tail in cephalaspids. *Colloques Int. Cent. Nat. Res. Scient.* **163**:21–35.

Hennig, W. 1966. *Phylogenetic systematics.* Urbana: University of Illinois Press. 263 pp.

Herald, E. S. 1961. *Living fishes of the world.* London: Hamish Hamilton; Garden City, N. Y.: Doubleday. 304 pp.

Herald, E. S. 1965. Studies on the Atlantic American pipefishes with descriptions of new species. *Proc. Calif. Acad. Sci.,* Ser. 4, **32**(12):363–375.

Herald, E. S. 1972. *Fishes of North America.* New York: Doubleday. 254 pp.

Herre, A. W. [C. T.] 1939. The genera of Phallostethidae. *Proc. Biol. Soc. Wash.* **52**:139–144.

Herre, A. W. [C. T.] 1953. Check list of Philippine fishes. *U. S. Fish Wildl. Serv. Res. Rept.* 20. 977 pp.

Hesse, R., W. C. Allee, and K. P. Schmidt. 1951. *Ecological Animal Geography.* New York: Wiley. 715 pp.

Hikita, T. 1962. Ecological and morphological studies of the genus *Oncorhynchus* (Salmonidae) with particular consideration on phylogeny. *Sci. Rep. Hokkaido Salmon Hatchery,* No. 17:1–97.

Hildebrand, S. F. 1938. A new catalogue of the freshwater fishes of Panama. *Zool. Series, Field Mus. Nat. Hist.* **22**(4):219–359.

Hildebrand, S. F. 1946. A descriptive catalog of the shore fishes of Peru. *Bull. U. S. Natl. Mus.* **189.** 530 pp.

Hoar, W. S. and D. J. Randall (Eds.). 1969–1971. *Fish physiology.* Vol. 1 (1969). Excretion, ionic regulation, and metabolism. Vol. 2 (1969). The endocrine system. Vol. 3 (1969). Reproduction and growth, bioluminescence, pigments, and poisons. Vol. 4 (1970). The nervous system, circulation, and respiration. Vol. 5 (1971). Sensory systems and electric organs. Vol. 6 (1971). Environmental relations and behavior. New York: Academic.

Hollister, G. 1936. A fish which grows by shrinking. *Bull. N. Y. Zool. Soc.* **39**(3):104–109.

Hora, S. L. 1936. Siluroid fishes of India, Burma and Ceylon. II. Fishes of the genus *Akysis* Bleeker. III. Fishes of the genus *Olyra* McClelland. IV. On the use of the generic name *Wallago* Bleeker. V. Fishes of the genus *Heteropneustes* Müller. *Rec. Indian Mus.* **38**(2):199–109.

Hubbs, C. L. 1941. A new family of fishes. *J. Bombay Nat. Hist. Soc.* **42**:446–447.

Hubbs, C. L. 1945. Phylogenetic position of the Citharidae, a family of flatfishes. *Misc. Publs. Mus. Zool. Univ. Mich.* **63.** 38 pp.

Hubbs, C. L. 1952. Antitropical distribution of fishes and other organisms. Symposium on problems of bipolarity and of pantemperate faunas. *Proc. 7th Pac. Sci. Cong.* **3**:324–329.

Hubbs, C. L. and R. M. Bailey. 1947. Blind catfishes from artesian waters of Texas. *Occ. Pap. Mus. Zool. Univ. Mich.* **499.** 15 pp.

Hubbs, C. L., T. Iwai, and K. Matsubara. 1967. External and internal characters, horizontal and vertical distribution, luminescence, and food of the dwarf pelagic shark, *Euprotomicrus bispinatus. Bull. Scripps Inst. Oceanogr.* **10.** University of California Press. 64 pp.

Hubbs, C. L. and K. F. Lagler. 1964. *Fishes of the Great Lakes region.* Ann Arbor: University of Michigan Press. 213 pp.

Hubbs, C. L. and I. C. Potter. 1971. Distribution, phylogeny and taxonomy. In M. W. Hardisty and I. C. Potter (Eds.), *The biology of lampreys:* 1–65. London: Academic.

Hubbs, Clark. 1952. A contribution to the classification of the blennioid fishes of the family Clinidae, with a partial revision of the eastern Pacific forms. *Stanford Ichthyol. Bull.* **4**(2):41–165.

Hulley, P. A. 1972. The family Gurgesiellidae (Chondrichthyes, Batoidei), with reference to *Pseudoraja atlantica* Bigelow and Schroeder. *Copeia* **1972**:356–359.

Hynes, H. B. N. 1970. *The ecology of running waters.* Toronto: University of Toronto Press. 555 pp.

Inger, R. F. and C. P. Kong. 1962. The freshwater fish of North Borneo. *Chicago Nat. Hist. Mus. Fieldiana, Zool.* **45**:1–268.

Ishiyama, R. 1967. Rajidae (Pisces). *Fauna Japonica.* Tokyo: Academic Press of Japan. 162 pp.

Ivanov, A. 1955. Pogonophora. Translated by A. Petrunkevitch. *Syst. Zool.* **4**:170–178.

Ivanov, A. 1963. *Pogonophora.* London: Academic. 479 pp.

Jain, S. L. 1973. New specimens of Lower Jurassic holostean fishes from India. *Palaeontol.* **16**(1):149–177.

Jardine, N. 1969. The observational and theoretical components of homology: a study based on the morphology of the dermal skull roofs of rhipidistian fishes. *J. Linn. Soc.* (*Biol.*) **1**:327–361.

Jardine, N. and R. Sibson. 1971. *Mathematical taxonomy.* New York: Wiley. 286 pp.

Jarvik, E. 1968a. The systematic position of the Dipnoi. In T. Ørvig (Ed.), 1968 *Current problems of lower vertebrate phylogeny:* 223–245. New York: Wiley-Interscience.

Jarvik, E. 1968b. Aspects of vertebrate phylogeny. In T. Ørvig (Ed.), *Current problems of lower vertebrate phylogeny:* 497–527. New York: Wiley-Interscience.

Jayaram, K. C. and N. Majumbar. 1964. Siluroid fishes of India, Burma and Ceylon. 15. Fishes of the genus *Chaca* Gray, 1831. *Proc. Zool. Soc., India* **17**(2):177–181.

Jefferies, R. P. S. 1968. The subphylum Calcichordate (Jefferies 1967) primitive fossil chordates with echinoderm affinities. *Bull. Br. Mus. Nat. Hist.* (*Geol.*) **16**(6):243–339.

Jefferies, R. P. S. and R. J. Prokop. 1972. A new calcichordate from the Ordovician of Bohemia and its anatomy, adaptations and relationships. *J. Linn. Soc.* (*Biol.*) **4**(2):69–115.

Jensen, D. D. 1963. Hoplonemertines, Myxinoids, and vertebrate origins. In E. C. Dougherty (Ed.), *The lower metazoa:* 113–126. *Comparative biology and phylogeny.* Berkeley: University of California Press. 478 pp.

Johansen, K. 1968. Air-breathing fishes. *Sci. Am.* **219**(4):102–111.

Johnson, R. K. 1970. A second record of *Korsogaster nanus* Parr (Beryciformes: Korsogasteridae). *Copeia* **1970**(4):758–760.

Jordan, D. S. 1905. *A guide to the study of fishes.* New York: Holt. 2 Vols.

Jordan, D. S. 1923. A classification of fishes including families and genera as far as known. *Stanford Univ. Publs., Biol. Sciences* **3**:77–243.

Jordan, D. S. and B. W. Evermann. 1896–1900. The fishes of North and Middle America. *Bull. U. S. Natl. Mus.* (47), pt. 1–4:1–3313.

Jordan, D. S., B. W. Evermann, H. W. Clark. 1930. Check list of the fishes and fishlike vertebrates of North and Middle America north of the northern boundary of Venezuela and Colombia. 1962 reprint. Appendix X to *Rep. U. S. Comm. Fish.* for 1928. 670 pp.

Jubb, R. A. 1966. *Freshwater fishes of southern Africa.* Cape Town: A. A. Balkema. 248 pp.

Karrer, C. 1968. Über erstnachweise und seltene arten von fischen aus dem Südatlantik (Argentinisch—Südbrasilianische Cüste). *Zool. J. Syst. Bd.* **95**:542–570.

Kerkut, G. A. 1960. *Implications of evolution.* London: Pergamon. 174 pp.

Khalaf, K. T. 1961. *The marine and fresh water fishes of Iraq.* Baghdad [The Author]. 164 pp.

Kiener, A. and G. Richard-Vindard. 1972. Fishes of the continental waters of Madagascar. In G. Richard-Vindard, and R. Battistini (Eds.), Biogeography and ecology of madagascar. *Monographiae Biol.* **21**. 764 pp.

Kleerekoper, H. 1969. *Olfaction in fishes.* Bloomington: Indiana University Press. 222 pp.

Kozhov, M. 1963. Lake Baikal and its life. *Monographiae Biologicae,* Vol. 11. The Hague: Dr. W. Junk. 344 pp.

Kozlowski, R. 1966. On the structure and relationships of graptolites. *J. Paleontol.* **40**:489–501.

Lachner, E. A. 1955. Populations of the berycoid fish family Polymixiidae. *Proc. U. S. Natl. Mus.* **105**:189–206.

Lagler, K. F., J. E. Bardach, and R. R. Miller. 1962. *Ichthyology.* New York: Wiley. 545 pp.

Lake, J. S. 1971. *Freshwater fishes and rivers of Australia.* Melbourne: Nelson. 61 pp.

Leim, A. H. and W. B. Scott. 1966. Fishes of the Atlantic coast of Canada. *Bull. Fish. Res. Bd. Can.* **155.** 485 pp.

Liem, K. F. 1963. The comparative osteology and phylogeny of the Anabantoidei (Teleostei, Pisces). *Illinois Biol. Monogr. No. 30.* 149 pp.

Liem, K. F. 1967a. Functional morphology of the head of the anabantoid teleost fish *Helostoma temmincki. J. Morph.* **121:**135–158.

Liem, K. F. 1967b. A morphological study of *Luciocephalus pulcher,* with notes on gular elements in other recent teleosts. *J. Morph.* **121:**103–133.

Liem, K. F. 1968. Geographical and taxonomic variation in the pattern of natural sex reversal in the teleost fish order Synbranchiformes. *J. Zool.* **156:**225–238.

Liem, K. F. 1970. Comparative functional anatomy of the Nandidae (Pisces: Teleostei). *Fieldiana: Zool.* **56.** 166 pp.

de Ligny, W. 1969. Serological and biochemical studies on fish populations. In H. Barnes (Ed.), *Oceanography and Marine Biology Annual Review* **7:**411–513. London: Allen and Unwin.

Lindberg, G. U. 1971. *Families of the fishes of the world; a checklist and a key.* Leningrad: Zoological Institute, Akademii Nauk SSSR. 472 pp. (in Russian); *Fishes of the World: A Key to Families and a Checklist.* New York: Wiley. 1974. (English translation.)

Lindberg, G. U. and M. I. Legeza. 1965. *Fishes of the Sea of Japan and the adjacent areas of the Sea of Okhotsk and the Yellow Sea.* 2 vols. Translated from the Russian by Israel Program for Scientific Translation. Jerusalem.

Lindsey, C. C. 1955. Evolution of meristic relations in the dorsal and anal fins of teleost fishes. *Trans. R. Soc. Can.* **49,** Ser. 3, Sect. 5:35–49.

Lindsey, C. C. and C. S. Woods (Eds.). 1970. *Biology of coregonid fishes.* Winnipeg: University of Manitoba Press. 560 pp.

Lindström, M. 1964. *Conodonts.* Amsterdam: Elsevier. 196 pp.

Lindström, M. and W. Ziegler (Eds.). 1972. Symposium on conodont taxonomy. *Geol. Palaeontol.* Spec. Vol. 1. 158 pp.

Lissman, H. W. 1963. Electric location by fishes. *Sci. Am.* **208**(3): 50–59.

Love, R. M. 1970. *The chemical biology of fishes.* New York: Academic. 547 pp.

Lundberg, J. G. and J. N. Baskin. 1969. The caudal skeleton of the catfishes, order Siluriformes. *Am. Mus. Novit.* **2398.** 49 pp.

Makushok, V. M. 1958. The morphology and classification of the northern Blennioid fishes (Stichaeoidae, Blennioidei, Pisces). *Proc. Zool. Inst. (Trudy Zool. Inst. Akad. Nauk SSSR),* **25:**3–129. Translated from the Russian, U. S. National Museum, 1959.

Mansueti, A. J. 1963. Some changes in morphology during ontogeny in the pirateperch, *Aphredoderus s. sayanus. Copeia* **1963**(3):546–557.

Marshall, N. B. 1961. A young *Macristium* and the ctenothrissid fishes. *Bull. Br. Mus. Nat. Hist. (Zool.).* **7:**353–370.

Marshall, N. B. 1962. Observations on the Heteromi, an order of teleost fishes. *Bull. Br. Mus. Nat. Hist. (Zool.).* **9**(6):249–270.

Marshall, N. B. 1965. *The life of fishes.* London: Weidenfeld and Nicolson. 402 pp.

Marshall, N. B. 1966a. *Bathyprion danae* a new genus and species of alepocephaliform fishes. *Dana Rep.* **68:**1–10.

Marshall, N. B. 1966b. The relationships of the anacanthine fishes, *Macruronus, Lyconus,* and *Steindachneria. Copeia* **1966:**275–280.

Marshall, N. B. 1971. *Exploration in the life of fishes.* Cambridge, Mass.: Harvard University Press. 204 pp.

Marshall, T. C. 1965. *Fishes of the Great Barrier Reef and coastal waters of Queensland.* Wynnewood [Narberth], Pa.: Livingston. 566 pp.

Masters, C. O. 1968. The most dreaded fish in the Amazon River. *Carolina Tips* **31**(2):5–6.

Matsubara, K. 1943. Studies on the scorpaenoid fishes of Japan (I and II). *Trans. Sigenkagaku Kenkyusyo.* 486 pp.

Matsubara, K. 1955. *Fish morphology and hierarchy.* Pts. I–III. Tokyo: Ishizaki-Shoten. 1605 pp. (2nd ed. 1971) (in Japanese).

Matsubara, K. 1963. Pisces. In T. Uchida (Ed.), *Systematic Zoology.* Tokyo: Nakayama Shoten. **9**:197–531 (in Japanese).

Matsubara, K. and T. Iwai. 1952. Studies on some Japanese fishes of the family Gempylidae. *Pac. Sci.* **6**(3):193–212.

Matsubara, K. and T. Iwai. 1959. Description of a new sandfish, *Kraemeria sexradiata* from Japan, with special reference to its osteology. *J. Wash. Acad. Sci.* **49**:27–32.

Matthes, H. 1973. *A bibliography of African freshwater fish.* Rome: Food Agric. Organ. United Nations. 299 pp.

Maul, G. E. 1957. Further additions to the previously revised family Searsidae. *Bol. Mus. Municip. Funchal.* **10**(25):5–21.

Mayr, E. 1963. *Animal species and evolution.* Cambridge, Mass.: The Belknap Press, Harvard University Press. 797 pp.

Mayr, E. 1969. *Principles of systematic zoology.* New York: McGraw-Hill. 428 pp.

McAllister, D. E. 1960. List of the marine fishes of Canada. *Bull. Natl. Mus. Can.* **168.** 76 pp.

McAllister, D. E. 1963. A revision of the smelt family, Osmeridae. *Bull. Natl. Mus. Can.* **191.** 53 pp.

McAllister, D. E. 1968. Evolution of branchiostegals and classification of teleostome fishes. *Bull. Natl. Mus. Can.* **221.** 239 pp.

McAllister, D. E. 1971. Old fourlegs. *National Museums of Canada, Odyssey Series* 1. 25 pp.

McAllister, D. E. and R. J. Krejsa. 1961. Placement of the prowfishes, Zaproridae, in the superfamily Stichaeoidae. *Nat. Hist. Pap., Natl. Mus. Can.* **11**:1–4.

McAllister, D. E. and E. I. S. Rees. 1964. A revision of the eelpont genus *Melanostigma* with a new genus and with comments on *Maynea. Bull. Natl. Mus. (Zool.), Can.* **199**:85–110.

McClane, A. J. (Ed.). 1965. *McClane's standard fishing encyclopedia and international angling guide.* New York: Holt, Rinehart and Winston. 1058 pp.

McDowall, R. M. 1969. Relationships of galaxioid fishes with a further discussion of salmoniform classification. *Copeia* **1969**(4):796–824.

McDowall, R. M. 1970. The galaxiid fishes of New Zealand. *Bull. Mus. Comp. Zool. , Harv.* **139**(7):341–432.

McDowall, R. M. 1971a. Fishes of the family Aplochitonidae. *J. R. Soc. N. Z.* **1**(1):31–52.

McDowall, R. M. 1971b. The galaxiid fishes of South America. *J. Linn. Soc.* **50**(1):33–73.

McDowall, R. M. 1972. The species problem in freshwater fishes and the taxonomy of diadromous and lacustrine populations of *Galaxias maculatus* (Jenyns.) *J. R. Soc. N. Z.* **2**(3):325–367.

McDowall, R. M. 1973a. The status of the South African galaxiid (Pisces: Galaxiidae). *Ann. Cape Prov. Mus. (Nat. Hist.)* **9**(5):91–101.

McDowall, R. M. 1973b. Relationships and taxonomy of the New Zealand torrent fish, *Cheimarrichthys fosteri* Haast (Pisces: Mugiloididae). *J. R. Soc. N. Z.* **3**(2):199–217.

McDowell, S. B. 1973. Order Heteromi (Notacanthiformes). Family Halosauridae. Family Notacanthidae. Family Lipogenyidae. In Fishes of the western North Atlantic. *Mem. Sears Found. Mar. Res.* **1**(6):1–228.

McKay, R. J. 1971. Two new genera and five new species of percophidid fishes (Pisces: Percophididae) from Western Australia. *J. R. Soc. Westn Aust.* **54**(2):40–46.

McPhail, J. D. and C. C. Lindsey. 1970. Freshwater fishes of northwestern Canada and Alaska. *Bull. Fish. Res. Bd. Can.* **173**. 381 pp.

Mead, G. W. 1957. An Atlantic record of the zeoid fish *Parazen pacificus*. *Copeia* **1957**(3):235–237.

Mead, G. W. 1965. The larval form of the Heteromi. *Breviora* **226**, 5 pp.

Mead, G. W. 1972. Bramidae. *Dana Rep.* **81**:1–166.

Mead, G. W. and G. E. Maul. 1958. *Taractes asper* and the systematic relationships of the Steinegeriidae and Trachyberycidae. *Bull. Mus. Comp. Zool., Harv.* **119**(6):391–417.

Meek, S. E. and S. F. Hildebrand. 1916. The fishes of the fresh waters of Panama. *Field Mus. Nat. Hist. (Zool.) Publ. 191.* **10**(15):1–374.

Meek, S. E. and S. F. Hildebrand. 1923–1928. The marine fishes of Panama. *Field Mus. Nat. Hist. (Zool.)* **15**: pts I–III.

Menon, A. G. K. 1951a. On a remarkable blind siluroid fish of the family Clariidae from Kerala (India). *Rec. Indian Mus.* **48**:59–66.

Menon, A. G. K. 1951b. Distribution of clariid fishes, and its significance in zoogeographical studies. *Proc. Nat. Inst. Sci. India* **17**(4):291–299.

Menon, A. G. K. 1963. A distributional list of fishes of the Himalayas. *J. Zool. Soc. India* **14**(1):23–32.

Miles, R. S. 1973. Articulated acanthodian fishes from the Old Red Sandstone of England, with a review of the structure and evolution of the acanthodian shoulder-girdle. *Bull. Br. Mus. Nat. Hist. (Geol.)* **24**(2):111–213.

Miller, P. J. 1963. Taxonomy and biology of the genus *Lebetus* (Teleostei–Gobioidea). *Bull. Br. Mus. Nat. Hist. (Zool.)* **10**(3):207–256.

Miller, R. R. 1958. Origin and affinities of the freshwater fish fauna of western North America. In C. L. Hubbs, (Ed.), Zoogeography: 187–222. *Publ. 51 Amer. Assoc. Ad. Sci.,* Washington, D. C.

Miller, R. R. 1966. Geographical distribution of Central American freshwater fishes. *Copeia* **1966**(4):773–802.

Miller, R. R. and J. M. Fitzsimons. 1971. *Ameca splendens,* a new genus and species of goodeid fish from western Mexico, with remarks on the classification of the Goodeidae. *Copeia* **1971**(1):1–13.

Misra, K. S. 1969. *Pisces, Fauna of India and adjacent countries.* Vol. 1. Elasmobranchii and Holocephali. New Delhi. 2nd ed. 300 pp.

Moore, G. A. 1968. Fishes. In W. F. Blair, et al. (Eds.), *Vertebrates of the United States:* 22–165. New York: McGraw-Hill. 616 pp.

Moore, W. S., R. R. Miller and R. J. Schultz. 1970. Distribution, adaptation and probable origin of an all-female form of *Poeciliopsis* (Pisces: Poeciliidae) in northwestern Mexico. *Evolution* **24**:789–795.

Moreland, J. [M.] 1960. A new genus and species of congiopodid fish from southern New Zealand. *Rec. Dom. Mus.* **3**(3):241–246.

Moreland, J. M. 1967. *Marine fishes of New Zealand* (illustrated by E. Heath). Wellington: A. H. and A. W. Reed. 56 pp.

Mori, T. 1952. Check list of the fishes of Korea. *Mem. Hyogo Univ. Agric.* 1(3):1–288.

Moy-Thomas, J. A. and R. S. Miles. 1971. *Palaeozoic fishes.* London: Chapman and Hall; Philadelphia: Saunders. 259 pp.

Munro, I. S. R. 1955. *The marine and fresh water fishes of Ceylon.* Camberra: Department of External Affairs. 349 pp.

Munro, I. S. R. 1964. Additions to the fish fauna of New Guinea. *Papua New Guinea Agric. J.* 16:141–186.

Munro, I. S. R. 1967. *The fishes of New Guinea.* Port Moresby, New Guinea: Department of Agriculture, Stock and Fish. 650 pp.

Myers, G. S. 1937. The deep-sea zeomorph fishes of the family Grammicolepidae. *Proc. U. S. Natl. Mus.* 84:145–156.

Myers, G. S. 1938. Fresh-water fishes and West Indian zoogeography. *Ann. Rept. Smithsonian Inst.* 3465:339–364.

Myers, G. S. 1958. Trends in the evolution of teleostean fishes. *Stanford Ichthyol. Bull.* 7(3):27–30.

Myers, G. S. 1960a. The genera and ecological geography of the South American banjo catfishes, family Aspredinidae. *Stanford Ichthyol. Bull.* 7:132–139.

Myers, G. S. 1960b. A new zeomorph fish of the family Oreosomatidae from the coast of California, with notes on the family. *Stanford Ichthyol. Bull.* 7(4):89–98.

Myers, G. S., 1966. Derivation of the freshwater fish fauna of Central America. *Copeia* 1966:766–773.

Myers, G. S. and W. C. Freihofer. 1966. Megalomycteridae, a previously unrecognized family of deep-sea cetomimiform fishes based on two new genera from the North Atlantic. *Stanford Ichthyol. Bull.* 8:193–206.

Nelson, G. J. 1966. Gill arches of teleostean fishes of the order Anguilliformes. *Pac. Sci.* 20(4):391–408.

Nelson, G. J. 1967. Gill arches of teleostean fishes of the family Clupeidae. *Copeia* 1967:389–399.

Nelson, G. J. 1968a. Gill-arch structure in *Acanthodes.* In T. Ørvig (Ed.), *Current problems of lower vertebrate phylogeny:* 129–143. New York: Wiley-Interscience.

Nelson, G. J. 1968b. Gill arches of teleostean fishes of the division Osteoglossomorpha. *J. Linn. Soc. (Zool.)* 47:261–277.

Nelson, G. J. 1969a. Gill arches and the phylogeny of fishes, with notes on the classification of vertebrates. *Bull. Am. Mus. Nat. Hist.* 141(4):475–552.

Nelson, G. J. 1969b. Infraorbital bones and their bearing on the phylogeny and geography of osteoglossomorph fishes. *Am. Mus. Novit.* 2394, 37 pp.

Nelson, G. J. 1970a. The hyobranchial apparatus of teleostean fishes of the families Engraulidae and Chirocentridae. *Am. Mus. Novit.* 2410, 30 pp.

Nelson, G. J. 1970b. Gill arches of some teleostean fishes of the families Salangidae and Argentinidae. *Jap. J. Ichthyol.* 17(2):61–66.

Nelson, G. J. 1972a. Observations on the gut of the Osteoglossomorpha. *Copeia* 1972(2):325–329.

Nelson, G. J. 1972b. Cephalic sensory canals, pitlines, and the classification of esocoid fishes, with notes on galaxiids and other teleosts. *Am. Mus. Novit.* 2492, 49 pp.

Nelson, G. J. 1972c. Comments on Hennig's "Phylogenetic Systematics" and its influence on ichthyology. *Syst. Zool.* **21**:364–374.

Nelson, G. [J.] 1973a. Notes on the structure and relationships of certain Cretaceous and Eocene teleostean fishes. *Am. Mus. Novit.* **2524**, 31 pp.

Nelson, G. [J.] 1973b. Relationships of clupeomorphs, with remarks on the structure of the lower jaw in fishes. In P. H. Greenwood, R. S. Miles, and C. Patterson (Eds.), Interrelationships of fishes: 333–349. *J. Linn. Soc. (Zool.)* **53**. Suppl. 1. New York: Academic.

Nelson, G. [J.] and M. N. Rothman. 1973. The species of gizzard shads (Dorosomatinae) with particular reference to the Indo-Pacific region. *Bull. Am. Mus. Nat. Hist.* **150**:131–206.

Nelson, J. S. 1968. Hybridization and isolating mechanisms between *Catostomus commersonii* and *C. macrocheilus* (Pisces: Catostomidae). *J. Fish. Res. Bd. Can.* **25**:101–150.

Nelson, J. S. 1971. Comparison of the pectoral and pelvic skeletons and of some other bones and their phylogenetic implications in the Aulorhynchidae and Gasterosteidae (Pisces). *J. Fish. Res. Bd. Can.* **28**:427–442.

Nichols, J. T. 1943. The fresh-water fishes of China. *Natural history of central Asia,* Vol. 9. American Museum of Natural History. 322 pp.

Nicol, J. A. C., H. J. Arnott, and A. C. G. Best. 1973. Tapeta lucida in bony fishes (Actinopterygii): a survey. *Can. J. Zool.* **51**:69–81.

Nielsen, J. G. 1968. Redescription and reassignment of *Parabrotula* and *Leucobrotula* (Pisces, Zoarcidae). *Vidensk. Meddr. Dansk. Foren.* **131**:225–249.

Nielsen, J. G. and V. Larsen. 1968. Synopsis of the Bathylaconidae (Pisces, Isospondyli). *Galathea Rep.* **9**:221–238.

Nikolskii, G. V. 1961. *Special Ichthyology.* Israel Program for Scientific Translation. Department of Commerce. Washington, D. C. 538 pp.

Nikolskii, G. V. 1963. *Ecology of fishes.* Translation. New York: Academic. 352 pp.

Nikolskii, G. V. 1965. *Theory of fish population dynamics.* English edition, 1969. Edinburgh: Oliver and Boyd. 323 pp.

Norden, C. R. 1961. Comparative osteology of representative salmonid fishes with particular reference to the grayling (*Thymallus arcticus*) and its phylogeny. *J. Fish. Res. Bd. Can.* **18**(5):679–791.

Norman, J. R. 1934. A systematic monograph of the flatfishes (Heterosomata). *Br. Mus. Nat. Hist.* **1**:1–459.

Norman, J. R. 1957. A draft synopsis of the orders, families and genera of recent fishes and fish-like vertebrates. Unpublished photo offset copies distributed by British Museum of Natural History. 649 pp.

Norman, J. R. and P. H. Greenwood. 1963. *A history of fishes.* London: Ernest Benn. 398 pp.

Northcote, T. G. (Ed.). 1969. Symposium on salmon and trout in streams. H. R. Macmillan lectures in fisheries. Institute of Fisheries, The University of British Columbia, Vancouver. 388 pp.

Nursall, J. R. 1956. The lateral musculature and the swimming of the fish. *Proc. Zool. Soc. London* **126**:127–143.

Nybelin, O. 1971. On the caudal skeleton in *Elops* with remarks on other teleostean fishes. *Acta R. Soc. Sci. Litt. Gothoburg, Zool., Stockholm* **7**:1–52.

Ochiai, A. 1963. Soleina (Pisces). *Fauna Japonica.* Tokyo: Biogeographical Society of Japan. 114 pp.

Bibliography

Okada, Y. 1955. *Fishes of Japan*. Tokyo: Maruzen. 434 pp.

Okamura, O. 1970. Macrourina (Pisces). *Fauna Japonica*. Tokyo: Academic Press of Japan. 216 pp.

Olson, E. C. 1971. *Vertebrate paleozoology*. New York: Wiley-Interscience. 839 pp.

Omarkhan. M. 1950. The development of the chondrocranium of *Notopterus*. *J. Linn. Soc. (Zool.)* **61**:608–624.

Orton, G. L. 1963. Notes on larval anatomy of fishes of the order Lyomeri. *Copeia* **1963**:6–15.

Ørvig, T. (Ed.). 1968. Current problems of lower vertebrate phylogeny. *Proc. 4th Nobel Symp.* New York: Wiley-Interscience. 539 pp.

Ovchynnyk, M. M. 1968. Annotated list of the freshwater fish of Ecuador. *Zool. Anz.* **181**:237–268.

Paetz, M. J. and J. S. Nelson. 1970. *The fishes of Alberta*. Edmonton: Queen's Printer. 282 pp.

Palmer, G. 1961. The dealfishes (Trachipteridae) of the Mediterranean and north-east Atlantic. *Bull. Br. Mus. Nat. Hist. (Zool.)* **7**:335–351.

Parr, A. E. 1960. The fishes of the family Searsidae. *Dana Rep.* **51**:1–109.

Patterson, C. 1964. A review of Mesozoic acanthopterygian fishes, with special reference to those of the English Chalk. *Phil. Trans. R. Soc. London.* Ser. B, **247**:213–482.

Patterson, C. 1965. The phylogeny of the chimaeroids. *Phil. Trans. R. Soc. London* **249**:101–219.

Patterson, C. 1967a. Are the teleosts a polyphyletic group? *Colloq. Int. Cent. Nat. Res. Scient.* **163**:93–109.

Patterson, C. 1967b. A second specimen of the Cretaceous teleost *Protobrama* and the relationships of the sub-order Tselfatioidei. *Ark. Zool.* **19**(2):215–234.

Patterson, C. 1968a. *Menaspis* and the bradyodonts. In T. Ørvig, (Ed.), *Current problems of lower vertebrate phylogeny:* 171–205. New York: Wiley-Interscience.

Patterson, C. 1968b. The caudal skeleton in Lower Liassic pholidophoroid fishes. *Bull. Br. Mus. Nat. Hist. (Geol.)* **16**:203–239.

Patterson, C. 1973. Interrelationships of holosteans. In P. H. Greenwood, R. S. Miles, and C. Patterson (Eds.), Interrelationships of fishes: 233–305. *J. Linn. Soc. (Zool.)* **53**. Suppl. 1. New York: Academic.

Patterson, C. and P. H. Greenwood (Eds.). 1967. Fossil vertebrates. *J. Linn. Soc. (Zool.)* **47**(311):1–260.

Paxton, J. R. 1972. Osteology and relationships of the lanternfishes (family Myctophidae). *Bull. Nat. Hist. Mus. Los Angeles County, Sci.* 13. 81 pp.

Penrith, M. J. 1972. Earliest description and name for the whale shark. *Copeia* **1972**(2):362.

Pfeiffer, W. 1963. Alarm substances. *Experientia* **19**:1–11.

Phillipps, W. J. 1926. New or rare fishes of New Zealand. *Trans. Proc. N. Z. Inst.* **56**:529–537.

Pietsch, T. W. 1972. A review of the monotypic deep-sea anglerfish family Centrophrynidae: taxonomy, distribution and osteology. *Copeia* **1972**:17–47.

Poll, M. 1947. *Poissons marins*. Faune de Belgique. Mus. R. d'Hist. Nat. de Belgique. 452 pp.

Poll, M. 1964. Une famille dulcicole nouvelle de poissons africains: les Congothrissidae. *Mém. Acad. R. Sci. Outre-mer, N. S.* **15**(2):1–40.

Poll, M. and J. P. Gosse. 1969. Revision des Malapteruridae (Pisces, Siluriformes) et description d'une deuxième espèce de silure électrique: *Malapterurus microstoma* sp. n. *Bull. Inst. R. Sci. Nat. Belg.* **45**(38):1–12.

Poulsen, T. C. 1963. Cave adaptations in amblyopsoid fishes. *Am. Midl. Nat.* **70**:257–290.

Quast, J. C. 1965. Osteological characteristics and affinities of the hexagrammid fishes, with a synopsis. *Proc. Calif. Acad. Sci.* Ser. 4, **31**(21):563–600.

Ramaswami, L. S. 1957. Skeleton of cyprinoid fishes in relation to phylogenetic studies. 8. The skull and Weberian ossicles of Catostomidae. *Proc. Zool. Soc., Calcutta, Mookerjee Mem.* **1957**:293–303.

Randall, J. E. 1963. Review of the hawkfishes (family Cirrhitidae). *Proc. U.S. Natl. Mus.* **114**:389–451.

Randall, J. E., K. Aida, T. Hibiya, N. Mitsuura, H. Kamiya, and Y. Hashimoto. 1971. Grammistin, the skin toxin of soapfishes, and its significance in the classification of the Grammistidae. *Publ. Seto Marine Biol. Lab.* **19**:157–190.

Regan, C. T. 1911. The classification of the teleostean fishes of the order Ostariophysi. 1. Cyprinoidea. *Ann. Mag. Nat. Hist.* Ser. 8, **8**:13–32.

Regan, C. T. 1913. The classification of percoid fishes. *Ann. Mag. Nat. Hist.* Ser. 8, **12**:111–145.

Regan, C. T. 1929. Fishes. *Encyclopaedia Britannica,* 14th ed., **9**:305–329.

Rhodes, F. H. T. (Ed.). 1972. Conodont paleozoology. *Geol. Soc. Am. Spec. Paper 141.* 296 pp.

Ridewood, W. G. 1904. On the cranial osteology of the fishes of the families Mormyridae, Notopteridae, and Hyodontidae. *J. Linn. Soc.* (*Zool.*) **29**:188–217.

Ringuelet, R. A., R. H. Aramburu, and A. Alonso de Aramburu. 1967. Los peces Argentinos de agua dulce. *Comision Invest. Cient., La Plata.* 602 pp.

Rivas, L. R. and S. M. Warlen. 1967. Systematics and biology of the bonefish, *Albula nemoptera* (Fowler). *U. S. Fish Wildl. Serv., Fish. Bull.* **66**:251–258.

Roberts, T. R. 1969. Osteology and relationships of characoid fishes, particularly the genera *Hepsetus, Salminus, Hoplias, Ctenolucius,* and *Acestrorhynchus. Proc. Calif. Acad. Sci.* Ser. 4, **36**(15):391–500.

Roberts, T. R. 1971a. *Micromischodus sugillatus,* a new hemiodontid characin fish from Brazil, and its relationships to the Chilodontidae. *Breviora* **367,** 25 pp.

Roberts, T. R. 1971b. The fishes of the Malaysian family Phallostethidae (Atheriniformes). *Breviora* **374,** 27 pp.

Roberts, T. R. 1971c. Osteology of the Malaysian phallostethoid fish *Ceratostethus bicornis,* with a discussion of the evolution of remarkable structural novelties in its jaws and external genitalia. *Bull. Mus. Comp. Zool., Harv.* **142**(4):393–418.

Roberts, T. R. 1972. An attempt to determine the systematic position of *Ellopostoma megalomycter,* an enigmatic freshwater fish from Borneo. *Breviora* **384,** 16 pp.

Roberts, T. R. 1973a. Interrelationships of ostariophysans. In P. H., Greenwood, R. S. Miles, and C. Patterson (Eds.), Interrelationships of fishes: 373–395. *J. Linn. Soc.* (*Zool.*) **53,** Suppl. 1. New York: Academic.

Roberts, T. R. 1973b. Osteology and relationships of the Prochilodontidae, a South American family of characoid fishes. *Bull. Mus. Comp. Zool., Harv.* **145**(4):213–235.

Robertson, D. R. 1972. Social control of sex reversal in a coral-reef fish. *Science* **177**:1007–1009.

Robins, C. H. 1971. The comparative morphology of the synaphobranchid eels of the Straits of Florida. *Proc. Acad. Nat. Sci. Philad.* **123**(7):153–204.

Robins, C. H. and C. R. Robins. 1970. The eel family Dysommidae (including the Dysomminidae and Nettodaridae), its osteology and composition, including a new genus and species. *Proc. Acad. Nat. Sci. Philad.* **122**(6):293–335.

Robins, C. H. and C. R. Robins. 1971. Osteology and relationships of the eel family Macrocephenchelyidae. *Proc. Acad. Nat. Sci. Philad.* **123**(6):127–150.

Robins, C. R. 1966. Additional comments on the structure and relationships of the mirapinniform fish family Kasidoroidae. *Bull. Marine Sci.* **16**:696–701.

Robins, C. R. 1973. [Review of] Opredelitel' I Kharacteristika Semeist' Ryb Mirovoi Fauny. *Copeia* **1973**:635–637.

Robins, C. R. and J. E. Böhlke. 1970. The first Atlantic species of the ammodytid fish genus *Embolichthys*. *Not. Nat. (Philadelphia)* **430**:1–11.

Robins, C. R. and D. P. deSylva. 1965. The Kasidoroidae, a new family of mirapinniform fishes from the western Atlantic Ocean. *Bull. Marine Sci.* **15**:189–201.

Robins, C. R. and J. G. Nielsen. 1970. *Snyderidia bothrops*, a new tropical, amphiatlantic species (Pisces, Carapidae). *Stud. Trop. Oceanogr. Miami* **4**(2):285–293.

Robins, C. R. and C. H. Robins. 1966. *Xenoconger olokun*, a new xenocongrid eel from the Gulf of Guinea. *Stud. Trop. Oceanogr. Miami* **4**(1):117–124.

Rofen, R. R. 1959. The whale-fishes: families Cetomimidae, Barbourisiidae and Rondeletiidae (order Cetunculi). In *Galathea Report*, Scientific results from the Danish deep-sea expedition round the world 1950–52. Copenhagen. **1**:255–260.

Romer, A. S. 1966. *Vertebrate paleontology*. 3rd ed. Chicago: University of Chicago Press. 468 pp.

Romer, A. S. 1970. *The vertebrate body*. 4th ed. Philadelphia: Saunders. 601 pp.

Rosen, D. E. 1962. Comments on the relationships of the North American cave fishes of the family Amblyopsidae. *Am. Mus. Novit.* **2109**, 35 pp.

Rosen, D. E. 1964. The relationships and taxonomic position of the halfbeaks, killifishes, silversides, and their relatives. *Bull. Am. Mus. Nat. Hist.* **127**(5):217–268.

Rosen, D. E. 1971. The Macristiidae, a ctenothrissiform family based on juvenile and larval scopelomorph fishes. *Am. Mus. Novit.* **2452**, 22 pp.

Rosen, D. E. 1973. Interrelationships of higher euteleostean fishes. In P. H. Greenwood, R. S. Miles, and C. Patterson (Eds.), Interrelationships of fishes: 397–513. *J. Linn. Soc. (Zool.)* **53**. Suppl. 1. New York: Academic.

Rosen, D. E. and R. M. Bailey. 1963. The poeciliid fishes (Cyprinodontiformes), their structure, zoogeography, and systematics. *Bull. Am. Mus. Nat. Hist.* **126**(1):1–176.

Rosen, D. E. and P. H. Greenwood. 1970. Origin of the Weberian apparatus and the relationships of the ostariophysan and gonorynchiform fishes. *Am. Mus. Novit.* **2428**, 25 pp.

Rosen, D. E. and C. Patterson. 1969. The structure and relationships of the paracanthopterygian fishes. *Bull. Am. Mus. Nat. Hist.* **141**(3):357–474.

Rosen, D. E. and A. Rumney, 1972. Evidence of a second species of *Synbranchus* (Pisces, Teleostei) in South America. *Am. Mus. Novit.* **2497**, 45 pp.

Rosenblatt, R. H. and J. E. McCosker. 1970. A key to the genera of the ophichthid eels, with descriptions of two new genera and three new species from the eastern Pacific. *Pac. Sci.* **24**:494–505.

Rosenblatt, R. H., J. E. McCosker, and I. Rubinoff. 1972. Indo-west Pacific fishes from the Gulf of Chiriqui, Panama. *Contrib. Sci., Nat. Hist. Mus., Los Angeles County* **234**:1–18.

Rounsefell, G. A. 1962. Relationships among North American Salmonidae. *U. S. Fish Wildl. Serv., Fish. Bull.* **62**(209):235–270.

Rutenberg, E. P. 1962. Survey of the fishes of family Hexagrammidae. In T. S. Rass, (Ed.), Greenlings: 1–103. *Trans. Inst. Oceanol.* Translated from the Russian, *Israel Program for Scientific Translation,* Jerusalem, 1970.

Schaeffer, B. 1947. Cretaceous and Tertiary actinopterygian fishes from Brazil. *Bull. Am. Mus. Nat. Hist.* **89**(1):1–40.

Schaeffer, B. 1967. Osteichthyan vertebrae. *J. Linn. Soc. (Zool.)* **47**(311):185–195.

Schaeffer, B. 1968. The origin and basic radiation of the Osteichthyes. In T. Orvig, (Ed.), *Current problems of lower vertebrate phylogeny:* 207–222. New York: Wiley-Interscience.

Schaeffer, B. 1972. A Jurassic fish from Antarctica. *Am. Mus. Novit.* **2495,** 17 pp.

Schaeffer, B. 1973. Interrelationships of chondrosteans. In P. H. Greenwood, R. S. Miles, and C. Patterson (Eds.), Interrelationships of fishes: 207–226. *J. Linn. Soc. (Zool.)* **53.** Suppl. 1. New York: Academic.

Schaeffer, B. and D. E. Rosen. 1961. Major adaptive levels in the evolution of the actinopterygian feeding mechanism. *Am. Zool.* **1**(2):187–204.

Schmidt, P. Y. 1950. *Fishes of the Sea of Okhotsk.* Akademii Nauk SSSR. Translated from the Russian, Israel Program for Scientific Translations, Jerusalem, 1965. 392 pp.

Schultz, L. P. 1957. The frogfishes of the family Antennariidae. *Proc. U. S. Natl. Mus.* **107:**47–105.

Schultz, L. P. 1958. Review of the parrotfishes family Scaridae. *Bull. U. S. Natl. Mus.* **214.** 143 pp.

Schultz, L. P. 1961. Revision of the marine silver hatchetfishes (family Sternoptychidae). *Proc. U. S. Natl. Mus.* **112:**587–649.

Schultz, L. P. 1969. The taxonomic status of the controversial genera and species of parrotfishes with a descriptive list (family Scaridae). *Smithsonian Contrib. Zool.* **17,** 49 pp.

Schultz, L. P. and Collaborators. 1953–1966. Fishes of the Marshall and Marianas Islands. *Bull. U. S. Natl. Mus.* **202.** Vol. 1 (1953), 685 pp., Vol. 2 (1960), 438 pp., Vol. 3 (1966), 176 pp.

Schultz, R. J. 1973. Unisexual fish: laboratory synthesis of a "species." *Science* **179:**180–181.

Schwartz, F. J. 1972. *World literature to fish hybrids, with an analysis by family, species, and hybrid.* Gulf Coast Research Laboratory, Ocean Springs, Miss. 328 pp.

Scott, T. D. 1962. *The marine and fresh water fishes of South Australia.* Adelaide: Government Printer. 338 pp.

Scott, W. B. and E. J. Crossman. 1973. Freshwater fishes of Canada. *Bull. Fish.Res. Bd.Can.* **184.** 966 pp.

Scott, W. B., A. C. Kohler, and R. E. Zurbrigg. 1970. The manefish, *Caristius groenlandicus* Jensen (Percomorphi: Caristiidae), in Atlantic Waters of Canada. *J. Fish. Res. Bd. Can.* **27:**174–179.

Sillman, L. R. 1960. The origin of the vertebrates. *J. Paleontol.* **34**(3):540–544.

Simon, R. C. and P. A. Larkin (Eds.). 1972. *The stock concept in Pacific salmon.* H. R. Macmillan lectures in fisheries. Institute of Animal Resource Ecology, The University of British Columbia, Vancouver. 231 pp.

Simpson, G.G. 1961. *Principles of animal taxonomy.* New York: Columbia University Press. 247 pp.

Singh, B. N. and J. S. Datta Munshi. 1969. On the respiratory organs and mechanics of breathing in *Periopthalmus vulgaris* (Eggert). *Zool. Anz.* **183:**92–110.

Smith, C. L. and E. H. Atz. 1969. The sexual mechanism of the reef bass *Pseudogramma bermudensis* and its implications in the classification of the Pseudogrammidae (Pisces: Perciformes). *Z. Morph. Tiere* **65**(4):315–326.

Smith, C. L. and R. M. Bailey. 1961. Evolution of the dorsal-fin supports of percoid fishes. *Pap. Mich. Acad. Sci. Arts, Lett.* **46:**345–363.

Smith, C. L. and R. M. Bailey. 1962. The subocular shelf of fishes. *J. Morph.* **110**(1):1–18.

Smith, D. G. 1968. The occurrence of larvae of the American eel, *Anguilla rostrata,* in the Straits of Florida and nearby areas. *Bull. Marine Sci.* **18:**280–293.

Smith, D. G. 1969. Xenocongrid eel larvae in the western North Atlantic. *Bull. Marine Sci.* **19:**377–408.

Smith, D. G. 1970. Notacanthiform leptocephali in the Western North Atlantic. *Copeia* **1970:**1–9.

Smith, D. G. and P. H. J. Castle. 1972. The eel genus *Neoconger* Girard: systematics, osteology, and life history. *Bull. Marine Sci.* **22:**196–249.

Smith, G. R. and R. K. Koehn. 1971. Phenetic and cladistic studies of biochemical and morphological characteristics of *Catostomus. Syst. Zool.* **20:**282–297.

Smith, H.M. 1945. The fresh-water fishes of Siam, or Thailand. *Bull. U. S. Natl. Mus.* **188.** 622 pp.

Smith, J. L. B. 1940. A living coelacanth fish from South Africa. *Trans. R. Soc. S. Afr.* **28:**1–106.

Smith, J. L. B. 1950. *The sea fishes of Southern Africa.* South Africa: Central News Agency (5th ed., 1965). 550 pp.

Smith, J. L. B. 1952a. The fishes of the family Batrachoididae from South and East Africa. *Ann. Mag. Nat. Hist.* Ser. 12, **5:**313–339.

Smith, J. L. B. 1952b. The fishes of the family Haliophidae. *Ann. Mag. Nat. Hist.* Ser. 12, **5:**85–101.

Smith, J. L. B. 1954. The Anisochromidae, a new family of fishes from East Africa. *Ann. Mag. Nat. Hist.* Ser. 12, **7:**298–302.

Smith, J. L. B. 1955. The fishes of Aldabra (Seychelles). *Ann. Mag. Nat. Hist.* Ser. 12, **8:**304–312.

Smith, J. L. B. 1960. A new grammicolepid fish from South Africa. *Ann. Mag. Nat. Hist.* Ser. 13, **3:**231–235.

Smith, J. L. B., 1966. Fishes of the sub-family Nasinae with a synopsis of the Prionurinae. *Ichthyol. Bull. Rhodes Univ.* (32):635–682.

Smith-Vaniz, W. F. and V. G. Springer. 1971. Synopsis of the tribe Salariini, with descriptions of five new genera and three new species (Pisces: Blenniidae). *Smithsonian Contrib. Zool.* **73,** 72 pp.

Sneath, P. H. A. and R. R. Sokal. 1973. *Numerical taxonomy.* San Francisco: Freeman. 573 pp.

Sokal, R. R. and P. H. A. Sneath. 1963. *Principles of numerical taxonomy.* San Francisco: Freeman. 359 pp.

Solomon-Raju, N. and R. H. Rosenblatt. 1971. New records of the parasitic eel, *Simenchelys parasiticus,* from the central North Pacific with notes on its metamorphic form. *Copeia* **1971:**312–314.

Southward, E. C. 1971. Recent researches on the Pogonophora. In H. Barnes (Ed.), *Oceanography and Marine Biology Annual Review* **9**:193–220. London: Allen and Unwin.

Spillman, C. J. 1961. Poissons d'eau douce. *Faune de France* **65**. P. Lechevalier (Ed.). Paris. 303 pp.

Springer, S. 1966. A review of western Atlantic cat sharks, Scyliorhinidae, with descriptions of a new genus and five new species. *U. S. Fish Wildl. Serv., Fish. Bull.* **65**:581–624.

Springer, V. G. 1968. Osteology and classification of the fishes of the family Blenniidae. *Bull. U. S. Natl. Mus.* **284**. 83 pp.

Springer, V. G. 1970. The western south Atlantic clinid fish *Ribeiroclinus eigenmanni,* with discussion of the Clinidae. *Copeia* **1970**(3):430–436.

Springer, V. G. 1972. Synopsis of the tribe Omobranchini with descriptions of three new genera and two new species (Pisces: Blenniidae). *Smithsonian Contrib. Zool.* **130**, 31 pp.

Springer, V. G. and W. F. Smith-Vaniz. 1972a. Mimetic relationships involving fishes of the family Blenniidae. *Smithsonian Contrib. Zool.* **112**, 36 pp.

Springer, V. G. and W. F. Smith-Vaniz. 1972b.A new tribe (Phenablenniini) and genus (*Phenablennius*) of blenniid fishes based on *Petroscirtes heyligeri* Bleeker. *Copeia* **1972**:64–71.

Stahl, B. J. 1967. Morphology and relationships of the Holocephali with special reference to the venous system. *Bull. Mus. Comp. Zool., Harv.* **135**(3):141–213.

Starck, W. A., II, 1968. A list of fishes of Alligator Reef, Florida, with comments on the nature of the Florida reef fish fauna. *Undersea Biol.* **1**:1–40.

Starks, E. C. 1930. The primary shoulder girdle of fishes. *Stanford Univ. Publs. Biol. Sci.* **6**(2):147–239.

Stauch, A. and J. Cadenat. 1965. Révision du genre *Psettodes* Bennet 1831; (Pisces, Teleostei, Heterosomata). *Off. Rech. Sci. Tech. Outre-mer., Fort-Lamy Tchad.* **3**(4):19–30.

Stensio, E. A. 1963. Anatomical studies on the arthrodiran head. Pt. 1. *Kung. Svenska Vetensk. Akad. Handl.* 4th ser., **9**(2):1–419.

Stensio, E. [A.] 1968. The cyclostomes with special reference to the diphyletic origin of the Petromyzontida and Myxinoidea. In T. Ørvig (Ed.). *Current problems of lower vertebrate phylogeny:* 13–71. New York: Wiley-Interscience.

Sterba, G. 1966. *Freshwater fishes of the world.* London: Studio Vista. 879 pp.

Stokell, G. 1969. New Zealand Retropinnidae. *Rec. Canterbury Mus.* **8**(4):379–381.

Strasburg, D. W. 1964. Further notes on the identification and biology of echeneid fishes. *Pac. Sci.* **18**(1):51–57.

Sufi, S. M. K. 1956. A revision of the Oriental fishes of the family Mastacembelidae. *Bull. Raffles Mus.* **27**:92–146.

Svetovidov, A. N. 1948. Gadiformes. In E. N. Pavlovskii and A. A. Shtakel'berg (Eds.), *Fauna of the U. S. S. R., Fishes* **9**(4):1–304. Zoological Institute, Akademii Nauk SSSR. Translated for the National Science Foundation, and Smithsonian Institution, Washington, D. C., 1962.

Svetovidov, A. N. 1952. Clupeidae. In E. N. Pavlovskii and A. A. Shtakel'berg (Eds.), *Fauna of the U. S. S. R., Fishes* **2**(1):1–428. Zoological Institute, Akademii Nauk SSSR. Translated for the National Science Foundation, and Smithsonian Institution, Washington, D. C., 1963.

Taliev, D. N. 1955. *Sculpins of Baikal (Cottoidei).* Akademii Nauk, SSSR, East Siberia Branch, Moscow, Leningrad. 603 pp. (in Russian).

Tarlo (Halstead), L. B. 1960. The invertebrate origins of the vertebrates. *Int. Geol. Cong.* **21**(22):113–123.

Taverne, L. 1968. Ostéologie du genre *Gnathonemus* Gill sensu stricto [*Gnathonemus petersii* (Gthr) et espèces voisines] (Pisces Mormyriformes). *Mus. R. Afr. Cent. Ann.* (Ser. 8, Zool.) **170**:1–91.

Templeman, W. 1968. A review of the morid fish genus *Halargyreus* with first records from the western North Atlantic. *J. Fish. Res. Bd. Can.* **25**:877–901.

Templeman, W. 1973. Description and distribution of new specimens of the fish *Lipogenys gilli* from the western North Atlantic. *J. Fish. Res. Bd. Can.* **30**:1559–1564.

Thomson, K. S. 1962. Rhipidistian classification in relation to the origin of the tetrapods. *Breviora* **177**, 12 pp.

Thomson, K. S. 1968. A critical review of the diphyletic theory of rhipidistian-amphibian relationships. In T. Ørvig (Ed.), *Current problems of lower vertebrate phylogeny:* 285–306. New York: Wiley-Interscience.

Thomson, K. S. 1971. The adaptation and evolution of early fishes. *Quart. Rev. Biol.* **46**(2):139–166.

Thomson, K. S. 1973. Secrets of the coelacanth. *Nat. Hist.* **82**:58–65.

Thomson, S. M. 1964. A bibliography of systematic references to the grey mullets (Mugilidae). *Div. Fish. Oceanogr. Tech. Pap. 16, Commonwealth Sci. Ind. Res. Org., Australia.* 127 pp.

Thorp, C. H. 1969. A new species of myrapinniform fish (family Kasidoridae) from the western Indian Ocean. *J. Nat. Hist.* **3**:61–70.

Thorson, T. B. 1972. The status of the bull shark, *Carcharhinus leucas,* in the Amazon River. *Copeia* **1972**:601–605.

Thys van den Audenaerde, D. F. E. 1961. L'anatomie de *Phractolaemus ansorgei* Blgr. et la position systématique des Phractolaemidae. *Mus. R. Afr. Cent. Ann.* (Ser. 8, Sci. Zool.) **103**:101–167.

Thys van den Audenaerde, D. F. E. 1967. *The freshwater fishes of Fernando Poo.* Brussels: Paleis der Acad. 167 pp.

Tominaga, Y. 1965. The internal morphology and systematic position of *Leptobrama mülleri,* formerly included in the family Pempheridae. *Jap. J. Ichthyol.* **15**(2):43–95.

Tominaga, Y. 1968. Internal morphology, mutual relationships and systematic position of the fishes belonging to the family Pempheridae. *Jap. J. Ichthyol.* **15**(2):43–95.

Trautman, M. B. 1957. *The fishes of Ohio.* Columbus: The Ohio State University Press. 683 pp.

Tucker, D. W. 1954. Fishes. Part 1. In The "Rosaura" expedition. *Bull. Br. Mus. Nat. Hist.* (*Zool.*) **2**(6):163–214.

Tyler, J. C. 1968. A monograph on plectognath fishes of the superfamily Triacanthoidea. *Acad. Nat. Sci. Philad. Monog.* **16.** 364 pp.

Tyler, J. C. and C. L. Smith. 1970. A new species of blennioid fish of the family Notograptidae from eastern Australia. *Notul. Nat.* (*Philad.*) **431**:1–12.

Ueno, T. 1970. Cyclopteridae (Pisces). *Fauna Japonica.* Tokyo: Academic Press of Japan. 233 pp.

Vladykov, V. D. 1962. Osteological studies on Pacific salmon of the genus *Oncorhynchus.* *Bull. Fish. Res. Bd. Can.* **136.** 172 pp.

Vladykov, V. D. 1963. A review of salmonid genera and their broad geographical distribution. *Trans. R. Soc. Can.* Ser. 4, Sect. 3, **1**:459–504.

Vladykov, V. D. 1964. Quest for the true breeding area of the American eel (*Anguilla rostrata* Le Sueur). *J. Fish. Res. Bd. Can.* **21**(6):1523–1530.

Vladykov, V. D. 1973. A female sea lamprey (*Petromyzon marinus*) with a true anal fin, and the question of the presence of an anal fin in Petromyzonidae. *Can. J. Zool.* **51**:221–224.

Waite, E. R. 1923. *The fishes of South Australia.* Adelaide: British Scientific Guild. 243 pp.

Walker, B. W. 1952. A guide to the grunion. *Calif. Fish and Game* **38**(3):409–420.

Walters, V. 1955. Fishes of the western Arctic America and eastern Arctic Siberia. Taxonomy and Zoogeography. *Bull. Am. Mus. Nat. Hist.* **106**(5):255–368.

Walters, V. 1960. Synopsis of the lampridiform suborder Veliferoidei. *Copeia* **1960**(3):245–247.

Walters, V. 1964. Order Giganturoidei. *In* Fishes of the western North Atlantic. *Mem. Sears Found. Mar. Res.* **1**(4):566–577.

Walters, V. and J. E. Fitch. 1960. The families and genera of the lampridiform (Allotriognath) suborder Trachipteroidei. *Calif. Fish and Game* **46**:441–451.

Watanabe, M. 1960. Cottidae. *Fauna Japonica.* Biogeographical Society of Japan. Tokyo: News Service. 218 pp.

Watson, D. M. S. 1937. The acanthodian fishes. *Phil. Trans. R. Soc. London,* Ser. B, **228**:49–146.

Weatherley, A. H. 1972. *Growth and ecology of fish populations.* New York: Academic. 294 pp.

Weber, M. and L. F. DeBeaufort. 1913–1962. *The fishes of the Indo-Australian Archipelago.* Vols. 2–11 (various authors). Leiden: E. J. Brill.

Weitzman, S. H. 1954. The osteology and the relationships of the South American characid fishes of the subfamily Gasteropelecinae. *Stanford Ichthyol. Bull.* **4**(4):213–263.

Weitzman, S. H. 1960. Further notes on the relationships and classification of the South American characid fishes of the subfamily Gasteropelecinae. *Stanford Ichthyol. Bull.* **7**(4): 217–239.

Weitzman, S. H. 1962. The osteology of *Brycon meeki,* a generalized characid fish, with an osteological definition of the family. *Stanford Ichthyol. Bull.* **8**(1):1–77.

Weitzman, S. H. 1964. Osteology and relationships of South American characid fishes of subfamilies Lebiasininae and Erythrininae with special reference to subtribe Nannostomina. *Proc. U. S. Natl. Mus.* **116**:127–169.

Weitzman, S. H. 1967a. The osteology and relationships of the Astronesthidae, a family of oceanic fishes. *Dana Rep.* **71**:1–54.

Weitzman, S. H. 1967b. The origin of the stomiatoid fishes with comments on the classification of salmoniform fishes. *Copeia* **1967**(3):507–540.

Wenz, S. 1967. *Compléments á l'étude des poissons actinoptérygiens du Jurassique francais.* Edition du Centre national de la Recherche Scientifique, Paris, 1968. 276 pp.

Wheeler, A. 1969. *The fishes of the British Isles and North-West Europe.* London: Macmillan. 613 pp.

Wheeler, A. C. 1955. A preliminary revision of the fishes of the genus *Aulostomus. Ann. Mag. Nat. Hist.* Ser. 12, **8**:613–623.

White, E. G. 1937. Interrelationships of the elasmobranchs with a key to the order Galea. *Bull. Am. Mus. Nat. Hist.* **74**:25–138.

Whitehead, P. J. 1962. The species of *Elops* (Pisces: Elopidae). *Ann. Mag. Nat. Hist.* Ser. 13, **5**(54):321–329.

Whitehead, P. J. 1963a. A contribution to the classification of clupeoid fishes. *Ann. Mag. Nat. Hist.* Ser. 13, **5**(60):737–750.

Whitehead, P. J. 1963b. A revision of the recent round herrings (Pisces: Dussumieriidae). *Bull. Br. Mus. Nat. Hist.* (*Zool.*) **10**(6):305–380.

Wiley, M. L. and B. B. Collette. 1970. Breeding tubercles and contact organs in fishes: their occurrence, structure, and significance. *Bull. Am. Mus. Nat. Hist.* **143**(3):143–216.

Wilimovsky, N. J. 1954. List of the fishes of Alaska. *Stanford Ichthyol. Bull.* **4**:279–294.

Woods, L. P. and R. F. Inger. 1957. The cave, spring, and swamp fishes of the Family Amblyopsidae of central and eastern United States. *Am. Midl. Nat.* **58**(1):232–256.

Woods, L. P. and P. M. Sonoda. 1973. Order Berycomorphi (Beryciformes). In Fishes of the western North Atlantic. *Mem. Sears Found. Mar. Res.* **1**(6):263–396.

Woodward, A. S. 1889–1901. *Catalogue of the fossil fishes in the British Museum.* London: British Museum of National History. Vols. 1–4.

Woolcott, W. S. 1957. Comparative osteology of serranid fishes of the genus *Roccus* (Mitchill). *Copeia* **1957**(1):1–10.

Wynne-Edwards, V. C. 1952. Freshwater vertebrates of the Arctic and subarctic. *Bull. Fish. Res. Bd. Can.* **94**. 28 pp.

Yarberry, E. L. 1965. Osteology of a zoarcid fish *Melanostigma pammelas*. *Copeia* **1965**:442–462.

Zangerl, R. 1973. Interrelationships of early chondrichthyans. In P. H., Greenwood, R. S. Miles, and C. Patterson (Eds.). Interrelationships of fishes: 1–14. *J. Linn. Soc.* (*Zool.*) **53**. Suppl. 1. New York: Academic.

Zangerl, R. and G. R. Case. 1973. Iniopterygia, a new order of chondrichthyan fishes from the Pennsylvanian of North America. *Fieldiana, Geol. Mem.* **6**:1–67.

Index